Marriage and the Post Office

One is a fundamentally protected right that has been a part of the United States of America since its founding.

The other... well... it is not even mentioned once in the entire Constitution nor all the Amendments.

Do you know which one is which? And, more importantly, why that is? What were the architects of our country trying to do when they laid out particular rules and rights? Or to put it another way:

> Why did the Founding Fathers believe the Post Office was so important while Marriage—with all its societal implications—did not even warrant the smallest of mentions?

New and Improved: The United States of America is an exploration of what the law of the land is and what needs to happen in order to even have a conversation about how it can be changed for the better. Inside is not the answers to every problem we have in America, but instead are the tools to make it possible to even talk about our issues and do something about them.

In order to have a true and just representative democracy, much must metamorphosize in our policies, laws, and—most of all—the Constitution itself. That said, will our representatives in government have the patriotism to put the benefit of the nation and its citizens above themselves and their personal ambitions? It is a lot to ask, but as the saying goes:

"We the people..."

TABLE OF CONTENTS

ON A VELLUM PARCHMENT

"The good news is that, if life is long enough, you can learn... that you need to change..."
— Brad Smith

PREAMBLE AND SOME REGULAR RAMBLE

In the years since the Constitution of the United States of America was written, it has been amended a mere 27 times. Are we saying that there are only 27 faults in a document that is over 230 years old? Actually, the 21st Amendment repeals 18th Amendment—the prohibition of the sale of alcohol—so then there would only be 25 corrections! Lest we forget, this a document that thought a fair compromise on slavery was to allow it in certain areas and count people as 3/5th a person in order to gain further power in the House of Representatives.

Granted, some of these amendments have corrected terrible mistakes like having slavery (13th), expanding the right to vote (15th for race, 19th for women), and guaranteeing free expression (1st). However, some have quite questionable value. Are the citizens of the United States truly happy that the 16th Amendment gave Congress the ability to levy an income tax? Was it absolutely necessary for the functions of government to change the date the President, Vice President, and members of Congress started work (20th)?

Even those who wrote the Constitution were not entirely happy with it, which began even before the process started. What commenced with 74 delegates quickly dropped to 55 as a group rebuffed attending for various reasons (aside from Rhode Island which declined to assign delegates at all, but more on them in a moment). To sum up their feelings, elected delegate Patrick Henry refused to attend because he "smelt a rat" in the whole ordeal. This was because the country was run under the Articles of Confederation and there was nothing in the Articles that gave the States or delegates the right to abandon them and form a new government. And even though some tried to do this on the sly, the first group of dropouts realized what was happening and wanted no part in it.

Then, as the process of developing a completely different government moved along, another 13 delegates dropped out leaving just 42. Three of the delegates who stuck around through the entire process did not concur on their collective work leaving just 39 of the delegates—a little over half of the original—to literally sign off on the Constitution. These three refusers could not get past the obvious compromises and bending of moral beliefs, and desperately were looking for protections for the average citizen that would not come until later, if ever.

Dedication Plaque to the signers of the Declaration of Independence at the National Mall in Washington, DC in December 2019. Just six of the men who signed the Declaration of Independence were part of and signed the Constitution: George Clymer, Benjamin Franklin, Robert Morris, George Read, Roger Sherman, and James Wilson.

Once the States got involved in the actual ratification process, the gaps began to be noticed quickly. While Delaware, Pennsylvania, New Jersey, Georgia, and Connecticut were quick to ratify and did so within a couple of months of being presented the final draft; the rest were not so hasty. Despite this, even vehement anti-federalists were eventually turned with the promise of amendments to come, the majority of which became the first ten amendments: The Bill of Rights.

This showed, though, how deficient the document was and what changes already needed to be made. Afterall, the entire Constitution was written in less than four months and at just 4,543 words (including the signatures of the delegates) it is today the shortest Constitution in effect. True, there were few examples at the time to base the Unites States Constitution on, but this amounts to under ten single-spaced pages in a word processor today! The 27 Amendments have added just another 3,048 words, or an additional six pages. Of course, we probably need to subtract out the amount of words removed by the Amendments as well, but this is not an exercise in detailed algebra!

With those promised changes and implied others, Massachusetts, Maryland, South Carolina, and New Hampshire came on board and the Constitution was officially set to become the law of the land. At this point it was June 1788 and it was agreed that that the government would begin on March 4, 1789. In the time in between, more oaths and treatises were made which brought Virginia and New York into the fold. North Carolina held out more for caution and anti-federalist concerns, but still acted as if in the union anyway. Once the Amendments passed through Congress in September 1789, North Carolina had no more arguments and officially joined the union in November 1789.

Then there was Rhode Island.

On March 24, 1788 the people of Rhode Island were given a chance to vote in a popular election to decide the fate of the Constitution. In a lopsided 92.6% landslide, Rhode Islanders rejected the very idea of this particular document. Why was Rhode Island so vehemently opposed to the end-product of developing a new nation?

As previously noted, Rhode Island was the only state to not even send a delegate to the Constitutional Convention. Despite being the smallest of the former colonies, Rhode Island had a long history of anti-authority sentiment and freedom of expression. Founder Roger Williams and his followers escaped the religious persecution of Massachusetts Puritans to form a place where all could come. While William Penn in Pennsylvania would take this a step much further by actively recruiting religious undesirables, Roger Williams and company laid the groundwork for what would become many of the amendments on personal freedom.

More so, Rhode Island's Royal Charter of 1663 established by King Charles II of England granted the colony the ability to govern itself and guaranteed religious freedom to all people. This was the first document in the *world* that granted people the ability to follow the faith of their own choosing without persecution and without a government being able to set an official religion. This separation of church and state is considered obvious for most modern western democracies today, but it was unique in the 1600's and was still not guaranteed by the late 1700's.

You see, the Royal Charter on which Rhode Island was governed actually guaranteed more freedoms for Rhode Islanders than the Constitution granted. By signing the Constitution, Rhode Island would, in reality, forfeit rights that their founders had fought and negotiated for. Literally, progress in personal freedom would be sent backwards a hundred years.

First page of the Royal Charter of Rhode Island on display at the Rhode Island State House in the capital of Providence on March 1, 2016.

Ten of the Twelve proposed Amendments passed by Congress were ratified by enough States to become law on December 15, 1791. One of those other two Amendments did eventually pass—202 years and 223 days later on May 5, 1992. This Amendment is in fact the last to have been added to the Constitution (27th) and stops Congress from giving itself a pay raise. Congress can now only give a pay raise to the next Congress, of which since 1964 has re-election rates usually above 75% (and generally in the 80%-95% range). In 2018, the House of Representatives had a 91% re-election rate and the Senate 84%. One must remember that a fair amount of incumbents also chose not to run in 2018, thus excluding those former representatives would make these numbers even higher. Essentially, the current Congress is in the next Congress and is giving itself a pay raise, so the 27th Amendment is doing nothing.

The other Amendment not to pass was related to how members of the House of Representatives were distributed among the States and specifically a focus on making sure smaller groups and areas were still represented as the population grew. Whether this particular Amendment would have limited the gerrymandering of today's electorate is debatable, but it shows that even over 230 years ago these concerns were coming to the forefront.

However, even the ten remaining Amendments still did not completely add up to what Rhode Island was losing. Despite this, Rhode Island ratified the Constitution on May 29, 1791—well before the Bill of Rights was certified by the States on December 15, 1791. Why did Rhode Island get on board without protections it held out so long for? Eleven times Rhode Islanders voted down the Constitution and its nascent amendments including the ratio of votes shown before. What changed?

The answer was a threat.

Rhode Island is surrounded by its neighbors with Massachusetts to the north, Connecticut to the west, New York across the bay to the south and the ocean to the east. Even today, no matter where someone is in Rhode Island, they would at most be 18.5 miles from another State or the Atlantic Ocean. Being small and trapped, Rhode Island's neighbors decreed they would treat Rhode Island like a foreign country and impose taxes on all its exports. Basically, Rhode Island was threatened with financial destruction and the choice was to give in or collapse.

And with that act of economic terrorism, the last of the original thirteen colonies signed up to create the United States of America under the Constitution. The holdouts began the process of becoming a unified nation not because the guiding document was everything they needed or dreamed of, but because it met their needs well enough to be acceptable. It was an imperfect union and came together under imperfect conditions.

This is not to say the Constitution does not have value and is not a strong and well-reasoned governing document overall. Despite the flaws and limited updates, it has provided the backbone to create, support, and stabilize this nation. Where it lapses, laws, policies, and judicial decisions fill in with an attempt to make a more just and free nation.

But that does not mean it should be accepted as-is or believed infallible. The Constitution and the Amendments to it have not created a perfect system, but instead created one with flaws, bureaucracy, bias, imbalance, and—most of all—intransigence.

The Founders were not all-knowing oracles and they did not have a guidebook. As such, they made mistakes that have had many unexpected (and some quite accurately predicted) repercussions rippling down through time. Beyond that, there have been changes in societal norms, technology, and the political layout of the world that they never could have accounted for.

Nor are we more perfect beings than the Founders were. As fellow flawed human beings, we will make mistakes while trying to correct the missteps of the past and create many unintended consequences of our own. Despite that, this is our first step as with any process: acceptance. We must accept that any form of government is only as well developed as its people, and that it must always be a work in progress to reach a more perfect union. And note that the Preamble to the Constitution calls for the creation of a "more perfect Union" and not a "perfect Union"; just the same as the Declaration of Independence calls for the "pursuit of Happiness", not the guarantee of one. Happiness is always a journey of the individual just as a perfected Union is the journey of a government.

Now if we accept that our Union is imperfect, and that anything we create will still have flaws, what then are our goals for modifying a system that works well enough? What do we actually want to accomplish?

We want to create a system of government that expands upon the ideals and intents of the Founders while also incorporating a modern understanding. This includes having an active, engaged, and represented citizenry that not only feels but is a part of the governmental function. At the same time, we want to prepare for future eventualities that make the government flexible enough to respond but rigid enough to stay by its principles. Beyond all that, we do not want to break what works and what is understood by 230 years of tradition.

In order to do this, there are specific goals that must be kept in mind and adhered to:

- Maintain a three-part government split between the Legislative Branch that creates the law, the Executive Branch that enforces the law, and the Judicial Branch that interprets the laws and hands out punishments for violation of the law. Each branch must be modified to have the appropriate checks and balances over the other branches with the intent of limiting overreach by any other area.

- Checks and balances should be extended to within each branch to limit individuals from controlling the entire government process and fate of the Union. Similarly, the federal government and those who work within it must have the appropriate checks and balances by the State and local governments and the individual people of the United States.

- A representative democracy—a republic—is still the ideal and intended approach, but the representation must be a true mix of the different people and perspectives of the land and not limited by oligopolies and limited choice. Everything must be done to have an actively engaged citizenry who trust that their perspective has a proper voice and that their vote truly matters.

- The intents of the Founders must be modernized to align with current technologies and be made more generic to account for technologies that have yet to be created. However, we must be willing to completely sweep away conventions that are shown to have limited to no value, especially those that add burdens to the people who have implicitly outsourced certain roles to their representatives.

- All changes are to be made to improve discourse and respect the rights of individuals. Wherever possible, specifics of types and monetary levels must not be fixed to exact values and instead be made on equations or definitions that can be derived. This way, the intent of law, spending, and other functions can remain the same while sliding with the changes in definition and needs over time without debate.

- The world will continue to be mutable and so will the needs of the people and governments. Methods for limiting, revisiting, and modifying decisions must be made in order to have flexibility far beyond what is available today. At the same time, flexibility must not be unlimited in order to have stability, and that means vetting processes and other checks that limit the burden on individual people and groups before decisions are enacted.

With these intents in mind, it is now time to lay out the specific policies, laws, and constitutional amendments to fundamentally change the conversation in government. And when these are adopted, there will be a **NEW AND IMPROVED: UNITED STATES OF AMERICA**!

A COVID NOTE

As a quick note and as can be seen in the <u>Version History</u> in the <u>Afterwards</u>, this book was written between May and October 2019 with content updating going on from then until February 2020. Since that point, the book was only modified with minor grammar and formatting considerations as they were discovered, reaching the form when this note was written in May 2020. Because of this, the entire book has been written and is still presented without the perspective of going through the COVID-19 pandemic and the subsequent aftermaths—including on people, the economy, the democratic process, government spending, emergency declaration, et al.

However, despite this, everything prescribed in this book is just as valid as it was before the pandemic, and in many ways is more so. Some of the facts— especially around employment numbers—may be a bit dated, but that may also depend upon when you are reading this. It may be that the economy is bursting at the seams even more than before the pandemic and the issues caused by those circumstances are more prevalent. The changes to our system of government as laid out within these pages are meant to function in all conditions and be a lither, more universal approach. As such, the exact examples used may not be what is happening "now", but it has happened in the past and will happen again in the future. Further, I have always tried to present the opposite situations to show the full impact and consequences of these changes.

Beyond those points, potentially there may be some comments and analysis that may seem insensitive given the pandemic and its aftermath. For instance, there is a discussion late in the book about what to spend to save an individual life due to a very specific situation. This is presented as a question, not an answer, but it is there. That said, this area—and others like it—was always meant to be provocative and would have been painful for many people to contemplate anyway. In other words, even without COVID-19, some (all?) people are bound to be offended at some point. Even I am offended by some of my own analysis!

This is the real challenge of what lies within these pages. As such, all I ask is that you do not get too hung up on the particulars of the world going on around you at the moment you are reading this. **NEW & IMPROVED: THE UNITED STATES OF AMERICA** is about changing and creating a flexible and fully representative system of government so that we can better respond to both extreme events like COVID-19 and mundane events like interstate highway maintenance. Once again, this book is not the answer to all the problems we have in America; it is the method and framework by which the conversations can finally happen and beneficial action can be taken for all!

J.P. Prag
May 18, 2020

PLEASE YIELD THE FLOOR

The United States Legislative Branch is broken up into two pieces: The House of Representatives and the Senate. Each has a unique method of their makeup and how individuals are elected. Despite being the guiding force in deciding the laws of the nation, the Constitution is rather vague or silent in how these areas are set up.

With the House of Representatives, we might call it the "Legislature of the People" because the amount of people in a State determines how many members will be elected. Today, there are 435 Representatives allocated to the States. Each State must get at least one and it is otherwise proportionality done by population according to the Census. While there is some left over language on how to count slaves ("other Persons") and non-taxed Indians that were overwritten by future amendments, the core of the setup is still there (spelling, punctuation, and grammar here and throughout this book are exactly as originally written):

> The Number of Representatives shall not exceed one for every thirty Thousand, but each State shall have at Least one Representative;

> The Times, Places and Manner of holding Elections for Senators and Representatives, shall be prescribed in each State by the Legislature thereof; but the Congress may at any time by Law make or alter such Regulations, except as to the Places of chusing Senators.

Notice what is not in there? Where did this 435 number come from? And anyone who votes should note that they elect a representative from a Congressional District—even if their State only has one district.

The estimated population of the United States at the end of 2018 was 327.2 million people. If there was a representative for every 30,000 people, then there would be over 10,900 Representatives; not the most efficient of meetings. After the first census of 1790, there were just shy of 4 million people in the United States and the number of Representatives increased from the initial 65 just the year before to 105, which is still below the 133 the math would call for. That is because of two factors: (1) Congress gets to choose how many people each Representative stands in for and (2) 30,000 is the minimum number of people, not the maximum.

As such, over time, that number has gone up. Something interesting happened in 1929, though. In 1913, Congress increased the number of seats to 433 to represent the latest 1910 census results (and 2 additional seats were added when New Mexico and Arizona became states in 1912), but a severe pushback began. The United States was becoming more urbanized and more industrialized, both of which drew in immigrants. Fearing this foreign influence, a piece of legislation called the "Permanent Apportionment Act" was passed that—as the name suggests—permanently set the number of Representatives and the method by which the House is "appointed". In a stroke, Congress gave up ones of its main roles and created a method by which one group of people (Rural/Nativists) could have disproportionate representation over another set of groups (Urbanites and Non-natives).

As noted above, it was up to the States to decide how their Representatives were elected. In many cases, States set up systems to elect Representatives in a "multi-member" district—being that multiple people were elected over an area. That all changed in 1967 when Congress created a law declaring that all States must make districts and that those districts must be "single member".

Before this, in 1964, the Supreme Court had made two rulings that said Congressional Districts must be roughly equal in size, which also helped lead to some interesting lines that are not based on town and county borders but instead on how to get the populations roughly equal so that each area has around the same amount of voters behind it. This would extend further with the Voting Rights Acts of 1965 that tried to stop breaking up districts to limit the power of people by Race and Ethnicity. It should be noted that this does not extend to any other grouping of people.

The bottom line of all of this is that Constitution does not lay out any of these decisions about how the House or Representatives should work. These are all methodologies that were developed by Congress or imposed by the Courts over time, and that the only thing stopping Congress from fixing inequities in how it is set up is Congress itself. All of the rules, procedures, and methods of passing a law are all made up and could be thrown away at any time. Yet, they are not, and they have become tools and weapons to be used for political purposes instead of the function as laid out by the Constitution: to pass laws.

While not going as deep, the Senate is the same way. Each State gets two Senators, but according to the original Constitution they were to be appointed by the State Legislatures. This was one of the many compromises in the Constitution that was put in to get it passed. If the State Legislatures felt like they had direct control of a federal institution then they were more likely to get on board. Over time, this became problematic and many states passed initiatives to have people directly elect their Senators (and then the Legislatures would certify that vote). This all changed with the 17th Amendment which modified the original text to make all Senators elected by the people.

This begs the question, then: what is the difference between the Senate and the House of Representatives?

There is also a question of disproportionate power. While the size disparities between the States is similar today (Virginia was the largest because it still had West Virginia and defiant Rhode Island was and still is the smallest), the population disparities were not as severe. They were still there, and again Virginia was at the top and Rhode Island was second to the bottom (Delaware, the next smallest State, had that distinction), with a range of roughly 60,000 to 750,000 people. The Senate was supposed to be a check on the Federal government by being a control of co-equal States. Since Federalist essentially won out and Senators are purely Federal employees, this distinction does not exist.

If we consider the Senate to be the "Legislature of the Land", then it is incredibly disproportionate today. Rhode Island at 1,034 square miles (at low tide) and Delaware at 1,955 square miles have the same say as California (155,973), Texas (261,914), and Alaska (570,641). If we think that population within a landmass makes more sense, California had roughly 39.5 million people in 2018 and Wyoming had less than 0.6 million. What gets interesting is if we combine these two statistics and get population per square mile; by 2015 statistics Rhode Island ranked 2nd (1,021 people per square mile), California 11th (251), and Wyoming at 40th (6). What is clear is that no matter which way you slice it (size, population, density), the Senate is not representing an original intent of being a Federal check.

And really, this is just the beginning of our issues with how the Legislature of the country is set up. There are a number of topics to contend with; that is why more than any other part of government the Legislative Branch requires the greatest amount of overhaul. While some may want to nitpick over slight adjustments within the existing framework, it is truly past time to consider the silence of the Constitution to be a detriment. Ideas that made sense for an era or were done just to win over State Legislatures do not align to the centralized Federal government that exists today. Nor have the stopgaps added over time led to a well and fully represented populace. Instead, more ways of skirting the letter of the law continue to be implemented despite the chilling effects on democracy.

No, in order to truly make an impact, the Legislative Branch needs a complete overhaul on all levels, and these levels must be controlled at the Constitutional level to make sure that Congress cannot create escapes for itself. In order to do this, several areas need to be locked up beyond their control:

- The makeup of Congress to represent the various viewpoints in the country

- The balance between Federal needs and State checks

- Stop legislative tools from ending the discussion and movement of bills

- Limit single party power to move or halt bills

- Have bills be more clean and specific

- Make sure laws are relevant and legal (re: Constitutional) today and in the future

- Get new people in Congress on a regular basis so it is not a long-term career

- Eliminate self-interest and add accountability for legislators

This is how it can be done...

WIN, LOSE, OR... ACTUALLY, IT'S ALWAYS LOSE

When we elect Representatives and Senators today, it is the will of the people... right? After all, we go to the polls and vote for a person, and that person who wins has the will of the people.

Except, they do not.

In the 2018 House of Representatives election, all 435 seats were available. Of those, over 20% of the races were decided by a 10% margin or less. Digging even deeper, almost 10% were decided by a 5% margin or less and 2% were decided by a 1% margin or less. If we say a margin of 10% or less means basically the race was even, then in 20% of available positions half of the people who backed the losing candidate(s) are receiving no representation whatsoever.

We have created a system of "winning", and winning means just doing better than opponents. It does not mean moving ahead with campaign promises or being the will of the people; it just means getting barely enough votes to get or maintain your job.

That is not an indictment on the motives of those who run for office or their intentions—it is simply the truth. Having a system of legislature where only a single person is supposed to represent a diverse and divergent group of people is inherently flawed. Even in a race like NY-15 where the Democrats won with 96% of the vote, the 4% of people who voted Republican are left out of representation of any kind. Or how about WA-02, where there was no GOP challenger but a third-party candidate received nearly 29% of the vote? And then there is UT-15, where the Republicans won about 62% of the vote, but Democrats had nearly 25% and Independents had nearly 14%? Sure, it was a solid Republican victory, but there in a so-called Republican stronghold nearly 2/5ths of people have no one to express their views in the federal legislature.

Their opinions and beliefs are effectively suppressed just because of where they happen to live.

Despite what you may have heard on cable news, there is no such thing as a "Red" (Republican/Conservative) or "Blue" (Democrat/Liberal) State. Each state has a plethora of political beliefs that run the gamut, and it shows up in the results. In the 2018 House of Representatives election, the most "Blue" State was Massachusetts with 78% among 9 districts, leaving 22% of Massachusetts voters with no representation. However, despite being a deep Blue state by this figure, in the same election Massachusetts re-elected a Republican Governor with 67% of the vote!

Eight of the top ten largest 2018 House of Representatives victories went to purported Blue states. In reality, the first eight went towards Blue with ranges from 78% in Massachusetts to 64% in Delaware. Even California—considered to be the most liberal state—came in with just 66% Democratic votes, leaving almost 4 million conservative voters and 200,000 independent voters without a voice.

The first Red State also had just 64% voting for the winner in the single district that makes up Wyoming. The largest Red State (both by area and voting population) in Texas had the GOP win just 50% of the vote leaving another 3.9 million liberals and 215,000 independents without any say in the federal government. The next largest State was Florida with just a 52% Republican victory. We could go with the pundits and say that Florida is a swing state, but what about their northern neighbor Georgia? Georgia had almost the exact same result with 52% going to the GOP, leaving 1.8 million liberals without a voice. If Georgia's and Florida's results are almost the same, then why is one considered a "Red" State and the other a "Swing" State?

It is because of our "Winner Takes All" system and the setup of the districts. If we look at each State's results and say that a winner within 50-60% of the vote is a close race, then 34 of the 50 states were that close. Yet, looking at a political map on TV, one would believe that these massive areas are solidly behind a single party. This could not be further away from the truth and reality, something that can be quickly verified in how people vote. Among those close States, 20 went Republican and 14 went Democrat. However, not all States are equal as some have one district while others have dozens. In districts, 177 went Republican and 107 went Democrat.

As noted above, those maps are also misleading due to the size of the States. There are seven States with just one district, and of those five are Red States. Some of those Red States are physically massive: Wyoming, North Dakota, South Dakota, Montana, and Alaska. The two Blue States like this—Delaware and Vermont—are tiny by comparison and create a very false impression on the maps. Among the top ten States with the highest number of districts (and therefore the most amount of people), seven of the races were in our close criteria, and of those close ones, five went the way of the GOP. Vast amounts of people are lacking a voice because of a myth that a State fully supports one political party or another.

The average margin of victory among all the districts was 30.2%, which means that same percentage of people have no representation. Of course, this is only of people who voted. Many voters in non-competitive districts don't bother to vote at all because the result is pre-ordained (or so they believe). How many more people have no representation at all based on that factor? Of eligible voters, 53.4% showed up in 2018, which—sadly—is a 50-year record high for a non-Presidential year. People not feeling like their vote matters and not bothering to show up because of that is a form of voter suppression.

All right, let's sum this up. Around half of eligible voters don't have any representation because they don't feel like they matter. Even if we say that at least half of those would vote for the eventual party winner in their district, we are still saying that a quarter of all Americans have no representation just from not voting. Add that back to the margin of victory, and we are back to over half of America having no representation in the House of Representatives.

This is a problem, but it goes even deeper than that. Even with those who do win, they do not come close to representing the makeup of the American people. What does Congress look like? How can we make it a better and true reflection of the will of the people?

WHO ARE THESE PEOPLE?

While Congress was elected by around half of the eligible people in our country, the half that did vote is severely underrepresented just by the sheer number of returns received for each party. But does it go beyond that? Well, let us start off at a basic question: How does representation align to political affiliation?

	House	Senate	Total Congress	2018 House Election Results	People of the U.S.A.
Democrat	54%	45%	52%	53%	31%
Republican	46%	52%	47%	44%	28%
Independent / Other	0%	2%	0%	3%	39%
Vacant / No Answer	0%	1%	0%	0%	2%

As can be seen above, even in the election where third parties like Libertarians, Greens, and others received 3% of the votes, they saw no seats in the House of Representatives. The Senate has two Independents that function as

Democrats and caucus with them, so there is hardly a balance in that chamber. You may think 3% seems like not much, but that amounts to nearly 2 million people who voted.

What is much more telling on that front, though, is how people are affiliated. Looking at a 2018 Gallup Poll on political affiliation (which aligns closely to numbers seen in States that have party registration), the largest political party is none or all other political parties! Think of it this way: if 39% of people are not Democrats or Republicans, then nearly 2/5th of people have absolutely zero representation in Congress.

Keep this in mind in for the next section while we now turn towards a closer look at the makeup of Congress. First, let us look at some rather surface elements of Gender Identity and Sexuality:

	House	Senate	Total Congress	People of the U.S.A.
Male Heterosexual	75%	74%	75%	47%
Female Heterosexual	23%	23%	23%	49%
LGBTQ+ / All Other	2%	3%	2%	4%

This Congress (especially the House of Representatives) has been celebrated as the most female and most representative of other Gender Identities and Sexualities ever. In truth, it is exactly that. However, it is far away from being a true mix of American society. This is a male heterosexual dominated institution that lacks a proper balance of viewpoints on something as basic as the makeup of births (LGBTQ+ numbers are estimated off of self-reported data). In this same vein, let us poke at race and ethnicity:

	House	Senate	Total Congress	People of the U.S.A.
Caucasian / White	75%	91%	78%	61%
African American / Black	12%	2%	10%	13%
Hispanic / Latino	9%	4%	8%	16%
Asian / Pacific Islander	3%	2%	3%	6%
Native / First Nation	1%	0%	1%	1%
Mixed / Unknown / Other	0%	1%	0%	3%

If you believe race and ethnicity have an impact on thoughtful representation, these numbers should be chilling. Every single group is underrepresented except for Caucasian / White which sees a +17% distribution towards that group at the expense of all others. That Congress is mostly male, heterosexual, and white is not a surprise to most people, but when you look at how far it is off from the population it does look a lot like a suppression of all other groups. Mind you again, the Congress elected in 2018 is the most diverse ever and it still does not even come close.

While the House of Representatives' makeup being created from smaller districts is closer to the actual population, the Senate does not nearly align due to each State having just two seats and the voting being done in a way that limits representation. Note: this is not claiming malicious intent (though many court cases have found malicious intent), but just a symptom of how Congress and voting is set up.

Now, let us go below the skin and look at religious affiliation. Though the First Amendment of the United States prohibits the establishment or suppression of any religion, religion is a powerful force in the country that informs many people's belief structures in how a nation should be run.

	House	Senate	Total Congress	People of the U.S.A.
Christian (Total)	89%	86%	88%	70%
Protestant (All Kinds)	*54%*	*60%*	*55%*	*48%*
Catholic	*32%*	*22%*	*30%*	*21%*
Mormon	*1%*	*4%*	*2%*	*2%*
Orthodox Christian	*1%*	*0%*	*1%*	*0%*
Jewish	6%	8%	6%	2%
Buddhist	0%	1%	0%	1%
Muslim	1%	0%	1%	1%
Hindu	1%	0%	1%	1%
Unaffiliated	0%	1%	0%	23%
Other Faiths	0%	0%	0%	2%
Unknown	3%	4%	4%	1%

A dispute could be made about Christian groups having far outstripped influence over other religions, but there is one much more important number to take away:

	House	Senate	Total Congress	People of the U.S.A.
Organized Religion	97%	95%	96%	76%
Unaffiliated / Unknown	3%	5%	4%	24%

The United States is not supposed to be a country where religion sets the agenda, but frankly it does. One quarter of people do not associate with an organized religion, and arguments could be made that many more that do so are not religious believers. Congress, on the other hand, is completely the opposite with a massively over-dominating presence of the religious believers. While many religions can claim persecution in this country, there is definitive decision-making being done against the non-religious the most. This group of people are discriminated against simply by not having a voice to counter the religious aspects of the current Congress.

Again, this is not an attack on religion; this is an attack on the lack of fair representation. When we talk about basic fairness, how can your view be heard and your concerns taken seriously when you have no say in how the country is run? Do not believe that this ends here as we move on to the age of Congress:

	House	Senate	Total Congress	People of the U.S.A.	Exclude Under 18
Under 18	0%	0%	0%	23%	-
18 to 24	0%	0%	0%	9%	12%
25 to 34	3%	0%	3%	14%	18%
35 to 44	14%	4%	12%	13%	16%
45 to 64	52%	50%	52%	26%	33%
65 to 79	28%	41%	31%	12%	15%
80 and Above	2%	5%	2%	4%	5%

We should get a few things out of the way. First, by the Constitution, Representatives must be at least 25 years old and Senators must be 30 years old. However, no member of either chamber comes close to those minimum ages. Instead, most people are far older with the 45 to 64 and 65 to 79 age groups representing 83% of Congress while only 38% of all people (and 48% excluding under 18 years old). Why is age so important, though?

Well, you will notice that the groups above are not broken up into even ranges. Instead, they represent phases of life, whether it be a child or young adult versus a middle career professional or a retiree. This is not an exact science and everyone's path in life is different, but this gives a general overview of where people stand. Now, we are not going to have children in Congress, so we can exclude them and still see the massive disparity between Congress and the people. The reason why I talk about "phases of life" is that people have different concerns as they age, what is most important to them, and what they need from the government. Younger people may care more about education, work opportunities, and access. Older people may care more about social welfare programs, security, and international relations.

Either way, if a group does not have representation then its concerns can be ignored. This may not be a willful ignoring, but more of an ignorance of what is important to a person at a different time in their life. How does a 75-year-old in Congress relate to the needs of a 19 or 25-year-old? How can younger candidates become known and get the resources to even run for Congress when they are eligible?

Also, if you think one party skews far older than another, you are correct. Democrats have far more elder members including 6 older than 80 compared to 2 for Republicans. Oh, you thought the Conservative Party was going to skew older than the Liberal one? This shows why you cannot make assumptions on how people want to be represented. But this also shows the challenges that different age groups face while trying to get into Congress. The Senate skews even older than the House because it is difficult to break in to limited seats, which means that those who do get elected have often already served in many other parts of government and have made a career out of it. Thus, not only are they not representing the ages and concerns of those age groups, but they are not involved in the everyday experiences of the age groups.

This lack of the average person's experience extends to pay. There is no need for a chart here as members of Congress make a minimum of $174,000 per year—where leadership positions pay more. Members of Congress are limited in how much direct pay they can make in outside jobs, but there are no limits on what their spouses can make, what can be made in non-monetary (re: stocks, real estate, intangibles, etcetera) compensation, and what can be done in a trust in their name for future payments. Just for comparison, 42% of households make under $50,000 a year and 30% make between $50,000 to $100,000. It is fair to say that member of Congress makes significantly more than at least 80-85% of Americans. However, annual income is only the beginning.

What is a better and more accurate measurement is household wealth. This is a measure of all assets (think cash, real estate, stocks, etcetera) minus any debts. This way, it is not just about what an individual is making in a single year, but where they stand over their lifetime.

	House	Senate	Total Congress	People of the U.S.A.
$0 or Less	7%	0%	6%	11%
$1 to $20K	1%	0%	1%	19%
$21K to $100K	4%	1%	4%	21%
$101K to $300K	12%	8%	11%	21%
$301K to $1.0M	24%	20%	23%	17%
$1.1M to $2.0M	13%	12%	13%	5%
$2.1M to $6.0M	17%	26%	19%	5%
$6.1M or More	22%	33%	23%	1%

Congress is full of very, very wealthy people. While over half of Americans have less than $100,000 in net worth, over half of Congress has over $1 million in net worth. And due to these starting points, with smart investments those with high net worth continue to grow exponentially faster than those without. Now, again, this is not an attack on wealth. Nor is this an attack on any political party because the figures are very similar between Democrats and Republicans. Simply, as most congresspeople make a large income and have incredibly high re-election rates (recall that is 80-95% likely), even if they start off with a low net worth that completely changes the longer they serve.

Yes, many of these congresspeople have worked incredibly hard outside of government to make their wealth. One could say a significant number of them have made a sacrifice to give up a lucrative career in order to take a lower paying job with severe limitations and almost no mobility. However, this is not an attack on wealth, but an attack on lack of representation. How can these people possibly understand the plights and needs of the average person when they are not in those groups? One can sympathize, one may even remember once being in that group, but experience will temper an opinion and urgency. The people in charge of all tax policy and spending cannot relate and effectively represent the people who are most impacted by those laws.

And it is not just straight wealth that is an indicator, but one of the precursors to wealth: education. Congress is by far more highly educated than the American people. While there is a direct correlation from higher education to higher earnings in the current American socio-economic climate, this only further exacerbates the situation of lack of prudent representation.

	House	Senate	Total Congress	People of the U.S.A.
No Degree	0%	0%	0%	12%
High School	4%	0%	3%	27%
Some College / Associate's	1%	0%	1%	29%
Bachelor's	25%	21%	24%	20%
Post-Grad	70%	79%	71%	12%

Being well educated is nothing that should be attacked and these congresspeople should be lauded for their accomplishments. Some would even argue that we should want Congress to be more highly educated than the populace in order to understand and make law. Though there may be some weight to that argument, it is again a question of understanding constituents. If 68% of Americans have an Associate's degree or less and 71% of Congress has a Master's degree or more, how can their perspectives and needs be in line? They have totally different experiences and expectations in life!

Congress is not the will of the people because it does not successfully represent the people. These are but a few ways of slicing the American populous up to show how Congress does not align. This could go much deeper into specific policy beliefs, desires for the direction of the country, and other socio/economic/physical differences, but that is unnecessary. The point is just to show that no matter which way you slice it, Congress is not in line with those they are supposed to stand for. If the will, setup, and diversity of the people is not reflected in the government, then how can the government give back to the people what is needed?

To be clear, much of this is not Congress's fault. Members of Congress should not feel shame or be diminished because they happen to be part of group that is severely overrepresented. Being more educated, making a fair wage, following your beliefs, expressing your culture and ethnicity—these are all things that should be followed by those who desire it. In a way, Congress is as much of a victim as the citizenry because if there are no representatives to express other views, how can these groups possibly respond? If it is not part of their life experience and there is no one in Congress to express this, how would they know?

No, there is a systematic issue here. There is no amount of law, policy, redistricting, quota filling, or any other method that can change the current situation. All of those methods can make slight tweaks but will still leave at least half of America without someone to speak on their behalf. The Legislature of the United States of America is broken at its core because of the compromises that were made to get 13 former colonies to agree to join and stay in a single a federalist union. We have had over 230 years to see the consequences and above shows them in plain numbers.

In order to fix these base concerns, we need to rewrite most of Article 1 of the Constitution through a set of Amendments.

A WHOLE NEW DISTRICT

One of the core arguments I have been making is that the "Winner Takes All" system through districts is not getting us anywhere near the breakdown of the American populace. While we have looked at education, wealth, age, race/ethnicity, gender/identity/sexuality, and other measures, the core one is political affiliation. The purpose of a political party is to group together like-minded people into a single force. Yet, the two main parties in America are so large that there is no way they can cover these nuanced and various viewpoints. And this can be seen in States where one party dominates the legislature and there is still great discord.

Though the Founders wanted to avoid political parties, it is just not in human psychology. Humans will create groups no matter what, and we must accept that this is going to always be the situation. While there will be outliers that are complete loners, even that is a group of just one (or often, few similar minded people). Most other western democracies have accepted this fact and allow legislatures to be proportionately driven. That is why earlier I said to think of the House of Representatives as the "Legislature of the People" because that is what it is supposed to do. The House should be the reflection of the people's will at the Federal level, and the only way to do that is with direct votes of a party and eliminating other factors.

Some thoughts on government from George Mason as he waits for a bus at his own memorial in Washington, DC (near Thomas Jefferson's) in December 2019. He is one of the three delegates who refused to sign the Constitution because of these beliefs, among others not pictured.

In order to make that happen, we need to start making Amendments to the Constitution right near the beginning. For this and all Amendments, additions are in **Bold** and removals are ~~crossed out~~. Sections that have already been removed or modified by prior Amendments are not shown and are assumed to already be the current version of the text, though can be reviewed in the Appendix. Any Amendment, law, reference, or statement throughout this document that uses a seemingly masculine singular pronoun should be considered to represent all people—it is just that this author prefers using a singular pronoun (and not multiple singular pronouns slashed together, which could be read plural and still be exclusionary) that cannot be confused for a plural one (especially when keeping in line with the original language of the Constitution and law) and English lacks a generally agreed upon gender-neutral singular pronoun, otherwise.

By Amendment to the Constitution of the United States, Article 1, Section 2, Clause 1 shall read:

The House of Representatives shall be composed of Members chosen every ~~second~~ **fourth** Year **on the even years opposite elections for President and Vice President** by the People of the several States **and Territories**~~, and the Electors in each State shall have the Qualifications requisite for Electors of the most numerous Branch of the State Legislature~~. **Political Parties shall create Lists of one hundred persons in order of preference to be considered for Membership. The Government of the United States and the Governments of the States and Territories shall provide no support to Political Parties for determining their Lists and the Political Parties are solely responsible for determining the method of developing their Lists. Nor shall the Government of the United States nor the Governments of the States and Territories provide any other type of support or resources for internal Political Party decisions. The people of the United States and its Territories shall vote for the Political Parties directly. There shall be no criteria for a Political Party to appear on the ballots save producing the List of candidates, though the List must be limited to those people who meet the criteria for the House of Representatives as written in the Constitution.**

Let us go through these various revisions in order.

First, currently the entire House of Representatives is re-elected every two years, with plenty of special elections to fill vacated seats. Because of this two-year cycle and the focus on individual races, most Representatives spend a majority of their time campaigning and fundraising. This is hardly a way to govern, so let us first aim to smooth out the schedule to make it every four years for elections of the House of Representatives. Later, this same recommendation will be made for the Senate, meaning that the entire legislature will be replaced on a four-year cycle.

That is why the next point is on the timing to have these elections be opposite the elections for the Executive Branch. That will give the people a voice during the middle of a President's term to have a say about what priorities are: do they want more legislators in line with the President and push forward the Executive agenda, or do they want to rein the office in? Since the legislature truly creates the laws and processes of the country and the President is supposed to execute those rules, this means the legislature will always be a check just by being elected. Additionally, with both the House and Senate being completely re-elected, it makes every election very important as all locations will be having their major races at the same time. This will maximize voter turnout in each of the Federal election cycles with so much at stake each time.

Next is a small change in the wording of who elects the House of Representatives. Right now, the Constitution talks about the "People of the several States" and similar phrases not just here, but repeatedly throughout. The issue is that around 4.4 million Americans live in "Territories", not "States" (though this number may be several hundred thousand fewer as people have fled Puerto Rico in the wake of Hurricane Maria—and other disasters that have followed—and have not returned). When the United States came together, the States controlled territory that might not be contiguous (IE, Massachusetts controlled what is now Maine) or was in conflict with neighbors (Vermont was carved out of disagreements between New Hampshire, New York, and others). However, over time, the United State via partition, purchase, treaty, and warfare acquired lands that were not part of any States.

Today, there are 16 recognized territories where 6 have regular populations— Puerto Rico, Guam, U.S. Virgin Islands, North Mariana Islands, American Samoa, and Washington, D.C. (Washington, D.C. is actually a "Federal District" which is different than a "Territory", but for the sake of simplicity we'll call it a "Territory" anyway). While some may claim that these locations do not lack representation because they can send Delegates to the House of Representatives, the Delegates have no ability to vote on legislation. Nor can any of these locations except for Washington, D.C. vote in Presidential elections as they do not have Electoral College members (the 23rd Amendment granted this special status to "The District constituting the seat of Government", which is currently Washington, DC). And to add further insult, unlike the rest of these territories the people of American Samoa (nearly

56,000) are not considered citizens and do not have the free movement rights that the other locations have. Instead, they are considered "American Nationals", which basically means they are treated like foreigners even though they are under American control. We will come back to them later, as well.

> In September 2019, the Cherokee Nation decided for the first time to enforce a clause in the 1835 Treaty of New Echota (that subsequently led to the Trail of Tears, a forced mass relocation of natives from their lands to less desirable areas and also accounted for a significant number of fatalities) that allows the Tribe to also send a non-voting Delegate to the House of Representatives. At the time of this writing, Congress has not passed the necessary legislation to accept this Delegate, but it is expected to do so. That said, it remains an open question in this redesigned House of Representatives how a Delegate like this one would fit in or if such a Delegate should exist at all. If the latter situation, the Treaty of New Echota would need to be renegotiated. Since natives make up only around 1% of the population, even if every single one voted for the same Party, it would still be challenging to get a single voting Representative elected, thus making the case to still include the non-voting Delegate.

In the meantime, it is most important to note that that among around 4.4 million people there is no representation and say. At this juncture, we are not talking about the territory system, just that people who are citizens or protectorates of the United States should have a voice in the Federal Government. They are directly impacted by every government decision yet have no say in how those decisions come together nor how they are enforced. This is patently discriminatory to a large group of people who should have some input.

Furthermore, even estimating that Puerto Rico has a population of 3.2 million at the end of 2018, that would be nearly 1% of the entire population in what would be the 29th largest State or Territory. In other words, similar and smaller states Utah (3.1 million), Iowa (3.1 million), Nevada (3.0 million), Arkansas (3.0 million), Mississippi (3.0 million), and Kansas (2.9 million) all have a say with four Representatives and two Senators each while Puerto Rico has no say whatsoever. What is the difference between Puerto Rico and the people of those States? Why should Puerto Rico not have equal representation in the Federal Government?

No, in order to get equal representation all people must be counted, and that extends further into the next and most sweeping change.

The crux of all arguments until this point have been that the win/lose by district method is eliminating representation. Many other western-style democracies elect their legislature by political party and not directly of individuals that cover specific odd-shaped slices of the country. The House of Representatives should follow a similar methodology in order to align to the will of the people directly. In other words, it will not be a zero-sum game of winning and losing, but a distribution game by the intent of the people. This would bring further engagement of the populous because people would have actual representation no matter where they live and what their beliefs are.

Here, let us return to an earlier chart with some modifications. If you will recall when we last looked at party preference, we stated that the election did not align to either how people voted nor how they identify. If we extrapolate a few assumptions, we can see a couple of different scenarios in how a straight party election would result in a very different distribution of the House of Representatives:

- **Scenario 1:** 95% of Democrats and Republicans vote for their preferred party, 2% of Democrats and Republicans vote for the other party, 3% of Democrats and Republicans vote for 3rd Parties, 40% of Independents vote Republican, 40% of Independents vote Democrat, 20% of Independents vote for 3rd Parties, and all Unknowns vote for 3rd Parties.

- **Scenario 2:** 95% of Democrats and Republicans vote for their preferred party, 2% of Democrats and Republicans vote for the other party, 3% of Democrats and Republicans vote for 3rd Parties, 20% of Independents vote Republican, 20% of Independents vote Democrat, 60% of Independents vote for 3rd Parties, and all Unknowns vote for 3rd Parties.

In this, we get two Scenarios where Scenario 1 is most Independents lean either Democrat or Republican and Scenario 2 where a small majority of Independents lean 3rd Party. This results in a striking re-adjustment of the House:

	House	2018 House Election Results	People of the U.S.A.	Scenario 1	Scenario 2
Democrat	54%	53%	31%	46%	38%
Republican	46%	44%	28%	43%	35%
Independent / Other	0%	3%	39%	12%	27%
Vacant / No Answer	0%	0%	2%	0%	0%

Even in Scenario 1, neither the Democrats nor the Republicans would have been able to take single party control of the House. In order to pass legislation, they would have to work with others! This, most of all, is the utmost critical element of this process: breaking up the oligopoly of the two major political parties and getting more competition and diversity. Instead of extremists of either the left or the right being able to control the agenda for as long as they are in charge, discussion and deals among many parties with particular needs would be necessary.

This brings us full circle back to the methodology. We will return shortly to determining the total number of members, but in this Amendment we establish how the Parties should prepare, and that is by creating a list of 100 members in order of preference. Since the suggestion is not to have voters pick an individual person, then they are aligning to a Party based upon a platform. Within the Party, though, there should be a list of the people intended to fill the positions in the House of Representatives and voters should be familiar with those people to make a decision on the group as a whole. The particular number will also be covered in detail ahead, however the important part here is the generation of the List in order to determine who the Parties are putting up for election. Therefore, even though it is voting for a platform, there are still specific people attached to that platform. The 100 number is also a good way to make sure a Party has enough people involved in order to stand a chance of electing a person and gaining enough of the populace.

Further through this Amendment is what has been discussed above; people will vote directly for the Parties and that all people will be included. Sandwiched in between these thoughts is another concept: getting the Federal Government out of Party business. Part of the issue with the Democrat/Republican oligopoly is that they have created rules that have the Federal, State, and local governments spending time, money, and resources on what should be internal Party responsibility. In particular, the fact that Primaries are conducted as if they are part of the election system and that government should support them is completely the antithesis to equal protections.

Why should the Government spend any time and resources on helping a Political Party decide who is going to run in their spot for an election? That is purely a Party responsibility, and as such this Amendment makes it clear that there is a separation of roles between the Government and those running to be in it. The act of coming up with a list of candidates and putting them in order of preference is a methodology that the Parties must decide themselves. If they need to go through a Primary process, it is up to them to create a voting process and pay for that process. Neither the United States government nor the governments of States, Territories, Counties, Cities, or any other division should have a responsibility for determining how an—essentially—nonprofit organization makes management decisions.

Finally, in order to fully remove the Government from being involved with Political Parties, all criteria for what is a "Political Party" needs to be removed. One of the major issues for third parties like Libertarians, Greens, and others is that they must go State-by-State and meet criteria that may be impossible unless they were already on a ballot. And even after they pass that criteria, they can still be removed and have to go through the process all over again.

Take for instance Maryland in March 2019. Libertarian and Green Party members—those registered with the State through their voter registration system—received a letter stating that their parties no longer met the criteria and their registration was being changed. Meanwhile, the Parties would have to go through a process to get themselves re-established at great cost of time and money. One of the criteria is to get 10,000 signatures from voters. Meanwhile, the Libertarians already had 20,000 registered voters before this purge, so it created an unnecessary re-verification of what should already have been known.

At the same time, the Parties are suing the State costing the taxpayers money. What it comes down to is a simple set of questions:

- Why is the Government in the business of defining what is a Political Party?

- Why is the Government limiting choices of the voters for any reason?

- Why is the Government wasting taxpayer resources to determine what Political Parties should be in or out?

If Apple, Google, and Microsoft got together and had the government agree that they were the only three companies you could buy technology from unless other companies passed some capricious criteria that the large companies designed, it would rightfully be called collusion and be struck down. Yet here we have the same situation where the Democrats and Republicans have done exactly that in order to limit their competition, just at the political level. There is no hope for other voices to be heard so long as Lucy is holding the football and can move it any time.

As shown in the prior section, it is not just political affiliation that is a cause for concern, but other odd limitations put in place by the Constitution. With that, the next small Amendment can be made:

By Amendment to the Constitution of the United States, Article 1, Section 2, Clause 2 shall read:

No Person shall be a Representative who shall not have attained to the Age of ~~twenty-five Years~~ **voting maturity as defined by the Constitution and Congress**, and been seven Years a Citizen of the United States, ~~and who shall not, when elected, be an Inhabitant of that State in which he shall be chosen~~.

We have previously noted that Congress does not match up into the ages of the people of the United States and therefore cannot represent the differing concerns of each age group. Why were these particular age limitations put in place in the first place? Because the Founders feared a youth (re: poorer) movement would not understand the functions of government. But removing this criterion is akin to saying, "If you are old enough to vote, you are old enough to be able to serve in government." Since the 26th Amendment lowered the voting age to 18, then this would align with that. However, it is always possible that could change in any direction in the future and as such the age listed for voting should be used everywhere and this directive should be tied to that number, not a separate listing that has to be modified.

Going back to the function of how the candidates would now become part of the House of Representatives, this Amendment basically replaces an entire Clause and part of an existing Amendment:

> **By Amendment to the Constitution of the United States, Article 1, Section 2, Clause 3 shall read:**
>
> ~~The actual Enumeration shall be made within three Years after the first Meeting of the Congress of the United States, and within every subsequent Term of ten Years, in such Manner as they shall by Law direct. The Number of Representatives shall not exceed one for every thirty Thousand, but each State shall have at Least one Representative; and until such enumeration shall be made, the State of New Hampshire shall be entitled to chuse three, Massachusetts eight, Rhode-Island and Providence Plantations one, Connecticut five, New-York six, New Jersey four, Pennsylvania eight, Delaware one, Maryland six, Virginia ten, North Carolina five, South Carolina five, and Georgia three.~~ **The number of Members of the House of Representatives shall be no less than one hundred. The Members shall be determined by taking the number of votes for a Political Party and dividing among total votes to get a proportional vote. Those attaining at least one percent of the vote shall receive a Seat and shall receive an additional Seat for each percentage point above that. Partial percentages shall always be rounded up to the next highest full number. With the number of Seats by each Party set, the Members shall be filled by the Lists provided by the Political Parties.**

> **Further, Article/Amendment 14, Clause 2 shall exclude the following statement:**
>
> ~~Representatives shall be apportioned among the several States according to their respective numbers, counting the whole number of persons in each State, excluding Indians not taxed.~~

Just to clear this all up, there are currently 435 members of the House of Representatives as that is what Congress decided it should be. Further court and Congressional decisions set up the districts we have today. Since this would be a direct vote, districts would not be needed at all nor minimal numbers for each Representative. This is about creating something akin to proportional representation while also minimizing the size of the House. Let us go through a few situations to see how these numbers come out:

- If one party receives 99.00...1% or higher of the vote, they would receive 100 Seats, which would be the absolute minimum. Since no other Party will have passed the 1% threshold, they would be alone in the House of Representatives; thus showing why a list of 100 people is necessary because it is the maximum number of potential Members that a Party can receive.

- If 99 Parties receive 1.00...1% of the vote, then any other Party cannot reach the 1% threshold. Since all percentages are rounded up to the nearest whole number, each of the 99 Parties would receive 2 Seats. Therefore, the House of Representatives would have a maximum of 198 Members.

- Both of those situations are highly unlikely. In the 2018 election, no third party made the 1% threshold by themselves so that election would have ended up with 55 Democrats and 46 Republicans.

- However, as previously established, third parties receive so few votes because of the various methods of suppression. Since there is not good enough data on third parties, if we go back to Scenarios 1 and 2 we may have ended up with either...

  - 46 Democrats + 43 Republicans + 12 Other Parties = 101 Members
  - 38 Democrats + 36 Republicans + 28 Other Parties = 102 Members

Either of these situations and how many seats the Other Parties have may completely depended upon how small a percentage each one gets. If there are 28 parties with 1.00...1% of the vote a piece, they would each get 2 seats. As such, a potential maximum in these cases would be...

- 46 Democrats + 43 Republicans + 24 Other Parties = 113 Members
- 38 Democrats + 36 Republicans + 56 Other Parties = 130 Members

The latter situation is particularly interesting in that it makes all Other Parties the largest party by Members. While none individually would the largest Party, by design it gives them an outstripped power so that the larger parties cannot run roughshod over them and dismiss their claims. In other words, it is a check within the House to make sure those in the minority are still heard and must be worked with.

Right now, with a large number of members, the House of Representatives is also quite inefficient. It is difficult to work with—nonetheless meet and know—so many other people. By pruning the size of the House, it is an attempt to make it more efficient and reasonable to work in, especially considering the disparity in opinions this system would set up.

Finally, there is one bit of housekeeping for the House:

> **By Amendment to the Constitution of the United States, Article 1, Section 2, Clause 4 shall read:**
>
> When vacancies happen in the Representation ~~from any State, the Executive Authority thereof shall issue Writs of Election to fill such Vacancies~~ **the Parties elected shall fill those vacancies from the next eligible and available names on their Lists**.

Basically, instead of expensive new elections in an area and a long time without some people having representation, a stability is created. With the pre-defined Lists, the next people in line are already there and if for any reason a replacement is needed, it is a simple measure to put a new person in place.

With that, we have covered all the main areas that completely changes the House of Representatives into the "House of the People". The only Clause not discussed is the 5th one that covers selecting the Speaker of the House and other Officers. Again, there are no Constitutional rules to contend with, so the Clause shall remain unchanged. That said, the process will be much more interesting with more parties involved because if no party ever has the majority then no one can just be "made" the Speaker.

It will be a lot more interesting getting to take over the Speaker of the House office in the U.S. Capital Building in Washington, DC as pictured here in December 2019.

This brings up interesting parallels to the Parliamentary Democracies around the world. Unlike the United States, countries like the United Kingdom, Israel, Norway, and others do not have a strong or any type of Executive system and instead the Legislature is almost purely in charge. The Legislature goes through a process of forming a "coalition" of parties and those parties vote on the Prime Minister who is essentially the true Head of State. Here, the power would be completely limited to just being the Speaker of the House, so the deal-making for determining Speaker would most likely come down to those "other Officers"—what we know today as committee heads (another fabricated function that is not part of the Constitution).

How the House of Representatives intends to organize and govern itself should be left mostly up to itself. However, there will be certain provisions we will review later to ensure a smooth process and the ability of legislation to be able to come to the floor. Congress has many self-inflicted hurdles that require dismantling, but for the moment we will continue to focus on the makeup of the body.

The last right the House of Representatives has in the 5th Clause is the Power of Impeachment. While the language is still rather vague, the process makes sense throughout the rest of the Constitution with the Senate. What does not make sense is the makeup of the Senate itself, and that is the next stop on our journey.

TWO IN THE HAND

As set up today, the Senate makes absolutely no sense. Every State has two Senators despite any and all factors. As previously discussed, that means that small States with more sheep than people have as much say as a State with largest amount of people and almost the largest amount of land. Meanwhile, the largest Territories that are physically and population wise bigger than half the rest of the country have no say whatsoever. It is an incredibly imbalanced solution to a real concern.

The genuine issue that the Senate tries to resolve is that Federal Government needs a check on it from the States so that the former does not become too powerful and trample on their rights. While this was the gravest concern in the late 18th century, this is still a logical—though not as pronounced— consideration even today. In order to balance out the will of the Federal Government, there must be a counter. However, the counter needs to be fair to all constituents within it.

More so, demographics are making it so that the Senate is becoming even more unfair and lopsided. A University of Virginia study estimates that by 2040 around half of the population will be living in only eight states. Since each State has two Senators no matter what, that means that half of the country would be represented by just 16 votes while the other half from sparse states will have 84 votes! Now, we could go further into political affiliations with sparsely populated areas, but as has been shown in previous sections that is too simplistic of a story on voting patterns. The real takeaway is the population disparity alone.

In case this is not obvious, the first thing that must change is the makeup the number of Senators and how they are distributed:

By Amendment to the Constitution of the United States, Article 1, Section 3, Clause 1 shall read:

The Senate of the United States shall be composed of **at least** two Senators from each State **and Territory with permanent population, elected by the people thereof,** for ~~six~~ **four** Years **on the even years opposite elections for President and Vice President**; and each Senator shall have one Vote. **The total number of Senators received by each State and Territory shall be one Seat for each State and zero Seats for each Territory; plus a proportional distribution of one hundred Seats based upon the total population of the States and Territories; plus a proportional distribution of one hundred Seats based upon the total land area of the States and Territories; such that each State shall have no less than three Senators and each Territory shall have no less than two Senators. The legal body of each State and Territory shall determine the method by which Senators are elected.**

Further, Article/Amendment 17, Clause 1 shall exclude the following components:

~~The Senate of the United States shall be composed of two Senators from each State, elected by the people thereof, for six years; and each Senator shall have one vote. The electors in each State shall have the qualifications requisite for electors of the most numerous branch of the State legislatures.~~

Since the House of Representatives has become a mechanism to reflect the Federal will of the people, the Senate should be a reflection of the States to keep in check the Federal Government, but still be a fair and balanced to what they represent. As such, the Senate can be thought of as the "Legislature of the Land", where the borders—as artificial as they are—determine an area that needs a say. Yet despite that need, the Senate requires a check within itself so that undersized and underpopulated States cannot have outsized influence over larger ones, and at the same time making sure the larger ones cannot act with impudence over the smaller ones. And on top of that, everyone must think of making sure all Americans are represented in the Senate.

Given those criteria, the first change is the relative number of Senators by saying that each State and Territory must have at a minimum two. Once again, Territories are included so that the millions of people living in those places and the thousands of square miles are not excluded. However, unlike the House of Representatives Amendments, there is an important distinction in Territories that have a permanent population. As previously noted, there are several more Territories that do not have populations and therefore are truly under the direct control of the Federal government. These areas do not need special attention because there is no one to represent!

Continuing on this path, there is then a distribution of available Seats. While we have condensed the House of Representatives, we have expanded the Senate within certain confines. While the House of Representatives needed pruning for efficiency, the Senate needs expansion to limit power mongering.

The first part was saying that if the location were a State it would receive a Seat and that if it was a Territory with Permanent Population, it would not. While much of this document so far has been discussing the importance of including Territories and the populations within, there are certain rights and responsibilities that come with being a full-fledged State. This is one of those areas where it makes sense to put a distinction to incentivize Territories to become full States and to make sure Territories do not have an outstripped role. This is yet another check on the system, constraining States and Territories with each other.

That is not to say Territories would not receive full representation, though. As the next part lays out, there would be 100 Seats to be distributed by physical area and another 100 Seats to be distributed by population. Given the current layout of the United States, this would result in a total of 250 seats—which would go up slightly by 1 as Territories became States or a new State were admitted to the Union. One of the main concerns right now is what if Texas or California split into many States and each State received two Senators. This would give these new States a massive amount of voting power, especially if they voted as a block or close to it. Instead, having more Senators to curb the impact of additional ones while also limiting what one gets just for being a State makes this a more smoothed-out growth and distribution curve.

The distribution curve is the most important part, as well. If California or Texas were to split up, the percentage of the land and population each new State were carrying would limit the power of each one. The total number of Senators would be slightly higher, but the distribution would reflect what is within the border of each. On the other side, if a new State joined the Union, then there would be a redistribution and some States may lose a Seat so the new ones could gain.

What you will notice is that this reimagining of the Senate is rather silent on the method by which the distribution is to happen, and this is intentional. If you take a straight percentage—and say those below one percent must at least get one of each Area and Population and round the rest—this will not work and you will end up with far too many Senators. If you keep the 1% rule but round down, you may end up with too few. Instead, certain other criteria need to be put in place in order to determine how the States receive their Senators.

In this example, I have used a method where each State must get at least one Senator in each Area and Population, even if their percentage is below 1%. Then, the threshold for rounding Area was set whereby 0.87+ will round up and everything below will round down. This yielded the perfect 100 Senators for Area. A similar method was tried for Population, but due to some tight numbers even a 0.999999999 rounding requirement still yielded 101 Senators. In the end, Indiana being the state with the least population and more than 3 Senators had to have one removed. Apologies to Indiana. The result was this:

	Is a State	Area Distribution	Population Distribution	Total Senators
Alabama	1	1	1	3
Alaska	1	17	1	19
American Samoa	0	1	1	2
Arizona	1	3	2	6
Arkansas	1	1	1	3
California	1	4	11	16
Colorado	1	2	1	4
Connecticut	1	1	1	3
Delaware	1	1	1	3
District of Columbia	0	1	1	2
Florida	1	1	6	8
Georgia	1	1	3	5
Guam	0	1	1	2
Hawaii	1	1	1	3
Idaho	1	2	1	4
Illinois	1	1	3	5

	Is a State	Area Distribution	Population Distribution	Total Senators
Indiana	1	1	1	3
Iowa	1	1	1	3
Kansas	1	2	1	4
Kentucky	1	1	1	3
Louisiana	1	1	1	3
Maine	1	1	1	3
Maryland	1	1	1	3
Massachusetts	1	1	2	4
Michigan	1	2	3	6
Minnesota	1	2	1	4
Mississippi	1	1	1	3
Missouri	1	1	1	3
Montana	1	3	1	5
Nebraska	1	2	1	4
Nevada	1	3	1	5
New Hampshire	1	1	1	3
New Jersey	1	1	2	4
New Mexico	1	3	1	5
New York	1	1	5	7
North Carolina	1	1	3	5
North Dakota	1	1	1	3
Northern Mariana Islands	0	1	1	2

	Is a State	Area Distribution	Population Distribution	Total Senators
Ohio	1	1	3	5
Oklahoma	1	1	1	3
Oregon	1	2	1	4
Pennsylvania	1	1	3	5
Puerto Rico	0	1	1	2
Rhode Island	1	1	1	3
South Carolina	1	1	1	3
South Dakota	1	2	1	4
Tennessee	1	1	2	4
Texas	1	7	8	16
U.S. Virgin Islands	0	1	1	2
Utah	1	2	1	4
Vermont	1	1	1	3
Virginia	1	1	2	4
Washington	1	2	2	5
West Virginia	1	1	1	3
Wisconsin	1	1	1	3
Wyoming	1	2	1	4

Of the 56 States and Territories, exactly half (28) ended up with 2 or 3 Senators. Among the States and Territories at the top of the charts, Alaska is by far the biggest winner expanding to 19 Senators based almost solely on its massive land area (which might make a case for splitting Alaska up, but that is not a concern for this particular argument). Outside of Alaska, though, the real winners were as expected with California and Texas each receiving 16 Senators—the exact outcome one would surmise for States with such vast amounts of area and populations to go along with them. The next highest States were Florida at 8 Seats and New York at 7 Seats. Though a precipitous drop off, it does reflect fairly the two factors of population and size. From there it continues to drop off so that States with large populations and small sizes (like Massachusetts) share the same number of Senators with those that have small population and large sizes (like South Dakota). None of the Territories escaped their 2-Seat minimum.

Note that this is just an example and Congress may make other decisions on distribution, but it shows the methodology in play. It makes sure States and Territories that have more land and people in turn have a large say while also making sure that no area has too little say or blocks of votes. There may be slight modifications to the method based on how large populations and land are in the future, and as such this modified Clause now allows the flexibility while giving a more equal distribution of power. Again, it is not completely even, nor is it 100% fair; it is just intended to level the playing field without going overboard to create perfection.

Beyond the setup, much like the House of Representatives, the Senate should be elected every four years in totality and once again on the even years opposite the Executive Branch. This would ensure that the entire Legislature is renewed during the term of the President and serve as a check on power or a will of the people. And again, this would make each 2-year cycle for elections incredibly important because so many positions would be being filled.

Critically different, though, is that the Senators are selected in a method decided by the States and Territories themselves. Once they know how many Seats they have, the method they choose to fill them is up to them save for being elected by the people. Now, it would be hoped that they would fill them in distributed manner akin to the House of Representatives, but that is a regional decision that must be up to each locale, as is the right of State/Territory.

These particularities were pulled up and out of the Amendments and into the main document; and were additionally further clarified. For instance, before the 17th Amendment, the Constitution made it sound like the largest party in each State's Legislature could come up with some way of deciding who could be a Senator. This has now been laid out to specifically say the "legal body" of each State or Territory in general decides the method for electing Senators, within the confines of elections by the people.

Of course, now that we have a larger number of Seats and method to fill them, the occasional vacancy will happen. As such, the next Clause covers how that is resolved:

> **By Amendment to the Constitution of the United States, Article 1, Section 3, Clause 2 shall be merged with Article/Amendment 17, Clause 2 and together shall read:**
>
> ~~Immediately after they shall be assembled in Consequence of the first Election, they shall be divided as equally as may be into three Classes. The Seats of the Senators of the first Class shall be vacated at the Expiration of the second Year, of the second Class at the Expiration of the fourth Year, and of the third Class at the Expiration of the sixth Year, so that one third may be chosen every second Year;~~
>
> When vacancies happen in the representation of any State **or Territory** in the Senate, the executive authority of such State or Territory shall issue writs of election to fill such vacancies: Provided, **t**hat the legislature of any State may empower the executive thereof to make temporary appointments until the people fill the vacancies by ~~election as the legislature may direct~~ **the method chosen by the State or Territory**.

With elections now happening every four years in totality, there is no need at all for the original statements in Clause 2 that cover Senator expirations from the time of the signing of the Constitution to today. Instead, the Clause can pick up what is already in Amendment 17, Section 2 to discuss filling vacancies. The only updates are technical, with a note to include Territories and removing that the specific method for voting for Senators to the method chosen by the State or Territory. This is important in case the State chooses a List-type method like with the House of Representatives. The Constitution should not be telling the States and Territories what their method is; the States and Territories should be informing the Federal government.

The pre-existing clause also allows the Executive Branch of States and Territories to fill vacant Senate seats on a temporary basis if allowed by their Legislatures (or Constitutions). This is maintained as a logical clause because it already has the out of being a decision left entirely to the States/Territories. Because the Senate is about the State's/Territory's power to check the Federal Government, then this should remain unchanged.

As with House of Representatives, there are some arbitrary age requirements for being a Senator that should be removed:

> **By Amendment to the Constitution of the United States, Article 1, Section 3, Clause 3 shall read:**
>
> No Person shall be a Senator who shall not have attained to the Age of ~~thirty Years~~ **voting maturity as defined by the Constitution and Congress**, and been nine Years a Citizen of the United States, and who shall ~~not, when elected, be an Inhabitant of that State for which he shall be chosen~~ **be a citizen of the State or Territory chosen during the election and throughout service to the Senate**.

The story is the same: if you are old enough to vote, you are old enough to serve. Additionally, the language of Clause 3 is rather obtuse, so this update clarifies that one must be a citizen of where they represent both at the time of election and during the entire course of their service to the Senate. However, the rule for "nine Years a Citizen of the United States" has been left in place. Although this is an anachronism left over from the Revolution and fear of foreign powers taking over the Senate, it is not distinctly a poor rule like the age requirement. All that statement does is another check to make sure those who serve meet the requirement of working for the country, and this is a test thereof.

A similar test does exist in the House of Representatives, but it is fewer years because foreign nationals may make a percentage of the populace and deserve representation that speaks to their needs should such a party arise. The Senate—being the check on the House of Representatives—should have a stricter rule in place. There is no functional reason to remove this particular wording, so for now it can stay as is. An argument could be made for the number of years in both situations, but that is up for debate and could be modified (and perhaps even eliminated from the House).

Finally, there is one minor change that is a preview to come:

> **By Amendment to the Constitution of the United States, Article 1, Section 3, Clause 4 shall read:**
>
> The Vice President of the United States shall be President of the Senate, but shall have no Vote~~, unless they be equally divided~~.

The only change here is that Vice President can no longer cast a tie breaking vote. Why this is will become very clear in the next section, but the crux of it is that no legislation should need a tie-breaker vote in order to proceed. Also, there is some oddity to having an Executive stand in a Legislative body for any reason, but there may be a use for this that will also be covered in a future section. Therefore, for now, we leave the Vice President in place and do not strip him of one of his limited duties!

From here, there is no need to get involved in the rest of Section 3. The next Clause discusses the President of the Senate pro tempore (the person who theoretically runs the Senate when the Vice President is not there, which is almost always, but more on this role shortly), and the selection of officers as the Senate sees fit. The next two clauses then cover impeachment which by itself is written out fine and with reason. The execution over the past couple of centuries leaves much to be desired, but that may change with a different makeup of the Legislature to begin with. As such, we again leave those alone and prepare to move on to how Congress functions.

LET'S TALK ABOUT IT

As we move through the remainder of Article 1 of the Constitution and the Amendments that impact it, there is not much that needs to be modified. We definitely need to look at Article 1, Section 4, Clause 1 because it relates to the day when Senators and Representatives are elected, but that is part of a bigger discussion on how elections should happen in general. Instead, let us focus for now on the duties of the legislative division of government.

Section 5 covers how Congress decides its own rules and procedures for doing business, making sure that there is a record of their activities, and keeping both chambers of Congress in session with each other. Moving on to Section 6, it straightforwardly notes that Congresspeople should be compensated for their services (more on this later) and makes sure they are not taking payments from places they should not. Section 7 is procedural dealing with how bills work through Congress and Section 8 covers the specific responsibilities Congress has. The next two sections are much the same, with 9 putting limitations and control on Congress—especially on trade, foreign influence, and honoring the law already established—and 10 making sure the States defer to the Federal government in matters of trade, coin, treaty, and war. All seems pretty cut and dry.

As such, you may be asking: what is the problem?

There is no doubt that Congress has become broken from the simple fact that so little legislation gets through; there is more time spent on using the made-up rules of Congress as weapons and technicalities than on organization and process; and that the items that do pass often are going through only on party lines or a thin margin with the other party involved. With few to no individually minded Congresspeople thinking of their constituents instead of their own party politics, we are in an era of stall and go-go-go that ebbs only as one party receives a small level of control of both chambers of Congress and the Presidency.

This is no way to govern.

While the changes made to the makeup of Congress and how Senators and Representatives are elected seem rather massive, they are relatively small tweaks to an existing process. At the end of the day, it is still a two-chambered legislature that has the same responsibilities, controls, and self-imposed rules that follows a process to shepherd a bill to a law. Yes, the intent was to limit the control of one party or another and get more voices in government, but it is not enough by itself that it could force Congress to act reasonably and accomplish their jobs.

That is why more than tweaks are necessary here. Instead, we need to add whole additional sections to the Constitution to not just change who is having the conversations, but how they are having them and what the rules should be. The original Constitution was silent on most of the procedures of Congress, but we have already dealt with the long-term issues of Congress's lack of oversight on that process. No, here we need to make sure we add language that forces Congress to be a thoughtful legislature and pay the price if they do not. In other words: Congress needs real accountability.

A view of the U.S. Capital Building in the National Mall in Washington, DC in December 2019. The House of Representatives and Senate meet here, but what is accomplished when they do so?

CRAZY IDEA: ACTUALLY VOTING!

You have seen the headlines: The House of Representatives or the Senate has passed a piece of legislation and it is moving on to the other chamber. And then... nothing... absolutely nothing. There was great fanfare; this was an important piece of potential law that would cause a paradigm shift. Yet, despite all of this, it simply died and went away, never to be discussed again. What happened?

Article 1, Section 5, Clause 2 states:

> Each House may determine the Rules of its Proceedings, punish its Members for disorderly Behaviour, and, with the Concurrence of two thirds, expel a Member.

And that is it. There are very few rules about how Congress is supposed to function and as such Congress has made up its own process over time. Whenever the news is talking about Congressional procedures and requirements, it is important to keep in mind that these are entirely fabricated by Congress and are inherently mutable. There is nothing in the Constitution that states how a bill is supposed to be presented, discussed, and passed on through each step of the system to become law. The few exceptions include Article 1, Section 7, Clause 1 that says, "All Bills for raising Revenue shall originate in the House of Representatives" and Clauses 2 and 3 that cover the bill moving from Congress to the President. These also cover how to deal with vetoes but are silent on any other part of the process.

Notice what is missing? There is not a mechanism to move legislation from one chamber to the other. That is where many of these Congressional rules have come into place and why legislation can die without ever being heard. It puts tremendous power in two peoples' hands: The Speaker of the House and the Senate Majority Leader. Each has effectively complete control over the agenda in their chamber and if they decide that a piece of legislation should not be heard, then it will not be. This includes anything passed by the other chamber or even the concerns of the majority of the chamber. There is just no way past these two gatekeepers and thus they have vastly overarching power that was never granted vis-a-vie the Constitution.

It is also important to note that nothing in the Constitution nor the Senate rules give the Senate Majority Leader any type of power or control; that has only come about from tradition and precedent. From a Constitutional perspective, the President/President pro Tempore of the Senate should be the one in charge, yet that position has become almost completely ceremonial.

Therefore, we have a problem where two people have a monopoly control over the country that was never granted to them and power over other legislators that are supposed to be their equals. It does not matter if a Representative is 25 years old and just elected or been serving for 50 years, they are 100% equal in the eyes of the Constitution. As such, we need to make some changes to the Constitution in order to rip back what never should have taken root in the first place and make sure Congress can function nominally.

Article 1 currently ends at Section 10. Amendments to the Constitution have been written as their own Articles which is inherently confusing because the Constitution is written in an order of specific themes. By tagging Amendments as Articles and not adjusting the original text, it makes a disjointed read and difficult to discern which is current law. As shown in the prior section, it will be more helpful to adjust the original text and merge the Amendments in where plausible (see the Appendix for a complete view of this in a finalized re-written Constitution). In this case, we are going to add an entirely new section to the existing documentation with its own clauses.

Clause 1 shall read:

The Speaker of the House of Representative and the President or President pro Tempore of the Senate shall be responsible for scheduling all debate and voting of their respective chambers.

While the positions of Speaker of the House and President/President pro Tempore of the Senate are laid out in the Constitution, there is nothing that states what those responsibilities include. This Clause is focused on giving them a very specific responsibility: setting the agenda and calendar for debate and voting. Notice, as well, that is it the President of the Senate (the Vice President of the United States) or the President pro Tempore who are setting the agenda in the upper chamber and not the "Majority Leader". Being that that Majority Leader is not a recognized position, we should work in the framework of the Constitution to grant responsibility to an existing position.

Thus far, this codifies what is happening today in the House and shifting the responsibility in the Senate—yet to the same result. Here, two people still have control over what their respective chamber is doing at any time. Therefore, the rest of the Clauses need to limit that control and make sure all Representatives and Senators are equal, as well as create checks on power overall from other branches of the government.

> **Clause 2 shall read:**
>
> Any legislation proposed by individual members of each chamber should be considered for schedule and voting by the leaders of the respective chambers. The leader of the chamber may refuse to add the legislation to the schedule, however if the legislation is sponsored by ten percent or more of the chamber it must be added to the schedule within thirty days of presenting the required sponsorship to the leader of the chamber.

Basically, this is a codification of how an item is going to come up for vote. The leader of each chamber should act as a gatekeeper because someone needs to be operations manager. But at the end of the day, they are subordinate to the will of all other legislators. The first part of this Clause makes it so anyone can present an item to the leader and the leader can just add it to the agenda with no questions asked. However, given there is a possibility for extreme fringe views to make it into a chamber (especially the House of Representatives), the leaders do have a filter mechanism to control what would ultimately waste time.

That is where the next override comes into place where the legislator who proposed the item need only get 10% of their chamber to say they want it on the agenda. Important to note that is not 10% of the chamber supporting the legislation, just that they agree that it should be heard on the floor and debated. Following that, there is a time limit for the leader of the chamber to get it on the agenda so they cannot stonewall the desires of a minority position. The threshold is large enough to remove the most fringe elements while at the same time allows those with a minority opinion to be heard and received in a timely manner.

> **Clause 3 shall read:**
>
> The Vice President of the United States—as President of the Senate—may propose legislation that must be added to the schedule and voted on within thirty days.

While it is an odd bit of the Constitution that the Vice President of the United States is the President of the Senate, there is a reason for this. Remember that we always want to make sure one branch of government should not have complete power over the other and that each is constantly kept in check by the other two. This position of the Vice President is a check of the Executive Branch on the Legislative Branch by making sure the legislature takes into consideration the concerns of the Executives. Much like minority representation in the prior Clause, this one gives executive representation in the law-making process.

Here, let us reiterate that that the Vice President is still a non-voting member and can only act basically as a meeting organizer. The tie-breaking voting power he did have we removed earlier, for reasons that will become clear shortly.

> **Clause 4 shall read:**
>
> Any order by the Supreme Court or delegated Federal Court to create new law or modify existing bills and law must be done within the timeframe designated by the Court.

Much later in this treatise we will return to Judicial Branch and its rights, responsibility, and limits thereof, but this is a taste of what is to come. Much like the Legislature, nothing in the Constitution has told the Judicial Branch how to function and what it can do. One of the abilities the Judicial Branch has granted itself is the ability to create law via judicial review. While judicial review is important in determining if a law is Constitutional or in violation of another law, it is an overreach by the courts to take on the task of determining what the legislation should have been when the Constitution or law is silent.

As such, a barrier needs to be put in place that stops the Judicial Branch from creating law because that is not their job. However, the courts should have the ability to compel the legislature to create law based upon the discoveries of the court. If the courts find that the law is lacking in a situation or the law as written has flaws, then the courts should have the ability to demand that the law-making body itself revisit and fix this.

Much leeway should be given to the courts in these decisions and in what timeframe they want Congress to correct the issues. Therefore: minor legislators, the executive branch, and the courts would have the ability for bills, laws, and adjustments to be introduced. But at the end of the day, it would still be 100% the responsibility of the Legislative Branch to make the law (and in this case the President to sign off on the updates). This separation of responsibility is critical to removing overreach by any branch and keeping roles completely distinct.

Meanwhile, the courts will need a mechanism to enforce this and other rules, but we'll return to that in Clause 10. In the meantime, there is more to the process that must be considered before we look at enforcement of said process.

> **Clause 5 shall read:**
>
> Any legislation that shall pass through either chamber of Congress must be scheduled and voted on by the other chamber within ten days.

Here we move into the process whereby the leaders nor the majority party of an individual chamber of Congress cannot stop legislation from moving through the next step. While in Clause 1 we established the responsibility of setting the schedules, here we taper that power further by making it clear that there is a responsibility to call a vote on something that has passed. In this way, this clause will remove the un-Constitutional power that the Speaker of the House and the Majority Leader of the Senate have bestowed upon themselves and level the playing field between each chamber. No matter what, then, a piece of legislation must be heard in the other chamber and voted upon.

One of the tools that Congress uses to stop legislation both as it moves between chambers and even within its own chamber is the process of adding amendments to make it undesirable. This is the next procedural move that must be stopped.

> **Clause 6 shall read:**
>
> All legislation must consist of single clauses directly related to the same subject at hand. Each clause and amendment must be passed separately in its own approval process.

Much as this section has been written in individual clauses, so, too, must Congress write their bills. Then, it is not voting on a bill in totality if there is just one part that is objectionable. Instead, each part would be open for debate, voting, and sending to the President for signature or veto. As written, this would also give the President line-item veto power since each clause would be presented individually and therefore would require sign-off on each.

At the same time, if there are differences between the House and the Senate, the differences will come through Amendments that would move through their own process so as not to stop the individual clause if there are no threshold objections. More important than all of that, though, is the end of pork packages. It is a common practice for Congress to attach some unrelated spending to a bill as a matter of compromise in order to get a particular person's or group's vote. More often than not these add-ons have nothing to do with the legislation at hand and everything to do with securing funding for the Representative's or Senator's home area and score brownie points with the voters.

If we eliminate the ability to just attach anything as a package deal and make it be voted on individually, then it will simply be on the merits of the item alone. True, the legislators could just make the same type of deals and agree to vote for each other's items, but at least this way it would be clean and there would be as many checks as possible between the two chambers and the President. Since each clause would be voted on individually, all members could be held accountable for their vote to that single line item. However, in order to do that requires getting every vote on the record.

> **Clause 7 shall read:**
>
> All Representatives and Senators, save for vacancies or physical inability, are required to cast a vote on all legislation presented before that chamber of Congress.

This may seem an odd item, but theoretically a Representative or Senator could just walk out of the room (or never show up to the room in the first place) and not vote on an item. Abstaining (voting "present") is a tool commonly used to avoid the appearance of taking a stand or getting on the record of exactly where a person or organization aligns. Often this is done in arenas like the United Nations in which a nation does not support some specific resolution but will not vote against it in order to not appear to be taking sides or to appease some opposing party. The standards of the U.N., though, are outside the purview of what is needed for the United States of America.

Within the confines of the United States, our elected officials must be held accountable, and the only way to do that is to have them on the record. This is how the voters in the country get to check on those representing them because there is a definitive record of not just where they stand on a bill in total, but on each clause and adjustment of that bill. It is the official record that can be used for or against an individual that is supposed to be the will of the people they were elected to represent.

The exceptions for not voting should be few and far in between. In the prior section, we have tried to eliminate times of vacancy as much as possible, even if it is with a temporary person. However, it is always possible that among nearly 400 people that a vacancy can happen at any time and that is understandable. That said, the idea of "physical inability" is speaking not of absence but of being in a hospitalized situation. As we will get to shortly, we will need to make sure Congress is always able to vote when necessary. Before that, it is time to severely limit what legislation can even move forward.

> **Clause 8 shall read:**
>
> All legislation must have at minimum sixty-one percent of the vote of all legislators in the chamber in order to pass to the next phase of the bill's process.

Here is the biggest rub of all. Today, legislation can pass from one chamber to the next and up to president with a simple majority. As the last twenty years have shown, this means the majority of legislation was passed on party lines. When one party had control of all chambers of Congress and the President, they were able to get their special interest items through. This includes recent massive items like the Affordable Care Act of 2010 and Tax Cuts and Jobs Act of 2017.

The Affordable Care Act was pushed through by Democrats with 51% of the House of Representatives, 60% of the Senate, and 53% of Congress in total. The Tax Cuts and Job Act was pushed through by Republicans with 54% of the House of Representatives, 51% of the Senate, and 53% of Congress in total. In other words, both were equally forced through by one side or another simply because of their majority at the time and their control over the White House at that moment. More so, in both cases no member of the other party voted in favor of the other's legislation. In reality, several Democrats voted against the Affordable Care Act and several Republicans voted against the Tax Cuts and Jobs Act.

Going back to the prior section of trying to limit the powers of one party and setting procedures that will hopefully limit one party from majority control, this clause is the next step in that process. Based upon voting patterns, bare majority should not be enough to move a piece of legislation ahead, especially in a country so evenly split. As has been seen with the Affordable Care Act, once the other party gets enough control, they work to dismantle that legislation. It is not a stable environment for people, municipalities, companies, the economy, or any other metric.

Poignantly, Congress used to believe they should have certain items that reached a higher level of acceptance. This was especially true in appointments to the Supreme Court where Senate Rules required a "super majority" of 60 votes. However, with stonewalling and no discussions between parties, this requirement was removed in favor of a simple majority. Lest this be considered an attack on Republicans, Democrats have done or attempted similar measures, so both major parties have equal blame.

We need to take that choice out of their hands and make sure legislation that has passed already has at least a "super majority" so that it is not just a constant batter-up position. Engraving in the Constitution a 61% requirement for any bill to pass will be closer to getting real legislation into law and limit individual party power.

Further, the threshold is below the veto override. That remains at 2/3rd (66.66...7%) of the House of Representatives and the Senate, so there is a gap between passing and guaranteeing it become law. Even if the vote was with 67% of the vote, there is no guarantee that those who voted for it will override a veto as they may respect the President's wishes or have reservations to begin with. Either way, it would give a tool to make bills more worthy of consideration.

Finally, this shows why the Vice President no longer needs his tie breaking power. Only legislation with 61% is going to pass through to the next part of the process, so if the vote is tied at 50/50, then it has effectively failed.

With all of these clauses in place, all that matters is enforcing them in the strongest terms.

> **Clause 9 shall read:**
>
> Congress shall make no rules or exceptions to circumvent the process of scheduling and conducting a vote.

This one sentence expresses this thought: do not try to create loopholes! The bureaucracy in Congress is self-inflicted, but that does not mean that all of it is without value. These rules were created to bring order to what can be a chaotic process within a large body of people. The problem has been that over time these rules have mutated from helpful elements to weapons of war to make Congress not function in order to push (or suppress) a specific agenda. Here we have a Clause that is ambiguous as well as wide, making all of those rules reviewable under a single criterion: does it stop legislation from flowing naturally? If a rule does not, then there is no worry. If it does, then there must be consequences.

> **Clause 10 shall read:**
>
> Failure to follow the guidelines of Article One, Section Eleven of the Constitution and any future amendments shall be considered Treason of the United States of America. The Vice President of the United States is responsible for enforcement of this clause and bringing forth charges of Treason against individual members of Congress.

Does treason seem a bit harsh? Well, let us look at Article 3, Section 3, Clause

1 of the Constitution which is the only point in which Treason is defined:

> Treason against the United States, shall consist only in levying War against them, or in adhering to their Enemies, giving them Aid and Comfort. No Person shall be convicted of Treason unless on the Testimony of two Witnesses to the same overt Act, or on Confession in open Court.

The next Clause gives Congress the ability to define the punishment for treason, but as you can see treason is very tightly tied to just one thing. By the Constitution, treason is about supporting enemies of the country and... that is it.

At the time the Constitution was written, there was great concern about foreign powers attempting to take over the fledgling nation. These were well grounded fears and during the revolution they experienced such betrayals. Modern estimates put that only about a third of the nation supported separation from England and the creation of a new country, so there were plenty of leftover questions on loyalty. Others were not sure that anything in the Articles of Confederation allowed the founders to even throw that out and start anew (hint: there was not). Meanwhile, as covered when we started this journey, the States were not exactly sold on what the Constitution offered. In other words, there were lots of chances for someone to turn to the other side for support.

Over time, the United States has become a super-power and a beacon for how other nations can function in a representative democracy. Foreign powers do try to influence and impact what happens within the borders of the United States of America and people do fall under the spell of those powers for a variety of reasons. That definition of Treason should remain in place and prosecuted as normal.

What about the enemies within, though? What about putting oneself before the country? What about betraying the principles of the nation and pledges made when accepting office for personal or party gain?

Are these not attacks on the nation? Does not hurting the nation constitute support to enemies by default?

The point of this last Clause is to remove the shield of invincibility that members of the government have. If they do not follow the rules or abuse their positions, what is the consequence? Most of the time it is nothing at all, and at worst it is loss of job when the voters get a chance. As covered previously, most members of Congress get re-elected so the same problems continue generation after generation. There needs to be a real and tangible consequence to trying to abuse the trusted position of a Representative or Senator.

Therefore, the recommendation is to make it treason to try to stop legislation using rules and procedures and underhanded methods. There are succinct responsibilities and functions that the leaders of each chamber and the members within have, and if they refuse to do their duty then they need to be punished. The impudence must end. There is no better example of this than with the current Supreme Court.

A LEGO® display of the first four female Supreme Court justices on display at the Supreme Court of the United States in January 2020. As of that date, they remain the only women to serve in this role.

When Supreme Court Justice Anthony Scalia died in 2016, President Obama did his Constitutional duty by presenting a nominee to the Senate in Merrick Garland. The Senate's job was simple: interview and vet the candidate then cast a yay or nay vote. That is all there is to it! Instead, Senate Majority Leader Mitch McConnell decided to block the candidate from even getting a chance to talk to Congress, never mind voting for or against him. Then, after President Donald Trump took office, he in turn nominated Neil Gorsuch and McConnell immediately took up the nomination. When it became apparent he was not going to have the minimal votes required to instate Gorsuch, McConnell then changed the rules to push the nominee through with a simple majority. Finally, in May 2019 McConnell told various groups he would completely ignore his own reasoning for not bringing Obama's nominee to the floor (Supreme Court nominees should not be considered in a Presidential election year) if a Supreme Court position became available in the election year of President Trump.

Under this clause, that would all be Treason. Those actions were done with the malicious intent of personal party gain and had nothing to do with just doing the roles and responsibilities as laid out by the Constitution. Not taking up legislation within a required timeframe, ignoring the Executive Branch's ability to bring an item to the Senate Floor, pushing items through below an acceptable threshold, and capriciously changing rules in order to create a loophole around the intent of the Constitution—this is the exact reason that the entire Section 11 is needed.

By the Constitution as written, though, McConnell has done no wrong. He has worked within the framework of the law and manipulated it to his favor. Those like McConnell—whether Republican, Democrat, or otherwise—would also be within their rights to do exactly the same thing or something similar. Many have promised to do so, and others already have done so in the past. For example, in the 2014 Senate the Democrats had 53 seats plus 2 caucusing Independents to the Republicans 45. Meanwhile, in the House of Representatives there were 234 Republicans to 201 Democrats. By July 2014, Republicans in the House of Representatives were complaining loudly to the press of the of the over 300 bills the House had passed but the Senate had not taken up under the tutelage of Majority Leader Harry Reid.

And they were exactly right! Sure, those bills stood almost no chance to pass the Senate and—even if they did—would surely have been vetoed by President Obama. But that is not the job of the leaders of these chambers; the job of congresspeople is to fashion and vote on bills only, not to use legislative tools to avoid doing what they are Constitutionally obligated to do. Most certainly, their job is not to create never ending gridlock.

Actions like these are not in benefit to the people of the United States; they are in benefit to a single Party's power. Now, a Party may be doing what it thinks is best for all people, but as previously established Congress is not a representation of the will of the people. To bring it full circle, first Congress must become a more even distribution of the mix of views and peoples of the United States. Then, with that, Congress needs rules to function in benefit of the nation and not in benefit of themselves or their parties. And finally, when that fails, and they try to do something that is against the Constitution then a consequence needs to be available.

That consequence is the accusation of Treason. In a final check, only the Vice President would be able to accuse a Representative or Senator of Treason based upon breaking Section 11 of the Constitution, giving the Vice President oversight power that does not exist today, as well as someone outside of Congress to make sure they follow their own rules. Of course, being accused of treason is not the same as being convicted, and any person thus accused would have the ability to present their case to the courts. But should they be found guilty, then the repercussions become real.

STOP IN THE NAME OF LAW

With the shape of Congress changed and rules put in place to make it push legislation through without roadblocks, the next area to be addressed is limiting the impact of those laws. While much of the prior discussion is about how to make conversations happen and perhaps make them move quickly, this portion is the reality check to slow things down. That begins, once again, with adding additional clauses to the Constitution. This time, we can work within existing sections for organization's sake.

> **By Amendment to the Constitution of the United States, Article 1, Section 7, Clause 4 shall be added.**
>
> Any bill that thus has been passed by both Chambers of Congress and approved by the President of the United States, or reconsidered by Congress after the President has returned it shall then be sent to the Supreme Court or a Federal Court designated by the Supreme Court. The designated Court will review the bill and confirm that it meets the requirements of the Constitution and other relevant laws. No Bill shall become Law nor be in effect before this review.

Section 7 for the most part covers the process by which a Bill moves up to the President for approval or veto. As a matter of interest, the words "veto" and "override" are not part of the Constitution; they are words we have added when discussing these clauses in order to make them understandable. Instead, the President is to "return" a bill to Congress with objections, and in turn Congress may "reconsider" it with their two-thirds override. Just to be consistent with the original Constitution, we have used the same language in this clause.

As for this Clause itself, we are talking about another layer of checks before a law goes into effect. Giving the courts the ability to review a law before it is implemented is intended to limit harm and reduce court times. Right now, the government can pass any law and those who believe they would be harmed by it or believe that is violating their Constitutional rights are forced to take on the time and expense of suing, getting an injunction, and fighting the law. Further, all of those resources are going through the entire weight of the government that is responsible for upholding and defending the law. These cases can go on for years and cost significant funds that could be used for other purposes, even when the law is known to be troublesome just to get a court ruling in the first place.

By having the courts review laws before they are in effect will take the burden from average people or organizations and at least have an initial ruling. Now, if there are issues, the courts can return the law to Congress to fix it with their notes—a part of the Constitution that would exist if Article 1, Section 11, Clause 4 from before were added. If the courts are fine or at least find no major issues, then the law will go into effect as written. That is not to say that people or organizations could still not sue and try to have the legislation overturned, but at least the preliminary check would have already been done. In a way, this may allow skipping the long first part of a trial today and immediately get into the appeals process in order to have quicker rulings.

In either case, the main idea is to limit potential harm. If a law can go into effect that causes harm, even if the law is thrown out later much of that harm may be permanent. There is a need to get out ahead of that and hold the government in check in order to protect people. However, Federal Law is only a small part of these issues.

> **By Amendment to the Constitution of the United States, Article 1, Section 7, Clause 5 shall be added.**
>
> Any law that has passed the local process within each State or Territory shall be reviewed by the Federal Court designated by the Supreme Court before the law may go into effect. The designated Federal Court shall review that the new law does not violate the Constitution, existing Federal Law, existing State or Territory Law, or prior judicial interpretation of the law. Should the law be found in violation thereof, the Courts shall return the law to the State or Territory and not allow the law to go into effect.

Law that is passed at the State/Territory level is usually where these issues arise the most, especially when the State/Territory wants to challenge Federal Law or prior court rulings. Basically, this Amendment is an attempt to stop the States and Territories from creating a law that they know is against the Constitution, Federal Laws, or existing court decisions and waste the time and resources of the taxpayers and those who would be potentially harmed. That does not mean that States and Territories cannot challenge Federal Law or court rulings, but that creating contradictory law is not the appropriate venue to do so.

The Constitution is silent on how States and Territories are to function (save for being a "Republican Form of Government" in the case of States as laid out in Article 4, Section 4) and how laws are passed in each. Because of this, all the Courts can do is send the law back to State/Territory and say that it cannot pass. It is then up to the State/Territory to do whatever process they feel is necessary because State's rights are protected by other parts of the Constitution. While we have a laid out a specific methodology for the Federal Government, whatever happens at the local level is beyond the purview of the Constitution and the courts.

With that all said, there still needs to be a way to make sure laws can be challenged further. Just because something was passed into law a hundred years ago does not mean that it is valid today or that it would be written in the same way. That is why as an effort to make sure legislation happens within Congress and not the courts, another Amendment is needed to bring laws up for regular review:

> **By Amendment to the Constitution of the United States, Article 1, Section 7, Clause 6 shall be added.**
>
> Any law that has been put into effect shall expire twenty years past the day it was put into effect, unless another date prior to twenty years has been set for its expiration. The law must be repassed via the process as laid out for a new Bill by the Constitution and relevant law prior to expiration in order to remain in effect.
>
> Upon the passing of this Amendment, all existing laws shall expire on a schedule unless another date had already been set for its expiration within twenty years of its passing. Those laws that have passed in the prior twenty years shall come up for expiration as if this Amendment were already in effect. For those laws that passed prior to twenty years before this Amendment has gone into effect, each shall expire in the proceeding ten years such that the last digit of the year the law was originally passed in becomes the year in which the law shall expire.

We can call this the "Time Limit" Amendment for laws. Right now, there are laws on the books at the Federal and State/Territory levels that have been there for hundreds of years yet are not enforced or are patently un-Constitutional. However, someone could still be arrested for these laws and resources must be spent one way or another to keep them on the books. As an example, this is a real Federal Law that you could be found criminally guilty of:

TITLE 21--FOOD AND DRUGS
CHAPTER I--FOOD AND DRUG
ADMINISTRATION
DEPARTMENT OF HEALTH AND HUMAN
SERVICES
SUBCHAPTER B--FOOD FOR HUMAN
CONSUMPTION

PART 102 -- COMMON OR USUAL NAME FOR
NONSTANDARDIZED FOODS

Subpart B--Requirements for Specific
Nonstandardized Foods
Sec. 102.39 Onion rings made from diced
onion.

(a) The common or usual name of the food
product that resembles and is of the same
composition as onion rings, except that it is
composed of comminuted onions, shall be as
follows:

(1) When the product is composed of dehydrated
onions, the name shall be "onion rings made from
dried diced onions."

(2) When the product is composed of any form of
onion other than dehydrated, the name shall be
"onion rings made from diced onions."

(b) The words "made from dried diced onions" or
"made from diced onions" shall immediately follow
or appear on a line(s) immediately below the
words "onion rings" in easily legible boldface print
or type in distinct contrast to other printed or
graphic matter, and in a height not less than the
larger of the following alternatives:

(1) Not less than one-sixteenth inch in height on
packages having a principal display panel with an
area of 5 square inches or less and not less than
one-eighth inch in height if the area of the
principal display panel is greater than 5 square
inches; or

(2) Not less than one-half the height of the largest
type used in the words "onion rings."

How many of these are there? What even is the criminal code the United States? The answer is: we do not know! When Congress last tasked itself in 2013 to have a complete and organized listing of all laws, the Chairman of the House Over-Criminalization Task Force Jim Sensenbrenner said that they "lack the manpower and resources to accomplish this task." In other words, Congress does not even know what the law of the land is and cannot tell the Executive Branch what it is supposed to enforce!

Some people like to poke fun at the extreme specificity of some of these laws, but when you get into it one can see there are often intentions of safety, security, or other concerns that are just being overdone by someone who had a very, very specific situation. Other times, though, we do end up with rules on how to name different types of onion rings.

No matter the source or reasoning, a law should be reviewed on a regular basis for many reasons, not limited to:

- **Validation:** Make sure the law is still valid in today's environment or has not been superseded by another law.

- **Clarity:** In the time since the law was written, maybe specific cases or situations came up that require further clarification of intent.

- **Closing Loopholes:** A law may be able to be circumvented for reasons not seen before and can be made better.

- **Removing Unnecessary Features:** Perhaps a well-meaning law just got too much into the weeds and needed to be pulled back in order to allow leeway with execution.

- **Never Enforced:** A law was so impractical or the situation unlikely that it was impossible to even enforce the law.

- **Not Needed or Desired:** Societal norms and desires change over time and perhaps a law should be discarded entirely just for that.

Also, if we take this approach then all laws will eventually go through the court-level approval process from above (assuming it passes Congress and the President). As such, everything will get a further Constitutional review along with a check against all other law. In the end, this would be a great way to clear out old law and have a more reasonable, understandable, compact, and controlled penal code.

One thing to note from the way this is written is that a law expires 20 years from the date it is put into effect. Many laws are written with specific start dates, so those laws would not be due until they started as authored. Similarly, if at any point a law is modified then it is new again and countdown would restart. There is nothing in this that says laws cannot be revisited off-cycle, just that they must be visited on-cycle. In a similar point, some laws are already written with expiration dates (an annual budget, for instance), so those would not need to be revisited.

The real trick will be the first twenty or thirty years that this is applied because the workload would be tremendous for Congress. Of course, they would have the regular business of Congress in any year, and then on top of that they would have the laws expiring that had been passed in the last 20 years. Laws older than that, though, would require a great amount of time. Let us say this Amendment were passed in 2020. Then, in 2021, Congress would have to review laws passed in 2001 plus all the laws passed in 1991, 1981, 1971, etcetera, all the way back to 1791. Thankfully there are fewer and fewer Acts the farther back in time one gets.

Again, though, Congress's job is to legislate, and this will keep them very busy with doing just that. After 20 years—roughly the length of a generation—new members of Congress may be in play and all the same laws can be reviewed with a fresh light. While much of what has been put in place before this has been about keeping others out of the legislative process, this is the case where we are attempting to keep Congress within its own boundaries and busy with regular duties.

Yet, in order to be efficient and reasonable, there are more rules that need to be put in place. In the same vein, to keep Congress from trying to do too much, there are parts that need to be reined in. In the next section, we will conclude the role of Congress by cutting down their resources and firing them on a regular basis.

DAYLIGHT COMING

It has been a difficult journey to get to this part. Frankly, the Legislative Branch of the government by far needs the most amount of reforms. While Presidential candidates make all sorts of promises on how they will change the country and what they will make happen, it is Congress that does all that work. We will be sure to return the Executive Branch shortly, but for now we still need some final reining in of Congress.

What we have done to this point is redistribute Congress to be a closer alignment to the affiliation of the many different peoples on the United States (making sure all people were counted), try to limit the oligopoly powers of the Democratic and Republican Parties, balance Federal powers with State/Territories checks, force a process of legislation moving through Congress, make bills and laws reviewed automatically on many different levels and at many different times, and hold Congresspeople accountable for their actions or lack thereof. Despite all of this, Congress would still have too many tools available to it to avoid doing its job and reward itself for doing so. Now, we need to de-incentivize those who want to be in Congress for personal gain and power and make it desirable only for those who want to govern and serve. In other words, Congress needs to be a far less desirable job, yet more flexible for those with the aspiration to assist yet not the means.

PART TIMERS

How often does Congress work? By the Constitution, they only have to work once in the entire year. This is covered by Article 1, Section 4, Clause 2 and modified by the 20th Amendment. We'll make one more adjustment to that Clause directly—which partially discusses how legislators should get together:

> **By Amendment to the Constitution of the United States, Article 1, Section 4, Clause 2 shall be merged with Article/Amendment 20, Clause 2 and together shall read:**
>
> ~~The Congress shall assemble at least once in every Year, unless they shall by Law appoint a different Day.~~
>
> The Congress shall assemble ~~at least once in every year~~ **regularly once sworn into office**, and such meeting**s** shall begin ~~at noon~~ on the 3d day of January, unless they shall by law appoint a different day.

Just a little housekeeping to start us off: we have removed the "at least once in every year" component and just made it "regularly once sworn into office" to rid the Congress of having a fixed number of working occasions, especially one so open-ended. In modern times, Congress usually meets for about half of the working year in total. When averaged out, it comes out to less than 3 days per week. That is not to say that they are not working on other occasions as Congresspeople are supposed to be meeting with their constituents when not in Congress. Of course, the reality is much time is spent on fundraising and other election-related activities, so the true workload is harder to discern.

What is known is that when in session Congress can work insane hours. Sessions can go late into the evening and through the nights. Speech is used as a weapon to keep Congress in session and either wear down opponents or hope they leave long enough to get a motion passed. It takes away from the spirit of debate to make being in Congress an endurance test. Aside from removing the specific start time of noon in the above Clause, a new Clause is needed to help determine working hours:

> **By Amendment to the Constitution of the United States, Article 1, Section 4, Clause 3 shall be added.**
>
> Each chamber of Congress shall set a regular schedule for itself with specific days and hours in which its members shall meet. Once set, these days and times shall not be moved, cancelled, or extended unless an emergency is declared by the President of the United States.

Having this amendment would be the first step to controlling Congress using time as a weapon. Before, in the new Article 1, Section 11, we added functions that force a bill to keep moving through Congress. Here in the follow-up to that part, it states there are certain days and times set up for Congress to meet and those days cannot be modified except in the case of an emergency. In particular, the emergency declaration would have to come from the President, so this is a check on Congress from being able to force a change in schedule themselves.

The idea of this is that Congress will have regular and expected hours instead of going through endurance tests and other tricks. On the other end, it stops Congress from creating new sessions when no one is available in order to push through legislation. Bills should not be about circumventing the system to make them happen; but should be about closely following the process.

There will be more about this scheduling up ahead, but there is another key element and that is the method by which people can vote:

> **By Amendment to the Constitution of the United States, Article 1, Section 4, Clause 4 shall be added.**
>
> Congress shall make all methods of debate and vote available to its members such that members need not be in the Seat of Government or any designated location to perform legislative duties. All technologies as are available shall be allowed and required to be used to limit the need for each chamber of Congress to meet in person. Representatives and Senators may respond to roll call, debate, cast votes, or perform any legislative duty by any legal method available.

Right now, Congress has created a set of rules that say a Representative or

Senator must be in the chamber to vote. They cannot even vote by proxy or even vote while out in the hallway yet still in the same building. Even if their hologram were projected on the Senate floor, that person could still not vote by current rules. All the Constitution says is that Congress shall assemble at least once a year and that a quorum (that Congress can define) is needed to vote. It says nothing of the where, why, and how a vote is to occur and left that totally up to Congress.

Unfortunately, Congress has chosen to make their lives more complicated than necessary. In the late 1700's and early 1800's, having congresspeople in a specific location was needed because communication and travel was slow. By refusing to keep up with modern technology, Congress is costing American taxpayers money by forcing Congresspeople to almost always be in Washington, D.C.; and that in turn creates the need to pay Congress an even higher salary. It is a vicious cycle that just keeps repeating itself.

We will get a lot deeper into the cost savings and time savings for Congress shortly, but for now the focus is on methodology, and mostly allowing Congresspeople to be remote in order to do their job.

One of the core issues with the Constitution is that is it hyper-focused on the timeframe it was written. The founders could not imagine the possibilities we have now, and we may not be able to image the possibilities to come. When writing this amendment, the idea is that a Congressperson can engage in the process, debate, and vote from any location so that they are not tied to Washington, D.C.; instead, they can work from home, which will be especially important later in this section as we cut down their time working for the government. This would be especially beneficial and poignant for Senators as they are supposed to represent their State's interest directly. It is a lot more plausible for Senators to represent State interests if they spent the majority of their time in their home State and not in the District of Columbia. And the only way to do that is to allow proxy voting.

Proxy voting is a method by which a person can cast a vote without being present. This is often used in other fields, especially with corporations that have stockholders fill out their votes online or via mail and then a person collects those and vote their shares for them. There is no reason—with proper security protocols—that Congress could not do the same. Today, there are any number of methods by which Congress could participate. The most logical ones are the same ones used in corporations across the world: Teleconferences and Webinars (i.e., GoToMeeting), E-mail and Texting, Message Boards and Social Media.

These are the technologies the world over uses to communicate and conduct business, and not only is there no reason for the Government not to use them, the benefits far outweigh the costs and potential issues (with proper oversight and controls, of course). Though we cannot accurately predict the future, perhaps there will be reliable 3D holographic communication, or virtual spaces, or some other method yet conceived. We simply do not have enough foresight to see what will be available, so we need to leave it open to even better communication options to come.

Thus, Congresspeople will need to be in Washington, D.C. a lot less. For sure, there will be times when they do need and want to get together, or it is more beneficial to be together for a period of time. However, those times should be fewer and far between. Because of this, Congresspeople should not be expected to set up and maintain residents in Washington, D.C. (which in turn will lead them to needing far less pay, but more to come there momentarily):

> **By Amendment to the Constitution of the United States, Article 1, Section 4, Clause 5 shall be added.**
>
> The Federal Government shall purchase and maintain a property or several properties to house all members of Congress when they visit the Seat of Government of the United States. The property or properties shall be sparse and utilitarian to only serve the temporary housing needs of just the members of Congress when visiting the Seat of Government. In addition to room, the Federal Government shall provide board, transportation, and all other basic needs while members of Congress travel to and from and stay in the Seat of Government.

Congress already has a right to purchase and maintain property, as Article 1, Section 8, Clause 17 states:

> To exercise exclusive Legislation in all Cases whatsoever, over such District (not exceeding ten Miles square) as may, by Cession of particular States, and the Acceptance of Congress, become the Seat of the Government of the United States, and to exercise like Authority over all Places purchased by the Consent of the Legislature of the State in which the Same shall be, for the Erection of Forts, Magazines, Arsenals, dock-Yards, and other needful Buildings;

The first part of this clause involved the creation of Washington, D.C., while the latter part is about making buildings and other assets. Most of what was listed is military in use, that "other needful Buildings" component is broad enough to be quite useful today. Over time, the government has grown its functional duty and as such has needed more office space for its many, many purposes. Creating what amounts to a government-run hotel for legislators is no different than any of those and easily falls into this category.

However, we need an amendment to the Constitution to lay out purpose and restrict Congresspeople. What we are actually creating is two parts: the first part is non-monetary compensation for Congresspeople. If we are going to reduce what Congress is being paid, the cost of being in Congress needs to be covered another way. This is why the Amendment goes into items like "board", AKA food. "Transportation" would be the plane, train, taxi, and other automotive costs of getting to and staying in Washington, D.C. while "other basic needs" would cover things like the utilities and water to keep the living spaces going. With these basic costs covered, Congresspeople should need far less monetary compensation to take care of themselves.

The Library of Congress in Washington, D.C. (as pictured in December 2019) is—as the same suggests—a resource for Congress. However, even this institution has digitalized their entire collection in order to make it available without the need of physically being there.

The second part is limiting the legislators' exposure to outside influence. Every component of housing, food, and services leaves them vulnerable to manipulation and the potential of ethical violation of emoluments. By taking all of that away, all they need to focus on while on government business is the action of legislating. In a similar vein, with Congress in town far less frequently—and more regularly spread far and wide—lobbyists would not be able to exert as much influence. Lobbyists would have to travel the country over or wait patiently for Congress's limited returns to Washington, D.C. to try to make as large of an impact as they do today. Yet, Congresspeople would not be as open to non-monetary influences (and we will deal with their monetary ones shortly, as promised).

Furthermore, since Congresspeople do not need to move to Washington, D.C.

full-time, they do not need to bring their families with them and make sure that they are provided for. That is why this Amendment is specifically about housing just the members of Congress and that the space be sparse and utilitarian. As the Amendment states, this is just to provide a "temporary" location for the Congresspeople, so it does not need much except the basics of any modern hotel room. That is not to say it should be an uncomfortable Soviet-style cement block with a mattress on the floor, but that the Congresspeople do not all need multi-million-dollar brownstones. If a Congressperson wants to buy something like that with their own money outside of their Congressional salary, that is their prerogative; the cost just does not need to be shouldered by the taxpayers in one way or another.

Now, since we have covered the Congresspeople's non-monetary needs, we can at last turn to the other half. Leaving Article 1, Section 4, we head down to Section 6 and the related (and nearly useless) 27th Amendment to revisit what the 27th Amendment tried to fix: compensation.

> **By Amendment to the Constitution of the United States, Article 1, Section 6, Clause 1 shall be merged with Article/Amendment 27, Clause 1 and together shall read:**
>
> The Senators and Representatives shall receive a Compensation for their Services, to be ascertained by Law, and paid out of the Treasury of the United States. No law varying the compensation for the services of the Senators and Representatives shall take effect until an election of Representatives **and Senators** shall have intervened.
>
> **Direct monetary compensation shall be limited to and equal to the Living Wage rate in the Seat of Government commiserated with the hours scheduled by each chamber of Congress. Additional non-monetary compensation may only be awarded as designated in other parts of the Constitution.**
>
> They shall in all Cases, except Treason, Felony and Breach of the Peace, be privileged from Arrest during their Attendance at the Session of their respective Houses, and in going to and returning from the same; and for any Speech or Debate in either House, they shall not be questioned in any other Place.

As previously discussed, the average Congressperson receives $174,000 per year for their services, with additional pay for leadership positions. True, Congress has forgone their automatic pay raise they assigned themselves since 2010, so their pay has been stagnant for quite some time. And despite this large number being far above the national average, it is nothing compared to what it has been in the past. In 1969, Congresspeople were paid $43,500, which adjusted for inflation is $295,934 in 2019 dollars.

By that, one could say Congress has cut their pay nearly in half! However, if we go back to 1855 when Congress permanently changed from a per day to a per year system of compensation, they were making $3,000 which in 2019 would be $88,120. In other words, their pay is nearly double what it was when they first started using this system.

Let us go back even further. In 1815, Congress used the annual system for the first time and set wages at $1,500, which amounts to $24,891 in 2019 dollars. Now this is where it gets interesting! If we go back to 1790 during the first full year of Congress, the members met for 191 days for $6 per day. Six dollars in 2019 dollars would be $166.66, and if we divide that by eight hours of a standard modern workday that would be $20.83 per hour. If we multiple the daily rate by the number of days, we'll end up with $1,146 for the year, or $31,832 in 2019 dollars.

What does this all tell us? Well, if we go all the way back in time, it seems like the original members of Congress—many of whom helped write the Constitution—had a different idea about what compensation meant than later members of Congress. Of the 39 delegates who signed the Constitution, 41% were members of the 1st Congress. In other words, the pay scales we see in the late 1700's and early 1800's are in line with what the founders and writers of the Constitution intended, not what we see today.

When looking at that original $20.83 per hour, it looks very similar to living wage calculations. The Living Wage, unlike the Minimum Wage, is calculated to what it really costs to survive in a given area. The Massachusetts Institute of Technology has developed a Living Wage calculator that is readily available in a peer-reviewed methodology. For a single person living in Washington, D.C. in 2019, the Living Wage would be $17.76 per hour (compared to the Minimum Wage of $13.25 or the Federal Minimum Wage of $7.25). We will return and spend a great deal of time on Living Wage, but for now consider it the benchmark by which we will pay members of Congress.

If we accept that $17.76 per hour and take the 186 days that the Senate was in session for in 2018 (the House met for 171, but we'll go with the larger number for this example), and assumed an 8 hour work day—though some were 24 hours and some were 1—we would get a grand total of $26,427. Isn't it amazing how that comes almost exactly in line with 1790 to 1815 numbers?! Most importantly is that "limited to" additional phrase in there means that Congress cannot grant itself other monetary compensation in service to the Government (i.e., getting paid extra to serve on a committee or in a leadership position).

Now, we covered the "non-monetary" compensation before with the housing situation. One of the reasons Congresspeople are paid so much now is because of the high cost of housing in Washington, D.C., which of course is a trap of their own making. Therefore, if their lodging, food, transportation, energy, and all other basics costs are covered, they do not need much of a salary anyway. All of those non-monetary components do add up to quite a bit of real value, but at least it is being controlled at a Federal level so that individual Congresspeople are not being influenced by either what they can afford or the gifts and discounts given to them.

All of this is taking members of Congress away from having a full-time job in the official seat of government. It was never the intent of the Founders that members of Congress would be full-time legislators and with the proper scheduling and technology use at home they should not have to be. Instead, it is time to align them to the position as originally conceived: a part-time, citizen legislator.

As a matter of fact, making a legislature be a part-time job is not uncommon in our country at all. Among the States, 14 explicitly make their legislatures be part-time and another 26 have a system that makes it so legislators cannot earn a full income in their government jobs. In other words, only 20% of States have in place laws or Constitutions that make their Legislative Branch a full-time position.

When that does happen, the costs immediately skyrocket! In States where the legislature spends around half of their time working in the government the average compensation is about $19,000 per year. Yet even when not full-time, with an average time working in government of around 85%, compensation jumps to about $82,000 per year.

If you believe that only small and/or low population States would have part-time legislatures and that in the larger, more populous a State that more work would be required, the numbers do not completely line up. For instance, States large in area like Texas and Florida have a part-time legislature while on the other end Alaska, Wisconsin, and Hawaii are carrying full-time ones. There is not a direct correlation of any of those factors in how they function.

However, the more a legislature is in session, the more pressure it feels to pass bills or take on work so as not to feel like they are not wasting time. Need some proof of that? Well, you already got it in the Onion Ring definition law! You see that law and the many, many others are unable to be categorized because there are too many laws. This is a symptom of the issues of overcriminalization. Because Congress wants to make sure they do not look like they are doing nothing when they are in session—even if they have nothing to discuss—many of these minor, over-engineered laws get passed. We spend a great deal of time talking about Congressional gridlock, but there is plenty of speeding through legislation just because people are there.

Now that we understand the costs (both literally and figuratively) of having a full-time legislature, how do States with part-time legislatures approach this? Take a look at a couple of examples:

Wyoming Constitution

§006. Compensation of members; duration of sessions.

The legislature shall not meet for more than sixty (60) legislative working days excluding Sundays during the term for which members of the house of representatives are elected, except when called into special session. The legislature shall determine by statute the number of days not to exceed sixty (60) legislative working days to be devoted to general and budget session, respectively. The legislature shall meet on odd-numbered years for a general and budget session. The legislature may meet on even-numbered years for budget session. During the budget session no bills except the budget bill may be introduced unless placed on call by a two-thirds vote of either house. The legislature shall meet for no more than forty (40) legislative working days excluding Sundays in any (1) calendar year, except when called into special session. The compensation of the members of the legislature shall be as provided by law; but no legislature shall fix its own compensation.

Wyoming is rather strict in its language and specifically controls not only how many days, but what must happen in those days. That may be a little too rigid for an entire country, but gives an idea of how to control the total working days. Remember that we have previously set up an Amendment to make Congress work within a certain timeframe of their own volition, so now we are looking to limit what is their available timeframe at all. As such, Wyoming's Constitution may provide some guidance on how to do that.

Oregon Constitution

ARTICLE IV

LEGISLATIVE BRANCH

Section 10. Annual regular sessions of the Legislative Assembly; organizational session; extension of regular sessions.

(1) The Legislative Assembly shall hold annual sessions at the Capitol of the State. Each session must begin on the day designated by law as the first day of the session. Except as provided in subsection (3) of this section:

(a) A session beginning in an odd-numbered year may not exceed 160 calendar days in duration; and

(b) A session beginning in an even-numbered year may not exceed 35 calendar days in duration.

(2) The Legislative Assembly may hold an organizational session that is not subject to the limits of subsection (1) of this section for the purposes of introducing measures and performing the duties and effecting the organization described in sections 11 and 12 of this Article. The Legislative Assembly may not undertake final consideration of a measure or reconsideration of a measure following a gubernatorial veto when convened in an organizational session.

(3) A regular session, as described in subsection (1) of this section, may be extended for a period of five calendar days by the affirmative vote of two-thirds of the members of each house. A session may be extended more than once. An extension must begin on the first calendar day after the end of the immediately preceding session or extension except that if the first calendar day is a Sunday, the extension may begin on the next Monday.

Similar to Wyoming, Oregon also gets into not only the number of days, but the different number of days in varying years along with specific limitations on the number of days in a row. This may be helpful as well in order to limit the amount of time Congress can spend together in session.

Taking lessons from these two Constitutions and others, we can now apply it to our federal one:

> **By Amendment to the Constitution of the United States, Article 1, Section 6, Clause 3 shall be added.**
>
> Both the House of Representatives and Senate shall be limited in the number of days they may meet per legislative year and the number of hours they shall meet in any single day. While either chamber of Congress is in session, each shall meet no more than three days per calendar week. All sessions must begin after seven o'clock in the morning and must end before ten o'clock in the evening at the Seat of Government. Furthermore, each session shall last no longer than six hours. Additional days and times may only be granted if an emergency is declared by the President of the United States.

Before diving into this, let us do a little math. There are roughly 260 working days in any given year, give or take the particular rules of a company and when holidays falls. At 8 hours per day, that is 2,080 working hours, which is fairly typical. Now, there are 52 weeks in a year, so if we say that Congress can only meet 3 days per week, at maximum we are talking about 156 days, which would be 60% of the total number of working days. However, at 6 hours per day, that comes out to 936 hours or 45% of a working week. And just to wrap in the last section, at $17.76, Congress would receive a maximum pay of $16,623 in a year (not including the other perks and covered costs).

It is fair to note that there are other Living Wage rates that could be used, as well, since we have been focusing on the "Single Adult" rate. There are higher rates if thinking about one adult with children, two adults with one working, two adults with both working, and two adults working with children. The average of these various rates is $26.54 per hour, so if we went with that one it would be $24,841, which is still quite in the reasonable part-time range. At the end of the day, it would be up to Congress to pass what is the definition of a Living Wage to use, so they would still have some control over their pay scales. Much later in this document, we will give a definition for Living Wage in the law that still allows some Congressional control.

For now, the limits to keep Congress part-time include not just the number of days per week and the number of hours they can work per session, but also the times in which they can work. As discussed previously, one of the main legislative tools used is simply wearing people out by keeping sessions going. Also, because Congress does not have fixed days and times they must adhere to, legislation can often go to the last minute and beyond. In other words, there are no pressures to get anything done because there are no limits to the amount of time Congress can be forced in session. By giving parameters and limiting how often and how long Congress can get together, it will force them to use their time properly, prioritize, vote, and move on to the next. Some Congresspeople seem to take pride and brag about working on legislation until 3:00 a.m. when they should feel ashamed for procrastinating and not being able to accomplish their work in acceptable timeframes.

> *As an aside, the Constitution was written before there were time-zones or even the idea of standardized times. It would take the invention of the train for people to realize they needed standard clocks so that trains would not run into each other (several did) and people would know when a train was coming. Before then, all time was relative and local. The management of clocks and time is a concept that the founders could not have foreseen and as such is an example of technology that is old to us yet is revolutionary in terms of the Constitution being able to recognize it.*

Despite all this, Congress would still have a lot of leeway as the Constitution already gives Congress the ability to decide when it is in session and we added Clauses so that Congress is in charge of creating their own schedule. More so—without the need to be in Washington, D.C.—Congress has a lot of opportunity to schedule meetings for "standard off-hours" so Congresspeople can just take the session from home. Right now, Congress takes the entire month of August off as well as plenty of other one, two, and three week stretches. With the remote ability and scheduling control, Congress would have the ability to meet more regularly. Again, though, all of that would be up to each chamber to decide what works best. All they would have to do is stay within the limitations of their timetable.

And let us not forget all of Section 11 that forces legislation to be scheduled, debated, voted on, and moved through the chambers. Congress would not even have the luxury of dallying under penalty of treason, so again this is a forced method of limiting bureaucracy. No matter the situation, the methodology and decisions would still rest within the legislature.

Beyond the direct costs and times of the Congresspeople themselves, there is one other item that comes from being a full-time worker, and that is the apparent need for an oversized staff on the government payroll.

Going back to our States examples, the States with legislators working 85% of the time or more see staff numbers on average (not even on peak, but on average) of around 1,250. For those working half time, staff size is around 160 on average. We are talking a nearly 8 times difference just from working an additional half time. If support staff were exactly in line with hours legislators work, then doubling part-time work to full-time should just double the staff needs (around 320), yet an exponential relationship is seen instead. Or another way to look at it is that in the part-time States there are 1.2 staff per legislator and in the full-time States there are 8.9 staff per legislator. Why is that?

As noted above, since a legislature feels pressure to do work when they are in session all the time, then they need more staff in order to pull that off. These staff people are gathering information, doing analysis, crafting policy and actual bills, and doing much of the labor required because excess workload has been created. It is a chicken-and-the-egg situation, except we know that there is more work for staff because legislators are making more work for themselves by feeling their time needs to be productive.

Meanwhile, the actual Congresspeople spend significant amounts of their time doing non-government activities (mostly fundraising). As such, they need to further offload their work on to others. Congresspeople should be doing all of their own work and research (or at least using Executive Agencies to bring research and analysis to them, but more on that later) and employees of the legislature should be limited to the operational functions needed to run Congress and not personally work for individual legislators on the government dime. Afterall, the legislators were the ones elected to do the work. Why should they be allowed to outsource their workload to an unelected person?

> **By Amendment to the Constitution of the United States, Article 1, Section 6, Clause 4 shall be added.**
>
> Congress may appropriate funds for a staff to cover the organizational and functional needs of Congress. Organizational and functional staff shall be shared by all members of Congress equally. Congress may not appropriate funds for staff assigned to individual members of Congress or groups of members of Congress. No staff member of the Government of the United States may be assigned to a single Representative or Senator or any group of Representatives or Senators.

After the Civil War, the idea of staff was slowly added to Congress, where before then there were no staff to speak of and Congresspeople were responsible for their own way. By the year 2000 and up to at least 2019 there were about 24,000 people working for Congress, of which most (about 12,000) work in the personal staff of a Congressperson. There are specific limits as to how many people can be hired and into what type of positions, but those were all created by laws Congress passed itself. How much money each member gets is also set by a Congressional appropriations committee. So basically, aside from a Presidential override of the entire budget, Congress has complete control over how much staff and money they assign themselves.

Now, there is a need for a support staff. Someone needs to keep the building clean, turn the lights on, run the IT infrastructure, prepare materials, and do all the functions that would make any business run. There is a need for government employees to do the jobs that help everything flow as normal. There are also people that theoretically work for Congress but act in more executive roles like the Government Accountability Office. Even beyond all this, the Capital Police also officially work for Congress. Altogether, this is not to say that there should not be anyone working for Congress, only that Congresspeople should not have personal staff to do their personal bidding.

The person who should be responsible for the individual activities of the legislator is the legislator himself. This would also remove the temptation (re: real issue) of using support staff for activities outside of running a legislative session (i.e., having staff doing fundraising activity while taxpayers cover the costs despite the lowly enforced Hatch Act). The only assistance congresspeople need is to make sure they can attend a legislative session. That is the role of the support staff, and this Amendment will help make sure it is nothing more.

One of the other ways that staff have been hired is for committees. Committees are not part of the Constitution and are just made up by Congress for its own process purposes. But because Congress created the committee, they can currently hire people to just serve roles on the committee, again giving power to non-elected officials with very little oversight of their pay or ethics. This amendment also shuts down that process by not allowing employees to serve "groups" of Congresspeople either. At the end of the day, the staff are just there to make sure the Congresspeople can do their jobs, and the Congresspeople cannot parse their jobs or special benefits to others at the expense of the taxpayers.

TURNOVER, TURNOVER, TURNOVER

Finally, with Congress now being compensated less, forced to focus on the job of legislating, and being a greater representation of the people, there is one last area that needs to be tackled: longevity.

Among all that staff that works for Congress are about 600 who are in the employ of the Congressional Research Service which just started in late 2018 making its non-confidential publications available to the public (and not only to be seen by members of Congress). One of the first publications on January 3, 2019 was an analysis of the tenures of members of Congress over time.

According to this agency, in the 116th Congress the average years for members of the House of Representatives was 8.6 years while the Senate was 10.1 years. Average is an interesting statistic, but distribution gives a clearer picture:

	House	Senate	Total Congress
New (0)	20%	4%	17%
Regular (1 – 12)	56%	57%	56%
Long (13 to 24)	16%	23%	17%
Ultra-Long (25 to 49)	8%	16%	10%

To arrive at these numbers, we must include all time served in the House and the Senate. Within the Senate, 40% of the members have prior experience serving in the House at an average of almost nine years. Even ten members of the House have prior experience in the same chamber with an average additional nearly six years of time. But that is hardly the end of this! Many members of both chambers have large amounts of prior experience in government as legislators at the State level, Governors, appointed positions, and more. In other words, the vast majority of the Legislative Branch is filled with long-time employees of one government or another.

Even this year is a bit of an anomaly. If you recall, re-election rates are incredibly high among all members of Congress. The key factor that truly impacts tenure right now is the decision of the Congresspeople whether to run again or not. Just comparing the average tenures of this Congress to last would make you think it was dropping, but two years are not a trend. The CRS shows a chart that makes it clear: since the beginning of the first Congress the tenure time in the Legislative Branch has been on a straight upward trajectory. Sure, there are dips and bumps as you go, but tenure has been roiling upwards, most especially post the Civil War.

Are you starting to see the connection in timelines? Starting in the 1850's is when Congress gave itself full-time salaries, and that is when the shift began to happen. Before the 1870's the average tenure for Senators hovered around 4 years and the House around 2 years. Yet, as a full-time salary was created and further grown, the tenures started going up and up. Mind you, those earlier years were impacted by the large number of new States joining the union, so the average is depressed. But in general, we have incentivized the idea of making working in the legislature and government in general a career (a lucrative career at that) instead of a service.

To further demonstrate this point, the CRS looked at the rates by which Congresspeople sought re-election. From the first Congress through the 1850's, the rate by which people attempted another term was on a downward trajectory and had reached below 50%. Then, with the advent of a full-time salary there was a sharp turn that brought the rate we see today in the in the 80% to 90% range. Therefore, 80% to 90% choose to run for re-election, and get re-elected 80% to 95% of the time. As such, very few people are being removed by election and most are just by natural attrition. Some may not run because they believe they will lose and instead choose to retire, but that does not prove that they would have lost their positions in a full election.

Returning to time in office, we should pay particular attention to those who have served in Congress in the Long and Ultra-Long categories. Within all of Congress, 27% has spent more than 13 years (and currently maxing out at 46 years, though that will go up every year after this is written) in Congress— again not including time spent in other government positions. That is more than 2 full Senate terms and 6 full House terms. The CRS comes to many of the same analysis points and more; yet does not come to any conclusions.

Here is the conclusion that they refused to write: too much time in office is the antithesis of a representative democracy. Recall earlier when we looked at the average age of Congresspeople and how it does not come close to the alignment of the American people. That is because people join Congress and for the most part never leave. Being in Congress creates an inherent bubble around legislators that disconnects them from the actual concerns and opinions of their constituents. There needs to be turnover in order to get current perspectives and knowledge into the government.

This is even more important in the system we have laid out throughout this entire legislative-focused section, particularly with the House. If the Political Parties are responsible for creating Lists of who is going to sit in the House, they would just put their longest tenured and most powerful party members in those roles and leave them there forever. No, we need one final Amendment to Article 1 to add term limits to serving in Congress.

> ### By Amendment to the Constitution of the United States, Article 1, Section 6, Clause 5 shall be added.
>
> No person shall be elected to the House of Representatives more than twice nor to the Senate more than twice, and not more than four times for all of Congress. And no person who has held a position in Congress for more than two years of a term to which some other person was elected shall be elected to the House of Representatives or the Senate more than once. But this clause shall not apply to any person holding a position in Congress at the time of ratification until the end of his current term.

Does that read familiar? It is practically an exact crib (some would say plagiarism) of the 22nd Amendment that limited the President to two terms. Prior to Franklin Delano Roosevelt, no President had ever served more than two terms as they saw it a service point to leave. After FDR, it was clear that a rule was needed to force the issue and make sure that no one person could amass that much power and control of American policy and future. The progression to Ultra-Long serving members of Congress has been a much more gradual slide, so it has not hit as many people in the face like FDR did. Besides, Congress was on board with limiting the power of the President; they are not on board with limiting their own power and earning potential.

FDR and his dog Fala agree that a few individuals should not coalesce all power over themselves, else they will create tyranny. This and other similar themes are covered in-depth at FDR's memorial in Washington, D.C. as pictured here in December 2019.

This Amendment would limit employment to two terms in each chamber of Congress, but does allow a person to serve in both for up to two terms each. If we accept the prior Amendments to make the House and the Senate four-year terms that happen at the same time, it means a person could serve up to 8 years in the House and then potentially immediately after that another 8 years in the Senate for a total of 16 years (or vice versa). There is a sub-clause in there to make sure current members of Congress are not kicked out in the middle of their terms just because they have previously timed out but that they are allowed to serve their term out until its natural conclusion.

Sixteen years may seem long, but it only the potential and requires moving between two different chambers and winning in two different systems. Based on Lists for the House, people may lose their seat and have to come back in later or not at all, so overall it should still end up with a good amount of new blood while allowing a fair amount of long-term people to stay involved. After all, it is reasonable to have both brand-new people and those with experience on a regular basis, but at the same time make sure no one is serving for an entire generation.

However, as discussed, that has not limited how much time these people could spend in any level of government. With former State-level legislators, Governors, Presidents, Judges, appointed positions—there are just too many other nooks and crannies that a person looking to make a career out of politics could sneak in to and have the government cover the bill. If a Party wants to pay its members for its services, that is the Party's business. That does not mean that the government should be paying for the Party to retain and use its power and influence. Because of that, we need one last Amendment to make sure all of government is safe from the careerists:

> **By Amendment to the Constitution of the United States, Article 8, Section 1, Clause 1 shall be added.**
>
> No person shall serve more than a combined twenty-five years in total in any elected or appointed position or combination thereof within any part of government, with no differentiation between local, State or Territory, Federal, or Foreign government. But this clause shall not apply to any person holding an elected or appointed position at the time of ratification until the end of his current term. Additionally, this Clause does not apply to staff and civil servants that support the functions of Government, nor those serving in the military or militia.

It is worth noting that the Constitution only has 7 Articles (less the Amendments), so Article 8 would be a net new one. We are going to call this Article "Limitations of Government". This should not be a surprise at this point, but later in this document we will be adding several more Clauses to this section to further limit the Government and grant rights to the people directly through another Article.

For now, this first Clause for Article 8 is about limiting the total amount of time that someone can spend working in Government; not just the Federal Government, but all of Government in any role that is not a support staff or public servant position or involved with the military. Those people are employees, but when it comes to elected and appointed positions, they are supposed to be in service. As such, they need to time out so that we do not create despots. Despots need not be the dictator of an entire nation, but they can be someone who controls which legislation is available for debate, which organizations get money, or who can participate in the PTA bake sale. We need a function to clear away people who have served for too long not because they necessarily are bad people or have done anything wrong, but simply because service is supposed to be temporary and we need new and different ideas on a regular basis.

At 25 years, a person could spend 8 years serving in the House, 8 years serving in the Senate, and 8 years serving as President with one year left over. Or a person could spend 12 years as their Town Selectman, 10 years as Mayor, and 3 years as Governor. Or another person could spend all 25 years being a Judge. The possibilities and paths will be up to the individual if and how they want to serve. Do you want to spend your limited years as a Secretary for the President? Do you want to be a Judge when you might want to be Governor? Will you spend 20 years on the PTO even if your children are grown and moved on? It forces a changeover in every single organization within every level of government. There is some math that must be done and people will need to make decisions. What is most important to your service? Is it a local issue or a national one? When do you start? When do you finish? Do you take a break?

Most importantly, it limits (though does not eliminate, other laws would need to do that) a bit of cronyism. For instance, the President could not just appoint someone to a plush government position that has no turnover. That would not be a support or civil servant position, so that person would have to realize that if they wanted to do something else (like be a Senator), they could not stay in that position forever. These rewards would be fewer and further between.

When you lay it out, 25 years is roughly a generation. Someone could be in the eye of the public and in service to it for all that time, but then another generation can come in. It will not work out perfectly like that because everyone will be on different schedules and experiences, but there would be a constant sweep of new people ready to be in service to our country with fresh ideas and hopeful desires.

LADIES AND GENTLEMEN AND EVERYTHING IN BETWEEN

Time to watch the Presidential debates again!

One candidate is promising a fix to immigration, one with the ultimate tax policy, one ready with a plan for healthcare, and yet another one the answer to our infrastructure woes. They all have interesting positions, some that you agree with and others you vehemently oppose. Listening to each candidate, you make a decision on which one is going to create or modify the functions of government the way you desire them to go. But there is one small problem in that decision:

That is not the job of the President.

Almost everything Presidential candidates and active Presidents talk about is really the job of Congress. Changes to social programs, taxes, protections, illegal acts, immigration, wages... almost everything you can imagine is all within Congress's purview. Sure, the President has traditionally set an agenda that they would like Congress to follow, but Congress is under no obligation to follow that roadmap. In actuality, Congress is directed to be the check on the Executive Branch and make sure that the President and all of the departments under his authority are following the mandate as they have set out.

One might ask, then, what is the President of the United States truly responsible for?

Well, the Constitutions gives the President very few duties at all. In total for all of Article 2 of the Constitution (plus Amendments that impact Article 2), here is everything the President is supposed to do:

- **Section 1, Clause 1, Sentence 1:** Be the executive.

- **Section 1, Clause 8, Sentence 1b:** Follow his oath to "the best of my Ability, preserve, protect and defend the Constitution of the United States."

- **Section 2, Clause 1, Sentence 1a:** Be Commander in Chief of the Armed Forces—but only when Congress declares that Armed Forces can be used.

- **Section 2, Clause 1, Sentence 1b:** Act in a supervisory role to the heads of executive departments and have them submit written reports to him.

- **Section 2, Clause 1, Sentence 1c:** Grant reprieves and pardons, except in cases of impeachment.

- **Section 2, Clause 2, Sentence 1a:** Make an initial draft of a treaty that in turn must be approved by 2/3rd of the Senate.

- **Section 2, Clause 2, Sentence 1b:** Make nominations for ambassadors, ministers, officers, and judges that must be vetted and approved by Congress except if Congress grants the President direct rights to appoint people to "inferior" positions.

- **Section 2, Clause 3, Sentence 1:** Temporarily fill vacancies when Congress is not in session.

- **Section 3, Clause 1, Sentence 1a:** Give the "State of the Union" to Congress from "time to time".

- **Section 3, Clause 1, Sentence 1b:** Force Congress (or just one of the Chambers of Congress) to either convene or adjourn, but only in "extraordinary Occasions".

- **Section 3, Clause 1, Sentence 1c:** Receive foreign ambassadors and the like.

- **Section 3, Clause 1, Sentence 1d:** Execute the laws as created by Congress through whatever means are necessary to do so and have been granted.

- **Section 3, Clause 1, Sentence 1e:** Grant commissions to officers in the Armed Services or civilian equivalents.

- **Section 4, Clause 1, Sentence 1c:** If Congress cannot be convened, protect the States from "domestic Violence".

- **Amendment 25, Clause 2, Sentence 1:** Nominate a Vice President should there be a vacancy in that position, though the nominee must be approved by a majority of Congress.

- **Amendment 25, Clause 3, Sentence 1:** Notify Congress when he is unable to do his duties so that the Vice President can take over on a temporary basis.

And... that is it. Other than that, it is just what is the checks on Congress with Veto power and withdrawing funds from the Treasury to pay for the things Congress has approved.

What is not in there or anywhere else in the Constitution is "Executive Orders", or at least not the way we think about them. Orders from the President are needed so that he can do his job, namely because "he shall take Care that the

Laws be faithfully executed". In other words, for Laws and the Constitution to be executed the President must send out commands to other administrators and departments to give them a process or have them follow the law. If Congress's law or the Constitution is lacking, sending an order can fall in this bucket as a clarification.

Even first President George Washington submitted Executive Orders, with his first in 1789; although all that order did was tell the executive departments to submit a written report which is basically what Article 2, Section 2, Clause 1, Sentence 1b says is the President's job and right. As time has moved on—and especially starting in the early 20th century—the number of Executive Orders has drastically increased. Part of that is the President has taken on the role of "Agenda Setter" and is seemingly establishing the pace for what Congress should work on and what the rest of the agencies of the government should be doing. The mass bureaucracy that has grown out of the wars of the 20th century has carte blanche control to make rules of their own and act as if those are "law" even though the Constitution is very clear that only Congress can make law.

But how did the President and the rest of the Executive Branch get this power? The only answer is that Congress ceded responsibility through a combination of neglecting their duties and purposely handing them away. Party politics have made it worse because, as shown in the prior section, each group is just waiting until they have both houses of Congress and the Presidency to pass into law what they desire and do not want to slow down for any reason. Congress and the President are loyal to their party first and the nation second, and they are trying to work together as a team to do the bidding of the party.

As noted previously, having a healthy separation of powers and not ceding responsibility is an important check and balance, as is making sure no party can dominate both the legislature and the Executive Branch at the same time. The changes before this to Congress would leave a world where not only could no single party force a policy, but the existing laws would come up for review in short order and Congress could retake the powers it has given away.

Right now, the President can do many things that he should not be able to do like set tariffs, deploy the military in foreign lands, completely change the directions of federal agencies on a whim or new election, spy on American citizens, and many more. Each new Congress fails to reign in the Executive Branch because it is not in their best interests of their personal political careers. That is not to say there are not legislators who have not attempted or do not want to do this, just that they cannot given the current makeup of Congress.

What we have done to this point is hopefully create a legislature that can regain all their powers and restore the balance that was intended in the Constitution. Now then, we must do the same to the Executive Branch through a variety of changes that accomplish the following goals:

- Create a system of electing the President and Vice President that assures full participation of the electorate, reflects a positive and negative combined will of the people, and forces further separation of parties that are in Congress from those elected to lead.

- Reorganize the entire Federal Government and Armed Forces for efficiency, cost savings, simpler understanding, and to limit the scope and reach of these agencies so as not to violate the 10th Amendment that grants rights to the States and the people.

- Get even more explicit with the duties of the Legislative and Executive Branches, especially in relation to how the military is used and tools for the Executive Branch to make sure Congress does its job.

- An ability for the Executive Branch to use similar State resources to accomplish its duties instead of creating new Federal ones.

At the end of the day, the changes to Congress will still make a greater impact, but the Executive Branch deserves a compliment of changes all its own. More than all that, though, is making sure the people of the United States are a part of the election process, and they will not feel that way unless specific Amendments are made to make sure their voice is heard in the election of the President and all other positions.

THE TWELFTH MAN

In the third Presidential election in 1796, something went wrong. Attempting to remedy the situation with an extra-Constitutional solution, the 1800 election showed the problems persisted and were exacerbated. The trouble was the method by which the Constitution had laid out how the President and Vice President were to be elected.

Thus in 1804—in time for the next Presidential election—the 12th Amendment was passed to fix the major flaws written into the original Constitution. Mind you, the Constitution had just come into effect in 1789; as such a mere 15 years after that point it already was showing cracks around its core components. What we are talking about here in Article 2, Section 1, Clauses 2 through 4 (as well as relevant Amendments) is the Electoral College, which is charged with electing the President and Vice President of the United States.

It is difficult to get too close to the White House in Washington, D.C. in this photo from December 2019. It is also worth noting the building is only white because it was painted that way to cover scorch marks after the British burned it down during the War of 1812.

COLLEGE GRADUATION

Let us not beat around the bush here:

The Electoral College is horribly undemocratic and the antithesis to reflecting the will of the people in choosing their government and leaders.

At the time of the writing of the Constitution, the Electoral College was considered a "fairish" compromise between those that wanted a direct vote and those that wanted Congress to decide who should be President and Vice President. If the latter had won, the United States would have a system similar to many Parliamentary Democracies with Prime Ministers in which the Head of State is actually part of the legislature and there is no check between those creating and those executing the law.

The compromise consisted of each State getting Electors in the college equal to the total number of people they have in Congress. In turn, the States could then decide how their Electors voted—at least theoretically. During the first Presidential election, only 6 of 13 States even used some form of direct vote by the people to decide what the Electors did. That number decreased to 5 of 16 in the 1800 election, but it did otherwise rise so that by 1868 all States did some type of direct voting. Today, all States save Nebraska and Maine grant the winner within their State all their Electors while the latter two have created districts to decide how each vote should go.

Mind you, nothing is illegal or un-Constitutional about taking any approach to how Electors should vote. Nor is there anything illegal or un-Constitutional for Electors to go rogue and do whatever they want. Some States have laws to address this, but otherwise Electors can be "faithless"—break their pledges to how the States say their votes should go. And if you think this is a rare occurrence, there have been 167 times that Electors have gone off script as of 2016.

The 2016 Presidential Election saw the following:

- President
    - 3 votes for Colin Powel (did not run)
    - 1 vote for Bernie Sanders (lost Democratic Primary)
    - 1 vote for John Kasich (lost Republican Primary)
    - 1 vote for Faith Spotted Eagle (who became the first Native American to receive an Electoral vote because of this, much to her surprise)

- Vice President
    - 2 votes for Elizabeth Warren (did not run)
    - 1 vote each for Carly Fiorina, Maria Cantwell, Susan Collins, and Winona LaDuke (all who did not run)

- Three additional faithless Electors were attempted but they had their votes revoked

While this was the most faithless Electors in recent history, it is hardy a new thing. Sometimes, it is as simple as not casting a vote or misspelling the name of a candidate or reversing the President and Vice President. For the most part, Electors are appointed political positions to give favor to party loyalists. A few states allow an election of their Electors, but in reality they are held accountable to no one and are appointed by the States' legislatures to people of clout.

After this was originally written, in August 2019 the 10th U.S. Circuit Court of Appeals ruled that Faithless Elector Michael Baca of Colorado won his case to vote however he wanted as an Elector. When Mr. Baca voted for John Kasich instead of Hilary Clinton as directed, the Colorado Secretary of State nullified his vote and replaced Mr. Baca with someone who would cast the ballot as told. The ruling—which immediately applies to all the States in the 10th circuit—admonishes the State for its un-Constitutional action as there is nothing that says Electors cannot vote any way they please, at least from a Federal and Constitutional perspective. Additionally, there is no mechanism to "take back" and "nullify" a vote, so those actions

*should not have been allowed. Since this is in
conflict with a Washington State Supreme Court
decision in the same vein, the latter ruling is being
appealed to the Supreme Court where it will most
likely become official policy that Electors are free
to vote as they see fit and all of the limitations and
pledges that exist today will be rendered un-
Constitutional and unenforceable. In January 2020,
the Supreme court agreed to hear this case and a
ruling is expected in June, before the 2020
Presidential election.*

As time has gone on, the flaws have continued to show themselves. All the way back in 1824 Andrew Jackson won the popular vote with 41.4% to John Quincy Adam's 30.9%. However, in the end Quincy Adams won the runoff in House of Representatives after 4th place Henry Clay threw his support behind Quincy Adams (and in turn became his Secretary of State). However, this is not the best example because popular voting had not extended to all States yet. At that time, 6 States had no vote at all and another 12 had restrictions on candidates so that they did not even appear on the ticket.

The election of 1876 is a better example because it was after all States had direct voting within their borders and the vote-getter Samuel Tilden (50.9%) lost to Rutherford B. Hayes (47.9%). This happened again in 1888, 2000, and 2016. In the meantime, in 1961 the 23rd Amendment was passed to give Washington, D.C. the number of electors it would have as if it were a State. However, this just further proves how off this system is because the Amendment was passed so that those not living in a State would have a say in the Presidential outcome from which they were directly impacted.

By 2018, there were approximately 702,000 people living in Washington, D.C. to whom these three Electors were given. Meanwhile, the 3.6 million people living in the Territories (including 3.2 million in Puerto Rico alone) have no say at all in who is President. All the 23rd Amendment does is further lay bare the inequities of people depending upon where they live.

Going back to the "winner take all" system of the majority of the States, there is a further suppression. If you live in a State that is going to have all your Electors go to a Party you do not support (or one you wholeheartedly support) and the voting patterns make it unlikely your vote will make an impact, then you are more likely not to show up to vote. This is reflected clearly in the numbers when looking at voting age population (VAP) versus ballots cast (not looking at voter eligible population as that would exclude people who could vote in other States or in later election, like former convicts in Florida).

The United States in total had a VAP turnout percentage of 54.7%. However, if you look at the so-called 14 "battleground states" versus all others, there is a difference of 59.8% to 52.2%. If we exclude Arizona and Nevada from the "battleground" list because they were until the 2016 election seen as solidly single party, the numbers change to 60.9% versus 52.1%, respectively. These numbers do not lie; in States where voters are told they matter more and their vote has an impact, they show up more often than those in States that are not competitive. Among the non-competitive States, Hawaii bottomed out with a 38.3% rate and Minnesota topped out with 69.4%. Within the battleground States, Florida bottomed out with 56.9% and Maine topped out with 69.4%. Just to go one step further, 18 of the non-competitive States were at or below the national average with 10 of them having turnout rates below 50%. Among the battleground states, no State had a turnout below the national average. The bottom line is: if people do not feel their vote matters, then they do not vote.

And that is what makes popular vote not even a good measure. We do not know what the people who did not vote would have done. We can make assumptions, we can do projections, but none are real until we can get more people involved in the voting process. We will return to that point momentarily, but for now we need to completely end the Electoral College for the undemocratic process that it is. Just knowing that its very existence automatically excludes 3.6 million people from having a voice and potentially discourages another 113.4 million from voting should be enough to prove that this system is as broken today as it was in 1800.

Support of the Electoral College can only be given for self-serving or traditionalist reasons. If someone says that certain areas like cities will have too much influence (but for some reason it is okay for a handful of low population battleground States to have too much influence), they are simply lying because the easy math does not support it.

- Around 17% of the population live in the top 100 cities versus 20% for all rural areas.

- The top 5 cities are 6% of the population, top 20 are 10%, and the top 50 are 15%. From there, the numbers just slowly creep up.

- Even if you look at metro areas (cities themselves, surrounding areas, and other nearby smaller cities), the numbers do not come close. The metro area of New York City is still less than 20 million people, or 6% of the population. The top 5 metro areas are 17%, top 10 are 26%, and top 50 are 55%. And lest we forget that many metro areas will include rural areas because they are close enough to the cities to be included.

- For over 30 years, 38 States have voted for the same political party anyway (Although as noted, a couple of those States are likely changing). This has resulted in a starting point where Democrats have 242 Electoral College Votes to 102 for Republicans. More importantly, since it takes just 270 to win the election, Democrats would only need 28 more and could concentrate their efforts on just the most likely ways to get there.

The bottom line is that no one area or type of area can dominate others under a straight election, despite what fear mongers have to say about it. Contrary to this, the Electoral College has allowed this exact situation to happen. More importantly, though, is that we must always remember the foundation of this document is that the Constitution is flawed because fallible people wrote it and made compromises just to get 9 of 13 former colonies to agree to it. We have dealt with the impact for hundreds of years and know that in order to have a just process and engage the citizenry there must be massive changes. Therefore, let us make some:

By Amendment to the Constitution of the United States, Article 2, Section 1, Clause 2 shall be merged with Article/Amendment 23, Clause 1 and 2 and together shall read:

~~Each State shall appoint, in such Manner as the Legislature thereof may direct, a Number of Electors, equal to the whole Number of Senators and Representatives to which the State may be entitled in the Congress: but no Senator or Representative, or Person holding an Office of Trust or Profit under the United States, shall be appointed an Elector.~~

~~The District constituting the seat of government of the United States shall appoint in such manner as the Congress may direct: A number of electors of President and Vice President equal to the whole number of Senators and Representatives in Congress to which the District would be entitled if it were a state, but in no event more than the least populous state; they shall be in addition to those appointed by the states, but they shall be considered, for the purposes of the election of President and Vice President, to be electors appointed by a state; and they shall meet in the District and perform such duties as provided by the twelfth article of amendment.~~

~~The Congress shall have power to enforce this article by appropriate legislation.~~

The President and Vice President of the United States shall be directly elected by the people of all States and Territories here within.

There it is! That is it! The Constitution does not have to be complicated, but a single sentence saying all people have a say in selecting the President and Vice President. The method by which to elect them, though, is a different story entirely.

ANYONE BUT THAT GUY

Just saying that people should be able to vote for the President and Vice President directly does not actually resolve the issue because that could just mean directing the Electoral College to vote for the popularity winner. This is what has been going on through the date of this writing in 2019 with the "National Popular Vote Interstate Compact" in which States pledge that all of their Electors will go to the winner of the national popular election should the number of States in the compact meet or exceed the number of Electors required to elect the President. While a noble goal, it is still an end-runaround the Constitution and leaves all the same problems of excluding people. Additionally, there are many issues that continue to suppress turnout including when results are available. One of the other reasons why Hawaii has so low voter turnout is because the election is already decided in the middle of their voting day.

We will return to how to get more involvement, but for now the focus should be on how people would vote for the President and Vice President. This requires a complete re-write of a section of the Constitution and an Amendment:

> **By Amendment to the Constitution of the United States, Article 2, Section 1, Clause 3 shall be merged with Article/Amendment 12, Clause 1 and together shall read:**
>
> ~~The Electors shall meet in their respective states, and vote by ballot for President and Vice-President, one of whom, at least, shall not be an inhabitant of the same state with themselves; they shall name in their ballots the person voted for as President, and in distinct ballots the person voted for as Vice-President, and they shall make distinct lists of all persons voted for as President, and of all persons voted for as Vice-President, and of the number of votes for each, which lists they shall sign and certify, and transmit sealed to the seat of the government of the United States, directed to the President of the Senate; —The President of the Senate shall, in the presence of the Senate and House of Representatives, open all the certificates and the votes shall then be counted; —The person~~

having the greatest number of votes for President, shall be the President, if such number be a majority of the whole number of Electors appointed; and if no person have such majority, then from the persons having the highest numbers not exceeding three on the list of those voted for as President, the House of Representatives shall choose immediately, by ballot, the President. But in choosing the President, the votes shall be taken by states, the representation from each state having one vote; a quorum for this purpose shall consist of a member or members from two-thirds of the states, and a majority of all the states shall be necessary to a choice. —The person having the greatest number of votes as Vice-President, shall be the Vice-President, if such number be a majority of the whole number of Electors appointed, and if no person have a majority, then from the two highest numbers on the list, the Senate shall choose the Vice-President; a quorum for the purpose shall consist of two-thirds of the whole number of Senators, and a majority of the whole number shall be necessary to a choice. But no person constitutionally ineligible to the office of President shall be eligible to that of Vice-President of the United States.

The President and Vice President shall run together on a single ticket and there shall be no criteria for a President or Vice President to appear on the ballots save for meeting the criteria for each position as stated in the Constitution. Eligible voters of the States and Territories shall rank their top three choices for President and Vice President and shall also be granted a single vote against a choice for President and Vice President. A value shall be added to each vote such that the first choice gets three points, the second choice gets two points, and the third choice gets one point. Furthermore, the vote against shall subtract two points. The candidates that receive the net most amount of points shall be the President and Vice President of the United States.

Per usual, let us break this down in pieces.

First off, one of the reasons for the 12th Amendment in the first place was because of the 1796 Election when the President (John Adams) and the Vice President (Thomas Jefferson) were in different parties. This was because the original Constitution did not have the President and Vice President run together but that that the person with the most votes was President and the second most votes was Vice President (Electors had two votes). Even though Adams and Jefferson did have running mates that they intended to be Vice President the votes did not break that way and Adam's Vice Presidential pick had less votes than Jefferson.

When the Constitution was written, there were no political parties and George Washington did not align to any while he was President. Meanwhile, most thought this would not be an issue because the differences were merely ideological and that everyone would still work for what is best for the nation. Unfortunately, as has been proven time-and-time again, those with polar opposite political opinions will not work together unless forced to do so, and the President and Vice President do not have a mechanism that will make them. While what we have put in the first section of this document will force political parties in Congress to work together in order to make law, in order to Execute Law a single directive is needed.

Jefferson's Democratic-Republican Party figured this out for the next election in 1800 and planned to have one of the Electors miscast their vote intentionally so that Jefferson would be the President and Aaron Burr would be the Vice President. Unfortunately, miscommunication made it so nobody knew which Elector was supposed to do this and therefore Jefferson and Burr actually tied, requiring the House of Representatives to decide the election (which incidentally almost elected Burr as President, yet another flaw).

Because of all of that, the 12th Amendment was passed so that President the Vice President were voted on separately and it has generally been upheld to vote for a ticket running together. But we should close that loophole correctly and just say the President and the Vice President are a single ticket item that people are voting for. While it is tempting to force a second-place candidate to be Vice President, the inherent danger to the President of having an enemy be the next up in line overrides that thought.

Within this track, though, is the same situation faced with those being in a Party that the States decide to remove for capricious reasons. There is no reason to restrict any duo from running for President and Vice President save the criteria as laid out by the Constitution, that criteria being:

> **By Amendment to the Constitution of the United States, Article 2, Section 1, Clause 5 shall read:**
>
> No Person except a natural born Citizen, or a Citizen of the United States, at the time of the Adoption of this Constitution, shall be eligible to the Office of President **or Vice President**; neither shall any Person be eligible to that Office who shall not have attained to the Age of ~~thirty-five Years~~ **voting maturity as defined by the Constitution and Congress**, and been fourteen Years a Resident within the United States.

As with Congress, age should not be a restriction because if one can vote, one can serve. It is highly unlikely someone young and unknown would be elected President, but there is no reason to restrict that. However, we will maintain the other criteria of being a natural born citizen for now and been 14 years a resident (meaning the person needs to live in the country for the past 14 years in a row). While there may be arguments to allow foreign-born persons to be President and the risk would be minimal nowadays, it is not a requirement to make the country function well. Additionally, this could always be changed with another Amendment later, so we will leave it alone for now.

Now, with so many people on the ballot, how are voters to cast their decisions? Theoretically, Political Party is irrelevant as anyone could run. Perhaps Political Parties would still run primaries and make decisions about how many of their people will run, but per earlier Amendments the Government is out of the Primary game, so that will be up to them. If someone wants to run and meets the criteria, they are on the ballot everywhere. Does that mean hundreds of pairings could be on the ballot? Absolutely! Why should choice be limited?

Instead, we will take a cue from the 12th Amendment again. The way it is set up now is that if no candidate receives a majority of Electoral College votes then the top 3 candidates will be sent to the House of Representatives to decide which one should be President. This is exactly what happened in the aforementioned 1824 election where not only did the person with the most popular votes (Andrew Jackson) lose the election, but he also lost even though he had the most Electoral College votes!

	Popular Vote	Electoral College	House Vote
Andrew Jackson	41%	38%	29%
John Quincy Adams	31%	32%	54%
Henry Clay	13%	16%	17%
William H. Crawford	11%	14%	N/A
Other	4%	0%	N/A

Because Jackson did not make it over the Electoral College threshold, it forced a runoff between the top three, of which he massively lost. While this has not occurred again, the potential is still there for this to happen. Having the House of Representatives decide the Presidential Election has already shown it will go against the will of the people if the chamber of Congress so desires and therefore should be excluded as a valid method. However, we can take one of the ideas in a top three decision.

If we went with absolute majority of votes, in the 2016 Election Hillary Clinton had 48% of the vote and Donald Trump had 46% of the vote. Now, we cannot assume what the 113 million people who did not vote would have done, so we should assume for now this result reflects the overall desires of the nation. That said, if we extended the "absolute majority" rule with the popular vote, we'd end up in the exact same situation. Gary Johnson had 3% of the vote, Jill Stein had 1%, and everyone else (including Evan McMullin. Darrell Castle, Gloria La Riva, and Bernie Sanders [somehow]) had another 1%. If we wanted a runoff vote with the Top 3 people, it is possible Hillary could have picked up another 2-3%, but it is more likely that Gary Johnson would have picked up enough to still not elect her.

Meanwhile, the expense and time of putting on another election would have been phenomenal. Let us not forget that the election was in November and the President assumes office in January. That means a runoff election would have needed to happen somewhere between Thanksgiving and the winter holidays— and could still have resulted in no clear winner! Other countries and local areas in this nation have dealt with this exact issue and it can result in unfilled position for months on end. That is not acceptable for President the Vice President of the United States.

Instead, we can take the guessing game out by asking a different question: if your first pick for President cannot be elected, who is your second choice? Who is your third choice? With this, we already have the runoff election complete because we can assign a point value to each of these choices. Your first choice gets 3 points, your second choice gets 2, and your third choice gets 1. Whoever has the most points is the winner as the points would already reflect the backup and backup's backup will of the people!

Sometimes, people do not have a clear idea of who they want to vote for, but they do know who they do not want as President. That should be reflected in the vote, too, as an allowance for a negative vote. In this case, the voters could give their will to have a candidate lose 2 points. This would not completely negate someone's first choice vote but would partially remove it while allowing other points to accumulate.

If we make various assumptions, we can estimate how the results would have been for the 2016 Presidential election. Some of the assumptions include:

- Every candidate that received a popular vote was the first choice and got 3 points for that.

- 90% of Democrats and Republican votes will use their negative vote on the opposing Party, as will 40% of all other voters.

- Roughly 1% of votes cast by all other parties will be used against every Third Party and Independent.

- 5% to 10% of every group will use their second and third choice votes for major parties or third parties, depending on relative political alignment.

This could be modeled forever using a ton of other assumptions, but the idea is to get an impression of where this might fall out. Here is what we see:

	Party	Electoral College	Popular Vote	Net Point Vote
Donald Trump	Republican	57%	46%	39%
Hillary Clinton	Democratic	42%	48%	43%
Gary Johnson	Libertarian	0%	3%	10%
Jill Stein	Green	0%	1%	7%
All Other	Many	1%	1%	2%

As you can surmise, Hillary Clinton would still win the election compared to the popular vote, but the Third Parties would get a lot more attention and net points so that it is more likely they will be recognized in the future. Again, a major point of this document is to break the oligopoly of the Democratic and Republican parties and this Amendment is an important step to helping other Parties gain attention. It is worth noting that both Republicans and Democrats engaged in fear mongering during the election saying a Third Party vote would be a waste or—worse—that it would help their opponent get elected. This is just the oligopoly talking to maintain its power and has nothing to do with reality. With 113 million people not voting, nearly 4 million people not allowed to vote, and who knows how many people scared out of voting for who they wanted for fear of the candidate they least liked being elected, it is impossible to say how different these number would turn out. It does not necessarily mean a Third Party would have won, but perhaps the margins would not be so large. Maybe a significant number of people would have voted for Third Parties first, Major Parties Second, and used their negative vote for the other Major Party? We cannot tell until we make the change and allow it to happen.

The Negative Vote is incredibly important in this scheme because it frees people to vote for who they want. Giving people full control and meaning to their vote is the truly virtuous thing to do in a representative democracy. As mentioned earlier in this section, though, a lot more needs to be done to get everyone involved and engaged.

FIVE DOUBLE-U'S AND AN H

Now that the Electoral College would be no more, there are other parts of the Constitution that will need immediate cleanup. This begins with modifying the clause related to setting the election date:

> **By Amendment to the Constitution of the United States, Article 2, Section 1, Clause 4 shall read:**
>
> The Congress may determine the Time of ~~chusing the Electors~~ **holding elections for the President and Vice President**, and the Day on which ~~they~~ **the people of the United States** shall give their Votes; which Day shall be the same throughout the United States.

This is a pretty straightforward change making note that it is now the people of the United States who are voting for President and Vice President, but Congress still controls that day. If you recall, we did not address this with Congress, but now we should do so:

> **By Amendment to the Constitution of the United States, Article 1, Section 4, Clause 1 shall read:**
>
> The Times, Places and Manner of holding Elections for Senators and Representatives, shall be prescribed ~~in each State by the Legislature thereof; but the Congress may at any time by Law make or alter such Regulations, except as to the Places of chusing Senators~~ **by Congress and the Day on which the people of the United States shall give their Votes; which Day shall be the same throughout the United States.**

Right now, this is the law anyway. First, Congress set the day for the elections of President and Vice President in 1845 as the first Tuesday after the first Monday in November, the date we are all familiar with:

> **Acts of the 28th Congress**
> **Session 2**
> **Chapter 1**
> **January 23, 1845**
>
> Be it enacted by the Senate and House of Representatives of the United States of America in Congress assembled, That the electors of President and Vice President shall be appointed in each State on the Tuesday next after the first Monday in the month of November of the year in which they are to be appointed: Provided, That each State may by law provide for the filling of any vacancy or vacancies which may occur in its college of electors when such college meets to give its electoral vote: And provided, also, when any State shall have held an election for the purpose of choosing electors, and shall fail to make a choice on the day aforesaid, then the electors may be appointed on a subsequent day in such manner as the State shall by law provide.

Further clarifications were made as time went on, but it is important to note that the same day was extended to the House of Representatives in 1872 in time for the 1874 election.

> **2 U.S. Code § 7**
>
> The Tuesday next after the 1st Monday in
> November, in every even numbered year, is
> established as the day for the election, in each of
> the States and Territories of the United States, of
> Representatives and Delegates to the Congress
> commencing on the 3d day of January next
> thereafter.

Finally, this same law was automatically extended to the election of Senators
with the 17th Amendment in 1913.

As such, this Amendment is not impacting anything we already have, just
codifying it into the Constitution and further clarifying that Election Day on the
Federal level is the same day no matter what except whether it is a Presidential
year or a Congressional year. States, Counties, and other local municipalities
would still have the option of having their elections on other days, though it is
most likely that at least on the State-level that elections would try to align to
the same Federal dates to defray the costs and increase voter turnout.

To further drive this home, we now return to the new Article 8 of the
Constitution. Another Section is necessary to enumerate the rights and
expectations of the Federal elections:

> **By Amendment to the Constitution of the
> United States, Article 8, Section 2, Clause 1
> shall be added.**
>
> The Day chosen by Congress for holding Elections
> for Senators and Representatives shall be the
> same Day for holding Elections for the President
> and Vice President; only separated by the Years as
> prescribed in the Constitution and relevant
> Amendments.

Again, this is just a forced codification and makes sure the law is uniform
across the United States. Per the Constitution, Congress would still control
what the day the election is and there is no recommendation to change that
here. Many people complain that the day is stuck in a 19th century mentality of
market days and when agrarians would be available to vote. Others point to
the fact that almost all other western representative democracies have their
election on a holiday or a weekend. Of course, all these people are right!

So are the people who say that elections that are on a weekend would disproportionately eliminate poorer Americans who work Saturdays, Sundays, and "off hours" at a far higher rate that more well-to-do Americans. One way or another, some group of people is going to be negatively impacted by a single day election. Therefore, the problem is not the day, but the timeframe in which the election happens. We need to build on what is law with an Amendment to get more people involved, and we start with the timeframe of elections:

> **By Amendment to the Constitution of the United States, Article 8, Section 2, Clause 2 shall be added.**
>
> Elections for Senators, Representatives, and the President and Vice President shall start at least three weeks before the Day chosen by Congress for holding Elections. The Election timeframe may be extended by law but shall not be shortened for any reason. Election polling must be made available as most convenient for the People of the United States and include hours and days in which the majority do not make labor.

Elections being on one day is truly the issue at hand because it limits the options for people voting in person. Instead, elections should happen for at least 3 weeks before whatever day is chosen as the "official" election day. Based on the current system, this would put elections starting in mid-October and would go through several weekends. That is also where the second part of this Amendment comes into play to have polling stations available at a time that is "most convenient" in that it is the time that "the majority do not make labor", in other words: off-hours.

One of the issues in the past has always been pegging government functions to the behaviors and customs of the time, but those do change over the decades and centuries. The voting laws were set up with an agrarian society in mind and a much more limited voting pool. Our country now is a mostly service economy with a greatly expanded pool of voters (age, gender, race, etcetera), so the current setup does not completely make sense. Flexibility is key, so if Congress sets polling stations to be open between 12pm and 8pm every weekday and 10am and 4pm on the weekend, then it should cover the vast majority of Americans without as much interference in the workday (Potentially, Congress or a local polling authority could also alternate days with different hours to allow more flexibility for different groups of people). And if you will recall, the earlier Amendments forced any law to be reviewed every 20 years, so these days and times would at least be revisited that often as habits of society change.

The important thing is the plasticity of having voting available and good timeframes to get as many people involved as conveniently as possible. For those who scoff at the cost of doing this, my question for you then is: what should the government spend money on that is more important than having an active, engaged and represented populace? What is the point of having a government at all if it is not spending its funding on being involved with the people who are the true rulers of this country?

And do note that this Amendment does allow Congress (or any other local municipality) to expand the timeframe even further. Thus, if it makes sense to vote for two months, then that is what will happen; just at a minimum there should be three weeks. During that time, though, there might be a desire to release preliminary results, and this must be stopped at all costs:

By Amendment to the Constitution of the United States, Article 8, Section 2, Clause 3 shall be added.

The governing body of each election—Federal or otherwise—shall maintain the secrecy of ballot results until at least seven full days have passed from the Day of Election. This timeframe may be extended by law or in order to have the appropriate time to verify the results, but shall not be shortened for any reason. No member of the governing body of each election may share results or estimates of the elections during this timeframe under penalty of treason.

As previously noted, the turnout rates in Hawaii are far below the other States and Territories. While one part of this is definitely the "my vote does not matter" impact of having an area solidly with one political party, the other is the time-zone differential of the elections. Hawaii is six hours behind the East Cost of the United States and as the years have gone on news outlets have been declaring winners of elections within seconds or minutes of polls closing. If the President is already decided before you get a chance to go vote after work, why would you even bother to do so?

This plays out all over the country and even within States. Releasing even tentative polling results discourages people from going out and voting because there is a feeling of uselessness. While there is nothing that can be done to stop the press and other pundits from making estimates, taking polls of their own, and making projections, the government does not and should not be part of the process. Additionally, trying to put out election night results puts undo strain on workers that can create mistakes. The process of counting votes should be slow, deliberate, and careful such that by the time the official results are given they are 100% accurate, or as close to that as humanly possible.

Since the elections are in early November and the government does not take its positions until early January, what is the rush to get the results out the door? The only reason is because we are in a society that demands instantaneous satisfaction and information. Patience is a lost concept in a world where every bit of media is available by saying a few words to an Artificial Intelligence living inside of a hockey puck. To be fair and safe, ballots should be protected for a detailed count, re-count, and verification process. And there may be times to extend this process in incredibly close races or if absentee ballots have been delayed (such as when troops are deployed in a war zone). Every vote should have a fair chance, and every voter should have the feeling that their vote matters.

You will notice here that we have again added the penalty of treason. Doing anything to undermine the election, even the simple act of releasing polling information early, is an attack upon America. As shown, this release causes (at least in part) a suppression of voters and depresses turnout, and that should be discouraged at all cost—including the cost of being accused of treason. This penalty and all the other rules around election results would extend to all levels of government, ensuring that this same level of scrutiny would be applied to the local sheriff race as equally as the President of the United States.

However, there are other key elements that are used to stop people from voting, not the least of which is getting and staying registered:

> **By Amendment to the Constitution of the United States, Article 8, Section 2, Clause 4 shall be added.**
>
> All eligible voters of the United States shall be automatically registered to Vote and be provided all necessary materials and information in order to give their vote.

Why does anyone need to register to vote at all? There is nothing in the Constitution that says voter access should be restricted; quite the contrary, the 14th, 15th, 19th, and 24th Amendments all deal with removing restrictions on voting in one form or another. The 24th Amendment, Clause 1 in particular states:

> The right of citizens of the United States to vote in any primary or other election for President or Vice President, for electors for President or Vice President, or for Senator or Representative in Congress, shall not be denied or abridged by the United States or any state by reason of failure to pay any poll tax or other tax.

It could be (and has been) argued that registering to vote is yet another type of tax. Tax does not have to be money, but it can be time or meeting criteria that States set up. There are active lawsuits that deal with States setting up restrictions for voter registration, for purging voter rolls, and other forms of refusing people to vote due to so-called discrepancies. Voting should not be abridged in any way and the Constitution already does not give any leeway in this. Now, this Amendment would codify that certainty and not just sustain it implicitly.

The easier it is to register, the higher the turnout. Looking at the VAP turnout percentages for 2016, the eight States with the highest values all had same day voter registration (Maine, Minnesota, New Hampshire, Wisconsin, Iowa, Colorado, Vermont, and Michigan). Among all the States with same day voter registration, the VAP was 56.1% compared to 54% of those States without. If we exclude California and Hawaii—two of the three lowest VAP (Texas being the other) because of reasons of their geography and lack of competition—that value jumps to 61.7%. Those numbers are clear: the easier it is to register and vote without restriction, the higher turnout is. It is so clear that since the 2016 election, four more States have already added the same option.

Much later in this document we will return to how to better keep track of people so that voter rolls are accurate, but for now the focus is just on the fact that everyone should be set up with no effort as a service of the government. Also as a service of the government is a note above for all related material. In order to be an informed voter, the government often prints out materials to explain particular items or what is being voted on—in other words, a voter's handbook. Again, all of this should be readily available to the people.

That is not the only material that should be provided, though. One of the best ways to understand what is going to be on the ballot is to have the ballot, and as such the following Amendment should be added:

> **By Amendment to the Constitution of the United States, Article 8, Section 2, Clause 5 shall be added.**
>
> All eligible voters of the United States shall be provided a ballot at the commencement of the Election timeframe. This ballot shall be able to be submitted by all methods as have been made available by law during the Election timeframe.

There are not a lot of examples in the United States, but the three States that do have automatic mail ballot voting (Colorado, Oregon, and Washington) have a combined VAP of 61.2% compared to the rest of the States with 54.3%. It should be noted that Colorado also has same day registration and is a "battleground" State, so it is hitting all the right checkboxes. Additionally, another 19 States have laws that allow counties or other municipalities to have entirely vote-by-mail elections if they so choose, but it is up to each area. Altogether, the data is probably not enough to base a statistical analysis on, especially since that is not the complete point of this Amendment.

States like Colorado do not just force everyone to vote by mail. While the ballots are sent out to all eligible voters, the voters can then mail it back, drop it off at a designated polling box, or vote in person at a polling station. And that is what the second part of this Amendment is taking about. Today, the ways to vote might consist of by mail, by a drop-box, early in person at designated location, or directly at the polling stations. In the future, though, maybe elections via the Internet will be safe and secure. Perhaps there is another method we have not quite figured out how to implement yet that would be easier and more accurate. In any case, all methods should be made available to the people to vote.

Therefore, sending out the mail ballot ahead of time could be considered just another piece of election material. In the (at least) 3-week timeframe that voting would happen, voters could use any of the methods available to them, not just the mail ballot itself—which then could just be informational in that case. It will give voters the opportunity to be informed and no excuse that every opportunity was not granted to get their vote in.

That said, there is one last measure that can be used to increase turnout and participation.

> **By Amendment to the Constitution of the United States, Article 8, Section 2, Clause 6 shall be added.**
>
> All eligible voters within the United States are required to vote in Federal elections unless unable to physically or mentally do so or have been granted an exception by law. Congress shall lay a levy on those who fail to submit ballots without meeting an exception.

You did not think you were going to get away without having a responsibility in all of this, did you? Yes, for the past 99% of this document the onus has fallen on the government to change, but that does not mean there are not civic duties for the people.

Compulsory voting would be impossible in the United States right now because it would violate the 1st Amendment. One could easily argue that forcing someone to vote is a type of speech that someone may not want to give. Because of that, an Amendment would be needed to make it part of the Constitution in order to have equal weight.

Others think of compulsory elections like those used in North Korea. Yes, everyone must "vote", but there is only one item to vote on and the answer is "Yes" no matter what, so it is not a real democracy. However, countries closer to our own like Australia, Belgium, Brazil, and others do have a compulsory system and see voter turnout rates in the 90% or above range. One of the key difference makers is the fine for those who fail to vote. Many countries that have compulsory voting do not have a fine or do not enforce it, and the rates of participation are noticeably lower.

Some may fear the idea of an uneducated or uninterested class of people being involved in the voting process who would not otherwise do so. Studies show, however, that because of compulsion, interest in the political process and desire to have one's views be heard *increases*. If we look back at our legislative section and see how people with low net worth, low education levels, and young ages have no or almost on representation, one can see that compelling these groups to vote may actually create the type of party that expresses their needs. And yes, the correlation is there that those who are more disadvantaged are less likely to vote and thus perpetuate the cycle. Just giving them the ability to have their voice be heard is one step, but it is another entirely to fuse their voice to the chorus.

There are exceptions, of course, that must be accounted for. Being in a physical state where voting is impossible or having a mental debilitation could be reasons for exclusion. Others may have religious reasons for not voting, or there are laws that restrict certain classes of people (think people in prison). As such, Congress would be allowed to create and maintain that list of exceptions—which in turn would be reviewed at least every 20 years when the law came due.

Plus, nothing is stopping someone from returning their ballot blank or filling it in with nonsense. Nothing is stopping people from doing that now! There were over 763,000 write-in votes for President in 2016, and a large number of votes were for fictional characters like Mickey Mouse and Elmer Fudd, or non-humans like the deceased gorilla Harambe. Again, though, studies have shown that while disengaged people may start off this way, over time they tend to vote for real candidates. Consider the reason for many of these joke votes—even among the limited constituents—as a response to living in an area where their vote makes no impact on the outcome. If we add in proportional representation in Congress and ranked voting for President, if we keep voting figures tied down, and if we make everyone vote, suddenly these excluded people will carry a large weight and an impact.

Of course, there will always be jokers, anti-establishment types, and general protesters, but that is their right. Should we find that compulsory voting in actuality is not effective, Congress could always lower the fine to $0 and therefore there would be no compulsion mechanism. That is one of the reasons for allowing Congress to control the rate as opposed to building it into the Constitution.

The government has a responsibility to the people of the United States; but how can the government be responsible if the people do not fulfil their duty to it? And the duty of the people is to vote.

SHRINKAGE

According to the Administrative Conference of the United States (ACUS) Sourcebook – Second Edition (December 2018), pages 26 to 28:

> [T]he Administrative Procedure Act (APA), which governs most federal agencies, provides one of the broadest and most widely-used definitions for administrative agencies.
>
> ...
>
> Courts have recognized that the APA's definition of agency is not entirely clear, and there has been a substantial amount of litigation over which government entities fall within the various legal classifications of agency.
>
> ...
>
> [T]here is **no authoritative list of government agencies** {*emphasis added*}. Every list of federal agencies in government publications is different. For example, FOIA.gov lists 118 separate executive agencies that comply with the Freedom of Information Act requirements imposed on every federal agency. This appears to be on the conservative end of the range of possible agency definitions. The United States Government Manual lists 305 unique or sub-component units as agencies. An even more inclusive listing comes from usa.gov, which lists over 600 government departments and agencies.
>
> ...
>
> Disentangling which of these entities is an "agency" is difficult, particularly since many are wholly or partly owned and directed by private sector actors.

Incidentally, the ACUS (according to itself) is "an independent federal agency charged with convening expert representatives from the public and private sectors to recommend improvements to administrative process and procedure". Therefore, it is one of the impossible to catalogue agencies that exists within the nether that is the Federal bureaucracy—what the report itself calls a fourth branch of government that is not held accountable to democracy.

In case this is not abundantly clear, the United States government is a mess. How can one effectively manage and fund such a behemoth when one does not even know what is included and where? Up until this point, the focus of this document has been about changing the Constitution to have the voices of the people be heard and expounded upon. Yet, once the people have proper representation in the Legislative and the Executive Branches, what then?

Even if the United States government is being fundamentally changed in who is in charge, there is still over 230 years of law and bureaucracy that has built up. Yes, the 20-year check in on all law will still happen, but that will take time and, in the meantime, how do you manage it all? What is the organizational chart of the government?

Instead of trying to focus in on "what is" and "how we got here" like the ACUS, we will instead focus on "what should be, given what we have". This section will focus on merging the various department and agencies that do exist (as much as can be catalogued) into a more cohesive structure that can be used to set the basis for where all other agencies should align to. In other words, the idea is to create a framework and hierarchical structure to the government that can be understood and place all agencies within that.

As part of that process, we will explore the costs of all these various areas with the understanding that there is much replication of process and operations going on that could be eliminated. For instance, the ACUS mentioned several other agencies that also do a research project on the structure of government, so we can assume there is overlap and redundancy that can be eliminated.

This will extend very deep into all parts of the government, including the military and all other related federal law enforcement agencies. Again, the idea is to eliminate redundancy and waste, but there is more to it. If there are not competing priorities, then we are approaching all situations with a single mind and with all of the relevant data. As an example, how much data is locked away at the CIA or NSA that the FBI and U.S. Marshalls do not have and vice versa? If these were singular approaches, how much more could we know and understand?

Beyond this, we will want to re-establish further breaks between the legislative and executive authorities, making sure that some powers cannot be delegated or taken. The Constitution is very specific around certain duties, but it seems like additional enforcement may be necessary. In the same vein, there are executive resources that can be tapped in to in order to take on roles at the

Federal level instead of creating new agencies and positions. This is about how we can shrink the Federal Government into something manageable, understandable, and useful.

THE BOB'S

As previously discussed, Section 2, Clause 1, Sentence 1b of the Constitution states for the President:

> [H]e may require the Opinion, in writing, of the principal Officer in each of the executive Departments, upon any Subject relating to the Duties of their respective Offices[.]

And that is it as far as the Constitution is concerned on the structure of the Executive Branch for anything outside of the President and Vice President. What are the "Executive Departments"? How should they be organized? How much oversight by the President is needed? What does he do with that information?

These specific questions were left to Congress and they have answered it in a variety of ways. Sometimes there are leadership positions that require Congressional approval, sometimes there are appointments, sometimes there are career paths, and sometimes there are mechanisms outside of the government such as boards and private organizations. Yet the Constitution gives Congress the ability to do this and more, as stated in Article 1, Section 8, Clause 18:

> To make all Laws which shall be necessary and proper for carrying into Execution the foregoing Powers, and all other Powers vested by this Constitution in the Government of the United States, or in any Department or Officer thereof.

Because of this, Congress has divested many of their powers directly to the Executive Branch, which in turn has allowed the President to issue many Executive Orders to create, modify, and transfigure a vast amount of the executive positions we know today. Much of what we think of as the heads of government are situated within the President's Cabinet, but this is not an organization or a position recognized by the Constitution. Despite this, right back to the first President George Washington there was a Cabinet which had five members. Over time, positions have been added, removed, merged, or greatly changed beyond their original intent to where in 2019 there are 15 official Department Heads and 7 other people considered to be part of the President's Cabinet.

You might think that these positions are more fixed because the 15 official Departments Heads are part of the Presidential line of succession. However, the Constitution and Amendments give Congress the power to determine the line of succession, which is currently following the order set up in 1947 and last updated in 2006. After the Vice President comes the Speaker of the House, the President pro Tempore of the Senate (there is that official position again and not the majority party leader), followed by the official 15 Department Heads who are also confirmed by Congress.

For something so important and so ingrained in the rest of the Constitution and the Law, it would seem to be sorely missing. Therefore, we should make organization of the Executive Branch part of the Constitution officially:

> **By Amendment to the Constitution of the United States, Article 2, Section 5, Clause 1 shall be added.**
>
> The President, Vice President, and heads of the Executive Departments shall form a body known as the Cabinet that shall meet at the discretion of the President.

Please note that there is no Article 2, Section 5, so this would be a new section added to the Executive Branch portion. What we want to do with this section is start the definition of the Federal Hierarchy by establishing that there is an official order that is referenced elsewhere in the Constitution and the law.

This starts by defining what the Cabinet is, which is just a body that consists of the two Executives (President and Vice President) and the heads of the official Executive Departments. Elsewhere in the Constitution, Congress has the power to define what the Executive Departments are and who the heads of those Departments are, though both come at the recommendation of the President. This does not contradict any of that thus far, just codifies what happens afterwards. Also, this body does not have to meet at all and the schedule is totally up to the President, as is also in line with the Constitution as shown above.

Now the question becomes, what are these Executive Departments? Well, in 2019 we have the following:

1. State
2. Treasury
3. Defense
4. Justice
5. Interior
6. Agriculture
7. Commerce
8. Labor
9. Health and Human Services
10. Housing and Urban Development
11. Transportation
12. Energy
13. Education
14. Veterans Affairs
15. Homeland Security

Theoretically, these are the most important things in our country. No offense to Housing and Urban Development (HUD) or Agriculture or Transportation, but how are they equal to Treasury or Defense or Health and Human Services? And how do you even separate on these lines? How can you talk about Transportation without consideration for Energy or Urban Development? Why is Defense separated from Homeland Security? Or the same could be said for Commerce and Labor? And where are other key considerations like the Environment and Science or Arts and Culture (the latter of which is mandated by the Constitution)? The bottom line is: what should be the big buckets we care about?

We will return to this question in a moment, but for now it is important to note that there are several other people in the Cabinet today. They consist of:

1. White House Chief of Staff
2. Trade Representative
3. Director of National Intelligence
4. Director of the Office of Management and Budget
5. Director of the Central Intelligence Agency (CIA)
6. Administrator of the Environmental Protection Agency (EPA)
7. Administrator of the Small Business Administration (SBA)

Now we have compounded our issues because National Intelligence and the CIA would seem to have the same overall mission as Homeland Security and Defense, yet they are separate areas entirely. Trade and the SBA here are separated from Commerce and Labor, and with the SBA particularly, it is again a question of why it has as high a bearing as other official Departments—really the same question we have for HUD. The EPA's appearance shows some consideration for the Environment, but it is not at the level of a real Department. At the same time, it is far outnumbered by other similarly aligned causes and still excludes all other areas of science.

Well, this requires a more detailed organization, but first we must close in on what it means to be in the Cabinet:

> **By Amendment to the Constitution of the United States, Article 2, Section 5, Clause 2 shall be added.**
>
> The President may ask or appoint other officers or persons to take part in the discussions of the Cabinet, but these persons shall not be members of the Cabinet.

In other words, yes, the President can ask his Chief of Staff to be part of the Cabinet or could ask any or all Agency heads and/or directors to visit for specific meetings. But in order to be part of the Cabinet you must be a Department Head so it creates an official hierarchy. From the President to the Vice President and the Departments Heads directly should be the plan, and the Departments should represent the gross amalgamation of all Agencies underneath them.

> **By Amendment to the Constitution of the United States, Article 2, Section 5, Clause 3 shall be added.**
>
> All other agencies of the Federal Government shall be organized underneath the Executive Departments, or the President or Vice President directly. All other agencies shall be subordinate to the heads of the Executive Departments, or the President or Vice President directly.

What is an Agency? The Constitution does not ever mention the word yet it comes up repeatedly in law and when discussing the scope of the Federal Government. Here, we gain a definition of Agency as an area subordinate (or "inferior" as the Constitution often says) to another federal institution, particularly an Executive Department, the Vice President, or the President himself.

Important to note that today Congress has Agencies that do report directly to it instead of being part of the Executive Branch. This is a removal of that function and puts all executing actions under the Executive Branch one way or another. Most of these areas are rather benign—such as the Library of Congress. However, Congress has given itself a police force separate from the Executive authority as well as quality assurance agencies like the Congressional Budget Office and Government Accountability Office. These would seem to be the very definition of Executive function! Just as we demanded all decision-making move into Congressional hands, we must demand that all action on those decisions be part the President's responsibility.

The Library of Congress—as pictured here in December 2019—is independent and is held accountable to no Executive Department nor even the President himself. Who knows what mischief they are getting into in there without proper oversight?

No, Congress's job is straightforward: create and fund departments and agencies, not run them. But even deciding where they belong should be out of their purview as that is also an executive decision. In other words, it should not take an act of Congress to re-organize the government into more useful functions.

By Amendment to the Constitution of the United States, Article 2, Section 5, Clause 4 shall be added.

The President shall be responsible for organizing all Agencies within each Federal Department, or Agencies within Federal Departments, or to the President or Vice President directly.

Congress would still have the purse strings no matter where these Agencies end up, though it is a question of how granular Congress wants to be. Perhaps they would be happier in their limited role setting a bucket for each Department and then have the Departments decide how the funds will be distributed? Or perhaps Congress will fund some intermediary level between Department and Agency that does the same function? In any of these situations, it would be Congress's decision, but the President could align the Agencies as he sees fit. This organization may make Congress note the redundancies in the system. Another option might be to have a bottom's up approach to budgeting where Agencies ask for certain amounts that are reviewed first by intermediate levels and then by Departments before being shifted to Congress for final approval. Again, this may reveal unnecessary funding and redundancies in the system so that Agencies get merged or depreciated entirely.

No matter what, the President should be able to understand the layout of the Executive Branch and call forth those responsible for certain areas. And if there is a deficiency, the Executive Branch can make it clear and ask specifically for what they need and why it does not fit into an existing structure. This does not happen today, as noted:

> **Administrative Conference of the United States (ACUS)**
> **Sourcebook – Second Edition (December 2018)**
> **Pages 84 to 85**
>
> A political decision to create a new agency begs the question of why Congress does not delegate new federal responsibilities to existing agencies. Generally, Congress creates new agencies to carry out federal responsibilities when it does not believe existing agencies will effectively implement new policies. Existing agencies may not have the expertise to carry out new policies. Alternatively, existing agencies may resist the delegation of authority because the new policy deviates from what the agency perceives as its primary mission.
>
> ...
>
> In other cases, new agencies are the result of the larger struggle over the new policy. Proponents or opponents of new policies demand that new policies will be carried out by agencies with specific structural features in exchange for their support. The structural features they demand shape the ability of political actors to get access to agency decision-making. For example, some structures insulate the agency from the influence of the President or Congress. Others provide privileged access to agency decision-making for some groups and interests. In many cases, there would be no agency created at all unless the new agency included certain features that allow broad representation and regular review by Congress.

In other words, there is no rhyme or reason or methodology; Congress just does whatever it feels like at that moment and creates or destroys agencies. While not mandated by any Amendment, having a logical flow organization of the government may make arguments one way or another more apolitical and reasonable. Questions like establishing new Agencies or not or keeping an agency in an existing (or new) Department can be approached with more logistics planning instead of gut feeling.

While we have established that there are Departments and that Congress controls what they are, what should these Departments be? What should the top layer of executive government in the Cabinet look like? And how does everything else fit underneath it?

Position	Department of...	Portfolio(s)
President		• Strategy and Vision • Risk Management • Communications and Marketing • Press Relations • Inter-Branch Relations and Communications
Vice President		• Quality Assurance • Efficiency • Accountability and Ethics • Safety Checks and Validations • Executive Security
Department Head	Government Operations	• Shared Services (Human Resources, Information Technology, Material Acquisition, Finance and Accounting, etcetera) • Legislative and Judicial Support Services • Inter-Departmental/Agency Communications • Project Management
Department Head	Internal Relations	• State Governments • Territory Governments • Local Governments • Native American Tribal Relations • Internal Border Management and Districting • Elections
Department Head	Foreign Relations	• Foreign Governments • Hosting Foreign Dignitaries • Ambassadors • Non-Military International Organizations (IE United Nations) • Treaty Management • International Border Management

Position	Department of...	Portfolio(s)
Department Head	Safety and Security	• Military • Intelligence Services • Police/Investigative Services • Relief and Recovery Services • Veterans Services • Prisons and Parole
Department Head	People and Society	• Human Services • Social Services • Health Services • Housing • Education • Census • Citizenship and Foreign Nationals
Department Head	Interconnectivity	• Transportation • Communications • Postal Roads • Post Office • Interstate and Cross-State Connections
Department Head	Science, Technology, and Environment	• Land, Water, Air, Underground, Plant, and Animal Management • Environment • Space • Technology • Agriculture, Chattel, and Food Management • Health and Medicine Management Energy
Department Head	Resource and Asset Management	• Government Buildings and Lands • Government Leases • Seat of Government Management • Capital Planning and Management • National Park Service • Allowed Resource Extraction (Policy set by the Department Science, Technology, and Environment) • Transparency and Government Information Requests
Department Head	Commerce and Labor	• Consumer Protection • Occupational Regulation and Safety • Labor Protections • Labor Training • Economic Analysis • Business Administration and Support • Trade • Insurance

Position	Department of...	Portfolio(s)
Department Head	Arts and Culture	• Artistic Works and Publishing • Libraries and Museums • Public Broadcasting • Archives and Records • Patents, Trademarks, and Copyrights
Department Head	Freedom, Law, and Justice	• Attorneys • Lawsuits • Legal Assistance • Special and Legal Protections • Foreign Claims
Department Head	Fiscal Management	• Taxes and Revenue Collection • Treasury Management • Debt Management • Investment Management • Equities Management • Central Banking • Minting Money • Scholarship/Fund Management

What this does is make the Cabinet a decision-making body and process that has a top-level look at any impact areas. If the President is considering an action or Congress has passed or is considering an action, this group of people can present a specific perspective where one has an equal weight for consideration. Going down the list from the first Department we can ask the question:

- What changes to operating the government will be needed?

- Does this impact relations between States and the Federal Government? If so, how—and how will the Federal Government respond?

- Does this impact relations between the United States and a Foreign Government or organization? If so, how—and how will the Federal Government respond?

- Is there a danger to the safety and security of the United States, its people, and/or its property?

- How does this impact the various people of the United States?

- Does this in any way limit or add to the ability of goods, services, and data to easily move between people and organizations?

- Is there a technological and/or environmental impact to consider? What does scientific analysis say about this decision?

- Does this impact existing Government resources that are currently in use?

- Is there an economic or labor consideration?

- Is there an impact on arts and culture?

- What are the legal considerations and potential impacts?

- What are the monetary considerations?

While not every decision will have a bearing on all these areas—and many will impact only one—it provides the ability to have these distinct perspectives that cover a large range of subjects. Meanwhile, within each Department will be a variety of Agencies that cover the further wide ranges of the portfolios. Now, HUD would not make a decision on running a program without consideration for the impacts in all other social services. In a similar vein, all of the disparate military and intelligence agencies would speak with one voice and share information between themselves to come with a common perspective to the President instead of four that are currently sitting on the President's Cabinet.

Beyond these Departments, other Portfolios would belong to the Vice President and the President directly. Specifically, the Vice President would consist of a "quality assurance" check on all other Departments to make sure they are living up to their mandates and are not trying to skirt the system. These checks might be anything from making sure environmental inspectors are doing their jobs correctly to investigations on military leaders (and deploying the military police, if necessary).

At the top of the chain is the President who is given a CEO role of setting the strategy and vision for the entire Federal Government. Because the President is ultimately in charge, his portfolio would also include all communication channels so that anything coming out of the government to the people or the press would be cleared by him and considered to be official. Along those lines, the President would be responsible for being the conduit to the other Branches of government because he ultimately represents everything Executive and all other people are flowing up to him. In other words, the buck starts and stops with the President.

As mentioned before, there are hundreds of Agencies (depending upon the definition) throughout the Federal Government. Going through each Department and many of the major Agencies that would now be a part of it is not the exercise for today. As such, I invite you to read **NEW & IMPROVED: THE PRESIDENT OF THE UNITED STATES** to see a complete reorganization of theses agencies in as accurate as a manner as possible. In the meantime, please keep in mind that vast amounts of Agencies would need to move out of other Agencies/Departments or independent areas to end up inside the hierarchy and aligned to their purposes.

Meanwhile, something else to consider is that the U.S. Government budget (at the surface) is around $4.1 trillion (with a "T"), and often goes on to spend more. These expenditures may be closer to the $6+ trillion range depending on definitions of what is the government and what is revenue. For instance, rail passenger service Amtrak is a for-profit corporation that just happens to be 100% owned by the Federal Government. In Fiscal Year (FY) 2018, Amtrak took in $3.4 billion in revenue, of which it spent all of that and then some (the rest of its $4.8 billion costs were covered by various governments—including the federal government—as well as loans). However, that $3.4 billion does not show up in the Federal Budget, never touches the Treasury, and is missing from expenditures. Even though the Supreme Court ruled in 2015 that Amtrak is part of the Federal Government, each of these actions happen within the stand-alone entity and are therefore not put into the Budget created by Congress. Amtrak is hardly alone in this designation, leaving many questions as to what the government truly takes in and spends. We will return to this very point later in this document.

For now, let us take a deeper dive on the potential structure Federal Government...

DEPARTMENT OF GOVERNMENT OPERATIONS

Right now, the question of how to run the operations of the government are left to each individual agency. Some have answers, other do not, and among the ones that have answers some are more efficient and realistic than others. It is an inconsistency seen across the board and makes it difficult to manage the government as an organization in general. If the Federal Government is one single overarching entity, then it needs an area that has a singular focus on making sure things run as smoothly as possible across all other areas.

"Shared Services" is the idea that there are certain compartments within an organization that can be shared among all other compartments. For instance, whether you work in sales, the custodial staff, or are the CEO, you are going to use the same payroll department. So instead of each of these areas having their own payroll, payroll is shared between them. You might be asking yourself if the government has taken this common-sense approach? The answer is: sort of.

> **Administrative Conference of the United States (ACUS)**
> **Sourcebook – Second Edition (December 2018)**
> **Pages 38 to 39**
>
> Congress has mandated the creation of four "chief officer" positions (financial, information, human capital, acquisition) in major agencies, leading to the creation of new and similar offices in different agencies across the executive establishment. Other government-wide managerial mandates... lead to additional common offices across departments and agencies (e.g., FOIA offices, faith-based initiatives offices, and equal employment opportunity or civil rights offices). Common agency tasks and requirements such as the need for legal advice and review, congressional and public relations, budget, and program evaluation also lead departments and agencies to have common features (e.g., general counsel, office of legislative affairs, office of public affairs, budget office).

As you can see, they understood the idea of a shared service and to have accountability on common functions, but they still put it down at a very low level. Furthermore, Congress added other features:

> **Administrative Conference of the United States (ACUS)**
> **Sourcebook – Second Edition (December 2018)**
> **Pages 112 to 113**
>
> Congress has enacted a number of government-wide management and transparency laws to facilitate political control of federal agencies, to improve performance, and to root out waste, fraud, and abuse... The Chief Financial Officers Act of 1990 was intended to improve the financial management practices of federal entities. It required the designation of a chief financial officer (CFO), appointed by the President and confirmed by the Senate, with an appropriate managerial and financial management background in all large agencies. The statute also mandates that a CFO be installed in other, smaller agencies, but in these agencies CFOs are appointed by the agency head and are career political appointees either from the competitive service or the Senior Executive Service.

The Information Technology Management Reform Act, mandated the designation of a chief information officer (CIO) in federal agencies. The CIO is responsible for: (1) providing advice to ensure that each agency acquires information technology and manages information resources effectively; (2) developing, maintaining, and facilitating an information technology architecture for each agency; and (3) promoting effective and efficient design and operation of all major information resources management processes for each agency. The statute's information technology requirements apply broadly to "executive agencies" as defined in 41 U.S.C. § 133: any executive department, military department, independent establishment, or wholly owned Government corporation.

Finally, Congress enacted the Inspector General Act of 1978 to help root out waste, fraud, and abuse in federal management. The Act and its amendments mandated the creation of Offices of Inspector General in various large agencies, designated "establishments," across the executive branch. Each establishment's Inspector General (IG) is appointed by the President and confirmed by the Senate solely on the basis of "integrity and demonstrated ability in accounting, auditing, financial analysis, law, management analysis, public administration, or investigations."

Thus, the basis for having Shared Services already exists by law, but it is spread out all over the place and has lost any high-level ability to review the government in its entirety. Instead of having a CFO for the entire government that appoints lower level managers for various Departments and Agencies, there are instead dozens of CFO's littered throughout the government. This is seen on the Information Technology (IT) side as well, to the point where each and every government agency has its own technological approach and purchasing. As such, instead of the entire government buying the same Accounting Software or Cloud services, each part of the government decides its own Accounting Software and Cloud Services and often buy competing or incompatible products. There is no common approach from the top-down to these decisions besides guidelines and rules for acquisition processes and it has resulted in a further fractured government. At the same time, it has led to waste where the government could be using its mass buying power to get volume discounts that it cannot get because purchasing is being done piecemeal.

What the Department of Government Operations does is reverse that and brings all central needs into a single pass-through place. At the same time, it creates an area that is specifically responsible for managing the interactions between all of the other Departments and Agencies. This would include all Project Management (i.e., any initiatives that required the use of more than one Agency in order to be deployed would be coordinated from this group). Meanwhile, it would take over responsibilities from the Legislative and Judicial Branches for managing their day-to-day needs. All of this would also allow the other Departments to focus on their primary missions.

Currently, if one looks through the budgets and spending of the government Agencies, functions like HR, IT, etcetera are not broken out or are buried so deep to the point where it is unrecognizable. Suffice to say, each agency within the government can and should have all funds allocated for these Shared Services moved to this new department and then from there the cost could be reduced because—as you can imagine—there is significant overlap and redundancy.

Furthermore, the only department not to be included here would be the Office of the Inspector General. Recall from before that the Vice President would oversee and be in charge of anything that is dealing with quality assurance, ethics, and reviews in general. This creates an agency above all other agencies in order to review them. We will return to the Vice President and those offices shortly.

DEPARTMENT OF INTERNAL RELATIONS

One of the Federal Government's main concerns is the relationship with the governments for the States and Territories. At the end of the day, the Unites States is just that: a number of States united in a common federation. Although a strong Federal Government has grown over the past 230 years, the Constitution and Amendments are very specific that the States have rights and that the Federal Government must respect them. While we think of the Bill of Rights—the first 10 Amendments—as enumerating protections for the people of the country, that is not entirely true. The 10th Amendment in particular states:

> The powers not delegated to the United States by the Constitution, nor prohibited by it to the States, are reserved to the States respectively, or to the people.

This is in addition to the entirety of Article 4 on the States' relationships with the Federal Government. Therefore, this affiliation and working within it is a top priority. Because of this, an organization should be set up to manage the overall relationship, but surprisingly there are very few agencies that have specific responsibilities at this time, just more parts of other agencies.

One could say that most of this vital function is buried somewhere in the Executive Office of the President, so breaking it out would be a further activity. There are specific agencies working with Native Americans, but very little dealing with State and Territory management, and that should change as well.

Beyond working with States, Territories, and Native governments, the last area this department should focus in on is Elections. Especially with the changes made to the legislative elections that were inserted in the prior sections of this document, coordination with the States and ensuring results is going to be a massive responsibility, and one that crosses all political divides. As such, elections are a core competency that must be focused in on.

DEPARTMENT OF FOREIGN RELATIONS

Where the relationship within the various governments inside the United States is important, so, too, is the relationship of the United States with all foreign nations and extra-national groups. In the 21st century the world is much more intertwined than it was in the 18th century and what happens abroad has direct impacts at home and vice versa. While the existing Department of State covers some of these ideas, this expanded department fully fleshes out the roles and moves many disparate free-standing international interaction points under one roof.

Most important from all of this is pulling any interaction with a foreign government into one place, whether that is through diplomatic channels like ambassadors or the UN or through volunteer organizations like the Peace Corps. If the government is interacting with a foreign body, it must be as a united face with a singular message, otherwise agencies could be providing conflicting messaging.

DEPARTMENT OF SAFETY AND SECURITY

One would assume that the existing Department of Defense would cover all military functions within the United States, but it is not even close. Many military and military-like organizations are far outside and in other Departments entirely, especially with peeling off Homeland Security into its own area. Others, like the aforementioned CIA, are under no direct Department per se. When one asks the question "What does the government spend on military, security, and intelligence functions?" it is not a question that can be easily answered because these functions are spread out everywhere (hint: it is a trillion dollars).

Having a separation of all these functions has led to deadly consequences in the past and will again in the future unless changes are made. We will get much deeper into how to further resolve these disparities in the next section, but for now let us just concentrate on the idea of having a single front for all of these functions that focuses on the safety and security of the American people, our country's properties, and interests at home and around the world.

As such, this Department could be broken up into smaller sub-areas including:

- Operations and Management

- Military Organizations (i.e., Army, Navy, Air Force, etcetera)

- Investigations and Security (i.e., U.S. Marshalls, ICE, CBP, NTSB, Capital Police, Nuclear Facilities Safety Board, etcetera)

- Intelligence and Special Operations (i.e., CIA, FBI, NSA, Military Intelligence, Navy Seals, etcetera)

- Relief and Recovery Organizations

- Veterans Services

DEPARTMENT OF PEOPLE AND SOCIETY

It is difficult to imagine, but the interests of the people of the United States are not well represented in the current Cabinet. Parts of the Departments of Interior, Commerce, Agriculture, along with the Health and Human Services and HUD would seem to have this covered, but they are not strongly focused and are missing many key elements. For instance, the Social Security Administration—one of the largest parts of the entire government in terms of dollars spent—is not represented at all. And when you look at HUD you can see that although they have a seat at the table they are far too specialized to have a say in any decision making process. No, in order to have a complete understanding of the social needs and desires of the public, all these various programs need to come together in the wholistic view of people and the societies in which they live.

This works in both directions as well; not only does the President and Congress get a complete view of the programs supporting the people and communities of the United States, but the people themselves can have a single stop front office in this Department to bring their needs to. How those needs are parsed out is an internal decision within the Department and not something that the typical person need worry about. Therefore, a person with social needs can present a single case and the system can streamline the results and end much of the waste and redundancy—both for the government and the person.

In a similar vein, there is a purposeful intent in having the Census and Citizenship being part of this Department. Much later in this document we will return to this very point and why they are together in one place, but for now consider that in order to assist people, you need to know who they are. People who are citizens or want to be citizens (or at least guest workers) all have similar needs and therefore the actual management of keeping track of people can fall to the department that works with people.

DEPARTMENT OF INTERCONNECTIVITY

This is a subject we will return to later in great detail, but it is a question of government responsibility in how data, materials, and people flow throughout the country and beyond. There are very particular requirements in the Constitution around the "Post Office" and "Postal Roads", so this is just a slight preview of that. For now, let us consider that we are talking about the ease of movement of anything between people and organizations. To illustrate this, we have this example:

- In the early 1800's, if someone needed information they had to have a piece of paper written and then moved along postal roads by foot or horse and brought to the destination.

- By the mid-1800's, that process was sped up with the advent of trains and the building of the intercontinental railroad.

- Around the same time, the telegraph started to be refined and grew to be the method of fast communication. By the turn of the 20th century, telephones started to become available and became the method of quickly sending information.

- Later in 1935 the "telefax" was added so that original documents could also be sent using the same lines as telegrams and telephones.

- These uses continue to grow to where computers in the 1980's could dial into each other to share data. This would further explode in the 1990's with gateway internet services and the world wide web.

- Today, workers need not even go to an office and can remotely connect through cloud services to work-stations and share data across the world in real time.

What this shows is the same question has been answered differently over time and yet all are connected. The means by which information, goods, and people flow is completely entwined and cannot be separated, especially as technologies continue to change. These are concepts that cannot be unwound from each other and should be considered as resolving the same question: how do we move something from A to B? What that something is will change (or stay the same for centuries), but the answers cannot be considered fixed. Hence, there is an interconnectivity that cannot and should not be ignored.

Altogether, what this is trying to demonstrate is that the technology makes no difference, only the intent of getting people, data, or goods from A to B in the best, safest, and most economical ways. As mentioned, we will delve into this much deeper later in this document, so this is the preview to the question: Why did the Founders of the Constitution believe Postal Roads were so important?

Technology always changes and just a little more than 100 years ago mail started to be moved by airplanes, thus vastly speeding up the rate at which information could move and methods for collecting government forms. This plaque in Washington, D.C. pictured in December 2019 notes where that started—while in the background the airfield has been replaced by a road and baseball fields.

DEPARTMENT OF SCIENCE, TECHNOLOGY, AND ENVIRONMENT

Just as the management of the Post Office, internet, highways, and railroads should not be considered independently but instead ruminated as an overall policy, so, too, should be all of Science, Technology, and the Environment. How can you have an energy policy without consideration for the environment? How can you think about how food is produced without also thinking about forest management? How do you plan for the future of space exploration without considering the health and medical technology needed to make it happen or what impact Earth diseases could have elsewhere?

In today's Federal Government, that is exactly what happens as scientific and technological research is all separated from each other and, in many cases, from direct departmental oversight. Some is focused just on war and defense while others on agriculture and others yet on nothing at all but their own concerns. We cannot talk about the technology that is to change the world or protect the people of the United States without talking about the consequences and impacts of those technologies elsewhere, and vice versa. This is all about having a unified approach for all scientific discovery and management.

As should be noted, there is significant overlap in these areas as well. Many different organizations are responsible for various areas of regulation that a lot of funding is being wasted on operations and bureaucracy that could be used to further the scientific ambitions of the nation. At the same time, Departments that have been in direct conflict like Energy versus Health and Human Services become conjoined under this new Department. The issues of competing needs can be met and worked out from a more scientific perspective and less from a political one by placing these fields together into a single train of thought. It will not end all debate, but that has never been the point of this document. Remember: this is about how to have the conversations, not enforcing the answers of one interest or another.

DEPARTMENT OF RESOURCE AND ASSET MANAGEMENT

That is not to say that competing priorities cannot meet at the top level. Where a Department focused in on the optimal needs of science is helpful, so, too, is the practical side of implementing and managing the resources science intends to use and/or protect. That is where the Department of Resource and Asset Management comes into play. In the day-to-day world, there are natural resources that are harvested for use by the people, organizations, and governments of the country and these all need to be managed. Meanwhile, the government owns and leases plenty of buildings and pieces of land that also need to be worked on and maintained. This is the pragmatic side of dealing with the minutia of what it takes to oversee these disparate components.

There are also functions that are currently a part of every agency that would have to be split out. First is Capital Planning, which is about doing big projects that cost a lot of money (think building that new apartment complex for Congress). Capital costs are one-time (though maintenance and upkeep are not, but more on that later), and being finite are usually from special funds that need to be managed. Expenses are generally broken into two large buckets: Capital for the non-normal activity and operations for the day-to-day expenses. Most everything else is day-to-day, but these programs stand out.

And on the other end would be "Transparency". Each agency of the government is responsible right now for publishing its own materials and making available requests from the Freedom of Information Act. The idea is that all of that would be brought under one department/agency that would provide the insights into how the government is operating. Theoretically, this Department should be managing all the records of the government, and therefore can provide the data and the public portals for the people.

DEPARTMENT OF COMMERCE AND LABOR

The two existing Departments of Commerce and Department of Labor are in bubbles that are both quite limited and inconsiderate of the larger picture. Commerce focusses in on creating economic opportunity while Labor looks at some (but not all) of the concerns of wage workers. Meanwhile, there are a plethora of Agencies that are independent or parts of other Departments that deal with all the regulations and management of industries and workers. Instead, this Department is a way to bring that all under one house with both Commerce and Labor having three sub-areas:

- **Protections and Regulations** – Making sure companies are doing what they are supposed to by the laws and regulations of the United States, both specific to how companies are intended to function by factors such as financial controls, the environment, etcetera and in their treatment of workers.

- **Development** – Using programs to create opportunities for economic growth for community organizations, companies, and workers' skillsets.

- **Insurance** – Similar to Protections and Regulations, the government has a numerous insurance and safety net programs that are specific to protecting companies and workers.

Beyond these key areas, there are also Consumer protections to be considered, along with Economic Research to provide the arguments when necessary. Combining these elements brings together the full macro-economic view of the country along with the micro of how to implement the programs the government has deemed necessary for the safety of people and the development of markets.

One could argue that putting the people in charge of economic development in charge of all that regulation is a conflict of interest, and that is correct. However, this conflict is going to happen at some level, so the idea is that it should be happening within the Department. Additionally, the regulations in this Department are generally not generated internally, but instead come from Congress or other Departments (more on this later), so basically Commerce and Labor must enforce all protections and the buck stops there; it would not be spread around everywhere. Then, when working on analysis or attempting to create opportunity, they should be well aware of the considerations already in place and make recommendations for changes one way or another—but not be able to make those changes themselves.

DEPARTMENT OF ARTS, SPORTS, AND CULTURE

Despite having several agencies focused solely on various sub-components of security, the United States currently completely lacks a representative for Arts, Sports, and Culture. This is not because the United States does not spend money on these—far from it—but because the United States has never decided it is a top priority despite the billions of dollars people spend in and on these industries and the equal amount of income created for the government in taxes. The expression of culture has been recognized around the world as a core competency, yet the United States has never placed an emphasis on it for important decision making. As a matter of fact, Team U.S.A. posts on their donor website:

> The US Olympic Committee, unlike its competitors around the world, does not receive funding from the federal government for its Olympic programs. Instead, Team USA. athletes rely on the generosity of the American people to achieve their dreams.

In a country with so much emphasis on sports, there really is no agency in existence that specifically works on athletic concerns (and very limited ones on the Arts, but at least there is something). At the same time, there are any number of laws for how sports are supposed to be regulated and funding comes in one form or another from the Federal Government to sports organizations. Yet, who is looking in on these deals and coordinating with local governments? The answer is: it is all over the place and depends upon each deal while there is no accountability.

This Department is the sparsest of the new structure simply because it needs the most filled in. While it is rare that this author would recommend a growth in the size and scope of the Federal Government, there are notable gaping holes in how the Executive Branch deals with the management of culture in the United States.

As an added bonus to this Department are two key areas: Protecting Creations and Archives. If we are talking about creations (whether arts, technology, or amalgamations of both), there should be more than some disparate agencies that care about these. We will be returning to protections of creations much later in this document, but how copyright functions and how trademarks works is an area of great debate among those who are directly impacted.

On the other end is managing the history of our nation—both the creations that are made and the important documents that preserve the story of America. The creation of the Constitution and Law is a significant portion of our culture and as such should have an important say in what is to come and how the government functions. After all, someone must record it all and make sure history is true, not just a perspective. How can one learn from history if there is no one to preserve and teach it?

The Department of Justice that exists today is an odd bag in that it contains policing duties in areas like the FBI and DEA, executive duties by representing the United States in courts, judiciary duties in quasi-courts of appeal, and a smattering of other odds and ends. As seen in previous sections, anything having to deal with investigation, policing, and security would be moved into the Department of Safety and Security, so where does that leave this newly reformed Department? Well, that is where the name change comes into place as this Department is about law services.

Overall, there would be a few big buckets:

- Civil protections for the people of the United States
- Litigative services for the government
- Litigative services working with companies and other organizations
- Dealing with foreign law
- Quasi-judiciary agencies

This structure makes the Department not about searching for crime, but about being the interpretation of the law of the land—at least as far as the Executive Branch understands it. Now, there is a Constitutional argument whether these quasi-judiciary agencies have a Constitutional right to exist at all (separation of powers and all), but that is not the argument for this section (wait a few minutes more for that one). Right now, we are focused on how to even look and talk about the government. If they are all together, now the argument can be made as to what exactly the agencies in this pool are doing.

At the African American Civil War Memorial in Washington, D.C. in January 2020, the inscription brings forth the question of why those who fought for freedom are still being denied it? Should not those who are still missing their human and civil rights have a government agency that is aligned with fighting for them, not against them?

DEPARTMENT OF FISCAL MANAGEMENT

The last of the full Departments, then, is the Department of Fiscal Management—which would be responsible for how the United States deals with its money. Right now, the Treasury is a stand-alone area, but what we have in the bank is hardly the story of how funding flows within the Great Material Continuum. That is why Fiscal Management would be broken up into specific buckets:

- **Financial Oversight** – Understanding how changes to spending will impact a particular area and estimating the long-term consequences of those decisions.

- **Taxes and Revenue Collection** – How the government gets money.

- **Treasury** – How much money is on hand and how much is expected to be on hand.

- **Debt** – Both taking out loans and managing existing ones.

- **Investment and Equities** – Managing the various ventures the government makes with available funds.

- **Central Banking** – How the government controls the liquidity of money available in the market for people and businesses.

- **Minting Money** – Coins and bills need to be made sometimes!

- **Scholarship/Fund Management** – The United States has created many pools of funds that people and organizations can apply for, but there is no central administration of that right now.

What this all comes down to is the single question: how is the money managed?

It must be remembered that this is about organization, not control. For example, despite potentially putting the Federal Reserve System underneath this Department, it would not necessarily mean that the agency could not still run independently and away from Secretarial and Presidential influences (or political influences in general). Instead, it is a way to see and understand the government, and in this case about how money policy is controlled within a reporting structure.

OFFICE OF THE VICE PRESIDENT

With all the Departments in place, an area is needed to oversee that all those compartments are not abusing power and are doing what is expected of them. Yes, there are theoretically checks from the Legislative and Judicial Branches, but what about within the Executive function? That is where a Department of Quality Assurance would come into play. Yet that does not fit into the idea that Departments should be key considerations for decision making. As such, we will give the Vice President some responsibility to review all the other baskets and have a person who is outside the structure of those Departments check in on each of them. This is why it was important in the originally added Amendment to make sure Agencies could be organized underneath the Vice President and President directly.

Much like with the Department of Government Operations, many of these functions are split among all the agencies today, specifically the Inspector General Office. If you recall, Congress has mandated the existence of this office, yet it has wastefully allowed each agency to create its own. All of those agencies could have the funding pooled into a new singular agency that would be responsible for the Federal Government as a whole, not just small bits and pieces that have a conflict of interest by working within the agency they are supposed to inspect.

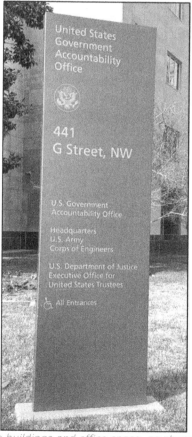

Many agencies currently share buildings and office space, as shown here in Washington, D.C. in January 2020. Unfortunately, as also shown here, those agencies may be completely unrelated due to lack of foresight. By re-organizing the government into like-agencies, they could also be physically moved so same functions are working together in the same space.

Similar to the checks and balances on the Department functions, the Vice President would also gain the various military police agencies. Right now, these "internal affairs-like" agencies exist within the respective branch of the military. While it may be tempting to keep them underneath the Department of Safety and Security as a sub-division, a true check would be completely outside the Department to ensure that the military is acting within expected parameters and then investigate and prosecute when not.

At the same time, the Vice President would gain control over the Secret Service as an agency that is to be separated from all the rest of Safety and Security. The Secret Service's function is unique in that it is a protective organization for members of the government, their families, and other important figures. As such, it should have a top-level coordinator in the Vice President so that the President can turn to a specific person when there are concerns or needs to be addressed.

OFFICE OF THE PRESIDENT

Finally, there is the President himself. Really, the President is the head of the Cabinet over all Departments. There is currently a White House staff, but even much of that would be managed by the Departments. However, there are a few areas of which the President should directly control. Much like with the Department of Government Operations and the Office of the Vice President, these functions exists within agencies independently and not within a single focal point. As such, the President will need new agencies created by Congress and to move the funding from existing agencies to have his agenda recognized.

Most important is that the President becomes the conduit for setting the Executive agenda, doing analysis on how the programs approved by Congress will be implemented, and being the voice between the branches of government, the people of the United States, and the world at large. While that does not necessarily mean the President has to be the person that says everything, each area of the Executive Branch should not be its own mouthpiece as there is an overall government agenda that must be considered. The President and his designated subordinates would instead be the filter for communications and ensure a singular message—with the exception of the transparency requests that anyone can make to find out how these decisions were made and who made them. This is the final check: the check of the people on the executive government.

On the other end, there needs to be a mechanism for civil servants and agency heads to be able to disagree with the official Presidential message. The message that the President puts out would be the official stance of the government, that is true, but that does not mean it is correct or that there are not other valid viewpoints. We have seen time and again Presidents and the Executive Branch in general attempting to suppress items such as scientific consensus or fiduciary concerns because they do not align to their particular political message or placate people who might vote for them. But that does not mean there needs to be anarchy in the system where different divisions in the government are presenting contradictory findings. There should be a single message, and an opportunity to respond.

That is why law would be necessary to solidify these ideas and provide protections from reprisal for anyone who cares to disagree with the official line. We will call this law the "Executive Branch Communications Act":

1: The United States Executive Branch shall provide singular messaging for the entire executive government through the President or the President's designated representative(s).

2: All communications to the public, other branches of government, foreign bodies, or any other like institutions shall go through the Office of the President or the representative(s) designated by the President. No Agency, Department, or any other sub-division of the Executive Branch shall provide its own communications outside of this method unless designated as a representative of the President.

3: Should the President or the President's designated representative(s) refuse to publish a communication authored by a person in the employee of the federal government, by an Agency, by a Department, or by any other sub-division of the Executive Branch, the communication may be presented to Congress and Congress may vote to release the communication under normal voting procedures. When voted upon, the President or the President's designated representative(s) must release the communication as originally presented.

4: Once the President or a designated executive representative has released a communication, that communication may be responded to by any employee, civil servant, contractor, appointee, or anyone else in service to the Federal Government whose work is directly impacted or referenced by the communication. If the communication was released against the President's wishes, the President may also respond to the original communication.

5: There shall be no restrictions on those persons responding to an executive communication save for reasons of national security. Elsewise, no person shall be restricted by any form for non-disclosure agreement.

6: The President, the President's representatives, supervisors, department heads, agency heads, or any other persons in the employ of Executive Branch shall be forbidden from making any reprisal for a person responding to an executive communication. Congress shall create law for the penalties of enforcement and the Judicial Branch shall adjudicate in claims of reprisal.

7: The President or the President's designated representative(s) shall create methods by which these responses can be attached to executive communications without restriction, censorship, editing, or any other constraint.

It is important to stay generic in "communications" because there could be press releases, speeches on television, tweets, or whatever else may come. The same with how to respond to them and the methods available; depending upon how a message was delivered means there might be different ways to respond. As shown in the law above, the President would be responsible to make sure there is a way for that to happen. Meanwhile, those in service to the government would not need to worry that they will face backlash from an employment perspective because the government is providing both the mechanism and the protections. Enforcement would be tricky, which is why it is important the checks come from the Legislative and Judicial Branches. This includes a way to circumvent the President entirely if the President is trying to suppress information that may not be beneficial to him or his Party. And only with Congressional approval would there be a government check. Note that this is separate from existing "whistleblower" protections as that is a disparate item that already has laws and protections in place (although those may need updating as well, but that is a reason we need Congress to be able to debate). Instead, this is about the work products of the Executive Branch and if there is a compelling case to overturn the President's decision to withhold an end-product. As always, the balance between each co-equal branch is important to maintain, as we will return to shortly.

ONE MAN ARMY

While organizing the existing government is helpful to understanding what is where, it does not answer the question of what should be done once organized. Nowhere is this clearer than in the Department of Safety and Security. Just by how it is laid out and the known agencies (and of course there are many more unknown or buried ones), as of 2019 there are:

- 6 types of armed forces
- 15 types of police and security agencies
- 17 types of clandestine and intelligence agencies

These numbers are astounding, but not as astounding as when you dig deeper:

- In 2015, the Air Force had 5,199 aircraft. At the same time, the Army had 5,117 and the Navy had 3,847. The Coast Guard also had about 210 of its own.

- The Navy has roughly 430 watercrafts (plus another 130 noncommissioned transport ships manned by civilians), the Army has about 120, and even the Air Force has 2! And of course, the Coast Guard has at least 2,000 of its own.

It is a very peculiar thing that the military has been set up to be separated by technology, especially when that technology is often purchased by the other divisions. In other words, there is a massive amount of waste and resource management issues in having a military that is separated along technological lines instead of on operations lines as we have laid out in the sub-divisions for the Department of Safety and Security. The amount of repetition among these agencies is vast and the duplicative efforts not only lead to waste but also to real security threats as information and resources are not shared and operations are not coordinated from a single station.

In December 2019, Congress authorized the creation of a sixth branch of the military in the Space Force, separating the function out of the Air Force where it had resided since 1982. Thus, Congress—at the urging of the President—have actually created more fracturing within the military and what will end up being more waste. As has been seen in the past and examples above, it should be expected that the Army, Navy, and Air Force will also want to do many space-based things themselves, such as maintain their own fleet of satellites. So instead of just having a single military that has its own satellites and share it among their internal divisions, each will pursue their own path while the Space Force also creates a new level of government all its own.

This would be like if a fast food chain had one division for cow beef, one division for chicken, and one division for fries, but they all buy fries because you can order fries with burgers or chicken patties. At the same time, said fast food restaurant would actually be competing for labor within itself as similarly skillset people would either work for the burger division, the chicken division, or the fries division instead of sharing the same labor across all.

You see where all of this is going? The military is a behemoth at nearly $1 trillion (with a "T" again!) in spending for the budgeted FY2019. Social Security is still the largest part of the budget at $1.1 trillion, but the military is not that far behind anymore. And this is probably a loose definition of "military" and not the entire definition of what we would put in the Department of Safety and Security. For now, it is as close to a number as we can get, so we will use it.

In order to be a streamlined operation, the components underneath the Department of Safety and Security need to merge into a singular approach for its namesake. One recruitment and career path through basic training to specialized services; one rank path so there is understanding of hierarchy that is vague between the branches today; one set of management for conflict engagement so that it is not a coordination effort between competing factions; one spending structure to make sure research and investment is for the entire organization and not repeated in several parts of it.

This document would not portend to have the entire structure that should be created and the solution to all the questions that need to be answered— everything from how housing to retirement benefits would work and how members of the former structure would be fit in. This would be the job of a President and his designated staff (most likely the Secretary of Safety and Security) to come up with a plan and lay out all of the real facts and figures of money saved, efficiencies gained, and overhead eliminated. To reorganize the entire military complex would take years to just analyze and even more years to implement. However, that does not mean it should not be done!

It is obvious from the numbers and structure alone that the military, intelligence, security, veterans, and other agencies are stepping all over each other's toes. Time and again has resulted in operational failures because of incomplete data, lack of sharing and coordination between agencies, and general bureaucracy that makes it impossible to know who is truly responsible. Much more should be expected from a $1 trillion in spending.

At the same time, it is amazing how large, expensive, and active the military is given the lack of war declared by Congress. As a reminder, Article 1, Section 8 of the Constitution says that only Congress has the ability:

Clause 11: To declare War, grant Letters of Marque and Reprisal, and make Rules concerning Captures on Land and Water;

Clause 12: To raise and support Armies, but no Appropriation of Money to that Use shall be for a longer Term than two Years;

Clause 13: To provide and maintain a Navy;

Clause 14: To make Rules for the Government and Regulation of the land and naval Forces;

Clause 15: To provide for calling forth the Militia to execute the Laws of the Union, suppress Insurrections and repel Invasions;

Clause 16: To provide for organizing, arming, and disciplining, the Militia, and for governing such Part of them as may be employed in the Service of the United States, reserving to the States respectively, the Appointment of the Officers, and the Authority of training the Militia according to the discipline prescribed by Congress;

In other words, only Congress can direct how the armed forces are to be used. The President is supposed to be Commander in Chief and follow the orders of Congress in use of the armed forces, but that has not happened for a long time. War has not been declared since World War II while Korea and Vietnam were more resolutions passed by Congress or actions taken unilaterally by the President through commitments to agencies like the United Nations (U.N.). However, Congress gave the President vast powers over the military in the 1973 War Powers Resolution, and that has mostly been used since, with Congress merely filling an appropriations role.

Stone soldiers march through the fields of the Korean War Memorial in Washington, D. C. in December 2019. Nearby is also the Vietnam War Memorial. Neither was a "war" declared by Congress.

No, it is time to also recreate that separation and use the Constitution to make sure Congress cannot give away its responsibility while also making sure the President has the tools to fulfil his own.

A PRESIDENT'S PURPOSE

Previously, we have made several Amendments to the Constitution to further define the role of Congress versus the role of the President. Many were about the President being able to make suggestions for law (through the Vice President) and making sure his recommendations for appointments were heard and voted on, all in specific timeframes so Congress could not abdicate its duty. Additionally, the Amendments gave the President (again through the Vice President) the ability to indict members of Congress for treason if they attempted to circumvent their Constitutional duties and roles.

There is more to this, and it begins with the abdication of duty. The aforementioned 1973 War Powers Resolution (AKA, the War Powers Act) allowed Congress to hand over military action—at least on a "temporary" basis. Although the law makes it clear that it is supposed to be about controlling the President from using the military indiscriminately, in reality that is exactly what has happened because it has given the President a 60-day window to do as he pleases due to a loose definition of what is an "emergency". At the same time, once involved, Congress has rarely pushed back and forced a President to return the military when this window was closed (and on a few occasions, Presidents have ignored Congress and paid no consequences for it). The Supreme Court has somehow managed to stay mostly uninvolved save for removing the "Legislative Veto" power in the law in an unrelated case, but that portion has never been tested. As such, the War Powers Act is the law of the land. While it is impossible to say what the Supreme Court would decide in a full trial, what is clear is that there is massive ambiguity in the Constitution itself that makes this particular law only "possibly" un-Constitutional instead of definitively.

As an alternative, we must return to Amending the Constitution to further build the wall between the Legislative Branch and the Executive Branch and clarify the points that are up for interpretation.

> **By Amendment to the Constitution of the United States, Article 8, Section 3, Clause 1 shall be added.**
>
> No Branch of the Federal Government may delegate any duties, responsibilities, or powers as laid out by the Constitution to any other Branch.

First is a new section of our brand-new Article 8. Section 1 was on limitations of those serving in government and Section 2 was on voting rights. In Section 3 is a focus on further cementing the boundaries between each branch of government to make sure each is doing its appropriate job. This starts with this specific Amendment of "non-delegation". It would seem obvious that the Legislature makes laws, the Executors implement laws, and the Judiciary interprets law, but that is not what has happened in practice. Thus, we must establish those boundaries anew.

To begin with, Congress has granted significant powers to the Executive Branch. For instance, the Environmental Protection Agency or the Food and Drug Administration can set standards that are to be followed, penalties for non-compliance, and act as the quasi-judiciary arm during appeals. Congress has actually passed very few laws in the 21st Century, but the Executive Agencies have passed hundreds of rule changes that act as laws because of this delegation. Executive Agencies are supposed to act out the will of Congress and be the enforcement arm, not the legislative one. As such, their power needs to be reined in and Congress needs to be forced to do its duty.

> ### By Amendment to the Constitution of the United States, Article 8, Section 3, Clause 2 shall be added.
>
> The Executive Branch and Judicial Branch may not create any new law or rules on top of existing law. Each may suggest and present wording for such laws to Congress, but only Congress shall have the ability to make changes to existing law and create new law.

As an extension to the earlier Amendments that stopped the courts from creating law and forced the issue into Congress (though with an enforcement mechanism of contempt and treason via the Vice President to wield), this Amendment extends the same ideals to the Executive Branch. What this effectively means, as an example, is that the EPA could not just capriciously change emissions standards as Presidents come and go. If one President wanted tougher standards and one wanted weaker ones, today it is a matter of the President getting their person in charge of the agency with a bare majority of the Senate or writing an executive order to the agency to do the same. Instead, the EPA would now suggest the change to Congress, present the evidence for it, and then Congress would vote (and that vote would be recorded for posterity).

One of the key reasons Congress has delegated so much of its power is that it does not have the technical knowhow of the many facets the government is involved in. No one person can be an expert on all scientific, financial, organizational, operational, military, cultural, and every other concern, and they should not be expected to be. The job of civil servants is to support the government in execution and in decision making, so on a case-by-case basis these agencies would be able to present their specific issue. The only "delegation" that would be happening is the due diligence necessary to present a case. And again, this would keep Congress in its lane of creating all laws and the rest of federal government in the role of executing, implementing, understanding, and interpreting those laws.

In the same vein, the Executive and Legislative Branches need to stay out of the way of being the juries for implementation of the law.

> **By Amendment to the Constitution of the United States, Article 8, Section 3, Clause 3 shall be added.**
>
> The Executive Branch and Legislative Branch may not create or run any judiciary function except where designated by the Constitution. Any judicial function must be vested within the Judicial Branch in the Supreme Court or an inferior Court as ordained and established by Congress.

There are many examples of this where the Executive Branch acts as a judicial unit. Thinking of the same agencies referenced before, if the EPA gives a company a civil fine (executing the law), the company can then go before EPA Administrative Law Judge. This judge is really an employee of the EPA and therefore part of the Executive Branch, no matter how much independence and lack of oversight the judge is given. The Constitution is very clear: Congress is supposed to set up "inferior" courts to the Supreme Court that are part of the Judicial Branch only. Yet the Executive Branch also has the Executive Office for Immigration Review and the Federal Mine Safety and Health Review Commission, both of which act as appeals courts within the Executive Branch. The Executive Branch cannot act impartially in a case because they have already interpreted and executed the law as they believe it is written. Only an independent court can say if that interpretation is correct with the will of Congress and in line with limitations of the Constitution.

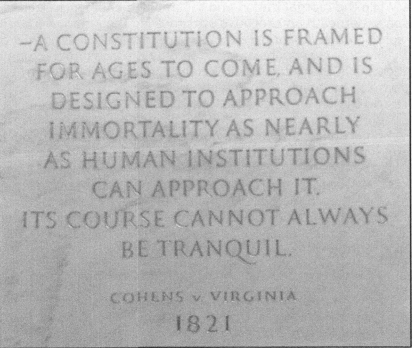

An engraving on the wall of the Supreme Court (as shown in January 2020) quotes the decision in a pivotal case that established the Supreme Court's right to review State laws and judicial decisions for their Constitutionality. Like many parts of government, the Constitution does not explicitly give this right. As such, clarifications are often needed to make sure each branch of government is doing its expected duty.

By the way, there are certain exceptions, as noted by this Amendment. Specifically, only the Senate can try all Impeachments (Impeachment being the accusation created by the House of Representatives, conviction or not is done by the Senate). Aside from this case, there is no point where Congress, the President, or their designees should be acting as judge and jury.

That is not to say that the Judicial Branch and the Legislative Branch do not step into the Executive Branch's role, and this must be stopped as well.

> **By Amendment to the Constitution of the United States, Article 8, Section 3, Clause 4 shall be added.**
>
> The Judicial Branch and Legislative Branch may not create or run any agency, department, or any other division of the Federal Government underneath each Branch save those granted by the Constitution.

While it was not a major component of the above re-organization of the government, there are several agencies that exist in the Legislative and Judicial

Branches. While the reorganization and the prior Amendments attempt to force organization underneath an executive structure lay the groundwork for this idea, the specific Amendment here makes sure that neither Branch is running an Agency. The only exceptions are as stated by the Constitution, namely the Supreme Court is in charge of all other courts and can create its structure there and Congress can have aids to manage the legislative process (through we severely restricted that earlier, as well).

Which now brings up back to how we got here: war. The Constitution says that only Congress can allocate funding for the military and determine if there is war, and that the President is Commander in Chief of the armed forces (in so many words). However, both are vague enough that there have been massive expansions of what each means and how the President can act without Congress. Sometimes, Congress has given great powers to the President both intentionally and unintentionally. Whatever the case, it needs to be reined in and fully clarified to explain the differences in responsibilities.

> **By Amendment to the Constitution of the United States, Article 8, Section 3, Clause 5 shall be added.**
>
> While acting as Commander in Chief of the Armed Forces of the United States, the President may not deploy any part of the military without the expressed consent of Congress. Should the President declare an emergency session, Congress must respond to a President's request for military services within forty-eight hours. Congress must renew any use of military services every ninety days or within the limits set by Congress at no more than ninety days. The President may only deploy military services without the expressed consent of Congress in Cases of Rebellion or Invasion as a defensive measure only, and then only until Congress is able to convene and officially declare intent.

There is a lot to unpack here, so let us go through it. First off, there is a vast array of changes to how the Constitution deals with the military in general. Most of the Constitution is talking about the Army, the Navy, and raised militias. At the time of the Constitution, there was not much of a standing army to speak of, nor were there necessarily intentions to have one. However, over time, that is exactly what has happened, as well an expansion through technology of what the military is capable of. Additionally, the military does a lot more than engage in battle. For instance, the military is involved in rescue, training, support of allies, building, and other non-destructive activities. As such, it is important here to pull back and broaden any activities that are done by the Armed Services, no matter what they are now or in the future. This is especially important as to extend beyond "war" and into anything the military can do so that it is definitive that Congress is the ultimate regulator of the military no matter the lexicon used.

Next, it would now be explicit that Congress must approve of any deployment of the military. The choice of deployment is deliberate as it implies sending troops to do an action no matter where that may be. This could be setting up a base in a peaceful ally, invading another country, going to the border of the United States, assisting with building a dam within the United States... really, anything that they do. That said, it is not to the level of detail of "how" the military is to do it. The President would not need to go to Congress with battle plans to get approval; he is still the Commander in Chief. That is the point of what the Constitution was originally saying: Congress tells the military to go somewhere to do something, the President commands the military in how and when to do that something once there.

Now, there may be times when the President believes it is necessary to engage the military for whatever reason. The War Powers Resolution unfortunately gives him the ability to do that for 48 hours, though the intention was to stop the President from using the military without Congressional approval. This Amendment reverses roles and makes it so the President must go to Congress for approval. One of the reasons Presidents have sidestepped Congress in the past has been because of Congresspeople's intransigence and slowness to act, so this again forces Congress to make a definitive decision quickly (in the same 48 hours). Despite that, Congress can still say "no" and the President will not be able to deploy the military.

And if he does such a thing? That is what the clauses for impeachment are for! The Constitution already has a mechanism for Congress to rein in the President. There is also the 25th Amendment, Clause 4 which could theoretically have the Vice President and the majority of the Secretaries declare the President unfit and remove him from office (though this is more likely to happen on television dramas than in real life). In either case, as with any reining in of overuse of the power of the Executive Branch, the mechanisms are already in place. They are not used because Congress is too politically aligned with or against the President one way or another, so the tools are useless unless the changes to Congress in the first section are implemented.

Finally, there is the exception when the President can deploy the military without Congressional approval—and that is in either a rebellion or an invasion, which is in line with the same wording of Article 1, Section 9, Clause 2 (suspension of the Writ of Habeas Corpus, or holding someone without their due process rights). But that does not mean the President can keep the military involved without Congressional approval; it is just until Congress can convene. In the case of an invasion, that may take some time, so it is important to be able to act without worrying about getting Congress together for a vote. However, if the "invasion" is not an imminent threat to life and property, then Congress should be able to meet and make its well known. A

President could not just declare a wayward single boat from Cuba an "invasion" and launch an offensive war; this is why it is specifically supposed to be only in "defense", as in the United States is being actively attacked and time is of the essence. And if the President and military were able to repel an invading force or put down a rebellion, then the action would be over—the military could not chase invaders back to their home country without Congressional approval.

In the end, as soon as Congress got back together, it could decide if it wanted to expand the scope and allow an offensive war or decide if enough was enough. Whether this case or a more "standard" declaration of military use, Congress would have a built-in clock on itself. Every 90 days (or less if Congress limited the action) Congress would have to re-approve the deployment of the military. If they did not like what the President was doing, they could rescind the deployment. If a new Congress came to power and did not like the direction and use of military, they could vote against it. Either way, it would force Congress to continually re-evaluate the use of military force and be responsible over-and-over again for current events. In that way, they could not just say it is the President's responsibility and wash their hands of it.

A quote from Martin Luther King Jr. at his memorial in Washington, D.C. as pictured in December 2019. Here we have a reminder that we are not just fighting to end an issue, but that we should be intending to create justice for all involved. This means having a plan, reason, expectation, and understanding of what we are doing.

With all that has been put on the President's plate both from the Constitution and the changes we have made above, there would not be a lot of time in the day. As such, the President may need some additional assistance with his duties. For instance, he may want someone else to represent the United States in an international arena or to greet with foreign dignitaries. But why should that just be someone who happens to work for the federal government? Why not another member of the executive government? As a further addition to the new Section 5 under the existing Article 2:

> **By Amendment to the Constitution of the United States, Article 2, Section 5, Clause 6 shall be added.**
>
> The President may temporarily delegate specific Executive Duties to a Governor from a State or Territory such that the Governor may act as the President in that regard.

The Governors of the States and Territories are closer to the function of the President and as such would be the most likely to act best in his regard. This would create a stronger relationship between the leaders of the Federal and State/Territory governments while still sticking to the same branch of government. It would also show a sign of seriousness to partners around the world by sending such high-level executive personnel instead of career dignitaries. Being leaders of States and Territories, they would also have an appreciation of what their area needs are and the pressures that go along with running a government that any agreement might impact. And thus, it would be a closed loop within executive authority and solidify those powers as laid out by the Constitution with the appropriate walls between the other branches.

At the same time, it would put to work existing agents of the government instead of creating yet more full-time positions. There are already a great number of people in the government just from being elected—why not have them take on a few more responsibilities and save the people of the United States some additional burden?

HITTING THE GAVEL

The sun rises on the Supreme Court in Washington, D.C. in December 2019.

Go ahead and read the Article 3 of the Constitution that establishes the Judicial Branch of the United States. Yes, please, just go right now, I'll wait...

Oh, you are back so soon? As you have noticed, there is not much to it! All of Article 3 can fit on a single page of paper yet contains the balancing control for a full third of the entire Federal Government. And just what is in this single page?

- **Section 1** establishes that there is a Supreme Court of the land that has "the Judicial Power of the United States". Furthermore, Congress can establish "inferior" courts and that Judges should not only be paid, but their pay cannot be diminished.

- **Section 2** establishes which groups may sue each other (hint: everyone/thing can sue everyone/thing else); that the Supreme Court is the ultimate appellate court but it is the original jurisdiction for cases involving ambassadors, government representatives, or when a whole State is a party; and that criminal cases shall be by jury (though not any details of what a jury looks like) in the State where the alleged crime happened.

- **Section 3** is about what is, how to try, and how to punish treason.

The End.

One can immediately see that there was some great concern about this light section that led to the Bill of Rights trying to create some boundaries within the judicial and law enforcement system:

- **Amendment 4** protected people from unreasonable search and seizure.

- **Amendment 5** laid out rules for how a person is to be charged through a Grand Jury, made it so a person cannot be charged for the same crime twice, prevented making a person testify against themselves, and protected a person and their property without due process and compensation.

- **Amendment 6** expanded Article 3, Section 2, Clause 3 with much of the same language but added additional ideas for a "speedy and public trial" and established various rights enjoined by the accused.

- **Amendment 7** said that if you sue someone for $20 or more, you have a right to a jury trial, too, if you want one.

- **Amendment 8** stopped excessive bail (and if $20 was enough to get you a jury, what do you suppose "excessive" means?).

Returning to the very beginning of this entire document, the Constitution was and still is incredibly flawed. But the flaws that were most prevalent made up 50% of the first batch of Amendments. Yet, that was still not enough as the very next Amendment passed by Congress in 1794 and ratified in 1795 made it so if someone wanted to sue a State they had to do it in the State's court, not in the Federal courts. It was a direct reaction to a rather minor court case where the executor of an estate (Alexander Chisholm) sued the state of Georgia for payments he felt he was due. Georgia refused to show up for the proceedings, so the Supreme Court ruled 4 to 1 in the plaintiff's favor. The States were so upset by what they perceived as an intrusion onto their supposed sovereignty that they helped get the 11th Amendment passed, including one of the few times a change to the Constitution had overturned a Supreme Court decision. The good news for Chisholm was that while all of this was going on and a jury was being summoned to determine damages, Georgia agreed to settle (although for pennies on the dollar of what they were being sued for, but it appears the plaintiffs were happy for anything at that point). Unfortunately for the four similarly situated cases coming up behind this one, the 11th Amendment preempted them from getting their day before the Supreme Court.

Although this was the last Amendment to directly address the courts and law, the 14th Amendment re-established due process and equal protection as the follow-up to the 13th Amendment ending of slavery and involuntary servitude. Despite this, we know the court system has far more levels, rules, and regulations than just what is in the Constitution. The districts of Federal Courts, the specialty courts, and appeals system and methodologies—all of this came about over time by the Courts themselves and acts of Congress. Add to that the jury system, how grand juries function, powers the courts have granted themselves, and the general time that a trial takes, and we are in a situation where almost an entire branch of government is built upon a house of cards.

As such, it is time to re-evaluate justice in America. This is not about whether specific laws are just, Constitutional, enforced evenly, or any of the standard arguments we hear about on a daily basis. Instead, this is about having a system that allows these conversations to happen and make a significant impact in how the people within the United States interact with the Judicial Branch. Included in this argument are the following:

- Examining how to make a jury system that is equitable to jurists and those involved in suits, but at the same time is knowledgeable about the law and does not interfere with the daily lives of citizens.

- Creating impartiality in judges despite whichever President and Senate appointed them, making sure judges do not get singularly associated and focused, and finally putting in rules that ensure turnover so that judges are replaced on a regular basis and no person can have massive power over long periods of time.

- Keeping the Executive and Legislative Branches out of the Judicial Branch and making sure the Judicial Branch has a power over them to enforce decisions made. At the same time, the other Branches need power over the Judicial Branch when it oversteps its bounds or when members need to be removed.

- Expanding and clarifying further what due process means and who it applies to.

- Making it so the Courts cannot be used as weapons with just time and money being the factors that determine how a case is going to be end, especially as a way to level the playing field between parties that have massive disparities in both.

With that in mind, you have received a summons in the mail, so it is time to go to court!

$15 A DAY FOR JURY DUTY

After going through the entire Constitution, do you know what right you do not have? There is no guarantee for a "jury of peers", an oft favored quote on entertainment programs. That idea comes from the Magna Carta, which for all intents here was the governing document of the Kingdom of England (that history is another story entirely). The United States Constitution only guarantees an "impartial" jury and nothing else. The Magna Carta, on the other hand, states:

By the way, the Magna Carta did not originally state this; it came through a process that we would consider an Amendment. Also, it was not written in English (This is a translation provided by the British Government from the original Latin. At the time, what we consider modern English did not fully exist yet, either). In either case, the references to juries come from:

- **Article 3, Section 2, Clause 3:** Crimes (except impeachment) are tried by a jury

- **Amendment 6:** Crimes are tried by an impartial jury

- **Amendment 7:** Civil trials over $20 can have a jury, if desired

Everything else dealing with juries has come from laws and judicial process that has developed over time. Even the idea of compulsory jury duty does not exist anywhere in the Constitution; yet it and the methods around jury selection have become the norm and expectation for American citizens. The overwhelming majority of Americans have trusted the messaging (re: propaganda) over the decades and believe that serving on a jury when called is an important civic duty, though the sentiment drops off precariously the younger the respondents is.

Despite that, most polls show that less than half of people bother to show up to jury duty when summoned (and in some areas the no-show rate can approach 90%), and of those who do arrive 95% of them will either find a way out or be dismissed. Because of these factors, more and more people are being summoned in order to get the potential pool of jurors up to a high enough number that will eventually result in the necessary quantity for a jury. Of course, that "necessary number" is again not in the Constitution, nor is there any reason for it other than the traditions borrowed from other countries at the time of the United States' founding.

While exact numbers on how American citizens feel about truly serving on jury are not readily available, anecdotal evidence of talking to your friends, family, and neighbors will most likely reveal very few people who want to serve on a jury under the current system. The reasons are varied, but most likely fall into the following categories:

- The amount of time taken from life, work, and family is unknown and can be potentially prohibitively long due to commitments with any or all these areas. There is also a large amount of waiting around doing nothing, usually awaiting other court procedures. Often during those times, jurors and potential jurors are not even allowed to read or look at their phones.

- People do not like that the service is compulsory and that they may face legal issues if they do not want to be a part of the process. In the same vein, being forced into servitude would seem to violate the 13th Amendment.

- Lost compensation cannot be made up and the compensation given for Jury Duty is a joke and well below even minimum wage levels. For some people, even the cost of getting to the courthouse can be greater than the compensation paid (which comes after—not during—the process).

- While people generally believe they understand the law and can be unbiased, they do not believe their fellow jurors are (hint: those people are wrong about their own abilities and correct about their fellow jurors). Overall, the average American citizen is not versed in the nuances and technical details that the law requires, as well as the Constitutional questions of if the law should even be allowed.

- Some people have a lack of belief in the justice system in general because enough innocent people have been convicted. This has happened because jury selection and presenting evidence is a manipulative process that both the prosecution and defense are attempting to do. While this manipulation may be solely based on a detached pure evidential standpoint, lawyers are still preying on how they can present that message to a specific audience.

What this is all coming down to is that American citizens are ill equipped and have little desire to be on a jury. But who, then, should serve as the decider of cases? Perhaps, the Judges?

> **By Amendment to the Constitution of the United States, Article 3, Section 2, Clause 3 shall read:**
>
> The Trial of all Crimes, except in Cases of Impeachment, shall be by **a panel of Judges acting as a** Jury; and such Trial shall be held in the State **or Territory** where the said Crimes shall have been committed; but when not committed within any State **or Territory or committed in multiples States and/or Territories**, the Trial shall be at such Place or Places as the Congress may by Law have directed.

There is an idea of creating a "Juror Bill of Rights" or something of the like to make Jury duty and the court system more palatable, but it is unnecessarily for the judicial process to directly include the citizenry. Instead of inconveniencing the American populace and breaking the 13th Amendment, we could instead vest the power completely in the judiciary itself. Yes, this will require a set of limitations and protections in order to ensure a balanced and less biased (Note: it is impossible remove all bias) pool of judges, but we will spend the vast majority of this section on those very principals. Indeed, what we have done here is change the definition of a "Jury" from being your average "peer" to a professional judge acting in a panel. We will address how many judges should be on a panel in the next section.

Judges, then, can fulfil the "impartial" component so long as they are not involved with the parties personally. With a better understanding of the law, they can apply it appropriately and test the Constitutionality of the laws to begin with. Per prior sections, we have already given the courts the ability to send laws back to the legislatures to be corrected for Constitutionality, so they are not making decisions on what the law should be, just what it should not be.

Meanwhile, since many cases require specific technical knowledge, judges may either specialize or learn on the job to understand issues. Much like Congress, judges cannot be expected to know everything about every subject and may also take advantage of specialized knowledge in the Executive Departments and Agencies, hence more reason for the Executive Branch to have Agencies specifically designed to support Judicial needs.

As for the other modifications, we must again expand the definitions of law to extend to the Territories. Further is the idea that if a law is broken in multiple States and/or Territories that a trial may take place in the best locale possible. Since most crimes that will be prosecuted at the federal level will generally meet this category, the system of courts will necessarily need places to go to (much of which already exists in the current system).

Considering the rest of the Amendments that deal with the Judicial Branch, it would be beneficial to move all of them into main part of the Constitution. This should be done with all Amendments, but these in particular are fairly clear on where they belong. The simplest solution is to just add an additional Section and stick them in there:

> **By Amendment to the Constitution of the United States, Article 3, Section 4 shall be added and consist of:**
>
> - **Clause 1:** Amendment 4
> - **Clause 2:** Amendment 5
> - **Clause 3:** Amendment 6
> - **Clause 4:** Amendment 7
> - **Clause 5:** Amendment 8
> - **Clause 6:** Amendment 11
> - **Clause 7:** Amendment 14, Clause 1

With that in place, we can move on to what was Amendment 5 and the particular phrase: Grand Jury.

The Grandy Jury is an idea that a jury will be selected before a trial process even starts to determine if a person should be indicted to begin with. At the time of the Bill of Rights, the thought was that someone should not be accused publicly until a Grandy Jury had the opportunity to review the particulars of the case in order to avoid any type of embarrassment or prejudice. In practice, however, this is not the case at all as it is very well known when someone has been brought in, arrested, and/or put before a Grand Jury.

Further, Grand Juries have no rules whatsoever and have pretty much become nothing but a tool of the prosecution. All those rules in the other Amendments—especially the 6th Amendment where a defense can present a case and confront/present witnesses—do not apply to a Grand Jury because it is not a trial. Instead, prosecutions just submit (or withhold) whatever they want to get the Grand Juries to agree to an indictment. How do we know this? Because Grand Juries indict 99.999999% of the time! They are a pass-through that does nothing in almost all cases (although they do have abilities to do their own discovery and get their own evidence, but most do not).

The idea of a Grand Jury was meant as a protection and it was based on similar systems around the world at the time. The United States, however, did not learn the same lesson as its peers and has held on to the system. Only one other country in the world still uses a Grand Jury system: Liberia. Most other places either have a direct trial or a preliminary hearing. Since the United States already uses preliminary hearings, the Grand Jury system is again redundant and unimportant.

> **By Amendment to the Constitution of the United States, Article 3, Section 4, Clause 2, Part 1 shall read:**
>
> No person shall be held to answer for a capital, or otherwise infamous crime, unless on a presentment or indictment of ~~a Grand Jury~~ **the appropriate and relevant Executive Department or Agency**, except in cases arising in the land or naval forces, or in the Militia, when in actual service in time of War or public danger; ...

We will return to the rest of this Clause shortly, however the relevant part is here: let us completely drop Grand Juries, the last vestige of the unaccountable citizen jury system. Instead, we'll put it on the Executive Department or Agency to present a case to a panel of judges on why someone should be charged. That is the point of the Executive Branch anyway, so let us set the direction properly, end the waste, and join the rest of the world (leaving Liberia well behind).

THE PEOPLE MADE THE CONSTITUTION, AND THE PEOPLE CAN UNMAKE IT. IT IS THE CREATURE OF THEIR WILL, AND LIVES ONLY BY THEIR WILL.

COHENS v. VIRGINIA
1821

Even the Supreme Court two hundred years ago agreed that the Constitution could and should change based upon the needs of the people. The quote pictured here in January 2020 is etched into the walls of the Supreme Court.

Now that we have removed you (you, personally) from having to go to Jury Duty, what do we require of our Judges to make this happen? First, we need to add some new Clauses to Article 3, Section 2 to describe what we expect from our "Panel of Judges" Jury:

> **By Amendment to the Constitution of the United States, Article 3, Section 2, Clause 4 shall be added:**
>
> The Panel of Judges acting as a Jury shall consist of an odd number of Judges. The lowest inferior courts shall consist of three Judges, the appeal courts shall consist of five Judges, and the Supreme Court shall consist of seven Judges.

Remember earlier that we noted that there is no reason for the number of judges in the Supreme Court or the Appellant Courts; they have all been decided on their own and can change over time. In 2019, some Democratic candidates have discussed increasing the size of the Supreme Court in order to staff it with judges they deem more palatable (assuming they could get the judges approved by the Senate). And why not, since this has been done in the past to get to the 9 members we have today? Here, though, we have simplified and solidified what should be expected of any level and eliminate much of that political interference. Instead, we break it down into a few easy levels:

- Whatever is the lowest "inferior" court (as the Constitution likes to call lower courts), would have a 3-judge panel. It is important to note that some courts are specialized to specific topics, so these would all fall into the "inferior" bucket.

- The middle appeals layer would consist of a 5-judge panel to expand the pool and even out decisions. While this does not particularly address how appeals work today, it does force going to a full appeals court instead of the intermediate appeals level before the full panel appeals that exists today.

- Finally, the Supreme Court would cap out at the 7-judge panel. This maximum would put in place the first of planned limitations to the Supreme Court to make it more impartial while also keeping the working group to a reasonable enough size.

But if we have these limiting sizes of the courts, how do we then create the impartialness as required by the Constitution?

> **By Amendment to the Constitution of the United States, Article 3, Section 2, Clause 5 shall be added:**
>
> All Judges shall be in a common Pool by area of the court or by type of court as determined by Congress. Each Panel of Judges shall be filled from these Pools; shall share cases except when a substitute is needed due to a conflict of interest, movement to a different Pool, personal leave, death, retirement, or any other reason determined by Congress; and shall serve for a term of five years. Assignment from the Pool to a Panel shall be at random in a method determined by the President. The Pool must consist of more Judges than necessary to fill Panels in order to have Judges in reserve in case a substitution is necessary. At the end of a five-year term, Judges are to return to the Pool for re-assignment or moved to another Pool and may not again serve in the same physical or specialized area.

This one is quite dense, so let us break it down.

First and foremost is the new concept of a "pool" of judges. Think of it this way: perhaps there are 15 "inferior" courts that would require 3 judges each. In total, that would mean we would need 45 judges. We should then have a pool of, say, 50 judges available so that we can assign the 45 judges we need and keep 5 in arrears when a substitution is needed. A substitution may be needed because there may be some type of conflict of interest or the judge had to leave for whatever reason (illness, vacation, death), or any other reason. Those other reasons would be determined by Congress as the check, but the idea is that a substitute should be able to be pulled in when necessary so that there is always a full panel. Currently in the appeals and Supreme courts, when a judge recuses themselves there is no one to replace them, and this can end up with an even number and a tie vote.

Now where this gets particularly interesting is how judges are assigned to a panel. The panels would serve for 5 years at a time and each judge would be assigned based upon a random method as determined by the President. If we go backwards, the President recommends to Congress a judge for a particular court (inferior, appeals, Supreme, etcetera) and Congress either approves or disapproves of the judge. Today, Congress approves the judge not only directly to a court, but often to a specific post in a court. Instead, here, Congress would be approving a judge to serve in a pool of judges that are available for a specific court. Congress already can create any inferior court it deems necessary and has done so. For instance, there is a court that focusses solely on bankruptcy, another on patents, and others that are just general concerns. These would be the various pools for each type of inferior, appeals, and Supreme Court created (the latter being only one, but worth noting as its own pool).

The judge would serve a 5-year term with the rest of their team; or if not assigned, be a substitute for other teams when necessary. At the end of five years, those on a panel would return to the pool for random re-assignment—assuming they are still eligible. A judge may reach retirement because we have already limited time served in government for any combination of elected or appointed position at any level of government to 25 years. That means if someone was a State judge for 10 years, they could only serve an additional 15 years in the Federal court system. Or similarly, if someone served in Congress or was in the Cabinet for 8 years, they would have a limited amount of time available to them to serve in the courts. This would be helpful to reduce cronyism and payoff jobs. It would not alone eliminate these situations but would be beneficial in at least making sure there is a turnover when someone gets through the cracks.

Assuming the judge were available for re-assignment, they could not again serve in the same physical or specialized area. In the latter case, if a judge served in bankruptcy court, they could no longer serve on that same court and have to move on to somewhere else. If it is desired to make a judge an appeals or Supreme Court judge, once approved by Congress they might be moved into those pools. But if they are staying in their assigned pool and the pool is more general or part of appeals, they must then move to a different physical area. Between the randomness of assignments and being forced to move on to a different physical district, no court area could have a certain style to it that lawyers could use to game the process. Today, lawyers file their cases in specific districts that they feel are more open to their arguments. This would reduce that by having a complete re-shuffling every five years.

While not on assignment, Supreme Court pool judges may enjoy some time in the courtyard at the Supreme Court building as shown here in January 2020.

Meanwhile, due to the five-year shuffle and the general timeout of service, the courts would constantly be changing their makeup. No President nor Congress would be able to stack a court to their favor, especially the Supreme Court. Not only would the Supreme Court turn over every five years, it would also need to have a pool of judges available for substitutions on particular cases. Even if a President and Congress added many judges to the pools, eventually they would time out or another President/Congress combination would add additional judges and the randomness would purge most of the situations that would be of concern.

At the same time, there is a need to further limit how much and how long judges can serve, even beyond the timeout limit created earlier.

> **By Amendment to the Constitution of the United States, Article 3, Section 2, Clause 6 shall be added:**
>
> A Judge may only act as a permanent member of four Panels over the course of the Judge's service.

If a judge never served anywhere else in any level of government, then they would be limited here to being assigned to 4 panels in total. Since each panel is 5 years long, that means a maximum of 20 years serving on a panel in total. In the remaining 5 years the judge could serve as a substitute—if they decided to stick around. And again, with the randomness, this judge could end up in 4 panels in a row or no panels ever or any combination in between. It is not something the judge should have control over, nor any other member of the government.

Between these conditions and the potential of having to move a family every 5 years, being a judge might be less appealing to many people. As a job of service, though, it is preferred to make a profession that is desirable by only the most dedicated. At the same time, all of this will force judges to not have the opportunity to get comfortable where they are and be prepared to change themselves and learn everything all over again—including working with different people.

All these changes amount to a redefinition of the court and jury system—but only at the Federal level. Most cases still at least start or take place at the local and State/Territory levels; and at those levels the rules may be quite different. As such, we must extend all these changes down to those levels in order to have an impact across all people and systems:

> **By Amendment to the Constitution of the United States, Article 3, Section 2, Clause 7 shall be added:**
>
> The States, Territories, and Local Governments shall have Court Systems set up in the same model as the Federal Court System as laid out in the Constitution and its Amendments. Any Amendment to the Judicial Branch at the Federal Level should be reflected at the State, Territory, and Local Level.

What this means is that all these changes for removing citizen jurors, ending Grand Juries, and creating pools for judges with turnover must also happen at the State, Territory, and local level. What it does not do is dictate how these non-Federal governments must set up their Judicial Branches but makes it clear that they should mimic the Federal system as laid out in the Constitution. It can then become a point of challenge if a State, for instance, is not following any of these rules and can be sued in Federal court to make that happens (once again with the Federal Courts making States write their own law). It is a guidance, but these lower governments could come up with their own language and address their own individual concerns.

With the Federal and Local courts in line, the question becomes: how do the courts enforce their powers over the other branches? And more so, how do the other branches hold power over the courts, keep them in check, and make sure the law is applied evenly, impartially, and to all?

DO YOUR JOB

Previously, in the legislative section, we added several Amendments that made it so that the courts could remand a law or approved bill back to the legislatures of both the Federal Government and the States/Territories. However, the courts lack a Constitutional enforcement mechanism to make that possible. The enforcement mechanisms that exists today are, for the most part, completely made up by the courts or Congress and are known as "contempt":

> **18 U.S. Code § 401**
>
> A court of the United States shall have power to punish by fine or imprisonment, or both, at its discretion, such contempt of its authority, and

none other, as—

(1) Misbehavior of any person in its presence or so near thereto as to obstruct the administration of justice;

(2) Misbehavior of any of its officers in their official transactions;

(3) Disobedience or resistance to its lawful writ, process, order, rule, decree, or command.

18 U.S. Code § 402

Any person, corporation or association willfully disobeying any lawful writ, process, order, rule, decree, or command of any district court of the United States or any court of the District of Columbia, by doing any act or thing therein, or thereby forbidden, if the act or thing so done be of such character as to constitute also a criminal offense under any statute of the United States or under the laws of any State in which the act was committed, shall be prosecuted for such contempt as provided in section 3691 of this title and shall be punished by a fine under this title or imprisonment, or both.

Such fine shall be paid to the United States or to the complainant or other party injured by the act constituting the contempt, or may, where more than one is so damaged, be divided or apportioned among them as the court may direct, but in no case shall the fine to be paid to the United States exceed, in case the accused is a natural person, the sum of $1,000, nor shall such imprisonment exceed the term of six months.

This section shall not be construed to relate to contempts committed in the presence of the court, or so near thereto as to obstruct the administration of justice, nor to contempts committed in disobedience of any lawful writ, process, order, rule, decree, or command entered in any suit or action brought or prosecuted in the name of, or on behalf of, the United States, but the same, and all other cases of contempt not specifically embraced in this section may be punished in conformity to the prevailing usages at law.

For purposes of this section, the term "State" includes a State of the United States, the District of Columbia, and any commonwealth, territory, or possession of the United States.

18 U.S. Code § 403

A knowing or intentional violation of the privacy protection accorded by section 3509 of this title is a criminal contempt punishable by not more than one year's imprisonment, or a fine under this title, or both.

The above is acceptable and makes sense (and surprisingly includes a definition of "State" that includes just about any other possession of the United States). However, this does not give the Courts the ability to hold Congress, the President, or the State/Territory legislatures in contempt. For that, we'll need some additional Amendments, starting with a new Section 5 in Article 3: the powers and checks on powers of the Judicial Branch.

By Amendment to the Constitution of the United States, Article 3, Section 5, Clause 1 shall be added:

When standing in judgement of a law or lack thereof, neither the Supreme Court nor any inferior court may create law, modify the meaning of existing law, or remove existing law. The Supreme Court or the designated inferior court must send the law or need for a law back to the appropriate legislature—whether that be Congress or the legislatures of a State or Territory—to create, modify, or remove the law entirely.

As noted, in the legislative chapter we gave the Supreme Court (or it's designated lower court) the ability to review laws that have been passed by Congress or the State/Territory legislatures and decide if they are Constitutional. However, should a law pass that initial process or was passed before that process existed, the Judicial Branch would need a mechanism to make sure they can review it. Here, we talk about "standing in judgement", which in this case means when a trial comes along that challenges a law (or lack thereof), we lay out that the courts cannot create their own law to fix or fill the gaps. Instead, the courts will always have to send orders back to the legislature from whence the law originated and the law must be fixed there. Of note, this also forces legislatures to write law to remove items officially instead of just being stricken by the court. Again, it is that line in the sand that only legislatures can create, modify, or annihilate law.

However, the Courts need a mechanism to force them to do any of those actions. Previously, we already gave the courts the ability to set a timeframe in which the legislatures would be allowed to work to get those updates in. But what would happen if the legislatures just ignored them? The Judicial Branch needs some teeth:

> **By Amendment to the Constitution of the United States, Article 3, Section 5, Clause 2 shall be added:**
>
> Should the Supreme Court or a designated inferior court send to Congress or the legislature of a State or Territory a demand for the creation, modifications, or removal of law within a specific timeframe and criteria, and the legislature does not act in accordance with the orders of the Supreme Court or designated inferior court, the Supreme Court or designated inferior court may hold any or all members of the legislature in contempt and implement any procedures and penalties as defined by law.

Now we are getting somewhere! Congress and State/Territory legislatures act with impudence because there are no personal consequences for them. We will return to this very idea later, but for now we introduce the first of what will be many personal risks an individual may take for being in a legislature. It is nice that someone wants to serve our government, yet that does not give them carte blanche to just do anything they want. Today, though, that is exactly what happens as it does not matter what legislators do or do not do since the biggest consequence they may face is not getting re-elected (and even that is relatively rare, as shown earlier).

With this Amendment, the Judicial Branch would have some real power over the Legislative one in that they could fine, imprison, or order both on the members of Congress or legislatures of the States/Territories for refusing their direction. It is still at the discretion of the courts to decide if and how much they want to implement this, but it means that members of Congress and the State/Territory legislatures face the exact same rules as regular people—which is precisely what they are. Congress defined "contempt" above, including how it can be implemented and what the penalties are. Why, then, cannot the same rules apply to them?

The reason these controls need to be specifically laid out in the Constitution is because some would consider being forced to vote for something one does not believe in as induced "speech". Since the 1ˢᵗ Amendment grants the freedom of speech to everyone, a separate part of the Constitution with equal weight would be needed to override that precise idea. Therefore, here, legislatures musts vote and come to a solution or face the potential wrath of the courts. With this Amendment, being a member of government restricts rights enjoyed by the masses.

And these controls and power of the Judicial Branch should not end here. Congress and—especially—State/Territory Legislatures have been known to take actions that waste the time and resources of the Courts. If they do so, they should face similar penalties.

> **By Amendment to the Constitution of the United States, Article 3, Section 5, Clause 3 shall be added:**
>
> Should Congress or the legislature of a State or Territory knowingly and willfully pass a law that is in violation of the Constitution, existing Federal Law, existing State or Territory Law, or prior judicial interpretation of the law—with the express intent of using the judicial system to challenge existing law and judicial interpretation—the Supreme Court or designated inferior court may hold any or all members of the legislature in contempt and implement any procedures and penalties as defined by law.

Whatever your politics, when a State passes a law that is knowingly un-Constitutional, they always pay a price by having to cover the court costs and some of their opponents' costs. Yet, time and time again, these legislatures feel it is their duty to pass laws they openly discuss as being created just to bring a challenge to the Supreme Court and overturn some other prior decision.

Now, we have made many changes already that every law passed is going to be reviewed by a court to begin with, so no law can come into effect without first passing muster. But that does not stop a State/Territory or Congress from passing the same or similar law over and over. Sometimes, a State/Territory or Congress is just picking a fight to change the definition of the world while the Supreme Court has made it clear: if you want a change, you need to go through a Constitutional Amendment process.

These laws are a waste of taxpayer dollars and time. When Mississippi passed a more restrictive version of a law that had been overturned the year before,

U.S. District Judge Carlton Reeves exacerbated:

> "Here we go again..."
>
> "Mississippi has passed another [similar] law... The parties have been here before."
>
> "Last spring, plaintiffs successfully challenged Mississippi's ban... The Court ruled that the law was [un-Constitutional] and permanently enjoined its enforcement. The State responded by passing an even more restrictive bill."
>
> "It sure smacks of defiance to this court..."

But what could Reeves do about it? All he could do was enjoin the defendant again and put the whole law into the process where it would not be heard by the Supreme Court. With this Constitutional Amendment, the Courts could hold legislators in contempt for just such an action. We will return to other ways legislators will have to pay for their choices, but for now we need to extend the same controls to the Executive Branch:

> **By Amendment to the Constitution of the United States, Article 3, Section 5, Clause 4 shall be added:**
>
> Should the President of the United States or the Governor of a State or Territory knowingly and willfully sign a law passed by their legislature or give an Executive Order that is in violation of the Constitution, existing Federal Law, existing State or Territory Law, or prior judicial interpretation of the law—with the express intent of using the judicial system to challenge existing law and judicial interpretation—the Supreme Court or designated inferior court may hold the President or Governor in contempt and implement any procedures and penalties as defined by law.

As can be seen here, the language is almost the same so that executives cannot simply sign-off or give an order and say they are not accountable. They will follow the same potential penalties for knowingly wasting the time of the courts and the money of the taxpayers.

That is not where oversight of the Executive Branch should end, though. There is another area that needs to be considered: abuse.

> **By Amendment to the Constitution of the United States, Article 3, Section 5, Clause 5 shall be added:**
>
> The Supreme Court or its designated inferior court may directly bring a criminal Case against the President, Vice President, Department Heads, Agency Heads, or any other person in the employ of the Executive Branch should—in the course of performing duties—that individual violate the Constitutional rights and rights granted by law to any person.

Right now, it is completely up to the Executive Branch whether to bring charges up against someone. However, that means the Executive Branch is also in judgement of itself and can choose to ignore issues, decide they are not issues, act in a judicial function and decide penalties, or—occasionally—decide to pass them off to the correct legal authority and act as the prosecution. The conflict of interest here is vast and does not provide the proper check. Many people are under the impression, for instance, that a sitting President cannot be indicted because of the Constitution. That could not be further from the truth. The Constitution says nothing about this, only stating in Article 1, Section 3, Clause 7:

> Judgment in Cases of impeachment shall not extend further than to removal from Office, and disqualification to hold and enjoy any Office of honor, Trust or Profit under the United States: but the Party convicted shall nevertheless be liable and subject to Indictment, Trial, Judgment and Punishment, according to Law.

In just the year 1973—in response to the Watergate scandal involving then President Richard Nixon—the Justice Department wrote a memo that said a sitting President could not be indicted. Then, in 2000, the Justice Department wrote another memo saying basically the same thing and that no court cases had overturned this prior memorandum. So, it was nearly 200 years after the Constitution was written that an Executive Department under the direct authority of the President unilaterally decided something that amounts not just to new law, but to new definition of the Constitution.

The Constitution—as shown above—is clear that that the impeachment process is only to include removing someone from office and can pursue no other punishment. An elected or appointed official can be indicted, tried, and found guilty of the same crimes and be punished under the criminal and civil code. The Justice Department seems to be implying that these are "in-order" items—that is, that the impeachment must happen first, then they can be charged. What was written here was stating just two separate facts: an executive can be impeached and can be indicted; these are mutually exclusive actions. While it seems unlikely that one would happen without the other, it is quite possible for a person to be found guilty of crime and sentenced to prison or some other penalty without losing their position and continuing to operate in their role.

That is why this Amendment is needed; we need to reaffirm first that the Courts have oversight over the Executive Branch and that the Executive Branch cannot have end-say supervision of itself. With that, we can then say the Court's job is to bring charges against the Executive Branch when the Executive Branch refuses to do it itself. That does not guarantee a verdict, but it does put that check in place and removes the idea that the Executive Branch can create its own law that gives itself immunity.

Think of a case like this: A United States Citizen has been detained under suspicion of being an undocumented immigrant. The person presents papers showing his legal status as a Citizen yet is still detained for several weeks. Finally, after a national news agency picks up the story, the person is released. This person has faced untold damage to time, health, wages, and has been attacked by his own government. His only recourse now is to sue civilly for what he has lost, but will anyone be held responsible criminally?

Unfortunately, the answer is "no". All will go on before no matter if this person sues or not and is successful or not. But what about the people that caused harm during this entire process who were negligent in their duties and have violated both the Constitutional and legal rights of this person? From the border agent that detained this person to the investigators at immigration services to the warden at the detention facility to the head of the department that has made these orders happen to the President himself who set the policy—are any of these people going to be held criminally guilty or civilly liable? Without this Amendment, all of them do not have to think or worry about consequences; they can just act with impudence for applying the law capriciously and maliciously. There is nothing that can be learned and there will be no personal responsibility so long as members of the Executive Branch have unchecked power.

But that does not mean that the Courts should have unchecked power of their own, either. If the Courts could do whatever they wanted, they would be a single endpoint with complete control of the country. No, as there are already Constitutional methods for the other Branches to hold the Judicial Branch in line, they must be expanded to make sure the Courts do not step over it.

We have often asked in this section: where do the rules of the courts come from? Why is there a prosecution and defense? Why does court happen at certain times and in certain places? Why are juries a certain size? Why is the appeals process the way it is? Why does it take years to work through the court system?

The answer is two-fold. First, Congress—and Congress alone—by Article 1, Section 8, Clause 9 has the ability "To constitute Tribunals inferior to the supreme Court". Therefore, the setup of what each court can do and how the appellant system exists is a matter of law. But all the processes have been decided by the courts themselves—with some law that has come up over time to enforce those unilateral decisions. But nothing can force the courts do to anything. Much like with Congress itself, the courts have created their own rules and regulations that slows down the wheels of justice. This is despite the fact the sixth Amendment specifically guarantees a "speedy and public trial". But that Amendment only mentions criminal cases, so perhaps we need some adjustments:

By Amendment to the Constitution of the United States, Article 3, Section 4, Clause 3 shall read:

In all criminal, **civil, or other judicial** prosecutions, the accused **and the accuser** shall enjoy the right to a speedy and public trial, by an impartial jury **of judges** of the State **or Territory** and district wherein the crime shall have been committed, which district shall have been previously ascertained by law, and. **Further, the accused is** to be informed of the nature and cause of the accusation; to be confronted with the witnesses against him; to have compulsory process for obtaining witnesses in his favor, and to have the Assistance of Counsel for his defence.

Here, we grant those speedy and public rights to both the accused and the accuser—for that person (using person to mean an individual, corporation, group, federal agency, or any other definition) may not want to spend years in the process either. At the same time, we have extended this to be for all types of cases so that the same rules apply evenly.

Here in the courtroom of the Supreme Court (pictured in January 2020), there are any number of rules the justices have come up with and maintain that are not based on laws or even logic. For instance, no recording devices are allowed, but people can still come in and draw pictures and write on a piece of paper. Perhaps requiring a camera in the room to record all proceeding and broadcast that to other rooms would free up some limited seats?

But what does "speedy" and "public" mean? Well, those are question or law, and only Congress can answer that. The afore created Amendment will now explicitly give Congress the ability to make decisions on how the courts should function so that they cannot go off on a rogue process. If Congress says each witness has 10 minutes to testify or that the prosecution and defense will be held on clock like in chess, then that is their prerogative. In the same vein, if Congress says that once someone has been sued civilly or arrested criminally that the trial must begin within a week, then that is what should happen. Just as Congress is to work for the people, so, too, are the courts supposed to do the same. The Supreme Court is still inferior to the people of the United States, and the will of the people should be reflected in how they operate.

This Amendment is open and gives great leeway, but also allows significant change. If something is not working out, the system can be updated easily by Congress. Just as the Executive Branch should not be held accountable to itself, nor should the Judicial Branch. With this specific Amendment, the courts would no longer be able to run (or slowly trot) amuck and expansive judicial reform can happen much more easily.

The Legislative Branch is not the only one who should have powers over the courts, as should the Executive Branch:

> **By Amendment to the Constitution of the United States, Article 3, Section 5, Clause 7 shall be added:**
>
> The President of the United States may order the Supreme Court or the appropriate designated inferior federal court to start a trial within the timeframe decreed by Congress when the court is in session, so long as the Supreme Court has not already ruled on the issue at hand.

As an expansion from the previous Amendment, there are times when the courts just sit on cases because they do not want to get to them in the current session. This can be massively frustrating for those who created the laws and those who enforce the laws because they have done their part while the last step in the process is refusing to do theirs. These types of delays can go on for years. Thus, should Congress choose, they could give the President the ability to make sure a case gets on the docket within, say, 30 days. That way, if the issue were pressing or involved a Constitutional question that must be resolved, the process could be pushed ahead within whatever other limitations Congress creates for the courts.

At the same time, there have to be limitations. If the Supreme Court has already ruled on a particular subject the President cannot force his hand here. For instance, the Supreme Court has already ruled that abortion is legal and Constitutionally protected within the United States. Now, the changes we made above will have forced Congress to write law making it so instead of only having a Court decree, but we have to deal with the here-and-now and all that came before such an Amendment existed. Since that is the law of the land, each time a State passes an anti-choice law, the federal courts immediately put it on hold and the appellant courts rule in favor of the plaintiffs fighting these laws. The decision has been made and the law is clear.

The hope of these groups is to make it to the Supreme Court and re-raise the discussion again. And let us be clear: there are times when getting back to the Supreme Court is necessary to overturn poor decision and this is a function we want to maintain. For instance, in 1944 the Supreme Court upheld the Constitutionality of the Japanese American Internment Camps in the case of Korematsu v. United States. This precedent has not been officially overturned to this day and it is technically still part of the books—although further laws, reparations, and the decision in 2019's Trump vs. Hawaii say this case was decided incorrectly (while at the same time using much of the precedent of that trial as reasons for ruling in partial favor of the President).

Over the years, the Supreme Court has reversed itself at least 230 times, and perhaps over 300 times depending upon how people interpret some arguments. Either way, it is around just 2% of all cases ever heard. Yet, many of these are even more amazingly disturbing, and not just with a lens of hindsight. In one example, in 1883, the Supreme Court ruled against Tony Pace for the crime of being a black man romantically linked with a white woman in the State of Alabama where the State created a law that said the two could not be married (the argument being that since the law applied equally to black and white people that it was not discriminatory). It took until the 1967 case in Loving vs. Virginia for the Supreme Court to overturn their own handiwork and say that State-sponsored racism cannot be argued as an interest of the State, no matter the "fairness" of the application of the law.

These are just a couple of examples of when the Supreme Court has and should revisit prior decisions and overturn them. Just because it is the moral, right, and correct thing to do, though, does not mean that the court should be forced to hear it again and again. If this is the first time an issue is coming before the Supreme Court, the President should have a right to make sure it is heard and heard in a timely manner. Once that has happened, though, only the Supreme Court itself should have the ability to decide if they will rehear an issue. This makes it so the same issue cannot be politicized by the Executive Branch and force the courts to do the work they have already done.

John Jay—the first Chief Justice of the Supreme Court—has a marble and bronze bust available in the in hallways of the Supreme Court building (as shown here in January 2020). Many of the rules and procedures still followed today were created by this man who resigned after five years to become the governor of New York.

Now, with turnover in the Supreme Court happening every five years, a Congress not dominated by a single party, a President that must compromise and collaborate with others, and time limits in government for all of these groups, the harm and ability to revisit issues should come up naturally on its own in regular cycles. Still, there may be abuse within the Judicial Branch itself, and there needs to be an enforcement mechanism when the Courts are in bold defiance. Luckily, we already have a mechanism to do that that just needs a bit of expanding:

> **By Amendment to the Constitution of the United States, Article 3, Section 5, Clause 8 shall be added:**
>
> Judges on the Supreme Court and inferior federal courts shall be removed from Office on Impeachment for, and Conviction of, Treason, Bribery, abusing the powers granted by the Constitution and law, failure to follow the procedural law as set by Congress, failure to start a trial when ordered by the President, or other high Crimes and Misdemeanors.

The wording here is almost exactly the same as what is written for the Executive Branch, with the additions of abusing power, failure to run as Congress has set by law, or failure to start a case under the direction of the President. The Constitution already covers that impeachment can only be started in the House of Representatives and tried in the Senate, and the only punishment is removal from office if voted guilty. This gives the Legislative Branch the ability to fully enforce all these new powers granted by the Amendments, but still maintain a high threshold to do so.

ONCE BITTEN, TWICE SHY

Returning to the existing parts of the Constitution, there are just a few clarifications that are necessary to make sure Article 3 aligns to all the other changes up to this point. First, we need to clarify the section on treason:

> **By Amendment to the Constitution of the United States, Article 3, Section 3, Clause 1 shall read:**
>
> Treason against the United States, shall consist only in levying War against them, or in adhering to their Enemies, giving them Aid and Comfort, **or any specific way defined elsewhere in the Constitution**. No Person shall be convicted of Treason unless on the Testimony of two Witnesses to the same overt Act, or on Confession in open Court.

As previously discussed, we have extended the definition of treason in a few specific ways. First, when Congress refuses to do its job and tries to circumvent the legislative process, that would be considered treasonous. Second would be violating the secrecy of election results. And thus far, that is it. That does not mean that there will not be more definitions later in this document or at some other point in the future, but treason is really the only crime in the Constitution and thus the definition of it must be restricted to the Constitution. This slight change to Article 3, Section 3, Clause 1 will allow additional definitions elsewhere in the Constitution to be reflected here without question.

Still, there are limitations to the application of any law. If someone is tried for a crime, no matter the outcome they cannot be charged for it again—at least as far as the theory goes. The previously partially updated 5th Amendment said that no person should "be subject for the same offence to be twice put in jeopardy of life or limb", what is commonly called "Double Jeopardy". However, this is not true as the Supreme Court reaffirmed once again in June 2019 that there is a way that this happens. If a person is charged with a crime at the State level, they could be charged with the same crime at the Federal level (or vice versa) and serve separate sentences for each.

This is called the "Separate Sovereigns Doctrine" (or "exception" as this case is) and it dates back to a case in 1847 when the Supreme Court ruled that the States and the Federal Government are different entities, and thus this Constitutional clause does not apply. In the previous section, we have discussed the need for the Supreme Court to be able to return to their decision and re-evaluate, yet this has happened many times with Separate Sovereigns and the courts keep coming to the same decision, with large margins (the last time was a 7 to 2 decision). The courts keep saying it is because of how the Constitution is written that they must rule this way, more than slightly hinting that the Constitution should be updated in order to have a different outcome.

And updating the Constitution to override Supreme Court decisions is not without precedent. We have already discussed the 11th Amendment being a response to a ruling by the Supreme Court, but so was the 26th Amendment that set the voting age for the entire country. In 1970, Congress passed the Voting Rights Act to lower the voting age to 18. However, Oregon said the law in their State asserted the voting age was 21 and Congress could not override the State's rights. In the end, they won at the Supreme Court. Not only would this create a patchwork of different voting ages across the country, but even in the same elections there would be mass confusion as the court ruled that the States could only control the age for State and Local election and not for Federal ones. This meant in a mixed Federal and State election, the Federal questions would go to those over 18 and the State ones would only go to those over 21. Immediately in March 1971, Congress passed the 26th Amendment to set the voting age for the entire country and it was ratified by enough States just 100 days later, the fastest any Amendment has ever been ratified. It is worth noting this is the last "real" Amendment that was ever passed as the 27th Amendment had been floating around for over 202 years. For those keeping track, that means in 2020 it has been nearly 50 years since a newly drafted Amendment has been passed.

Therefore, we return to the issue at hand of Double Jeopardy. This portion of the 5th Amendment was based on English Common law, but the difference being that in England there is no legal separation between the "Federal" and the "State" (or their equivalents) as there is in America, so it is not a question that needed to be addressed. Because of the unique and different circumstances of what the United States is, we need to modify the Constitution so that the courts can change direction:

> **By Amendment to the Constitution of the United States, Article 3, Section 4, Clause 2, Part 2 shall read:**
>
> ... nor shall any person be subject for the same offence to be twice put in jeopardy of life or limb **no matter if the offence was tried at the Federal, State, Territory, Local, or any other jurisdiction within the United States and foreign courts recognized and designated by Congress; nor shall be tried in a civil court when found not guilty in a criminal court;** nor shall be compelled in any criminal case to be a witness against himself, nor be deprived of life, liberty, or property, without due process of law; nor shall private property be taken for public use, without just compensation.

The first part is exactly as we have discussed: if a person (and thankfully the 5th Amendment already said "person" instead of "citizen" so that it applies to everyone regardless of legal status, but more on that later) is already tried for a crime no matter the court, they cannot be tried again for it. It is important to note that we have extended this further than Federal vs. State/Territory/Local, but also included definitions of any other legal body that Congress may create, as well as one additional area. In an increasingly connected world, crimes and civil infractions may take place across borders or in many countries. Most western-style democracies have a judicial system similar to our own; and thus should be trusted with their outcomes. As such, should Congress officially designate a foreign court as equivalent to our own, then its rulings should be respected as if they happened within the United States. In a practical sense, this means that if a person is found guilty and serves their penalty abroad, they could return to the United States without fear of facing the same trial again. Justice can only be served once and a United States' resident or citizen should not fear returning to the country or being made stateless.

That covers the criminal side of the house, but there is one more type of Double Jeopardy: civil liability. Even if a person is found not guilty for criminally committing a crime, they can be sued civilly for the same crime and be found liable. In a criminal affair the prosecution must prove their case "beyond a reasonable doubt" and that the defendant is "innocent until proven guilty". However, neither of these phrases are guarantees of the Constitution or the Amendments; they are just interpretations of the 5th and 14th Amendments. As such, there is an argument that could be made to make these functions part of the Constitution. For now, we will leave it as is and assume "due process" (the actual Constitutional guarantee) will need refinement over time.

Back to civil cases: in these the plaintiff need only prove a "preponderance of the evidence", or in the simplest terms that the defendant is at least 51% at fault. The burden of proof is far lower and is more about convincing a jury that your side is more correct than the other. This is the reason someone like O.J. Simpson could be found not guilty of murder but civilly liable for wrongful death. With the same evidence and a near repeat of the criminal trial, a different outcome was arrived at. No matter if the criminal court landed at the correct verdict or not, this was Double Jeopardy. While it may "feel" satisfying that an alleged murderer was at least punished in some way, it does not pass an objective legal standard.

If that can happen to O.J. Simpson, it can happen in many other cases. Take this hypothetical for instance: A protester is outside a government facility and is approached by a police officer to move. The protester refuses and notes that they are on public property (say the sidewalk) and not within the facility grounds. The police office decides to use physical force and in the scuffle is hurt by the protester with a blunt object the protester retrieves from inside his jacket. After being arrested and charged with assaulting a police officer, the protester is found not guilty of assault. However, the police officer faces severe medical bills and decides to sue the protester. That court rules in favor of the police officer and now the protester must pay the police officer's medical bills and court bills, as well as his own legal fees.

The circumstances do not seem as clear cut there, do they? And there are countless more situations like this. Even if a person is not found civilly liable as well, they still must go through all of the time and stress of the trial, losing wages, productivity, time with family, and anything else they hold dear. Even if in the end the plaintiff has to pay the legal fees of the defendant (which they may never be able to claim thanks to the monetary situation of the plaintiff in the first place), all of that time, effort, and anxiety can never be returned. Sometimes just the act of going through the civil trial as a punishment unto itself is all the plaintiff wants.

No, we cannot draw lines between people we want to find civilly liable those we do not; everyone has the right to be seen evenly and objectively in the eyes of the law, no matter the circumstances. As such, we must make sure that civil Double Jeopardy is removed as a possibility. But do note that this Amendment was specific if the person was found criminally not guilty. If the person was found criminally guilty, they could still be civilly sued! That is not Double Jeopardy, just continuation of the same crime and deciding additional penalties within the law.

Yet there is still one question of if these rights are enjoyed by all. "Due process" would seem to be guaranteed by the 5th Amendment above and the 14th Amendment, Clause 1. Despite that, the latter is lacking and allows certain groups of people to not receive protections—specifically non-citizens and those detained outside of the United States' official borders.

> **By Amendment to the Constitution of the United States, Article 3, Section 4, Clause 7 shall read:**
>
> All persons born or naturalized in the United States, and subject to the jurisdiction thereof, are citizens of the United States and of the State **or Territory** wherein they reside. No State, **Territory, Local government, or Federal authority** shall make or enforce any law which shall abridge the privileges or immunities of citizens of the United States **or any other person within or in the care of the United States**; nor shall any ~~State~~ **government or government body** deprive any person of life, liberty, or property, without due process of law; nor deny to any person within its jurisdiction the equal protection of the laws.

When the 14th Amendment was passed, it was a reaction to the post-Civil War America that still did not know how to deal with millions of people who were once slaves. Laws passed to protect the former slaves and grant citizenship did not seem to have any enforcement mechanism and conflicted with other parts of the Constitution and court cases on State's rights. In order to correct this, the 14th Amendment worked its way through Congress and the States. The other provisions are not controversial today in that they fixed the errors of how to count people for representation in the House, limited debt assumption due to the rebellion, and barred anyone who had engaged in insurrection against the United States from serving in the government. The first clause, though, was completely about trying to make sure all people were treated fairly under the law.

Unfortunately, it was not an immediate success and it would take generations to get due process and equal protection to most of the people. Yet today, the fight continues as groups of people are often attempted to be circumvented. We will return to this point later, but there is one significant area we need to address.

As written, the 14th Amendment is set up for the protections of citizens of the United States. Yet, there are almost 23 million non-citizens in the United States (including over 11 million undocumented), and the "due process" protections only say that a "State" cannot limit those protections, not the Federal Government. Even more than that, the United States government—and especially military—has looked for technicalities to avoid giving due process. This includes setting up detention centers like Guantanamo Bay in Cuba where the United States has held people indefinitely with no trial and no rights. The rational is that these are war efforts (Congress has declared no war, as previously covered) and that the Constitution does not apply to those outside of the United States.

The spirit of the 14th Amendment was about making sure all people had equal protections of the law. Since it was written in a volatile political environment with some compromises and some shortsightedness, the actual wording is missing that spirit. The corrections above ensure that all people—whether they are citizens or not, whether they are within the United States or not; just that they are "in the care of" the United States—have access to all of the same legal options and abilities to present their cases. The United States should not look for technicalities to get around its own rules; the United States should set the moral bar to exceed expectations and make sure rule and law are applied equally no matter the circumstances. To find a loophole and use it means that we have no values—period—and the Constitution is worthless. If we are just going to intentionally find ways to circumvent the rights of people to due process, then there is no point in having due process at all and we might as well adopt a fascist model.

ACE ATTORNEY

Even with granting "due process" and "equal protection" of the law, the approach on how to work within the court system is still not equanimous. While we have given Congress and the President the ability to speed up trials and make rules to even the playing field, that does not guarantee anything remotely close to equal access to and ability of representation. If a person has an issue with a major corporation, a hospital, or the government itself and they are of limited means, admittance to the judicial bureaucracy and having representation can eliminate them completely from receiving satisfaction. Meanwhile, their opponents may have armies of lawyers and near limitless funds to fight any battle, even bringing a case against an individual who would be completely overwhelmed.

The 6th Amendment (and its updated Article 3, Section 4, Clause 3 above) has only guaranteed that those accused have a right to "Assistance of Counsel for his defence [sic]". The Courts have interpreted this to mean that if a person cannot afford a lawyer for their own defense, one will be assigned to them free of charge. This idea came from the 1963 decision in Gideon vs. Wainwright and is once again not part of the Constitution or laws passed by Congress.

These appointed lawyers, however, have very limited resources compared to the prosecution and are often overloaded with too many cases. At the same time, the Courts are the ones who make the income determination, so if you are wrongfully accused and the Courts believe you are above a certain threshold, you will have to pay for lawyers out of pocket even if drives you to bankruptcy in the end. And if the government loses its case, it is not like they will pay you back!

Meanwhile, sometimes the fight is just about wearing out funds. In civil cases especially, a large group may use every judicial tool available to extend timelines and add work to the point where an opponent will not have enough funding. On the other end, someone may sue a corporation, a celebrity, or others because they know it will be less expensive for those groups to just settle for a much lower amount that would be satisfactory than to continue the trial process. Similar techniques are used in criminal cases just to get a plea deal agreed to instead of trying for justice (most estimates have at least 90% of criminal cases ending in guilty or no contest pleas). It is a massively imbalanced system where access to resources often determines outcomes. True, the little guy with enough gumption and persistence can succeed, but it is hardly guaranteed and will still leave permanent scars and costs.

There is no amount of law, incentives, debt forgiveness, or any other program that can fix these vast gaps. Access to the court system has become a question of haves versus have nots, no matter the circumstances. A much more radical stance needs to be taken, one that many would consider "nationalization" and "socialization" of the profession of being a lawyer. But without equal access to lawyers and resources, there is no way for parties to have equal protections and due process. For this, we will need a new Section 6 of Article 3 of the Constitution.

> **By Amendment to the Constitution of the United States, Article 3, Section 6, Clause 1 shall be added:**
>
> All parties presenting or intending to present a case—whether criminal or civil—to the Supreme Court, inferior courts, or any court belonging to a State, Territory, or Local government shall have a Counsel assigned to them by the appropriate government body.

The first element is that every party involved in a lawsuit would have attorneys assigned to them. As a process, a party would go to the appropriate government agency and file the paperwork to start a case. The agency would then assign the lawyer to the party and alert whatever other government agency would need to prepare the defendant. All of this aligns with the earlier Department of Freedom, Law, and Justice in which we set up buckets to handle law services for people and organizations. What that breakout may need to be at the lowest level is questionable and would require further refinement by Congress (i.e., criminal versus civil, prosecution versus defense, family law versus patent law, etcetera). Either way, this would be the first step to ensure that no matter the reason for the lawsuit, each party would have a lawyer that is assigned and not directly tied to each. But how do we ensure that these lawyers are objective and will not have additional help from those with massive resources?

> **By Amendment to the Constitution of the United States, Article 3, Section 6, Clause 2 shall be added:**
>
> All Counsel who are to present a case to the Supreme Court, inferior courts, or any court belonging to a State, Territory, or Local government must be in the employ of the Federal Government or the Government of a State, Territory, or Local municipality. The Counsel may not receive funding, services, or support of any kind from any party directly or indirectly involved with a case before any court system. Congress shall have power to enforce, by appropriate legislation, the provisions of this clause.

What we are saying here is that if you want to be a lawyer who presents to the courts, you must be either employed or a sub-contractor of the government. That does not preclude a lawyer from doing private work either independently or for an organization, but it means that if they intend to ever go before the court they cannot also have those responsibilities. It essentially creates a division between lawyers that provide services and consultation with those that practice trial law.

Further, in order to make sure each party has equal representation, the assigned lawyer is all that each party should have. If, say, a corporation wants to use its private lawyers to pour over documentation as a service to the assigned government lawyer, this would not be allowed because it would give that party an unfair advantage. If the assigned lawyer were to accept that help and try to hide it, Congress could have laws that make this a criminal action and send the assigned lawyer to jail, pay a fine, and overturn the results. Those laws would have to be determined and refined with time, but the overall idea is that each party will have an equal footing and must use the same types and level of resources. Enforcement would be especially important to ensure justice and maintain an impartial and incorruptible system.

The idea that there is a bar that determines if a lawyer can practice in a specific court is also not part of the Constitution. Thousands of lawyers are members of the Supreme Court Bar—as shown here in January 2020—even though very few will actually have the opportunity to argue before the court.

Yet, with basically free access to a lawyer to make any case someone wants, what is to stop someone or some group from filing frivolous lawsuits nonstop and abusing the system? Well, as with any system in the government, there must be a balance and check on that power.

> **By Amendment to the Constitution of the United States, Article 3, Section 6, Clause 3 shall be added:**
>
> Any party who prosecutes a case—whether criminal or civil—to the Supreme Court, inferior courts, or any court belonging to a State, Territory, or Local government shall be held liable if they do not prove their case and will pay reparations to the defending party, Counsel, and Court for the harms suffered as determined by the hearing Court. This only applies to the originating party and does include assigned prosecuting Counsel.

If you start a case and you lose, you will pay for it one way or another. The need to pay some type of penalty is valuable in many cases:

- The police arrest and charge a man on limited evidence and do not make their case.

- A person goes after a celebrity to try to bribe them into a settlement.

- A corporation goes after a former employee to enforce a non-disclosure agreement in an unenforceable situation.

- A homeowner wants to sue their neighbor for being a nuisance and cannot prove the charges.

These are a few small examples where the person or group doing the suing—whether it was for criminal or civil reasons—would be responsible for paying back the other party for their lost time, wages, and general stress. At the same time, they would also be responsible for paying the government costs of the case in the lawyers and the court, so this would theoretically be a system that should pay for itself. In reality, not everyone will be able to afford to pay and many would declare bankruptcy to protect themselves from reimbursing those costs, but at least it would hold some people and groups back from filing superfluous suits on a regular basis. Those with more money may be more willing to pay that price, but it is again up the Courts to recognize this and make sure the payment at least makes a noticeable dent, scaling with the party.

All of this can help clear up much of the backlog in the legal system as it would limit the government, corporations, organizations, and people from constantly abusing the system as it is today. Combined with the above, we could see a more efficient, fairer, and equally applied system of justice than anything that can ever be accomplished today.

WHOSE ROLE IS IT ANYWAY?

> **Federalist Papers**
> **Number 15**
> **For the Independent Journal**
> **Alexander Hamilton**
>
> Why has government been instituted at all?
> Because the passions of man will not conform to
> the dictates of reason and justice without
> constraint.

What is the purpose of the federal government? According to the preamble of the Constitution, it is to "establish Justice, insure domestic Tranquility, provide for the common defence *(sic)*, promote the general Welfare, and secure the Blessings of Liberty to ourselves and our Posterity". According to an interpretation by former Kansas City, MO mayor Mark Funkhouser in response to the same question, he stated that the federal government "is responsible for creating and sustaining markets, enforcing contracts, protecting private property, and producing systems of education and infrastructure that allow commerce to function efficiently". Those seem rather specific and, unsurprisingly, are not mentioned anywhere in the Constitution (though Congress does have rights to create laws around many of these, including commerce). Instead, those are roles the government has taken on among many others (protection of the environment, the welfare and health of the people, creating and maintaining lands for the public good, expanding science and technology).
These various roles are often in conflict with each other and cannot be undertaken by the same government at the same time without great friction.

When reading the Constitution, the first three Articles are specifically about the setup of the Legislative, Executive, and Judicial Branches, respectively. The next Article is about the Federal Government's relationship with the States and the fifth Article is about how to amend the Constitution. Within the sixth Article are clauses about assuming the debts the United States had in its prior form (Articles of Confederation), making sure the Constitution and Federal law are superior to State/Territory law, and that legislators and judges should take oaths of office that do not include religious affirmations. Finally, the seventh Article is just for ratification. After that are just the 27 Amendments that add to those themes... and that is the Constitution in a nutshell!

Throughout the entire Constitution, there are very few enumerated functions of the government. There is some on taxation and monetary policy, some on the judicial process, others on the power to raise and maintain a military, others yet on the rights of States, and some rules on the seat of government and government properties. There are also specific actions such as in Article 1, Section 8, Clause 8 that states:

> To promote the Progress of Science and useful Arts, by securing for limited Times to Authors and Inventors the exclusive Right to their respective Writings and Discoveries

This is what we consider copyright and trademark laws today. Otherwise, almost all other functions have been created because of Article 1, Section 8, Clause 18:

> To make all Laws which shall be necessary and proper for carrying into Execution the foregoing Powers, and all other Powers vested by this Constitution in the Government of the United States, or in any Department or Officer thereof.

This has given Congress the ability to create all the various Executive agencies and departments we have today which do all of those actions as exampled previously. In other words, the government has decided itself what the role, scope, size, and purpose of the federal government is. And it continues to change with time. Yet somehow, they have forgotten and misunderstood their most important roles of all.

SPECIAL DELIVERY

There is one special role that Congress has that stands out quite prominently in the Constitution via Article 1, Section 8, Clause 7:

> To establish Post Offices and post Roads

The Post Office? And Postal Roads?! Why are these so important that they are included in the Constitution? Everything else in the Constitution is much vaguer and gives great allowances, but the Post Office and Postal Roads is unusually specific.

In today's world of instantaneous video communications, the idea of the Post Office may seem antiquated and unnecessary. There are many that wonder why the government would support such an institution when the private market in companies like FedEx and UPS can take care of everything that the Post Office does (albeit at a higher cost). Many of these same people (re: politicians) have tried to craft the case by intentionally making the Post Office unprofitable by forcing them by law to pre-pay for retiree healthcare far into the future. The Post Office's operational finances are just fine and they are running at a profit, but the allocation of future expenses to the here and now is putting them under water.

Still, even without this manipulation, it would seem silly for the Government to have to maintain what should essentially be a private delivery company. After all, there are samples of other republics divesting their Post Offices and having it work out for the best. For example, after Japan privatized their Post Office it went on to become a top-20 Fortune 500 company. Therefore, we should amend the Constitution to drop this strange clause... right?

Wrong!

The problem is that we are just thinking about the Post Office as a stand-alone object in the modern context and not what it and postal roads meant in the 18th century. To state the obvious, there was no internet, no television, no phones, no radio, no telegraph, no interstate highway, no railroads, nothing at all that we would see as a method to communicate. There was only talking to people directly, writing letters, and printing (through laborious methods) books and articles. If you wanted to get any of those letters or parcels anywhere, there needed to be roads to move them from place to place. In other words, the Postal Roads were the World Wide Web of its day, the letter the text message, the pamphlet the website, and so on and so forth. The founders of the Constitution could not imagine the options we have now, so they were specific in what they thought was necessary.

We know much more now and realize that the Post Office is not the only way to communicate with people and move goods from place to place. That is why earlier we established the Office of Interconnectivity and it is for this same idea: people, goods, and communications needs to move from A to B with ease and it is the Government's responsibility to make sure that those are available. Why is communications and movement so important, though?

Because the Founders knew this simple truth: if you control communications and the movements of goods, you control the people. It is a common tactic in war and one we see in use in totalitarian regimes today. If a person or an army does not know what is going on and cannot get timely data, they can be much more easily controlled, dictated to, and defeated. During the Revolutionary War, the Founders experienced this firsthand when they were cut off from vast territories and imported goods by the British Army. They never wanted to be that far removed again and knew that in order to unify and protect the nation, they needed to safeguard communications and the free movement of people and goods. It was just that in their time that consisted of the Post Office and Postal Roads.

Let us be further clear as what these terms even mean, especially Postal Roads. Former law professor and Constitutional scholar Rob Natelson summed it up as follows:

> A "post road" was not defined as any road over which the mail was carried, as many have believed. Rather, a post road was a highway punctuated with stations called "posts"—much like a modern Interstate highway. The posts were places for the exchange of letters, rental of horses and vehicles, production of newspapers, and rest and refreshment at inns and taverns. The term "post roads" does not come from the mail. Just the opposite: The term "post" for the mail comes from fact that the mail traveled over post roads.

While highly partisan and sometimes seen as controversial in his perspectives (and using a quote from him is not an endorsement or agreement with any political stance), Mr. Natelson makes a clear historical point here on what the term "post" even meant. So, what we are talking about is the means by which we get to and reach hubs for communications and services.

Taking this history, what we know we have for technology today, and how changes in the future may impact what we need, we must broaden this clause tremendously in order to protect the original meaning of the Constitution.

> **By Amendment to the Constitution of the United States, Article 1, Section 8, Clause 7 shall read:**
>
> To establish ~~Post Offices~~, **maintain, and support the existence and safe usage of systems of delivering communications, goods, and people;** and ~~post Roads~~ **the methods by which those communications, goods, and people are moved between locations; and shall ensure both of these are available to all people at a reasonable expense without limitations and available equally without preferential treatment;**

If we return to the original intent of this chapter, the question that was asked is what is the purpose of the Federal Government? What is it that we expect from the government? As a "government of the people, by the people, for the people" (as said by President Abraham Lincoln at the Gettysburg Address, but cribbed from many other earlier sources dating back John Wycliffe's English translation of the Bible in 1384), what is it that is expected?

At the end of the day, there is a hierarchy to the Federal Government, but at the top of the hierarchy is the American people. The various persons residing within or in care of the country need a government that has one purpose: to serve the needs of the people. President John Kennedy said in his inaugural address:

> And so, my fellow Americans: ask not what your country can do for you — ask what you can do for your country.
>
> My fellow citizens of the world: ask not what America will do for you, but what together we can do for the freedom of man.
>
> Finally, whether you are citizens of America or citizens of the world, ask of us the same high standards of strength and sacrifice which we ask of you.

But people have misconstrued this sentiment to just the first part of the statement, where the question becomes what you can do to be in service to the country; what you can give of yourself to sacrifice and make the government better; how you can be subservient to the greater good of the country as a whole. That is not what Kennedy was asking here, though, and the next sentence shows this. Kennedy knew the simple truth that the American government was created to be in service to the people, not the other way around. The whole point of the United States is to provide a framework that represents the will of the people while also having a check on the will of the majority to suppress the minority. Everything the government does should be to make life more functional (re: not better, happier, or easier) for all people.

Kennedy was not asking in his speech to do everything the government desires and to be submissive to it. While that has been the modus operandi of the politicians in the government before and since, that is not what Kennedy was asking of the people. Instead, what he was saying is that if the government is to be the reflection of the will of the people, the will of the people should change so that it is not selfish but thinks of what good the government can do not just for Americans, but for the whole world. He is asking that the American people do not make the government just provide selfish services directly to themselves or do not eliminate or refuse to create services that can help others, but instead use their voice to make America provide helpful services to all.

It is easy to forget the context in which these words were made, but when Kennedy came into office the United States was deep into a recession and had a relatively high unemployment rate. Kennedy ran under the slogan "getting America moving again", so his inauguration speech was about that: how we are going to get America moving again through economic reform. What he was asking from the American people was that they were willing to make the sacrifices necessary to bring prosperity to all, not just the few. His successor Lyndon Johnson would take this much further, but we will return to that point later.

Kennedy may have been inspired by similar sentiments from FDR, as shown in the latter's memorial in Washington, D.C. in December 2019.

In a speech to the Economic Club of New York in 1962, Kennedy stated:

> There are a number of ways by which the federal government can meet its responsibilities to aid economic growth. We can and must improve American education and technical training. We can and must expand civilian research and technology. One of the great bottlenecks for this country's economic growth in this decade will be the shortages of doctorates in mathematics, engineering, and physics—a serious shortage with a great demand and an undersupply of highly trained manpower. We can and must step up the development of our natural resources.

> But the most direct and significant kind of federal action aiding economic growth is to make possible an increase in private consumption and investment demand—to cut the fetters which hold back private spending.

These are the ideas that Kennedy is putting forth; that the services the government supplies should expand the economic opportunities of the many peoples by the sacrifice of others. This specifically included a modified tax structure to free up capital. Though many cite Kennedy as a justification for every tax cut, Kennedy had very focused tax cuts and wanted the rates at levels much higher than seen in 2020. Just because Kennedy believed in some tax cuts did not mean he wanted all tax cuts and believed that tax cuts could provide all economic opportunity. Contrary, as shown above, he felt a government in service to people by providing the tools necessary for economic opportunity (capitalism through social services) was required, and that means having high enough taxes to support socialistic causes. This was the balance and was among the sacrifices he was asking for in his inauguration speech.

So, what does this all have to do with the Post Office?

Well, we needed to debunk the common misinterpretation of Kennedy's words to show that the government is in service to the people. The requests of the people can be moderated, but the function of the government overall is to provide the tools and framework necessary to function in life. And the key to doing that is to control communication and transportation. In the 18th Century, that meant the "Post Office" and "Postal Roads", but in the 21st Century that means so much more.

As written above, the Amendment to the Constitution not only gives the government charge over making sure the systems and methods by which communications, people, and good move exists as a possibility—it makes it a requirement. The arguments in 2019 around "Net Neutrality" and what role the government plays in making sure all internet traffic is treated equally is only a question because the government is not mandated to do so. While Net Neutrality enjoys an 80% approval rating in the polls (87% among Democrats, 77% with Republicans), it is not a requirement of the government. How the government treats the Internet, phones, railroads, highways, satellites, airlines, et al., is a matter of law now, a law that is mutable and contradictory.

The federal government is only mandated to have some type of postal service—and even that is a question of law because what we see as postal services in the 21st century is not what the founders thought of it as. Contrarily, the idea of postal service was not for the people, but for the government to send its communications, and possibly even to spy on post coming into the country from abroad. While the 4th Amendment would eventually stop that idea, that did not mean the government envisioned anything like the postal system today. There were many Supreme Court cases in the early country just trying to define if the government actually had the right to build the roads needed or if they could deliver a letter and what type of fees they could charge to do so. Despite what we see today, what "postal" means was not a definitive idea.

In a similar vein, though most people would argue that treating internet traffic equally and not allowing Internet Service Providers to have capricious rules about how they deliver traffic is a human right, frankly it is not. It is not a right because the Constitution is written poorly. The Amendment above makes it clear: whatever form communication or movement of people or goods, the government has a responsibility to manage it. That does not mean the government needs to "own" it as they do the post office and the highway system, but that does mean they need to regulate it.

There are two specific components in the Amendment above that are particularly important. First there is the part that states the government must make sure these components are available at a "reasonable expense". Now, expense could be a direct payment (think a toll on the highway) or could be through taxes (think a tax on gasoline to support a highway). In the case of the highway, though, that does not mean there can be a $10 toll every mile as that would be unreasonable and would make people who need to commute on those roads poor in short order. Or as another example, if an ISP were the only option in a town that would not give them carte blanche to charge $100 per month for basic access. While there could still be private corporations who own, manage, deploy, expand, and invest in the infrastructure needed, it does not preclude the government from regulating those prices to be "reasonable". And then, "reasonable" can also be fought in court to decide if there is a question. This is the point of law and order, and another reason for the government to exist.

On the opposite end, just because private industry may own the components of interconnectivity, it does not mean they should. Or perhaps even if they do own those for a certain period that does not mean that something should not be federalized at some point in the future. Roads used to be private, but the governments at both the Federal and Local level realized how much this restricted people and thus made most roads public. Yet even in this, the Federal government does not own the Interstate Highway system; the States/Territories own and maintain the roads under the direction of the Federal Government.

A form of interconnectivity can become so important and the private industry can abuse it so much that it may be necessary to federalize it in order to protect the people and ensure safe access. As of May 2019, 69% of Americans use Facebook as one of their primary forms of communication, and of those 74% use it at least once a day. It can be argued that Facebook is an important form of communication that needs to be regulated as the Amendment above is written because it has become critical. As a comparison point, less than 43% of Americans have landline phones yet that is one of the most heavily regulated areas of the United States government. Technology changes with time, and whatever form it takes the government needs to shift laws to manage them, and this Amendment would provide that impetus.

As the same time, recent data breaches and corporate tactics have shown that perhaps Facebook is not safe for the American people and the "expense" of using the service is not reasonable (personal data for the private profits of the corporation). In such a situation, the government would now have options to either regulate, semi-federalize (let it stay a private company or trust but severely curtail its activities and make the United States Government the primary owner), or completely federalize. There are arguments for each of these options, but at least the options would exist for Facebook and whatever else may come next.

The second component in the above Amendment is that the various forms of interconnectivity be "available equally without preferential treatment". For ISPs, this is specifically an allusion to make sure all access and bandwidth is treated the same—that AT&T could not decide that Netflix gets throttled while HBO Max (which they own) gets unlimited speeds and does not count against data caps. This also means that local residents and those from out of State would pay the same tolls on the highway, that the prices on airline tickets could not massively fluctuate by the minute, that Amazon could not charge itself nothing or anything different than it charges third parties for its freight services, and many more examples and potentialities. And again, should a service abuse this principle, the government would not just have a right, but a requirement to do something about it.

It is an interconnected world, and it will only continue to be more so in the future. We cannot maintain a patchwork of easily overturned policy in order to have a government that is in the employ of the people and nothing else.

WRITE, RIGHT, WRIGHT

While we have spent a great deal of time making sure all people within the United States have equal rights, representation, and access to the law, we have not defined what those rights are. It may seem that it is quite clear and intuitive what a personal right is, yet those do not have a definition. All the Constitution says about it via the 9th and 10th Amendments is that whatever the Federal Government does not control vis-a-vis the Constitution and related Federal Law is up to the States; and then the States if they do not have a particular law against an act are given and assumed by the people.

What does this actually mean? What types of laws are States/Territories allowed to create to control their population? And what happens when the laws in one State/Territory are significantly different than another neighboring area?

This has and continues to happen all the time, yet these governments live in some type of homeostasis with each other. In the year 2019, one of the key headlines was around States that have legalized recreational marijuana and opened stores on the border with States where it was not legal. But this is hardly extraordinary as there are many minor refractions of these issues. Where one State has a higher minimum wage than another State, if a worker lives on the border and crosses State lines, how should they be paid? They are supposed to pay taxes in their home State, so should their wage laws apply, too? Another example might be that one State has more stringent requirements in a home for the physically or mentally disabled, yet their higher standards do not apply just a mile away. On the other end of existence, a State like California can create emission standards for cars that must be met and because they are so large and control so much of the population and economy that the State effectively sets the minimum policy for the rest of the country, even if federal standards are lower.

These are a few examples of how States/Territories can differ from each other in significant and minor ways, and from a Constitutional perspective these variances are guaranteed. On the other end, States have been given carte blanche to decide what is right for their own people. The Supreme Court has had to step in on many occasions to say that a law is discriminatory or contradictory to federal law; but as discussed above, it has also failed in this role and not only allowed but actually enforced horribly inequitable and bigoted laws for sometimes over a century at end. Part of the reason for this is that there is no clear direction in the Constitution to determine what it is States can do and the Federal Law that has built up over time is extremely situation specific.

Take for instance Title VII of the Civil Rights Acts. All throughout and even via later amendments the classes that have protection are listed as an "individual's race, color, religion, sex, or national origin". Because it is so specific to these five categories of people, the Civil Rights Act has been used to discriminate against other groups such as age, sexuality, gender identity, citizenship status, economic situation, and more. Other parts of the law are similar, such as Title IX of the Higher Education Act that only protects gender access in education. Every time there is a problem due to discrimination, laws that are intensely specific are written and give rise to future abuses. Something much broader and simpler is needed to protect people from the various governments creating restrictions on them.

It would seem, then, that what we need is an "Equal Rights Amendment".

As many readers may be aware, there has been a potential Equal Rights Amendment available for the better part of a century, though the reader may believe that the term "equal rights" means that all were given equality of rights under the law. As will become clear, that is far from the case. This particular Equal Rights Amendment (updated from earlier drafts) that was proposed in 1943, passed Congress in 1972, and was—by the time it expired—ratified by 35 of the necessary 38 States was written as:

> **1:** Equality of rights under the law shall not be denied or abridged by the United States or by any State on account of sex.
>
> **2:** The Congress shall have the power to enforce, by appropriate legislation, the provisions of this article.
>
> **3:** This amendment shall take effect two years after the date of ratification.

This exact same Amendment has been re-proposed in every new Congress since originally expiring its time limit but has not moved ahead. There have also been many slight variations to the same theme, but this Amendment has been the main one since replacing the version first written in 1923.

> *Despite Congress putting an original expiration date of 1979—and extending it to 1982—for the Amendment to be ratified, debate has still continued in the State legislatures over the original text. Nevada passed the Amendment in 2017, Illinois in 2018, and Virginia in January 2020. With that, the necessary 38 States would seem to have been reached. However, four States rescinded their ratifications during the original ratification timeline (although it is a Constitutional question if they could even do that) and it is well past the expiration timeframe set by Congress. Virginia and others have argued that since the expiration is not in the text of the proposed Amendment that it is not binding. Meanwhile, the Office of Legal Counsel has directed the Archives to not add the ERA to the Constitution and some States have sued to enforce this idea. It seems that this case is destined to make its way to the Supreme Court, but it may be years before it is resolved.*

Thus, in the year 2020—almost a century removed—an Amendment guaranteeing equal protections based on gender has still not been able to pass. And frankly, it should not.

The reason that this Amendment should be abandoned is that it does not go far enough. Lest we forget, women had just achieved the right to vote 3 years before the first version of this Amendment was written. At the time, the beginnings of women's rights was just coming to the forefront and the idea of the rights of other groups (non-whites, foreigners, other gender identities, etcetera) were barely in consideration in the conscious of the mass populace (Of course, those groups were well aware of their own lack of rights and desperately desired to achieve equality. There was a lot of discrimination within the Suffragette movement against people of color, poorer women, homosexuals, and others that was often not successfully fought back against.). The focus became intense on just making sure this one group of people had equal protections and it has become an obsession to get something called the "Equal Rights Amendment" passed because it sounds noble and it is believed that it will even out the disparities between the two main genders.

In the proceeding century, we have learned a lot about discrimination in this county and how to unjustly apply it to groups of people. Unfortunately, the reality is that we have not found the bottom of this barrel and will continue to deny rights to groups of people, perhaps groups we do not even recognize on a mass scale today. An amendment that is to give equal rights to all people and be applicable now and in the future must be much broader and offer protections not just within the law, but within all parts of society. How can women, minorities, and all other designations of people reach parity in pay, opportunities, protections, and access if there are still loopholes to exploit and each group needs to individually fight their own battle? It is the same battle time after time, and it should not be. The United States and all public and private institutions within should treat people the same without having to always argue the point.

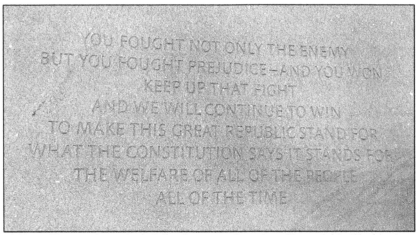

President Harry Truman is quoted at the Japanese American Memorial in Washington, D.C. in January 2020. Japanese Americans fight for equal rights has had to be repeated by others who continue to be oppressed. There is no end in sight so long as we can continue to sub-divide humanity or decree that the "other" is to blame.

As such, a different Equal Rights Amendment should be added to the Constitution:

> **By Amendment to the Constitution of the United States, Article 9, Section 1, Clause 2 shall be added:**
>
> No edict by any government nor rule—whether official or understood—by any private persons or businesses shall be created, maintained, or enforced that denies or abridges the equality in law and treatment of the many people of the United States and the people in care of the United States on the basis of age, ethnicity, race, color, physical attributes, religion or lack thereof, gender or gender identity, sexuality, language, origin, family origin, national origin, citizenship status, immigration status, political affiliation, group affiliation, personal affiliation, employment status, economic situation, or any other known or unknown way of categorizing people, except in cases where a person is unable to be treated equally due to physical or mental limitations, or where necessary knowledge and skills are required.

Once again, we have added a new Article to the Constitution in number 9. Article 8 was the new one we added to put in limitation on government, and this Article has a similar theme. However, it is closer to Article 4: State's Relations. As such, Article 9 is "People Relations", basically the contract the government would have to support and interact with people.

This specific Clause makes a broad setup of how people are to be treated and what that means. It is important to note that right from the beginning this Amendment is both for the laws any government may make and for any rule a business or person may make. Those rules do not have to be official or written down—even an unwritten rule that is enacted and can be proven as discrimination would be a violation. Think of this when someone is applying for a job and no one over 50 is hired into the position. While it is not official policy or written anywhere, age would appear to be a determining factor, and that would not be allowed.

Once more we delve into the fact that this would apply not just to citizens, but to all people, no matter where they are in society. The extension of this is again for those "in care of the United States", which is an allusion to any person the United States is holding in custody regardless of legal status (i.e., expired/undocumented immigrants or enemy combatants). As noted, this entire Article is about the relationship of the Government to the People, and the People come in many forms that the no government nor business should be able to distinguish between.

And creating (or rather eliminating) distinction is what makes this a truly Equal Rights Amendment. It is not about gender, it is not about race, it is not about religion, it is not about nationality. The larger issue at play here is the idea that people are categorized and placed into buckets at all. As an unfortunate psychological condition, humans will not only place themselves into groups, they will place others into groups. Being an impossible genetic condition to overcome, the law must make clear that no matter what way we divide people into smaller and smaller slices, the slice still is irrelevant. Anything that makes living more difficult for a person because another person has put them in a certain bucket is a violation. That is why in particular the Amendment ends with "any other known or unknown way of categorizing people"—because it is important to note that we will continue to figure out ways to classify people in manners we may not even be aware.

Each group has had to fight the same battle for equal rights. Whether people of color, women, homosexuals, transgenders, or whomever comes next, those who fear "the other" will always try to put a line in the sand and determine who should be allowed and should not be. This could be anything! Ultra-liberal people may want to ban extreme-conservatives, the poor may want to limit the rich, the blue collar may want to rein in the white collar, Star Wars fans may want to silence Star Trek fans—and all vice versa. Any group with sufficient clout can diminish the other.

The only exceptions we need to make is for those with physical or mental limitations or not having the needed skills. Now, this can take many forms. On the one hand, a construction job that requires walking on high beams cannot be done by someone in a wheelchair and the exception for unequal treatment in employment must be allowed. Similarly, the job of a nuclear physicist cannot be attained by someone without the proper education. On the other end, it also allows us to create unequal protections. The American Disabilities Act grants special rights and requires by law the treatment of individuals in a different way, but this is necessary to give them equal access and opportunity. All these exceptions are about creating opportunity without undue burden and having to hear all potential situations; that is a matter of law to be imposed.

Altogether, the important take away is that neither the government nor any company can refuse to work with or limit access to any person for any reason and needs to make accommodations for those who would otherwise be refused. Each group would not have to go through the same fight for rights as the privileges would be enshrined in the Constitution. Should any group be refused, they can point right to this Amendment. After all, just because you may be in the majority today, it does not mean you always will be, and that whatever group you belong to should not have to fight to get back rights that should never have been taken away in the first place.

While reviewing this, a quote comes to mind:

> When children learn to devalue others they can
> devalue anyone, including their parents.

This line was given by Patrick Stewart as Captain Picard in Season 6, Episode 11 of Star Trek: The Next Generation entitled "Chain of Command, Part II" and first aired on December 21, 1992. Thinking we should not take advice from fictional characters and want to hear from the Founding Fathers? Thomas Jefferson said in his inaugural address on March 4, 1801:

> All too will bear in mind this sacred principle, that though the will of the majority is in all cases to prevail, that will to be rightful must be reasonable; that the minority possess their equal rights, which equal laws must protect, and to violate would be oppression.

It is a nice sentiment and all, but it is just that: a sentiment. In order to establish this as a principal, let us make it law:

> **By Amendment to the Constitution of the United States, Article 9, Section 1, Clause 3 shall be added:**
>
> No law of any government, nor any Amendment to this Constitution, shall allow the will of the majority to hold tyranny over the minority.

To paraphrase John Adams, we do not want the majority to hold tyranny over the minority and that the minority—whatever it may be—must still have equal rights. There is a very particular limit to this that we must attend to, but there is first another issue to address. You most likely noticed that with the Equal Rights Amendment we added that it was Clause 2. So, what is Clause 1? Well, we return to our original Amendments and look through the ones we have not placed to date and see where they belong in the scheme of this Article:

> ***By Amendment to the Constitution of the
> United States, Article 9, Section 1 shall be
> added and consist of:***
>
> - **Clause 1:** Amendment 9
> - **Clause 4:** Amendment 1
>
> ***By Amendment to the Constitution of the
> United States, Article 9, Section 2 shall be
> added and consist of:***
>
> - **Clause 1:** Amendment 26
> - **Clause 2:** Amendment 15
> - **Clause 3:** Amendment 19
> - **Clause 4:** Amendment 24
>
> ***By Amendment to the Constitution of the
> United States, Article 9, Section 3 shall be
> added and consist of:***
>
> - **Clause 1:** Amendment 2
> - **Clause 2:** Amendment 3

The 9th Amendment specifically states that:

> The enumeration in the Constitution, of certain
> rights, shall not be construed to deny or disparage
> others retained by the people.

Thus if this Article is about aligning the rights of the people and their relationship with the Federal Government, the 9th Amendment actually is the most logical first one to set the tone, followed by the Equal Rights Amendment, the tyranny of the majority, and then the 1st Amendment granting a number of specific privileges like expression, religion, assembly, and petition.

The second section consists of voting rights: 26th for age, 15th for race, 19th for gender, and 24th for poll tax. Next, the third section is on other relations such as the 2nd Amendment for bearing arms (do not worry, we will discuss this later) and the 3rd Amendment preventing the forced quartering of soldiers under most situations (there are loopholes, of course).

And that is all the Constitution has to say on the rights of people. Yet, there is one other right of the people that should be put just as high as the first Amendment in protecting people from the overreach of government, and that is the right to self. This is the limit on equal protections that would give the government the right to make the laws that governs people's lives.

> **By Amendment to the Constitution of the United States, Article 9, Section 1, Clause 5 shall be added:**
>
> The rights of the people shall not be abridged or denied until the actions of the person brings harm to another. Each person has the inalienable rights to take any action with himself and his property, so long as that will does not violate the rights of another. No law shall be created, maintained, or enforced by any government that may abridge or deny the rights of a person unless this principal is taken into consideration.

Earlier, we said that the will of the majority cannot hold tyranny over the minority, but there are times when we want that to be so. For instance, a majority of people are not murderers and having murder be allowed because it is the will of some minority group is not conducive to a functioning society. The way we address this is through "harm". As laid out in this Amendment, a person has the right to do anything to their own body and their own property up until the point they do harm to another.

As an example of a benign way this could be interpreted, a town may have a law of how long you can keep your grass or how much scrap you can keep on your property. The reason for this is a public health concern where long grass and large piles of scrap attract rodents that in turn spread to neighbors and bring with them disease and destruction. In this case, your actions on your property are bringing harm to others and therefore can be regulated.

Similarly, a noise ordinance could be enforced because if you are playing loud music or having parties at 2:13am on a Tuesday night/Wednesday morning, your disturbance of your neighbors is brining harm. Harm can be minor; it does not always have to involve robbery, rape, or murder.

Moving up the chain, if you choose to imbibe alcohol or any other mind/body altering substance, you are only doing harm to your own mind/body and not anyone else. Anything you put in your body could not be stopped. However, a law can be made that if you get behind the wheel of a car while intoxicated you are putting others in potential harm and can be held accountable. Similarly, the government can regulate the quality (though not the existence, more on this later) of these substances to make sure they are not bringing harm to those who consume them.

At the end of the day, the idea is that the people have rights and those rights are not enumerated as stated by the 9th Amendment. We should not have to add rights to the Constitution or create laws whenever an exact circumstance comes up. Whatever you do to yourself and your property is your business and not the government's. The government should only be concerned when what you do impacts others, and there the government acts as the intermediary to make sure there is an appropriate response.

When something new comes along, the assumption should be you are free to do it until told otherwise. Laws are the balance to your freedom, not the definition of it.

Thomas Jefferson stands over his own memorial in Washington, D.C. in December 2019. Jefferson was a conflicted man who expounded the concepts of freedom and equality while having and raping slaves. Jefferson begged for Amendments that would take away his ability to own slaves and would grant complete equality to all people. Since they were not passed, he felt he had no choice but to use and abuse those systems. This is why Constitutional Law is so important and valid. Implied rights are not rights unless we specifically lay them out.

ON SOME ISLAND

Despite now making sure the rights of the people are respected and that everyone has a voice and equal protections, the 4.4 million people in the Territories still lack basic safeguards. It seems all we have done to make sure the Constitution applies to the Territories that the Territories would now be treated equally, but that is not the case in the least because there is Supreme Court precedent that says otherwise.

First, we must understand what the Constitution even says about Territories. Article 4, Section 3, Clause 2 states:

> The Congress shall have Power to dispose of and make all needful Rules and Regulations respecting the Territory or other Property belonging to the United States; and nothing in this Constitution shall be so construed as to Prejudice any Claims of the United States, or of any particular State.

And that is it! If you thought the Judicial Branch was sparse in concrete action and direction, this section is by far trimmer. The Clause prior to this makes clear that new States can be admitted and just that they cannot be created from existing States unless the States agree to it. The idea of territorial expansion was a foreign idea to the nascent nation that was just trying to get off the ground. Not to say there were not territories because the United States had at least partial control over most of the area east of the Mississippi River, and States started to be carved out as early as Tennessee in 1796 (Vermont and Kentucky were carved out of other States or claims by other States). Thus, the idea of creating new States out of territory was not unheard of, but the idea of gaining territory—especially ones with a population—was not fully explored.

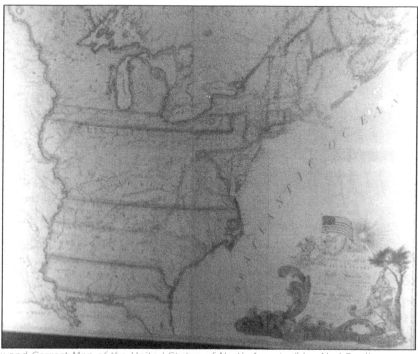

This "New and Correct Map of the United States of North America" by Abel Buell was on display at the Library of Congress in December 2019. According to the Library it is "the first map of the newly independent United States compiled, printed, and published in America by an American. This important early American map is known to exist in only seven copies." In this copy, we can see the territorial claims of the States extending outward in straight lines to the Mississippi River.

The shortsightedness of this came to a head almost immediately with the Louisiana Purchase in December 1803. At the time, even President Thomas Jefferson was unsure if the United States had the Constitutional authority to purchase the land from France. As a strict interpreter of the Constitution at its word, Jefferson had to fend off critics in his own party for a seemingly hypocritical stance. In the end, he was convinced that since the President was given the right to make treaties, and that the bill of sale was one, that this was well within his and the United States' allowed abilities, pending approval of 2/3^{rds} of the Senate.

But this only opened a further Pandora's Box into the question of how law applied to Territories, especially questions of the citizenship of the people living there. The Constitution is silent on this, thus the issue persisted when the Spanish-American War broke out in 1898. The causes, reasons, and actions of this war are chronicled in detail elsewhere, but for our purposes it ended with Spain ceding the territories of Puerto Rico, Guam, and the Philippines (as well at temporary control over Cuba) to the United States. Additionally, Spain sold the Northern Mariana Islands to Germany, which in turn was taken over by a Japanese invasion in World War I. In a similar turn, the Northern Mariana Islands came under the United States control at the end of World War II. Around the same time as the end of the Spanish-American War, the United States also engaged in negotiations with Germany and other powers—as well as forceful actions against the natives—to take control of part of the Samoan islands, eventually creating the territory we know today as American Samoa. The U.S. Virgin Islands, on the other hand, were acquired rather peacefully by a purchase from Denmark.

By the time the U.S. Virgin Islands entered the fray, though, the Supreme Court had already made numerous decisions collectively known as the "Insular Cases". In summary, the Courts created new extra-Constitutional categories for territory, specifically "unincorporated" and "incorporated" land. In the latter, Congress would pass "Organic Acts" that say the territory is considered an integral part of the United States and has all of the intents and purposes of becoming a State—such as with Alaska and Hawaii. With the "unincorporated" territories, Congress can pick and choose which parts of the Constitution apply with the exception of "Fundamental Rights" that must always be employed.

What is a "Fundamental Right" and how do we pick and choose which rights apply to territories and which do not? It is a difficult question to answer because it varies greatly between the populated territories. The bigger question is: how can we treat people differently just because of where they were born or happen to live, especially when they gain full rights when they come to the fully incorporated United States? Is this not just yet another form of discrimination? Let us see the Federal Government's response to these very questions:

United States General Accounting Office
Report to the Chairman, Committee on
Resources, House of Representatives
U.S. Insular Areas: Application of the U.S.
Constitution
November 1997
Page 23-24

The Constitution does not apply in its entirety to
territories solely by virtue of the fact that those
territories have come under the possession and
control of the United States. Whether rights under
the Constitution apply to a territory and, if so, to
what extent depends essentially on either of two
factors, according to a series of Supreme Court
decisions called the Insular Cases. The first is
whether the right in question is considered to be
"fundamental" or not; the second is whether the
Congress has taken legislative action to extend the
Constitution to the territory.

Most of the Insular Cases, which comprise the first
extensive consideration of the application of
constitutional and statutory rights within United
States territories, date from 1901 to 1904,
following a period of territorial expansion by the
United States. In these cases, the Supreme Court
developed the idea that, without any action by the
Congress, constitutional rights that are considered
to be "fundamental" are available in all areas
under the jurisdiction of the United States, but
that other rights apply only when extended to such
areas by law. The Court pointed out that even
though some of these fundamental rights may not
be expressly stated in the Constitution, it would be
wholly inconsistent with the principles that underlie
our government not to preserve them in the
territories. Thus, in one of the Insular Cases,
Downes v. Bidwell, the Court said that the
Congress, in creating governments for the
territories, could not do so in such a way as to
abridge fundamental rights.

The question whether particular rights are
fundamental has been answered only as specific
cases come before the Supreme Court. The Court
has identified the Fifth Amendment privilege
against self-incrimination as a fundamental right.

> On the other hand, the Court has said that the Sixth Amendment right to trial by jury and the Fifth Amendment right to indictment by a grand jury "are not fundamental in their nature, but concern merely a method of procedure...."
>
> Under the Insular Cases and subsequent decisions, rights other than fundamental rights, even though they may be stated in the Constitution, do not apply to the territories or possessions unless the Congress makes them applicable by legislation. The Congress can by law extend the coverage of the Constitution in part or in its entirety to a territory or possession, and has done so with respect to some territories. In the absence of such congressional action, however, only fundamental rights apply. The Insular Cases use the term "incorporated" to distinguish territories where all constitutional rights apply, because a statute has made them applicable, from "unincorporated" territories, where fundamental rights apply as a matter of law, but other constitutional rights are not available.

Recall when we stated that we need the Supreme Court to have the ability to revisit prior rulings: This is another example where the Courts have made a decision that is questionable at best on vast grounds. Whether it is a question of if Courts can create policy and terms, interpretations of the Constitution, deciding what rights are "fundamental" or not instead of saying all rights are "fundamental", or allowing discrimination by place born and lived—this is another example of why not only are the updates to the Constitution desperately needed, but also where additional changes are needed in order to override prior Supreme Court decisions.

Because of these factors, it is obvious that Article 4, Section 3 needs some immense expansion to answer all the questions that have been asked since the Louisiana Purchase, and most especially since the end of the Spanish-American War. This begins with the question: how does the United States gain territory?

> **By Amendment to the Constitution of the**
> **United States, Article 4, Section 3, Clause 3**
> **shall be added:**
>
> Populated Territory may be added to the United
> States only via a treaty—whether the treaty is
> made ensuing peace, surrender, intent to join the
> Union, purchase, or trade—and only if the majority
> of the population has voted to join the United
> States. Unpopulated and claimed Territory may be
> added to the United States through the same
> method and only requires the agreement of the
> governing body. Unpopulated and unclaimed
> Territory may be added to the United States
> through an act passed by Congress.

We make it explicit here that populated and claimed as well as unpopulated and claimed Territory become a part of the United States by a treaty. Since the Constitution already has a procedure for treaties (created by the President, approved by 2/3^{rds} the Senate), the same methodology can be followed. Those treaties can be peace treaties, surrender treaties from a conquered nation in war, an independent nation itself deciding it wants to join the United States, or purchase or trade with another country. Basically, if you can acquire it, it can become part of the United States. It seems so basic, but these functions do not exist in the Constitution and as such the actions taken since 1803 could be argued as un-Constitutional and eventually proven so in the Supreme Court.

While it may feel like there is no untouched and unclaimed land in the world, that is not entirely true. Right now, Antarctica is not allowed to be claimed by treaty, but that treaty expires in 2048 and there are already violations that make it clear that some nations may try to claim sovereignty there—notably with rising temperatures that expose more land and resources as the ice melts and coastal cities are inundated. Also, new islands are created above volcanos in the ocean—especially in the Pacific—on a fairly regular basis (geologically speaking). Finally, as technology expands, humans may create additional space stations and colonies on other bodies in the Solar System; so, too, could these be considered unclaimed and unpopulated lands. We do not know what the future holds, thus the need to be prepared for any eventuality in a way that the founders could not have imagined.

An important side note is that should a territory have people in it, the population of an area must also agree in the majority to become a territory. Thus, if the President tries to buy the Territory of another country (via a treaty), the transaction would be invalid unless a majority of voters in the territory agreed to become a part of America. Thus, we stop forced imperialism both from the purchase perspective and from the invasion perspective. There is a technical difference between an area being occupied by the United States and becoming a Territory of the United States. The key difference here is stated as the populous' agreement that they even want to be a part of our country.

This harkens back to the Philippines and Cuba both fighting revolutions to end Spanish rule and gain independence. Initially, the United States stepped in and seemed to be on the side of the revolutionaries, although for our own reasons. Those reasons quickly turned where—instead of helping the revolutionaries—the United States took control and suppressed the rebellion. While the Spanish-American War was short, the ensuing Philippine-American War lasted over 3 years and killed far more people—at least 200,000 Filipinos, possibly as many as a million. In the end, the United States occupied and controlled the Philippines until 1946, minus the time occupied by Japan during World War II.

As you recall, a great deal of this document has been about extending the rights assumed by American citizens and making sure they are applied to all people within the care of the United States. If the Philippines were occupied as a result of war, that does not mean it should become a territory or, even while occupied, had people treated any differently than any other person in the United States proper. What happened in the Philippines is the horrific example of what happens when the United States circumvents its own laws because of the technicality of how the Constitution can be applied.

Even partial application is a type of suppression because the decision on "fundamental rights" is vague at best. One important right that was decided as not fundamental was citizenship. While people in Puerto Rico, Guam, U.S. Virgin Islands, and even Northern Mariana Islands are citizens of the United States because of acts of Congress, the 56,000 people of American Samoa are not. As discussed earlier, they are considered "American Nationals". Unlike those other territories, if someone from American Samoa wants to come to the mainland United States and exercise full rights, they must actually "immigrate" and take a citizenship test after 3 months of being a "resident".

American Samoa proudly has a pillar recognizing the sacrifice of its people at the World War II Memorial in Washington, D.C. (as captured in December 2019). Yet despite these sacrifices, the people of American Samoa continue to be discriminated against by the Federal Government.

This is where we must stop the partial application of fundamental rights, of which citizenship should be considered one (but is not). If a people are a part of the United States through a Territory, they must be treated as full person under the law.

Here we make it clear that once a Territory is in the United States, its people are citizens with the full rights that ensures. However, it goes a step further in saying that citizenship is retroactive to birth, and this is for a reason. If their citizenship were only made active on the date they became a Territory, then every person—even a one week old baby—would not be considered to have been "born" in the United States and would be ineligible to run for President. Further, we currently have requirements that those who serve in Congress or as President must have resided within the United States for a certain amount of time. All people of a new Territory would be barred from service without accepting their birth and time spent in the new Territory as if it was already part of the United States.

> *The day after this was originally written in late August 2019, the lack of equality in citizenship that we currently have became clear when the U.S. Citizenship and Immigration Services sent out a policy alert to armed services members and government employees operating abroad. In the alert, children of naturalized citizens (such as American Samoans) who are born abroad due to their parents' deployment will no longer receive automatic citizenship as those born to parents in the United States proper would receive. This capricious rule change affects an estimated 100 babies a year, the very definition of splitting hairs to a tiny group that we wanted to protect in the prior section. So here we see both an attack on a small (baby sized) group and a reason that all Americans regardless of where they are born being in need of the full safeguards of citizenship.*
>
> *Yet there was hope as in December 2019 a federal court in Utah made a ruling that American Samoans are citizens and should be granted all rights of*

> *citizenship (in this case passports). Since this is in direct conflict with a ruling in the District of Columbia Circuit from 2016, it seems that the Supreme Court will be forced to intervene (they declined to in 2016).*

In order to have the equal protections of the Constitution, the people must be considered as if they were always a part of the country, otherwise it will take generations to get people of equal rights. On the same subject, the Constitution must apply in full, as well, not in part:

> **By Amendment to the Constitution of the United States, Article 4, Section 3, Clause 5 shall be added:**
>
> The entirety of the Constitution and the Laws of the United States shall apply immediately when any Territory is added to the United States. Any reference to a State within the Constitution or the Laws of the United States shall apply equally to all Territories.

In prior adjustments to existing Clauses, we have specifically added the term "and Territories" in order to make it clear that they were included. That said, there are still parts of the Constitution that say "State" and—more so—the majority of Federal Law also states this. While we saw an example where "State" was defined to include Territories, this Amendment makes it clear that in all situations that is true. At the end of the day, a Territory is just a State that has not been fully incorporated yet. However, that does not mean a Territory should remain that way forever. The goal of a Territory should be to have it fully incorporated, one way or another.

> **By Amendment to the Constitution of the United States, Article 4, Section 3, Clause 6 shall be added:**
>
> Once a Territory has been added to the United States, it may remain a Territory in perpetuity within its existing boundaries. By agreement of a majority of the people in the Territory, the Territory may become its own State, be added to an existing State, combined with another Territory to make a single Territory, or any combination thereof. Should a Territory have no population, Congress may make the same decisions for the Territory.

The first part of this thought is what a Territory can do—including becoming its own State, joining another State, or joining another Territory. The latter might be especially useful for smaller Territories like Guam that may want to join with the Northern Mariana Islands, American Samoa with the unpopulated Pacific island territories and perhaps Hawaii, and the U.S. Virgin Islands with Puerto Rico. Otherwise, a Territory could not grow and would have to remain within its original boundaries. Should there be no population, it would be up to Congress to decide what to do with the Territories. As with any bill, an act of Congress would have to go through the same procedures and be signed by the President (or have Congress override his veto).

That all said, it may not be possible for a Territory to become a State. While that is the ultimate goal, if the people continually reject becoming a State or part of another State or express a great desire for independence like the Philippines, then that should be granted. Right now, there is only a clause that says Congress "shall have Power to dispose... the Territory", and that is all it says about it. But since this did not consider a situation like the Philippines, it is questionable as to what Congress has already done.

Similarly, take a situation like Puerto Rico with its 3.4 million citizens. Since the Constitution is only partially applied and citizenship is only granted by the will of Congress, if the United States traded Puerto Rico to Denmark in return for Greenland, what would become of that citizenship? Do the people on the island on the day of the trade lose their citizenship while those who were born there but moved to another State or Territory get to keep theirs? Or do they, too, become citizens of Denmark and get deported? Would the United States—in contradiction to the Constitution and international agreements of which it is a signatory—make a whole group of people stateless?

The answer is: it is possible, unless there is a clear rule that says otherwise.

> ### By Amendment to the Constitution of the United States, Article 4, Section 3, Clause 7 shall be added:
>
> Over time, all Territory of the United States should be incorporated into the Union as a State or part of another State. Should it not be possible or desirable to maintain a Territory, a Territory may be divested by an act of Congress and—if populated—by a vote of a majority of the people in the Territory. Congress may grant the Territory to another nation or full sovereignty. Should the divested Territory be populated, the people shall remain citizens of the United States unless they individually relinquish that citizenship and all the rights that citizenship ensues.

One of the current powers of the Federal Government is that they can divest Territories, but they can only do so by trading to another nation. As far as the Federal Government is concerned, once a Territory has been gained it can only stay a Territory, become a State, or be traded away. As such, this Amendment makes it clear that self-sovereignty is an option. As the same time, it makes the people of the Territory key in making that decision since the people themselves should be in charge of if they want to be sovereign or part of another nation. And even if either of those situations happen, their citizenship is not lost unless they individually choose to relinquish it. That "individual" component is especially important because that means the decision to drop American citizenship cannot be forced on them by the tyranny of the majority— another important Constitutional right that we addressed above.

Yet there is one more form of separation and divestiture that was never addressed; not even in light of the Civil War.

> **By Amendment to the Constitution of the United States, Article 4, Section 3, Clause 8 shall be added:**
>
> Once a State is in the Union of the United States, neither the State nor any land within the State may secede or be divested to another nation.

The argument for the Confederate States and of separatists of today is that there is nothing in the Constitution that stops a State from leaving. Frankly, they are right. While the Civil War seemed to settle the issue, it did not. The Constitution is very clear that what is not controlled by the Federal Government is controlled by the States. In practical terms, the massive and powerful United States armed forces would consider this an insurrection, put it down, and occupy a State, but it is otherwise a theoretical possibility. As such, this Amendment finalizes that once a State has joined the Union, it is a part of the United States forever.

And this is the core difference between a Territory and a State. A State is here to stay no matter what; a Territory can still leave if things do not work out.

MERGING ASSETS

If that last sentence sounds a lot like a marriage, that is because it is. United States Federal and Local law are filled with marriages of all kinds, but we call them a different name: a merger. When two or more corporations, organizations, municipalities, or any other grouping decide they want to get together, a merger contract is created that combines these various entities into a new single one. True, not all mergers last, and many of these companies that come together split apart years later, although they are quite changed from their experiences of being conjoined.

The Supreme Court has ruled for years that corporations and other organizations are "persons" and as such the Constitution and all laws apply to them. Afterall, one does not normally sue the chief of research and development of a company for a failure of a product, but the corporation itself. Yet, in this case, corporations appear to have a right that human persons do not seem to have at all.

What is a marriage at the end of the day? In the most secular, broad, and copious definitions, marriage has nothing to do with love, making a family, religious edicts, creating a partnership, building an alliance between clans, settling feuds, protecting a bloodline, or any other such purpose for marriage dating back thousands of years. All marriage is, in the simplest of terms, is a merger of assets. One party and another party join and present themselves as a single unit for the purposes of asset and debt management. While this may sound unromantic, the purpose of the Federal Government is not to provide personal fulfillment, but is to provide services, methodology, and laws that allow transactions to happen.

This is exactly what corporations are doing when they merge; the assets and debts of the individual persons become a single unit with a combined set of assets and debts. When corporations break up, there is a split of those assets and debts. Sometimes there are contracts that say how the assets and debts should be split in the case of a dissolution, other times it must be negotiated. In either case it is rarely what the ratio was when they joined together.

Similarly, when people go through a divorce, they must split up their assets and debts (as well as future responsibilities to dependents). Divorce laws vary greatly from State to State, but 9 States have an automatic 50/50 split while most of the remainder have an "equitable distribution" clause that decides what the ratio will be. In nearly all these cases, the "communal property" is never split to exactly what each party brought to the marriage in the first place or added throughout its duration. Without a contract (generally a pre-nuptial, but others are possible), there is no other way to know how to break apart the combined property of the single unit.

The Constitution is completely silent on marriage/divorce and corporate mergers/dissolutions; all of this has been left up to State and Territory law. Because of this, the patchwork of laws across the country has been contradictory to the point where the Supreme Court has had to intervene. This has led to cases like the previously discussed ones where Corporations became people and homosexuals gained equal access to marriage (though continue to fight for equal access in other areas, like adoption, which the proposed Equal Rights Amendment would eliminate). We will discuss later whether the Federal Government should take on a direct role in areas it left to the States, but for now we have a much more specific question to ask: What should the Constitution say about marriage, if anything?

Today, we look at marriage as a union of two people, but that was not always so. The Supreme Court has upheld many times that the States have an interest in promoting and creating certain types of marriage, which allowed discrimination against people of color, homosexuals, and other groups for decades if not centuries. The question, though, is a much larger one: Why is the Government involved at all in defining relationships? What interest is it of the government how people live their lives?

Religion, tradition, and societal norms (of the current time) may push the idea that marriage is supposed to be a certain way, but it hardly is and just being married does not regulate behavior. All States have laws against polygamy, yet people still live in households with multiple spouses (if not spouses by law). Society has seemed to define marriage as a monogamous one, but some people have "open" marriages where spouses are allowed and sometimes encouraged to be physically intimate with other people. While these situations and many more are not the majority of cases, we have already said that the tyranny of the majority should not dictate to the minority so long as the minority is not doing harm to another person. Personal choices that one does to one's own body with agreement of those in spousal relationship are not harm. While you or I may not be able to live that lifestyle, that does not mean we should judge those who do, and vice versa. While extraordinary relationships may get a lot of media attention, those in monogamous relationships should not feel attacked for pursuing that lifestyle.

Back to the question at hand, then, is how the government can have an agnostic policy when it comes to marriage. The problem is thinking of it as "marriage" at all and what that word entails. Reading any marriage contract in any State should make it clear that what happens in a marriage from a relationship side has nothing to do with the union that is being set up on the personal side. Marriage contracts read the same way as another combinate contract—corporate mergers.

At the end of the day, what is marriage but a merger of assets and debts? Whether the things being merged are "people" or "corporations" does not matter; the role of the government is to make sure persons can merge together and present as a new single unit for the purposes of commerce. That is all! That is all marriage should be!

However, there is one other component to consider. If marriage is just a merger of property, and if corporations can merge multiple persons together at the same time or add other person(s) later, why cannot human beings do the same? Why would the merger of assets and debt be limited to just two people?

And let us be clear; this is not really about polygamy. Take for instance a situation where five older women who do not or no longer have spouses are living together in a home. They have a joint bank account that they pay the mortgage and all bills from. Yet, if one dies and there is no will with specifics, the remaining old ladies could lose the house, or the portion of the house belonging to the deceased as this could revert to a next of kin (as defined by the State). Why cannot the five old ladies, then, form a single unit for the purpose of owning and sharing their assets? Then, when one dies, nothing changes as the house still belongs to the shared unit and not to the next of kin of the dead person. Sure, they could form a shell corporation that owns the house for them, but the same situation may come up again with share ownership of the corporation.

Again, marriage is not about love, making children, or any other such reasoning. And even if someone gets married for those purposes, there is no justification for a law to exist that limits rational. If that were so, for example, a woman past menopause could never get married. The government should only be interested in providing a service to people that allows them to do commerce easily, as directed by the commerce related clauses in the Constitution.

Whichever ways people or corporations decide to get together and for whatever purpose is not the concern of the Government. The Government should be concerned when an integration creates a monopolistic situation that impacts commerce, but the combination of people into larger groups for the purposes of paying bills and having hospital visitation rights would hardly fall under this category. What this is all amounting to is that the Government should not be in the business of defining what is a "family". Sometimes a family is just a group of friends with no one else they would rather be connected to. Other times, a family is the nuclear one shown on television (although that is much rarer than television would admit).

Since we do not want the Government involved in those decisions, what do we want the Government to do? Simply put, the Government should create the mechanism by which persons can merge, in any way they see fit:

> **By Amendment to the Constitution of the United States, Article 9, Section 3, Clause 3 shall be added:**
>
> Congress shall create laws or direct the States and Territories to create laws that shall allow persons to combine into a single unit and present as a single person for the purposes of commerce and all other rights attained by such a union. No law shall limit the merger of persons save for those protected by other clauses of the Constitution. Further, Congress shall create laws or direct the States and Territories to create laws that shall allowed the dissolution of such unions.

After doing so, the Constitution will then cover both Marriage and the Post Office, yet not use either term, being a much more inclusive, generalized, and supportive instead.

I WANT TO TAX EVERYTHING YOU DO

MAKE IT RAIN

The idea of taxing income goes back to the early 1800's but was only implemented for a short time around the Civil War. For the early part of American history, government revenues mostly came from tariffs and excise taxes and all together were less than 5% of the Gross Domestic Product (GDP). The government does have expenses and needs to feed its treasury, so finding other sources would seem to be a necessary effort.

Despite this, aside from a short jaunt in the mid-1800's that was repealed by 1872, no income tax was levied at the federal level. The Populist Party especially was a proponent of graduated income taxes as they believed that tariffs put an unfair burden on the poor and they wanted costs shifted to wealthier people. Thus, in 1894 the Wilson-Gorman Tariff Act was passed that slightly edged down the tariff rates in return for an income tax of 2% on incomes over $4,000—the equivalent of $119,335 in 2019. Due to the high threshold and the relatively low incomes of agrarian America, this income tax would have only impacted 1% of the people.

However, one person that was tangentially impacted was Charles Pollack who was upset that an organization called Farmers Savings and Loan Company (of which he owned 10 shares) told shareholders that it was going to not only pay the tax but that it was going to tell the Department of Treasury the names of people it was acting on behalf of who would also owe the tax. He sued to stop this and—after losing in lower courts—the case made its way to the Supreme Court in April 1895. There, Mr. Pollack finally succeeded, but probably not in the way he intended.

Despite urban legend (that was echoed during the introduction of this document for dramatic effect, so no need to nitpick that), the Supreme Court did not find Income Tax itself as un-Constitutional. Instead, the ultimate judicial authority found the income tax violated Article 1, Section 2, Clause 3 which stated in part:

> ... direct Taxes shall be apportioned among the several States which may be included within this Union, according to their respective Numbers...

And further in Article 1, Section 9, Clause 4:

> No Capitation, or other direct, Tax shall be laid,
> unless in Proportion to the Census or Enumeration
> herein before directed to be taken.

What the courts actually stated was the income taxes in this case were "direct" taxes and as such had to be divided among the States based on the results of the Census. Since the United States wanted to use these funds for more general purposes on the Federal level, that meant that they could not collect them for those reasonings.

Interestingly enough, the courts did not find that all income taxes themselves were always direct taxes but could be indirect in certain circumstances (though those circumstances were not enumerated). Furthermore, the United States could collect an income tax that was direct so long as it was appropriated by the definition in the Constitution. Congress found this idea completely unworkable, though, and avoided any income tax for the next 13 years. In 1909, Congress passed the 16th Amendment and sent it to the States, which in turn passed the threshold for adding it to the Constitution in February 1913. The Amendment reads:

> The Congress shall have power to lay and collect
> taxes on incomes, from whatever source derived,
> without apportionment among the several States,
> and without regard to any census or enumeration.

This clause supersedes those two clauses above and made it so Congress could tax anything they wanted and use the tax money in any way they wanted. Thus, this began the modern mass tax centralized Federal Government. While the intentions may have been just, the timing could not have been worse.

Immediately in October of the same year, Congress passed the Revenue Act of 1913 that put a 1% tax on incomes above $3,000 ($77,749 in 2019 dollars) and an additional 6% on incomes above $500,000 ($12.5 million in 2019 dollars). As you can imagine, these thresholds did not hit too many people, so the tax seemed useful and basically fair. Then, on July 28, 1914, World War I started.

While the United States originally remained officially neutral in the war at the onset, they were a supplier to the Allied Powers and provided material support that the Central Powers saw as hostile. After the sinking of a merchant marine ship by a German submarine, the United States officially joined the war effort in 1917 (after an actual declaration of war from Congress). In order to fund the war effort, though, the United States needed more tax revenue, and they now had a way to get it. By 1918, incomes below $3,999 ($67,949) had a 6% tax rate, incomes starting at $4,000 ($67,966) jumped to 12%, and every couple of thousands of dollars of income increased the tax rate by 1% such that those earning over $1,000,000 ($15,991,457) were taxed 77%. Very suddenly, Income Taxes accounted for almost 5% of GDP itself, plus the additional tariffs and excise taxes bringing taxes up to 7% of GDP.

Though rates went down after the war, the government got a taste of extra, steady revenue that they could function with. As World War I gave way to the Great Depression and the New Deal, taxes continued to fluctuate. The New Deal created Social Security and what is known as "Payroll Tax", and this new tax again happened at the perfect moment: in time for World War II.

The second World War by far saw the highest jump in tax rates to the point where income and payroll taxes took up 17% of GDP and taxes in general reached 20% of GDP. After the war, taxes have trended overall downwards to this day in 2020, but income taxes have rarely dipped below 10% of GDP (usually because of a recession that meant less tax revenue could be collected) and expanded Payroll Taxes have accounted for another 5% to 7% of GDP. Even in 2019, combined taxes of income, payroll, and tariffs/excise account for around 15% of GDP, in line with spending levels after World War II. Once the Federal Government got used to this level of funding and the size of an expanded organization, they have not been able to give it up.

To be fair, communal programs like Social Security, Medicare, Medicaid, Supplemental Nutritional Assistance Program (SNAP), and other parts of the $2.8 trillion in "Mandatory Spending" have theoretically provided beneficial services that did not exist prior to the 16th Amendment. Thus, yes, the government is bigger and is doing more services. Still, should the government be doing 3 to 4 times more than it was doing prior to the 16th Amendment? That is a question of policy that can only happen with a Congress willing to work together and reach agreement.

In the meantime, we are stuck with a spending bill of nearly $4.8 trillion planned for FY2020. Unfortunately, as previously discussed, this is not all that will be spent as the government does not include organizations that are "self-funded" (i.e., Amtrak) such that there is over $6+ trillion in real spending. Until such a time as the government can be reorganized and shrunk, revenue is needed, and we need to cover this entire bill. How, then, can we accumulate revenue that is fair and equitable while also keeping fairly steady collections? And what else can we change to make transactions that involve money reasonable and understandable for the American people?

TAX EVASION GOT AL CAPONE

There is a common statistic in economics that consumer spending is responsible for around 70% of the United States economy. What this type of statistic leaves out is that if there were no consumers (i.e., people!), there would be zero spending by businesses, governments, investors, and other methods to make up the remaining 30%. In other words, people are responsible for 100% of the spending in the economy because we will not have an economy without people. It seems simple, but the idea is lost on a lot of macro-economists and pure industry-minded types. We need people to do anything and they cannot be abused by the system.

This number looks specifically at GDP, which is not as straight forward as it seems. For instance, when it comes to business expenditures, only when a business is creating a new item is it counted. So, if a company is replacing all of its computers, that is not counted towards GDP the same way buying a new computer for a new employee would be. As such, GDP does not capture total spending in the economy. And frankly, no one has any great measurement of what total spending is between consumers, businesses, and the government, and where all the overlaps are.

First off, people themselves spend around $14 trillion per year on goods and services of various kinds. Some of what is looked at as "people" spending is probably people acting on behalf of companies, governments, and other organizations. Yet, sometimes those organizations buy things of their own directly. Because of that, we'll go with GDP number of around $21 trillion as a placeholder for total purchases. Recall previously that the United States' total expenditures that are not self-paid come in around $4.8 trillion, or around 23% of GDP. Keep that 23% number in mind for a moment.

Now, let us go back to what people and companies pay in taxes on income. First off, you are most likely aware of the taxes the government withholds from you personally, but they also charge your company directly in a line item that you do not see on your paycheck. To break it down, the income tax buckets are:

- **Employee Federal Income Tax:** A variable rate depending upon income level (and at each threshold, different rates are paid)

- **Social Security:** In 2019, this was 6.2% of the first $132,900 of earnings. The Employee and the Employer each pay this separately.

- **Medicare:** In 2019, this was 1.45% on the first $200,000 in earnings, plus an additional 0.9% on earnings over $200,000. The Employee and the Employer each pay this separately.

- On the Federal level, the only other tax is FUTA which is related to unemployment. Since States generally have their own unemployment systems, this rate varies greatly depending upon where you work. For our purposes, we are going to ignore and think of it as a State tax.

- The other income taxes are all State related, including others like disability. Since this is a Federal question, we will not address those.

Now, if we look at various income levels, we can see what type of contributions can be expected. For the purposes of simplicity, we are using a salaried single person with no exemptions and no pre-tax deductions who gets one paycheck a year from a single regular job and will be taking just the standard deduction. This situation is fairly unlikely as most people are paid more frequently, higher earners may have more deductions, higher income people often get income from capital gains, and health insurance and 401K are pre-tax reductions that will reduce a tax burden—but we need to keep it very simple here.

	$32K Annual Income	$50K Annual Income	$100K Annual Income	$250K Annual Income	$1M Annual Income
Employee Federal Income Tax	$2,182	$4,342	$15,247	$58,424	$330,474
Employee Social Security	$1,984	$3,100	$6,200	$8,240	$8,240
Employee Medicare	$464	$725	$1,450	$4,075	$21,700
Employer Social Security	$1,984	$3,100	$6,200	$8,240	$8,240
Employer Medicare	$464	$725	$1,450	$4,075	$21,700

The employee part is what you see deducted from your paycheck, but the employer part is paid directly by the company you work for. Theoretically, if the company was not paying this tax, you would get it as income. As such, the table below shows what your income would be if you received that money and paid all the taxes yourself:

	$32K Annual Income	$50K Annual Income	$100K Annual Income	$250K Annual Income	$1M Annual Income
Revised Annual Income	$34,448	$53,825	$107,650	$262,315	$1.03 M
Total Single Tax Burden	$7,078	$11,992	$30,547	$83,054	$390,354
Single Tax Burden %	20.5%	22.3%	28.4%	31.7%	37.9%

Do those percentages look in line with something? Above, we said 23% was the federal budget in comparison to all spending (or at least the statistic we could use as a placeholder for it). What if the situation were this, then: instead of paying any income and payroll taxes at all, the Federal Government just had a sales tax? If we set the rate at, say, 25%, consumption would more than make up for the total expected budget. And should the government be able to rein in spending that rate should by necessity fall.

Meanwhile, people's net pay would go up and they could use that money as they saw fit. Since no Federal Taxes would be withheld (cannot speak for the States/Territories, that will be up to each one), everyone's pay would immediately rise. If a lower income person did not or could not buy many items, they would pay far less taxes. A person with more wealth who buys more expensive toys would in turn pay higher taxes. It is still a graduated tax system, but one that people have control over. Meanwhile, because we currently withhold taxes, we are giving the government a free loan every year that they can earn interest on. If people had those funds instead of the government, they could earn interest on their own money instead.

It is worth noting that people who live in the Territories often do not pay federal taxes. There are any number of unnecessarily complicated ways in which certain taxes are paid by specific people or businesses in particular situations, but it is too much to get into. The important idea here is that we could eliminate that mass confusion and make people in the territories also pay for the services provided by the Federal Government. If one is going to be treated fairly under the Constitution, one must also take the downsides!

In order to create this type of tax structure, we do not even need a new Amendment as we already have one with the necessary language. What we need to do then is to create a new law that we shall call the "Perpetual Consumption Tax and Price Requirements Act", perpetual being that it would not need adjustments every year (but of course would have to be reviewed at least every 20 years as we have previously established).

> **1:** The Federal Government shall lay no taxes directly on the income of workers, but instead shall tax consumption.
>
> **2:** The tax rate on consumption shall be set by Congress each year.
>
> **3:** All transactions—whether a good, a service, a fee, or any other method of selling—shall be taxed at minimum the rate set by Congress. No good, service, or any other type of transaction shall be exempt from having a tax on it. Only other taxes are exempt.

We start the law with laying out the intention: taxing consumption is to be in place of taxing income, not as a supplement to it. If the government could do both, they would certainly abuse both ends such that tax burdens would end up higher and be much more bewildering than they already are. The actual rate that is to be used is up for a debate with more detailed analysis, but it should always be a shifting target in that if the Treasury is collecting more than needed then the rate should go down the following year, and vice versa. Thus, if we said there are $21 trillion in transactions a year, and the rate was 25%, then the dollars collected in taxes would be $5.25 trillion. The government said it needed $4.8 trillion for FY2020, so perhaps the rate should be lowered to 23%, assuming a similar level of consumption.

Consumptions and transactions are the key to this. At the State level right now, sales tax is unnecessarily complicated. Depending upon where you are is not only differences in rates, but differences in what is taxed. In a state like Massachusetts, food and clothing are not taxed, except with clothing over a certain dollar threshold for a single item. Meanwhile, food service at a restaurant has a tax, but not home delivery, nor another service like a hair stylist or a consultant. Massachusetts' neighbor Rhode Island passed a law in 2019 to start taxing services provided over the internet like Netflix, but they do not tax the cost of access to the internet. The rules are convoluted when it can be simple: anything you sell is to be taxed. The only exception is if you are paying another tax (like State sales or income tax, or a municipal charge like an excise tax on a home or a car) since you should not be paying taxes twice by paying taxes on taxes.

This also means taxes happen in the entire chain of a product. When a company makes a product, they need to buy raw materials from another organization. Those raw materials will be taxed when sold by the provider to the company. Then, as a finished product, the company will pay the tax when selling to their wholesalers. The wholesalers, in turn, will pay a tax when selling to the retail outlets. Finally, the retail outlet will pay the tax when the consumer buys the product. As an aside, this also means that if a company sells something to itself, it will pay the tax on that. If there is a sale, it is taxed! If one wants to reduce the tax burden in the chain, one must do less transactions and be efficient.

Thus, if everything is taxed, how is the collection of the tax dollars handled? We continue the Act:

> **4:** Taxes shall always be collected by the seller and be the responsibility of the seller to withhold and transfer to the Treasury of the United States in the times, manners, and methods as defined by law.
>
> **5:** If a third party entity is acting as a seller or a marketplace for another seller and is collecting money for the initial seller, the third party entity shall be the party that is held responsible for collecting, withholding, and transferring the tax to the Treasury of the United States.

Right now, with income tax the earner and the company paying the earner are responsible for paying the tax. Here we make it quite simple: if you are selling it, you are responsible for the tax. That means that if you have a yard sale, whatever you make in that day you are responsible for paying the tax to the government. Should you be a retail outlet or a supermarket, then you pay the tax based on what customers pay you. If you are a law firm, you pay taxes on the fees you collect from clients.

An interesting provision in this, though, is if someone else is acting as the marketplace. For instance, if you sell something on eBay or Amazon, or you put your product in a consignment shop, that entity is acting as the seller since they are the ones collecting the cash. In those situations, the entity collecting the dollars is the one who is responsible for withholding the tax dollars. In other words, Amazon or eBay or the consignment shop must deduct the taxes from the sales amount before handing over the remaining dollars to you.

The method for handing over the dollars to the Treasury is another area that Congress would need to define. Should deposits be made once a year, quarterly, monthly, weekly, daily, or instantly? These are questions that Congress would need to answer and perhaps tweak with time. This specific act becomes the framework, but the details of operations can be updated on a regular basis (or never if a method works well).

With such high taxes, though, it may be difficult to understand costs. Even today, it is difficult to understand real costs because there are so many layers of hidden costs and fees that are not shown up front (think about Ticketmaster or a cable company). As such, this Act should correct all of that:

> **6:** Prices shown to consumers must always include taxes, fees, and any other additional costs—no matter the source or reasonings for those additional costs. When a price is shown, that is what the purchaser shall pay in total and no additional costs can be collected at any point before, during, or after the transaction.
>
> **7:** All types of legal tender shall be charged the same amount and no additional fees may be charged for using any specific form of payment.

This could not be more clear: if you go to an airline website or see a commercial for a home television and internet service, the price they put up on your screen is the price you will pay and not a penny more now or later. Most other countries have a similar concept and tourists to the United States are greatly confused when they come here because the price shown is not what is to be paid. In order to better manage personal finances, prices shown must be exactly what the consumer is expecting. This extends to the form of payment, such as a gas station saying there is a higher price for credit cards (or as they present it a lower price for cash). Charging more for a different type of payment is a form of discrimination for how people choose to or need to pay for items.

What this means practically is that if someone wants to charge, say, $100 they must back into the original cost. In this case, the item would be $80 with a 25% tax giving $20 to the Federal Government. Of course, if there were States Taxes and other hidden fees, that would further reduce the "base" cost of the item. At the end of the day, though, the consumer is still just paying $100 and does not need to worry about what comes before.

But how do we enforce this collection of taxes? If there are no income taxes, what would the Internal Revenue Service (IRS) do with their $147 billion budget? Well, hopefully the first thing would be to severely cut that budget down, but there would still be a need to perform certain functions of enforcement:

> **8:** Failure to collect and return taxes to the Treasury of the United States shall result in a penalty equal to double the original sale price including all taxes and fees.

There needs to a be a very real penalty for tax evasion and here we set it. Thus, if you sold that item for $100 but never turned over the $20 to the government, the penalty is double what you sold it for: $200—plus you would still owe the original $20 tax. And who better than the IRS to become an investigation and enforcement agency for those who try to skirt paying their consumption taxes? Afterall, this would be direct theft from the government.

The IRS has been very successful in this role in the past. In the 1920's, notorious gangster Al Capone was alleged to have been involved in many violent and non-violent crimes, but nothing could stick to him in court. In 1930, though, the IRS began a meticulous investigation, watching every ledger and purchase they could get their hands on. Taking into account what was spent, the IRS backwards calculated the necessary income for such expenditures and came the conclusion that Al Capone had been avoiding paying income taxes to the tune of over $200,000. While the FBI could not get Al Capone, the IRS did! Capone was subsequently found guilty of Tax Evasion on October 24, 1931 and was sentenced to 11 years in prison.

If the IRS could do this more often instead of making the average person concerned if they are going to be audited on their humble earnings because they do not understand the massively convoluted income tax scheme, would this not be a better use of their time? Would this not be a better reflection of the will of the people and further the government's role in protecting Americans instead of harassing them?

In the previous section, we set up the Act so that the tax rate set by Congress would be the minimum, but it would not necessarily be the maximum. Why would we want to have graduated taxes that are even higher? Well, we have them today—at least on the State level—for items that have a cost on society. For instance, cigarettes and other tobacco products are taxed theoretically not to make money for the government, but to dissuade people from buying them in the first place. Another example could be the tax on gasoline that is supposed to support roads and bridges—the thought being that the more gas needed, the more roads you are using and destroying (gas efficiency and non-gas vehicles has actually made this collection problematic). Whether these are particularly good methods to achieve these goals is up for debate, but it is a concept that could be extended further.

For instance, let us think about food. Perhaps we want people to eat less Cheese Its and Skittles and more fresh fruit. In that case, we could set up a graduated taxing system that perhaps has five levels, where the bottom level has no additional tax (fresh vegetables) and the top level has an additional 25% tax. This would make the total cost have a 50% tax on it. As an example, if a 12-pack of Coke cost $6.99 now and your State has a 5% sales tax, the base price is $7.34. If we just have the regular 25% sales tax, the price would be $9.17. But if we add an additional 25% on top that, the price would be $11.01. And lest we forget, that $11.01 is the price that would be seen by the consumer.

Here, then, we allow consumers to buy whatever they want. Just because a person may like their high sugar and fat items, that does not mean we need to support him. There is a cost to society in the additional healthcare expenses, at a minimum. The government may want to dissuade people from products that add to the obesity epidemic, but the government cannot ban what people do to their own bodies outright based on the previous Amendment we made.

Meanwhile, the Food and Drug Administration (FDA) could be charged with deciding which category a product belongs in. Additional law could make it a requirement that products prominently display their societal cost level as set by the FDA. Here would be a proper use of Congress' requirement of "carrying into Execution the foregoing Powers, and all other Powers vested by this Constitution in the Government of the United States, or in any Department or Officer thereof" as decreed by Article 1, Section 8, Clause 18.

With this in mind, we further build the aforementioned Act:

9: Congress may create levels for higher taxes on certain products, categories of products, services, or categories of services—or charge another Federal Department or Agency with creating higher taxes on the same—so long as the taxes are in addition to the standard tax that must be paid on all products and services.

10: Additional taxes put on certain products, categories of products, services, or categories of services may only be added if it is deemed that the same has a cost to society or the varied peoples of the United States.

11: Additional taxes put on certain products, categories of products, services, or categories of services shall be directed into regulation, education, and rehabilitation programs with the intent of lowering consumption of the same or paying for the costs of society because of the same.

Important in these clauses is a requirement for how this extra tax is to be used. If the idea is that we do not want people to smoke or drink 128 oz Monster drinks or any such thing, the money cannot go towards the general Treasury. If it does, the government is incentivized not to tax an item out of existence, but to tax it in such a way that will maximize profit. There is an equation that can be used that tests demand versus price, and taxes will be set at the level where demand and price yield the greatest profit (in this case, tax revenue for the government). This works well in business, but it should not be the defining characteristic of the government acting in the interest of the people.

Instead, the taxes would be put directly towards funds that serve a purpose: to regulate the items as much as allowed by law, educate people about the dangers of these items and why they should not be consumed (or at least limited), and providing support services when those fail. Thus if someone smokes tobacco, funds can be used to make sure cigarettes have the least amount of other harmful ingredients as possible, educate people on the dangers of smoking, and provide support services to get people to quit or with hospital bills related to health issues that may arise from smoking. The same could be said for anything such as food, pollution from energy sources, etcetera.

Which brings us to what has been alluded to since Article 9, Section 1, Clause 5 before. As a reminder, that Amendment would state:

> The rights of the people shall not be abridged or
> denied until the actions of the person brings harm
> to another. Each person has the inalienable rights
> to take any action with himself and his property,
> so long as that will does not violate the rights of
> another. No law shall be created, maintained, or
> enforced by any government that may abridge or
> deny the rights of a person unless this principal is
> taken into consideration.

What this would mean in a practical sense is the end of the war on drugs, at least from the consumption perspective. The government may make an argument that taking certain mind altering substances does cause harm to others, but that is a pretty far stretch especially when the argument can be made that the government allows some mind altering substances (alcohol, tobacco, caffeine, processed sugar), and could be fought in court. That said, this tax code may provide a better framework.

Instead of trying to control the flow of drugs and creating a black market, the government could bring it all into light and tax it like everything else. The spending on illegal drugs in the United States is estimated to be around $100 billion per year (as can be imagined, getting accurate numbers is rather difficult). Much like with Al Capone, all those sales are avoiding taxes. If we go with this model, that means $25 billion to the Treasury. Then, if we say that there is a societal cost, an additional $25 billion could be collected that could be used for regulation of quality, education on the honest dangers of consumption, and support services for those that have an actual problem. Not everyone who uses drugs has a drug "problem", but there are those whose use is abusive. Services could be paid for out of the money being made from these substances. Additional savings would be made on the vast number of non-violent offenders that would be sent to rehab instead of jail, so the net results would have extensive monetary savings and better outcomes.

Prohibition proved a century ago that moderation on personal behavior that mostly impacts the individual goes nowhere. Our best avenue of attack is understanding this fact and to engage with the people who use substances that certain other people or groups may not agree with. If we legalize, regulate, toll, educate, and provide the services necessary when all else fails, then we will not only be a much more supportive society, but one that approaches issues with the cold objective lens of tax policy.

HERE COMES THE MONEY

Of course, the question will return to what do we need all this tax money for? As covered briefly back in the Executive Branch chapter, there is a galaxy of departments and agencies with wildly different funding levels. Before getting to almost all those agencies, though, nearly 60% of costs are "mandatory", such as Social Security and Medicare/Medicaid (about $2.8 trillion in FY2020). There is no debate on these packages because Congress of the past adopted legislation that mandated Congress of the future to fund these programs no matter what. The only way to change that mandate is to change the programs themselves, and there certainly is not enough inter-party cooperation to do anything of the kind with the modern Congress.

Overlooking the Lincoln Memorial Reflection Pool with the Washington Monument in the background in December 2019. The Federal Government certainly needs money to maintain parks like this one, but there are other expenses to consider. Should they have free access to money to do as they see fit? Or should there be some limiting rules?

While not mandatory, another 10% of the FY2020 budget is planned to pay for interest on debt (around $479 billion). The government could choose not to pay this, but then we would default on our debt, the economy would completely collapse, the entire world would go into a multi-decade recession, and all the horrors associated with those conditions would ensue. As such, we do not want to default on our debt despite the high costs. Yet, those costs are only going to rise because the government is planning $1.4 trillion in discretionary funding for its agencies for a total $4.8 trillion budget based off $3.6 trillion in revenue. In other words, the government is planning to have a $1.1 trillion (don't mind the difference in rounding due to digits not shown here) deficit, a deficit that will have to be covered by debt. More debt means more interest on debt; means higher annual costs and less dollars for all other programs. It also means we are in a cycle of continually rising costs and debts that cannot stop, not without significant revenue increases (as shown would be possible in the last section) and a more rigorous and controlled budgeting process.

Part of the reason funding levels remain so high is that Congress is not actually mandated by the Constitution to make a budget of any kind. Instead, Congress is given the power to raise funds by collecting "Taxes, Duties, Imposts and Excises" (Article 1, Section 8, Clause 1), to borrow money (Article 1, Section 8, Clause 2), and to mint money and decide its value (Article 1, Section 8, Clause 5). However, nothing in the Constitution says they must plan for how much money they expect to have, how they expect to get the money, and what they want to use that money for. Instead, all that is said in Article 1, Section 9,

Clause 7 is:

> No Money shall be drawn from the Treasury, but in Consequence of Appropriations made by Law; and a regular Statement and Account of the Receipts and Expenditures of all public Money shall be published from time to time.

Other references in the Constitution also call for paying people like Senators, but otherwise Congress is free to do whatever it wants in the acts of raising money and spending money. While there is a general requirement for "[r]eceipts... from time to time", having tried to get that data is exceedingly difficult and obfuscated to the point of near uselessness for the average American. This author has a degree in business and 16 years of business consulting experience with a focus in financial technology and still had great difficulty finding, interpreting, and discovering just what is in the United States budget and actual spending. As has been discussed elsewhere in this document, even the definition of what is budgeted ($4.8 trillion versus $6+ trillion) is questionable, at best, and creates a complete lack of accountability for our elected officials.

Thus, some have called for a "Balanced Budget" Amendment. But like the Equal Rights Amendment, this idea does not go nearly far enough. Instead of one Amendment, below are twelve Amendments that completely change the budgeting process and bring real consequences to those who look to abuse it, or at the very least act negligent in their duties. Once again, the government is to be in service to the people, and we the people should demand they use our money correctly.

> **By Amendment to the Constitution of the United States, Article 8, Section 4 shall be added.**

Let us start right at the top; we need to make sure Congress really passes a budget!

> **Clause 1 shall read:**
>
> Congress shall pass an appropriations budget for the entire Federal Government before the start of the fiscal year.

This seems like a strange idea, but Congress has not passed a full budget before the fiscal year begins since FY2006. Instead, it has passed parts of it at various times, and often for short periods (although sometimes for a couple of years so they did not have to talk about it again during an election cycle). Known as "continuing resolutions", the government has largely been running on an ad-hoc basis with no accountability to getting a budget done. Since Congress is not looking at a "total expected revenue" versus "total expected costs", the costs keep getting passed in their own blind buckets. No one wants to look like they are taking money away from a beloved program (even if only beloved by a core voting group) and as such will keep funding without trying to make the government more efficient and accountable—or making the hard decision of cutting beloved programs simply because we cannot afford it.

Previously we have noted that 11% of Americans have negative net worth and another 40% have low net worth. If we excluded the value of non-liquid assets (those that cannot be turned into cash in a day or two, such as houses and cars), those numbers would be far worse. How can the government tell people to balance their own checkbook and live at or below their means when the government refuses to do so? The government is setting a poor example for financial management and needs to be forced into managing our house much better. That starts with making sure they have the tough talks about what we can and cannot afford, but it must not stop there.

Even though a budget was passed in FY2006 that accounted for all parts of the government, it was not a balanced one. Instead, it intended to take on debt, and therefore was not sustainable. The last time expected revenue was to match expected costs was in FY2001 (It did not work out due to a massive terrorist attack followed by a recession that in turn led to troop deployment in uninvolved nations with no exit plan or even proof of the reasonings for the deployment. And again, no war was declared, so the troop deployments were not Constitutional.). Taking on debt should not be a regularly planned occurrence and should be restricted to specific situations.

> **Clause 2 shall read:**
>
> The appropriations budget passed by Congress shall not exceed in total cost the amount of Taxes, Duties, Imposts, Excises, and revenue amassed by self-funded agencies collected in the prior fiscal year—though appropriated budget costs may be less than what was collected in the prior fiscal year. Taking on debt to cover the planned cost of the government is prohibited and the intaking of debt cannot be included in the planned budget.

> **Clause 3 shall read:**
>
> The United States may take on debt only in the event that war is declared by Congress or if the President has declared an emergency and Congress has passed legislation to support said emergency.

In FY2019 (which is ongoing at the time of this writing), the total revenue collected by the federal government is expected to be $3.4 trillion. Yet for the FY2020 budget, the expectations are for $3.6 trillion in revenue. While it is common in business and in personal finances to plan for a growth in revenue, the government should not be projecting that. Instead, last year should be used as the starting point and no more than that. In an ideal state, the next year's budget would be funded solely on what was collected the year before. In other words, the United States would get its single paycheck and then decide how to spend the money instead of guessing what it is going to be and paying its bills from that. Unfortunately, we are already 230 years into the United States, so we cannot get that going right away. Maybe after a few decades of a controlled methodology it could be done, but for now we must use last year to gauge this year.

That does not mean the budget could not be less than $3.4 trillion, though. Given the size of our government this would be beneficial. In FY2001, the budget was $1.99 trillion, which in 2019 dollars would be $2.88 trillion. Since the budget of FY2020 is $4.8 trillion, that is a 66.7% increase in real costs since before 9/11. Does a 66.7% increase in real costs in less than 20 years seem reasonable? And if we were still spending $2.88 trillion, we would have a tax surplus and could use that money for other purposes, either to return to the American people or pay down the massive debt we have accumulated.

There is a time when we need debt, but it should not be for normal operations. As you would tell your child, if you cannot afford to do it, then you cannot do it. The government needs to learn this lesson as well and live within its means. Yet, there are times when debt is unavoidable, but that is because something we were not prepared for happens. For instance, if there is a war (an actual declared war, not just a deployment) or a massive hurricane or earthquake hits. We can set aside money for these events and try to save up, but all those costs coming at once may be too much to handle. In a disaster situation, getting the funds immediately is far more important that worrying about the source. That is absolutely a reason to take on debt.

Once we have the debt, though, we need to set aside funding to pay it off. But because we have been using debt to pay for normal operations and have not been paying off our debt for decades, our liabilities continue to grow. The last time there was no national debt at all was in 1835! Congress keeps kicking the can down the road such that the public debt in FY2020 will be $18.1 trillion (you might note this is almost as much as all private sector spending). Based on the current type of budgets being passed by Congress, the national public debt will increase to $26.4 trillion by FY2026, with debt financing and interest amounting to 13% of the budget.

Going back to 1929 before the stock market crash and the forthcoming Great Depression, the amount of debt in the United States in 2019 dollars was $0.3 trillion. There had been a massive bump in debt from before World War I with $0.1 trillion in 1915 to $0.4 trillion by 1919. However, from that point on, the debt was being paid down. Once the Great Depression started and most of the agencies we know today came into existence, the debt began to creep up. Before the United States entered World War II, the debt had reach $0.9 trillion. The war itself almost quadrupled this number, bringing the debt to $3.7 trillion in 1945.

Yet here again, the United States began to pay it down so that by 1951 debt had been reduced to $2.5 trillion. This was despite starting the Korean War (not a declared war) and the recessions before and after it. This level held until 1976—after the Vietnam War (not a declared war) ended. Poor economic conditions caused a jump to $3.0 trillion, but it dropped again such that when Ronald Reagan entered office in 1981 the debt had shrunk back a bit to $2.8 trillion. So here again, since a couple of years after World War II and for another 35 years, debt was relatively stable. Then Reaganomics happened.

The year 1983 is a turning point where—under President Reagan—taxes were slashed and spending was increased all in the name of economic stimulation. At the same time, there was mammoth expansions in certain government agencies, notably the military. By the time Reagan left office in 1989 and George H.W. Bush came in, the debt had more than doubled to $5.9 trillion. Bush, his successor Bill Clinton, and Clinton's successor George W. Bush continued these same policies. Under Clinton, there were a few years of Budget surplus so there was a minor paydown on the debt. Thus, Clinton started with $7.8 trillion and ended with $8.5 trillion, but since then it has only skyrocketed. Starting in 2002, the debt has increased on average 6% per year, including two years under Barack Obama where one year was a 19% increase and the other one was 12%. At the beginning of Donald Trump's presidency, the growth had slowed to 1%, but the tax cuts that were passed under his tutelage immediately jumped the growth rate back up to the average.

For nearly 40 years now, debt has been growing on average 6% per year in inflation adjusted dollars. Some of that is just interest on unpaid debt, but the vast majority has been Congressional overspending. As such, Congress needs to be brought back in line not just with the purposes and reasonings for debt in the clauses above, but also what to do once debt is on the books.

> **Clause 4 shall read:**
>
> Once debt has been accumulated, Congress is directed to pay off the debt as fast as possible without limiting the operational functions of the Federal Government. This includes paying off principle debt ahead of schedule so as not to incur future interest fees.

What this saying is we have to actually pay off our debt... What a concept! Lest it is not that clear, the government has been using debt in part to finance the paying off of the debt, thus perpetuating this crisis. Congress needs a plan to not just pay off debt, but to pay it off ahead of time and bring us back to 1835, or at least to 1965. Even if we dedicated $1 trillion per year starting in FY2020 towards the public debt, it would still take nearly 20 years to pay it off. Being that figure is unrealistic, and assuming the prior Amendment stops the intake of new debt, it might take 50 to 100 years to completely pay off our debt (barring the need for any additional debt). Once the government does so, though, we will not only be more stable, but more secure. The debt is a weapon that other countries and private entities have over the government of the United States, and eliminating it should be a national security concern.

The United States government funds many worthy causes such as the Smithsonian Institute— represented in this photo from December 2019 in Washington, D.C. with the Smithsonian Castle and Enid A. Haupt Garden in the foreground. No Congressperson wants to take money away from beloved institutions, but sometimes hard decisions must be made when you are massively in debt. However, because Congress is not forced to have these difficult discussions, it is yet another conversation our government is not having.

Sadly, debt is not the only way Congress and, frankly, the legislatures of States/Territories and Cities/Towns plug the holes in their budgets. One other way that these various governments fill in their gaps is by using penalties and fees as part of the budgeting process. For instance, your local town expects the police to write a certain number of parking tickets and pull over a set number of people for speeding. They have created an equation of what is expected revenue based on the fees that are collected, and those fees are so expected that they are a budget revenue line.

This is what we will refer to as the "Blockbuster Video Model". Blockbuster Video was a chain of stores in which people went in and rented physical media for movies, video games, and the like. Christopher Harress of The International Business Times stated that:

> At its peak in 2004, Blockbuster had 60,000 employees and 9,000 stores worldwide with a market value of $5 billion and revenues of $5.9 billion.

Those revenue numbers are of particular interest. You see, because Blockbuster was renting physical media from a physical location, they needed their product returned so that the next customer could pay to rent it out. As far as Blockbuster was concerned, they only made money when the next person rented out the object. As such, they had a limited timeframe in which you could rent and created a set of late fees to incentivize customers to return their items.

In practice, though, they quickly saw something else; a certain subset of people never returned their items on time and paid double or triple their original cost. The fees started to become a steady source of income, so they broke it out as a line item and planned for it. In other words, they used bad behavior as an expected behavior so they could get revenue. By the year 2000, with $5 billion in revenue Blockbuster got $800 million from late fees, or 16% of total. This percentage was much higher than when Blockbuster started collecting late fees for one reason: Blockbuster saw a reason to incentivize bad behavior.

Once the executives saw that late fees could be a steady stream of income, they decided that they wanted to generate it more than they wanted to eliminate the bad behavior. Blockbuster created capricious and difficult to understand rules about the timing of returns in order to bill more late fees. They had zero tolerance and showed no understanding with their customers for any reason. No matter if it was a first offence for a customer of 10 years, the penalties were still applied without warning. The fees were also exorbitant where the they equaled the cost of rental for every day late. If the rental was $3 for 3 days and a person returned it two days late, they would have $6 in fees. These could add up quickly and potentially could cost more than buying the product.

Even after being sued on this and settling, Blockbuster continued the policy. Penalties were too important of a revenue source for them and, as such, they wanted to keep collecting them. In the world of business, though, they were eventually undercut by Netflix's at-home DVD delivery service that had no late fees and let you keep media for as long as you wanted. Then, streaming media hammered the final nail in the coffin of the greed of Blockbuster. They wanted to keep the model the same in a changing world and collect fees forever. In 2020, one Blockbuster location remains open.

While Federal, State, and Local Governments are unlikely to be surpassed by another competitive organization, they have all taken the lesson from the Blockbuster Video Model. As with Blockbuster, these governments create penalties to make sure behavior is correct. If you violate a safety code in a building, there is fine. This makes sense as a mechanism. However, these governments have decided their mission is not to moderate behavior for the benefit of society, but to maximize revenue. While they could charge exorbitant fees for a violation, the government intentionally sets fees at a level such that should a violation occur, a certain percentage of those fined will pay. This creates a revenue stream, thus the math continues with each successive budget: how do we get a certain percentage of our revenue from fees by having penalties set at such as level that it will dissuade some, but not all of violators?

All governments need to be told that this is not acceptable. Penalties are only for moderating behavior and ensuring compliance. Each agency of the government needs to not be incentivized to create fees that benefit themselves. For this, we will need serval Amendments:

Clause 5 shall read:

Expected and real penalties and fines collected by a government agency—whether a federal agency, State or Territory agency, or local agency—cannot be included in the appropriated budget of said agency or any other part of the same government. Penalties and fines are to be consider extraordinary income and shall not be included as planned income.

> **Clause 6 shall read:**
>
> Expected and real penalties and fines collected by a government agency—whether a federal agency, State or Territory agency, or local agency—may not be used at the agency that collects the penalties or fines, nor at any agency that receives direct or indirect benefits from the agency; nor may penalties and fines collected be transferred to the general treasury. Penalties and fines may be transferred to an unrelated agency for use as a one-time revenue for a specific purpose that will not directly or indirectly benefit the agency that originally collected the penalty or fine.

Of note, unlike many other Amendments in this Section, these Amendments apply to all governments—whether Federal, State/Territory, or local. This is especially important because the latter two are the ones most likely to benefit from fees being included in a budget. As an example, let us return to the police officers.

Police are incentivized to write tickets. In Chicago, IL in 2016, 7% of the entire general fund (about $264 million) came from traffic and parking tickets put out by the police. Thus, for the police to get funding to do police work, they have to be out there doing traffic and parking ticketing. But the more time they spend doing that type of work to raise revenue, the less time they are out doing actual police work. Not surprisingly, in Chicago the crime rate is well above the national average and in 2016 Chicago accounted for half of the net increase in homicides nationwide.

If we had the Amendments above, Police would have to be funded by the general treasury and all the fees and fines they collect would have to go somewhere else. Thus, if the police did not have an incentive reason to try to catch every minor motor vehicle infraction, they would be freed up to do other work. That is not to say there are not motor vehicle infractions that should be ticketed, just that the police should not be spending their time looking for them. If they come across a crime in the line of their regular duties or are called in, then it makes sense to do so. Otherwise, they are just harassing mostly law-abiding people for minor civil infractions.

What happens to the penalties and fees they do collect, though? Well, by the Amendments above they cannot keep them, and they cannot give them to the general treasury (thus, the Mayor/Governor and legislature do not have an incentive to pressure the police to write more tickets). They can give it away, but not to someone who benefits from them. For example, the money could not go to the Attorney General because their work is directly linked, and the Attorney General may exhort a pressure to write more tickets so that office can get additional funding. Similarly, it cannot go to firefighters and ambulances because they often respond to the same scenes. Even though their work is different, they are indirectly tied together.

Where could the money go? The answer might be nowhere, depending upon the agency. Everyone is impacted by the police. But what if it was a building code violation? Maybe that money would go to education and the schools. They are not directly connected and cannot then exert an influence. Still, the answer may be much simpler: give it back to the boss.

> **Clause 7 shall read:**
>
> Excess penalties and fines that have not been distributed, as well as excess tax collected but not needed to run federal agencies or held for a specific planned future use, shall be returned to the people of the United States or the local area from which the penalties, fines, or taxes have been collected and shall not be kept in the Treasury for general use.

Yes, the boss being the people of the United States! When someone commits a finable misdemeanor, who are they really harming? The larger answer is society and the government itself, and both only exist by the will of the people. If this were a civil court case, the people of the United States (or of the local area where the alleged offence has happened) would be suing for the harm caused to them. As such, should not these fees and penalties be distributed to the people, as if these fines were a class action lawsuit? Then the equation does not become what can be done to maximize revenue, but what level of penalties can be used to minimize the need to collect any because most parties will be doing what is expected?

This Amendment also extends the idea of refunding money left over in agencies to the people. Right now, an agency that does not spend all that is budgeted can put it in their own account and hold on to it for another purpose. Sometimes they use it, sometimes the government comes in and swoops it up for an unrelated use. Now, on occasion it makes sense to have excess budget in a year in order to save up for a large expense in the future. Other times, though, too much money has just been collected. If the government has not planned for it (i.e., appropriated), then the money should not be allowed to be free floating. Again, the government is there to serve the people, not use the people as a source to gouge.

On the other end, though, is that sometimes agencies are not careful with their money and spend more than they are appropriated. When this happens, generally there are no consequences. The government still must pay the bill, and does so, going further into debt. On occasion someone is fired or demoted or moved to a less harmful position, but not on a regular basis. And even if they are, is that a fair punishment? Cannot we hold the heads of agencies more accountable to the people and make some of the cushier jobs far less so?

Clause 8 shall read:

The heads of federal agencies shall be held personally financially responsible should the agency of which they have charge spends more than appropriated by Congress unless granted additional funding by Congress through legislation or a declared emergency. Congress may pursue the recovery of the excess spending directly from the agency head through the courts. Similarly, Congress may make an allotment such that if an agency spends below what is appropriated that a portion of the unspent funds may be distributed to the agency head and other members of the agency, with the remainder returned to the treasury.

First, we make sure it is clear that if you are running a federal agency that you have a stake in the process. While running an agency, you cannot act like the money is magic and just comes out of the ether, but that it is an appropriation of the funds given by the American people that you are responsible for. Should you want to spend more money than you were given, then you would have to pay for it out of your own pocket. As a safety mechanism, this would not be automatic. Instead, Congress would have to sue and pursue claims in the courts and the courts would have to make the decision. There may be a reason for the overspending that is beyond the control of the agency leader, such as the President directing other members of the agency to do activities over the head of the person actually in charge. Either way, it is not automatic, and it must be pursued. Also, there may be times when Congress does not want to pursue the funds for any reason. The important fact is that they can pursue overspending, just not the requirement to do so.

Similarly, there are exceptions such as an emergency or additional funding approved after the initial budget is passed. For instance, if there is a natural disaster or a terrorist attack, various agencies like the Federal Emergency Management Agency (FEMA), health services, and the military will respond and spend whatever is necessary to save lives and protect property. As such, the heads of those agencies should not be held responsible so long as they have been ordered to respond without consideration for funding. Should an agency decide itself it wants to respond without authorization, then the head could and should be pursued for unnecessary expense.

At the same time, there should be an incentive for saving money. If an agency was appropriated $5 billion and they only spend $4 billion, what happens to that extra $1 billion? In the prior Amendment, we said that was unneeded funding and that it should be returned to the American people. However, before doing so, there might be a benefit that could be done to incentivize the heads of federal agencies to find savings. With this Amendment, Congress could approve something like 5% of savings could be earmarked for bonuses to the employees of an agency, in this case resulting in $50 million in bonuses to be handed out for a job well done in saving the American people so much money. Again, it is not a requirement, just a tool that would allow Congress to create programs to realize cost savings. This is an extreme example, but despite the rhetoric of much of this document, some federal agencies do manage to spend below their allotted funds. Perhaps more could do so, as well, with the right motivation.

Besides managing funds, there are other concerns when it comes to the budget, mostly around understanding it. This begins with making sure the budget covers the entire scope of the federal government:

Clause 9 shall read:

All departments, agencies, companies, organizations, and any other entity that is run by or owned by the Federal Government must be included in the appropriations budget—even if the entity is self-funding. All sources of revenue must be shown in the appropriations budget, including expected revenue from self-funded entities.

This Amendment returns to our discussion around government organization like Amtrak, although Amtrak is not the only one. For instance, there is the Federal Deposit Insurance Corporation (FDIC) that according to its own website:

The FDIC receives no Congressional appropriations - it is funded by premiums that banks and thrift institutions pay for deposit insurance coverage and from earnings on investments in U.S. Treasury securities.

Other agencies like the National Credit Union Administration (NCUA), the Farm Credit Administration (FCA), the Federal Housing Finance Agency (FHFA), and a few others all have a similar situation in that they make their money as almost any private company would. The only real difference is that these organization are owned by the federal government. While it seems beneficial that the American people do not have to foot the bill for an agency, there is a dark side.

One of the main checks and balances in the Constitution is that Congress controls the funding even though the Executive Branch does the work. Thus, if Congress is not pleased with the performance of the executive agency, they can pull funding and control it that way. By having an agency completely in control of both its allotment and its spending, Congress has no control and has completely ceded a Constitutionally mandated role to the Executive Branch. To correct this imbalance, Congress needs to own the allotment to these independent agencies, even if they are allotting them funds they make themselves. At the same time, Congress may choose to allot these self-funded agencies less then they made in the prior year because Congress wants to reign in the scope of what these agencies do. As it is right now, self-funded agencies and others can act with impunity and do whatever they want with no oversight so long as they do not need to ask Congress for money.

The Amendment above re-establishes Congress' control over all federal agencies. This is also why way back in the Executive Branch chapter so much effort was put in to making sure every agency had a home underneath a Department. If these self-funded agencies are part of the greater mission of the American government, then they are less likely to work only in their own self-interests.

Yet, Congress cannot be completely trusted to do what is right. There are times when Congress and other legislative and legal bodies need to be told explicitly how they are going to act, especially when it comes to maintenance:

> ### Clause 10 shall read:
>
> With the erection of Forts, Magazines, Arsenals, dock-Yards, and other needful Buildings—or any other asset built by any government—the legal body responsible for the creation of the asset must also pass an act such that the costs of maintaining the asset for the asset's expected lifetime will automatically be a part of the appropriations budget of the future and cannot be diminished.

That language for "Forts, Magazines," et al comes from Article 1, Section 8, Clause 17 that describes the idea that the federal government can own assets. Although this clause was focused on the "Seat of Government", over time the government and the courts have expanded this definition to the idea that the federal government can own assets anywhere. We will not fight this because it makes sense; there are many places that the federal government should have buildings, lands, bridges, docks, and anything else necessary to run the nation or provide services to the people of the nation. This would also include intangible assets, AKA non-physical ones like a database program. Digital-only holdings have become much more common to be in the mix of owned assets.

But just because something is built it does not mean the costs are finished. As an example, at a university they may have a campaign to raise funding so that they can build a new campus center. The plans are drawn up and it is decided it will cost $25 million to build it. They raise the $25 million, congratulate themselves, thank their donors, and get on with building. Unfortunately, there is a major problem with this plan. By adding all of this square footage to campus, there are additional costs—it costs to heat, cool, and power the building; it costs to clean the building; the building has mechanicals that have to be maintained and replaced; a certain percentage of mishaps will happen over time; paint will peal; something will break; people are needed to staff the space; etcetera.

Creating an asset is not a one-time activity. If that building cost $25 million to build, it will probably cost another $25 million to run over the next 25 years. We see this today when the government has made one-time investments in bridges, schools, highways, monuments, and everything else. The money is found to make the original investment happen (usually through debt, but we have covered that), but no one is thinking about the costs of the actual owning, running, maintaining, and repairing these assets.

In the world of maintenance, preventative maintenance is usually the first thing to be cut. For instance, every year you are supposed to have your home heating system checked out. But if you have not had any issues, you think it unnecessary and do not bother paying for it. Why pay a few hundred dollars for a guy to come in, look at a few dials, turn a couple of wrenches, then leave? Because it is more akin to brushing your teeth. If you brush your teeth, floss, and use mouth wash you will help prevent tooth decay and gum disease. On the other hand, if you do none of these things you end up going to a dentist in an emergency situation and have to spend thousands of dollars for teeth extractions and follow-up care, more than if you had just done the preventative care in the first place. Sure, you saved several hundred dollars a year, but ended up paying thousands in the end, so it was a net loss.

This is exactly what happens with buildings. If a building has a chiller to run the air conditioning and it is never serviced in order to save money, it is guaranteed that that chiller will die earlier than expected, and probably at the peak of summer heat. And because it would be at the peak of summer heat, a replacement would have to be bought and installed at the highest price feasible with overtime to get it installed as fast as possible. By trying to save money not doing preventative maintenance, all that has happened is the costs happened all at once at the worst possible time.

This is why all governing entities—whether it is Congress, your State/Territory legislature, your city council, or the local PTA—that have the power of the purse to create an asset must also pass with the legislation for that asset the funding for years in the future to maintain it. It would become another piece of "mandatory" spending, much like Social Security. So instead of waiting for the next bridge to fall down and kill people, when the bridge is built it will come with funding to maintain and repair it on a regular basis. That funding will not be able to be touched by the next legislature, leaving them less wiggle room and not letting one legislature steal from the prior one (or this legislature not fund the next one) in order to fund their own pet projects.

Not only will this be less expensive in the long run, but it will make people safer and make purchasing decisions smarter. Yes, thinking about what it is going to cost to clean a building for 25 years is not something sexy a representative can hang their hat on; and you are not going to walk around in the mechanical room of a government office and be impressed by its grandeur. Sadly, though, those are the motivating factors for many decisions, so here we must force the ugly and unsexy considerations to be part of the decision-making process, and not something that can be swept away.

What is also not sexy is accountability and auditing. Earlier, we discussed Article 1, Section 9, Clause 7 that said that "a regular Statement and Account of the Receipts and Expenditures of all public Money shall be published from time to time". This statement, though, is not specific enough and only applies to Congress. In order to be rectify this, another Amendment is needed.

> **Clause 11 shall read:**
>
> All government authorities that collect Taxes, Duties, Imposts, Excises, Penalties, Fines, or Fees shall send to the people from which these were collected a receipt that fully lays out how the funding was collected and used. These receipts shall be made available at least once per fiscal year and be as specific to the individual as possible and be understandable to the layperson.

At a high level, what we are saying here is that any government entity that controls money—Congress, State/Territory legislature, city council, the PTA—must send a receipt that shows how much and by what methods the money was collected and then how it was used. Further, they must do this at least once per year and the receipt has to be in a format that the average person would be able to understand it (i.e., you should not need a specialized financial understanding like this author to unpack it). Further, if possible, the receipt should not be generic but tailored specifically to the individual. This might not be possible at the pure individual level, but it might be reasonable at the metro level to explain how funding from one area is collected and used elsewhere.

At a State level, studies like this have been done in the past. According to the Nelson A. Rockefeller Institute of Government, the distribution of federal taxes collected from a State and given to another have great disparity. The data here concerns FY2017. On one end is Connecticut that paid $55.5 billion in federal taxes and received back $41.1 billion in services for a Return on Investment (ROI) of -26% (that is negative, as in they lost). The complete opposite side is Kentucky that paid $30.1 billion in federal taxes and received back $70.8 billion for an ROI of 135%. As an interesting coincidence, the Majority Leader of the Senate Mitch McConnell was representing Kentucky in 2017 (and still is in 2020). Is there a correlation?

In all, 11 States pay more in federal taxes than their States gets back in programming: Connecticut, New Jersey, Massachusetts, New York, North Dakota, Illinois, Washington, Nebraska, New Hampshire, Colorado, and California. Make from that list what you will, but the important thing to note is that these 11 States are subsidizing the remaining 39—plus all the territories that do not pay federal taxes. Of course, to be fair, they did not 100% subsidize all costs because the government is running at a deficit, so the remainder was made up for in debt ($3.1 trillion collected vs. $3.7 trillion spent at the State level, with the rest of spending at the Federal level).

Thus, there are ways to create a receipt that are more tailored to a specific area.

As always, though, the issue becomes how can any of this be enforced? What happens if Congress refuses to pass a balanced budget and send receipts to the American people? Well, the answer is the same as before if they refuse to follow their oaths of office: treason.

Clause 12 shall read:

Failure to follow the guidelines of Article Eight, Section Four of the Constitution and any future amendments shall be considered Treason of the United States of America. The Vice President of the United States is responsible for enforcement of this clause and bringing forth charges of Treason against individual members of Congress or the responsible legal body forthwith.

Just as with Article 1, Section 11 from before, the representatives of the people have taken an oath, and violation of that oath should be considered treason. All other reasons are the same here whereby if members of Congress try to avoid their duties related to budgeting, then they should be held accountable. There must be a consequence, otherwise the temptation to continue doing all the harmful activities we do today will continue.

What is slightly different with this Amendment, though, is it extends outward not just to Congress, but other legal bodies that make budgets. As before, this could be a State/Territory legislation, a city council, a PTO, or any other organization. In any of those cases, though, it would still be up to the Vice President to bring those charges. The reason those groups are included here is that while many of the budgeting rules would apply to them, they will not feel obligated to follow them without a consequence. And since States' rights and autonomy is also paramount to the entire Article 4 of the Constitution, an Amendment is necessary to override anywhere the State may try to act in its government's own interests ahead of those of the people within.

A SIDE OF AVOCADO

What do wages, welfare, immigration, importation, and the counting of people have in common? The answer is a lot more than marriage and the post office.

While the counting of people is a fairly clear Constitutional requirement; the rest are actually other mandates that Congress does have in Article 1. Sure, there are not specific items called "wages" or "welfare for people", there are directives for commerce, for managing trade, and for creating rules of naturalization. At the end of the day, they are all mandates that Congress is to create laws on, the President and the Executive Branch are to enforce, and the courts to review and make sure the laws align with the ideals of the Constitution.

Despite this, most people consider these all separate issues that cannot be handled in a unilateral way. However, they are all intertwined in a complicated web. Why are wages low? To keep America competitive with the rest of the world and make our products desirable elsewhere. Why do people want to immigrate here? Because there are better opportunities for wages and less danger of personal self. But if someone immigrates here who is used to a lower standard of living, do they not depress wages? However, does not a State want more people—no matter their origin—because the more people they have the more representatives they will have in the House of Representatives? Yet if we keep people away, cannot they have even more reduced wages across the sea and produce products cheaper, thus increasing importation and lowering employment? And if there is less employment, does not the government need to provide more for the people through welfare?

This is the very delicate scale we are attempting to balance, but the current policies and reasonings are not working because each of these areas is being worked on in a vacuum. Some people are the champion of wages, some on immigration, some on imports, some on social programs, and some—yes, even this—on the counting of people. Still, because each one of these pieces creates a reaction in the other, they cannot be worked on independently. Instead, they must be thought of as one wholistic issue that can only be resolved together.

In order to accomplish this idea, two things are needed. First, we will need to update the Constitution for exactly what we need for proper and useful counting and tracking. Once we do that, though, we will need a new law, one that we will call the "Uniform Labor, Welfare, Immigration, and Imports Act". With these Amendments and this new law, the entire saga of managing people and commerce can be accomplished in rather simple ways comparative to the current solution, and one that does not require the regular interference of Congress. However, even when that is all said and done, we must question what happens when all of these systems and protections do not yield the desired results?

For those paying close attention, there is a part of Article 1, Section 2, Clause 3 that we did not account for—specifically this:

> The actual Enumeration shall be made within three Years after the first Meeting of the Congress of the United States, and within every subsequent Term of ten Years, in such Manner as they shall by Law direct.

You might recognize this as the decennial "Census" (again, not a word in the Constitution) which requires the government to count the people in the United States every ten years. The main reasoning for this was to determine how many representatives each State was to receive in the House of Representatives, but the data today is used for a host of funding distribution purposes. And really, that is fine, as the data on where people live should be used for many different purposes, especially at the expense of doing this counting.

While counting every ten years seems to have made sense in the smaller nation of the late 1700's (both physically and numerically), we have other options and better technology to make this not just a regular process of checking in, but a continual function of the government. Why just count the people when the Census can be a program that is useful to the people in their everyday lives? As such, we move the idea of the Census out of the Legislative section and make it part of the People Relations in our new Article 9 with the addition of Section 4.

> **By Amendment to the Constitution of the United States, Article 9, Section 4 shall be added.**

> **Clause 1 shall read:**
>
> An actual Enumeration or Census of all the peoples within the United States shall be made on a continual basis, in such manner as Congress shall by law direct through an agency created and assigned by Congress to do so.

First off, we need to re-establish the Census because we had removed it earlier (by changing the House of Representatives numbers and voting method). The language is similar to the previous partial clause but here we have made the adjustments to ensure the Census a continual effort. This Amendment also directs Congress to create an agency to do these actions. Luckily, we already have such an agency in the Census Bureau! If you recall earlier in the Executive Branch chapter that we placed the Census and immigration functions together under the Department of People and Society. The reason the two are together will be made clear as we move along through this entire chapter, but altogether the idea is that the Census Bureau is in charge of tracking people in the country—whether they were born here or are coming in through the borders.

Clause 2 shall read:

The Enumeration or Census of all the peoples shall include not just citizens, but shall also include all peoples who have made residence within the United States—whether on a permanent or temporary basis—as well as those calling upon the United States for an impermanent period of time.

Clause 3 shall read:

The agency assigned by Congress for the Enumeration or Census shall also be responsible for tracking all residents—whether permanent or temporary—that are not citizens and those calling upon the United States for an impermanent period of time to ensure compliance with the uniform Rule of Naturalization as defined by law by Congress.

These clauses combine together the idea of keeping track of all people falling to one agency with the express purposes of knowing where all individuals are. This is for everyone: citizens, foreign workers on a visa, and people just visiting. This means that when going through customs at a port of entry, the same scrutiny and tracking will apply to all people and ensure that even if someone is just visiting for a few weeks that we know where they intend to be and that they exit the country when expected. The largest group of immigrants in the country without documentation are not people who come over the southern border through desert impasses, but through legal ports of entry with valid visas. For instance, in FY2017 around 310,000 people were apprehended for undocumented border crossings (which is not illegal, as an aside), but over 700,000 people stayed in the United States beyond their visa limitations—both workers and tourists (which is illegal). This group of visa-overstayers are the ones that need to be catalogued, tracked, and have enforcement actions taken against them. Consideration for those who want to work in the United States will address them shortly. For now, the idea is simply that every person needs to be tracked.

Foreigners like this panda at the National Zoo in Washington, D.C. pictured in January 2020 should be fully documented whenever they come into the country—whether it is on a temporary or permanent basis.

It should be noted that Article 1, Section 8, Clause 4 of the Constitution states that Congress is "[t]o establish an uniform Rule of Naturalization", so that is where that particular language comes from.

Still, people do leave the United States—both citizens and visitors alike—and those people need to be tracked and remembered for a future return:

> **Clause 4 shall read:**
>
> Upon leaving the United States, a person shall not be struck from the Enumeration or Census but shall be maintained in a separate list such that the person is known not to be within the borders of the United States but may return in the future and continue as the same record—whether the person is a citizen of the United States or otherwise.

With non-citizens, it is important to be able to track that visitors and temporary workers have left when they were supposed to. And should people return, it is important to check that they are allowed back in under whatever reason they are coming. For instance, a student from a foreign country may leave and return several times a year or a consultant from Canada may come to the United States once a month. In any case, there should be a clear record of a person entering and leaving the country and where they have been.

For citizens, this is a way to track where tourists have gone, where expats may be living, and where each might be so that embassies can check in on them and provide services if needed. Additionally, if a person is not returning to the United States, they should not be included in the counts of the area they may maintain a house in since they are not within the United States. Keeping track of people's homes and contact information is not just useful for the Government, but it can be a tool that helps people directly.

Clause 5 shall read:

For the Enumeration or Census, the main domicile and pertinent contact information—as defined by Congress—for each person within the United States shall be maintained by the agency assigned by Congress and updated immediately upon a change to that domicile or any pertinent contact information.

Clause 6 shall read:

Upon the main domicile or any pertinent contact information being updated by the agency assigned by Congress, the agency shall in turn alert all government, public, and private institutions that use that domicile or pertinent contact information to update their records to align to the Enumeration or Census.

Have you ever had to change your name because you got married or know someone who has? It is a common occurrence in the United States, but it is a painful and expensive process. Every agency of the federal, State/Territory, and local municipal government; every credit company; every insurance company; every current and former employer; and so many more organizations need to be told of a name change. Many of these—such as Social Security, passports, and driving licenses—all cost money and take significant time. This process is so time consuming in a modern America that it can take years, which in turn makes some people not bother at all or maintain a mix of names for the remainder of their lives.

Why cannot the government work for the people, instead? If there were a single agency in charge of keeping track of every name and their contact information (i.e., address, phone, e-mail, etcetera), why cannot all other organizations that need this contact information be able to pull it directly from the source. Instead of going one-by-one every time you move or change a phone number, could not the government provide a useful service to the people?

This is the point of these two Amendments. Now, a person could just update with the Census Bureau and the Census Bureau would update all the other federal government agencies, all the relevant State/Territory/municipal agencies, and all private companies that are authorized to use this information. It becomes a one-stop shop to make the lives of people easier instead of the massive red tape that is expected of them now.

Of course, having such data and tracking all people is dangerous to just have available. Protections need to be put into place so it is up to the individual person how they want their data to be used, who they want to have access to it, and make sure there are penalties for unauthorized access by everyone—up to and including the President.

Clause 7 shall read:

The domicile and pertinent contact information maintained by the agency assigned by Congress shall be considered protected information and shall only be released to organizations agreed to by the person related directly. Congress shall make law such that individually identifying information within the Enumeration or Census shall only be accessible by those within the agency assigned and punishments for unauthorized access or release of this information up to and including treason.

So, if you want your credit card company to have access to this information such that when you update your records they get it automatically, that is up to you. If you do not want that and want to maintain the data individually, that is also up to you, too. At the same time, the Census Bureau could not just release information or someone else could not just steal it without consequence. Should the President order the Department Head of Safety and Security to get this information for the use in law enforcement, that would not be allowed. Even asking to do so is a cause for treason. The data should only be released in aggregate (i.e., how many people live in New Mexico) and no personally identifiable data should be made outside the agency for any reason that is not approved by the individual person.

When the minimum wage was created through the Fair Standard Act of 1938, the rate was set at $0.25 per hour, which would amount to $4.55 in 2019 dollars. In the ensuing years, the minimum wage has been updated 22 times, reaching $7.25 in 2009 (where it has sat since). It would seem based upon this quick math that minimum wage has actually done quite well and outpaced the original setting! Except, that is not the case at all because minimum wage was increased immediately the next year and continued to rise upward both in actual numbers and in real value compared to 2019.

As can be seen, the peak in value of the minimum wage came in 1968 when it became the equivalent of $11.80 in 2019 dollars or $0.65 in 1938 dollars. You see, what happened after the initial minimum wage was twofold. First, there was a realization that this rate was not enough. More than this, though, was the second component being the societal and political decision that minimum wage should cover the cost of living. In other words, the minimum wages that people should expect should cover a decent living.

Unfortunately, that idea was lost with time mostly for one factor: that the minimum wage had to be manually updated. As shown in the chart above, there are large gaps of time with no changes at all followed by several spurts of catching up slightly. In 2019, those pushing for a $15 per hour minimum wage are creating the same dire situations. Many States have picked up this mantle and created a path to $15 per hour, but what happens once they get there? Is the minimum wage always going to increase? And if so, based upon what?

The main issue is not just the purchasing power of a dollar, it is what it cost to live on that dollar. Every chart you can find will show you that the cost of living has increased at a rate far faster than adjusted real wages, nonetheless minimum wages.

The minimum wage is an antiquated solution to a problem that never actually solved the initial issue in the first place. Congress must be put into in a situation where they are required to not only review wages on an annual basis, but to make sure those wages cover the entire cost of living.

This is what is known as a Living Wage. Conservative minded folks will say that if everyone were making a higher wage then companies would have less employees. Well, this is true, but it is not the entire picture. Right now, people making below the Living Wage by necessity must have these dollars made up elsewhere in order to... well... live! These funds typically come from the government in the form of welfare, discounted healthcare, tax rebates, write-offs, and other measures. One way or another, the government is covering the cost of the people, which is part of the reason mandatory spending continues to skyrocket. Let us look at a particular example:

Say a large box store that we will call "Mal-wart" employs 100 people at $10 per hour. Where these people live, though, the cost of living is $15 per hour. As such, the government must make up the difference in subsidies that align to that $5 difference. Thus, there is $500 per hour the government needs to spend times 2080 working hours in a year to equal $1.04 million. Basically, this is welfare that Mal-wart is getting at the expense of other taxpayers.

So, we make a law that says Mal-wart has to pay their employees $15 per hour. Before, Mal-wart had $2.08 million in labor fees and now they will have $3.12 million. Conservative people say that Mal-wart will then layoff people to get back to their original labor fees. That would mean 34 people will be laid off leaving 66 working at Mal-wart. Those 66 people will cost Mal-wart $2.06 million while the government will need to hand out the $15 per hour for the 34 laid off people, resulting in a government payout of $1.06 million. In the end, it looks like a wash as Mal-wart and the government are paying roughly the same amount they were before, and less people are now employed.

Except that is not the end. You see, Mal-wart has minimum staffing levels necessary to run their stores and cannot lay off a third of their workforce. More likely, they could at most drop 15% of their workforce, which would end up with 85 people working at Mal-wart and 15 on the government welfare. Those 85 people would cost Mal-wart $2.65 million and the 15 people on welfare would cost the taxpayers $0.47 million, saving the taxpayers $0.57 million dollars. And this is just one store among thousands, among thousands and thousands of other companies. In other words, there are billions of dollars of savings to be had. The government is going to have to pay in one way another; should it not have to pay less?

Which is a better situation of the two below?

1. A low unemployment rate, but the majority of Americans make incomes below the Living Wage rate and are dependent upon government payments to make up the difference, thus giving welfare indirectly to employers.

2. All working Americans make a Living Wage and can support themselves and their families without government assistance, employers receive no welfare, but there is potentially a larger unemployment rate.

The latter is the direction we should be heading. Even the detriment of the higher unemployment rate is not necessarily a bad one because the current system creates an oft non-reported underemployment rate. We would need law to ensure all who are working are fully employed and making a wage to live so that the unemployment rate would actually be a useful measure instead of one that covers up our real problem: wages have not kept pace with the cost of living.

Thus, we return to the "Uniform Labor, Welfare, Immigration, and Imports Act" previewed in the introduction to this chapter. Unlike many other areas, we do not need a Constitutional Amendment because not only does Congress have the right to do this, they are directed to do so in Article 1, Section 8. Therefore, the first part of this Act will focus in on the Living Wage:

1: The laborers within the United States shall at a minimum make a *Living Wage*.

1-A: A *Living Wage* is defined such that a household that contains two adults and the average number of children within the county or equivalent area, and one adult is working *Full-time* for wages, the wage received shall cover the *Cost of Living* for all individuals within said household.

1-B: The *Cost of Living* is defined as the median cost of housing, food, clothing, utilities, healthcare, and any other such measure as deemed necessary by Congress.

1-C: *Full-time* is defined by Congress as the amount of time necessary for a laborer at a single job to be considered so.

2: The *Living Wage* for a laborer shall be calculated in the method as determined by Congress.

2-A: The *Living Wage* for a laborer shall be calculated at the county or equivalent level, such that all those who live or labor within a county shall have at minimum that Living Wage.

2-B: Should a laborer live in a county with a different *Living Wage* than the county that the laborer is employed in, the higher *Living Wage* of the two shall be required to be paid.

2-C: Should a laborer live within 20 kilometers of another or several counties, the highest *Living Wage* of all of the counties within 20 kilometers shall apply to that laborer.

2-D: Congress shall recalculate the Living Wage once per year such that the new *Living Wage* shall take effect on the date the last one has expired, as defined by Congress. The *Living Wage* shall automatically take effect without further legislation from Congress.

2-E: Should the *Living Wage* decrease from the prior calculation laborers may not have their wages reduced to match this lower amount. Should an employer attempt to do so or induce a laborer to accept a reduction, the employer shall be penalized twice the expected annual wages of the laborer.

3: The States and Territories—and the municipalities within those States and Territories should they be allowed to by the law of that State or Territory—may set a wage rate above the definition within this Act, but may not set a wage rate below the definition within this Act.

There is a lot to unpack here, so let us begin at the top. First, we even need to define what is meant by a "Living Wage". As discussed in the Legislative Branch chapter, there are several definitions depending upon how many people in the house are working and how many children they have. As such, we have gone with a definition that is one adult working in a household with two adults and having the average number of children. That latter number on children in 2018 was 1.9 at the entire country level and is continuing to decrease, though at lower levels there may be higher or lower numbers. More on that statistic later, but it is important not to create a fixed number on a variable that is in flux. If a variable is going to need updating on a regular basis, we cannot depend upon Congress to pass the legislation necessary to keep up with the times. This way, the equation is set so long as we get the figure from a trusted source.

And it would still be up to Congress what the equation should be. While the aforementioned MIT Living Wage Calculator is the industry standard, it is not the only potential option and Congress may decide to take its own approach. We will return to this point, as well, but for now we will go with the idea that a "full-time" employee (whatever "full-time" is) should make a living wage that is enough to support the cost of living for that person, their spouse, and a couple of kids. That does not mean that households will still not want to have both adults working, but that doing so should elevate them economically, not just be enough to get by that a single adult working would guarantee.

Next, we note that the level we are looking at is by county (or the equivalent of "county" because some places do not have this breakout below State but above town). Still, that is not enough in case someone lives in one county and works in another or lives/works within 20 km (12.5 miles) of another county. Whichever county has the highest Living Wage in those situations is the one that is going to be used. This is a stopgap to smooth out the issue of solid lines in a fluid system and make sure companies do not just set up shop in the cheaper counties to avoid paying fair wages.

Along those same lines, it is possible that a recalculation will end up with a lower cost of living. This might happen due to the average number of children decreasing, real costs going down, or any of the other variables. But just because the cost of living may slide down during a re-evaluation does not mean a company can scale a worker's wages downward or fire them and rehire them at the lower wage. While a new employee can be hired at a lower wage, an existing one cannot have their wages garnished. If a company attempts to do so, the government can penalize the company for double that worker's expected income. So if you were going to make $40,000 in your area and the company tried to compel you take a pay cut to $39,000, not only would the company still have to pay you $40,000, they would now owe the government an $80,000 penalty. And as the prior chapter covered, a penalty can be redistributed back to the American people.

Finally, nothing in this law would prohibit a State/Territory or local municipality (if a State/Territory allowed it) from creating an even higher required wage above the Living Wage; they just could not set a rate below it. Even if the specific area set a higher rate, the federal Living Wage is still the one that would apply in any given equation of what an employer should pay at minimum.

Still, employers are notorious for trying to circumvent the law. When the Affordable Care Act was passed, it had a clause that said an employer had to offer healthcare to any employee who worked over 30 hours a week. As such, the companies started limiting hours for employees to 29 per week and hiring multiple part-time workers instead of full-time ones. Here, we must correct that mistake and make sure that there are more fully employed people instead of having a large under-employed population and people stringing together multiple part-time jobs to make a full-time income (and not getting any of the benefits of full-time employment).

> **4:** An employer may not hire multiple *Part-time* laborers when a single *Full-time* laborer could perform the required tasks and a *Full-time* laborer is available for hire.
>
> **4-A:** *Part-time* is defined as any time threshold that eliminates any benefits provided by the employer or eliminates any taxes or benefits required by law for *Full-time* laborers as defined by either Congress, the State/Territory legislature, or the local municipal law-making body.
>
> **4-B:** Should an employer attempt to circumvent hiring *Full-time* laborers and instead hire multiple *Part-time* laborers, the employer shall be penalized twice the expected annual wages of each *Part-time* laborer as if each were a *Full-time* laborer, as well as pay any tax or benefit not paid because of not meeting the necessary threshold. Additionally, the employer shall pay each *Part-time* laborer the difference in wages from being *Part-time* to *Full-time* for the lifetime of that laborer's employment.

Here, we make it quite clear: if you try to circumvent something like offering healthcare, you are in violation of this Act. In violation, there is a penalty that would amount to quite a bit. Let us return to the prior example where a single employee is making $40,000 full-time. Instead, the employer hires two half-time people for $20,000 each. When the government discovers this, they charge the company $80,000 per employee for a total of $160,000. They will then have to pay the difference in wages to the employees for another $40,000, totaling $200,000 in fees. Secondly, they will have to pay any and all additional taxes, fees, penalties, and benefits they were trying to avoid, but those are variable by the situation. As a simple example, we will say whatever small amount of money they were trying to save (let us say $10,000) has instead cost them $210,000. Now, we have incentivized companies to play by the rules and fully employ and pay people because it is not cheaper to circumvent the rules—as it is today.

Still, there is a question of if the equations created by Congress are fair. Afterall, Congress may lean into a political belief or lobbyist group that says wages should be higher or lower and try to make the factors reflect that. Is high speed internet access a necessary cost of living in 2020? Is a smart phone? These are beliefs that will have to be argued and tested to determine a standard, and one that will have to change as what is needed for a "standard" living evolves with time. Because of this, the question needs to able to be challenged:

> **5:** The laborers and employers of the United States may bring a case to the courts of the United States if they surmise that Congress has incorrectly defined or calculated *Living Wage, Cost of Living, Full-time, Part-time*, average number of children, distance from county borders, or any other measure used in determining the Living Wage. Should the party bringing the case succeed, the Treasury of the United States shall be responsible for paying out the difference in either lost wages or cost of wages to the originating party.

Since Corporations are people, too, they may sue to say the definition is creating too high of a rate. If they are proven correct by the courts, they deserve restitution. On the other end, if employees are found to have lost wages because Congress has calculated poorly, then they are owed money. Since the employers did nothing wrong in that case, the government itself would owe the people. Further, since we previously made agency and department heads financially responsible for what happens under them, these heads may feel inclined to make sure Congress is using a rate that can withstand judicial review.

However, as discussed before, there will still be people who are unemployed. The federal and State/Territory governments have many forms of welfare to assist in these situations, but this has created a "hand-out" situation. Instead, we should look backwards to when these programs were created to give a "hand-up". The government did not just hand out money, they expected something in return. For eight years starting in 1935, what became known as the Work Projects Administration (WPA) did not just give money out to people; they demanded something for those wages (and the laborers desired to give something in return). Almost everyone who wanted a job could get one through the WPA, and in turn the country got bridges, roads, buildings, artistic establishments, historical sites, and more. The only reason it was disbanded was because of the depressed unemployment caused by World War II (reaching as low as 1.2%).

Much of what we consider the National Mall (much shown here in this photo from December 2019), monuments in and around it, and the streets giving access to it come from projects done during the New Deal period through organizations like the Public Works Administration (PWA), Works Progress Administration (WPA), and the Civilian Conservation Corps (CCC). The Living New Deal website quotes a newspaper of the time stating: "...the mile long park connecting the Capitol with Washington Monument and Lincoln Memorial probably would still be in an early stage of development but for the allocation of PWA funds to finish the project."

For whatever reason, no new version of the WPA has ever been created. Here, we should establish one, but we do not necessarily need it for infrastructure (although we do need it for infrastructure as so many WPA and other projects are falling apart). There is work that can be done from filing to stuffing envelopes to answering phones to data entry—there are many activities that do not require as physical an action if a person is not capable of it. At the same time, physical activities are needed, and those can be filled as well, even if it is something as straight forward as beautifying one's own local community. Even the act of being put into a furthering education situation (i.e., technical job training for new skills) would be a fair investment by the government.

In any of these situations, we extend this Act to include what we expect from welfare:

6: In the event a laborer is unable to find employment and decides to do so, the laborer may petition for the welfare of the government to provide a *Living Wage*.

6-A: The government is obligated to provide a *Living Wage* for any person that petitions and meets the criteria heretofore:

6-B: In return for a *Living Wage*, the government must require an act of labor or an advancement of education deemed necessary that is within the physical and mental capabilities of the laborer.

6-C: A laborer may only collect the *Living Wage* provided as welfare for a maximum of one (1) contiguous year. In the event of declared emergency or Act of Congress, this may be extended up to three (3) contiguous years.

6-D: A laborer may only collect the *Living Wage* provided as welfare once within a contiguous term.

6-E: At the end of collecting the *Living Wage* provided as welfare, the laborer must wait at least six (6) months before being allowed to collect the *Living Wage* provided as welfare again.

6-F: A laborer may only collect the *Living Wage* provided as welfare for a maximum of five (5) years within a lifetime.

6-G: The government may refuse to allow the *Living Wage* provided as welfare for a laborer if the laborer has refused to do assigned tasks or has fraudulently claimed completion of tasks when not done so.

7: A continuous *Living Wage* as welfare may be provided with no expiration only for a person without the physical or mental capabilities of doing any labor or will never be able to be hired by any employer for other reasons as defined by law.

7-A: In the event that a person will never be to be hired by any employer for any reason defined by law, but the person has the physical and/or mental ability to do labor, the government may assign labor to that person, though may not end welfare should that person not complete labor.

First, we have the clauses for the "able-bodied" person that says if they find themselves without work, the government is obligated to provide a full-time job with a living wage on a temporary basis. The person may take this job for up to a year at a time (or up to three years if extended because of an emergency or another Act by Congress such as during an extreme recession) and use these benefits multiple times over their lifetime. They can use it for up to 5 years in total but must wait at least 6 months between uses. The government will expect some labor or education by the person in return. Thus, if the person refuses to do the work or does a poor job, the government will not be obligated to continue providing this benefit.

Despite these limitations, there are reasons that these time confinements and expectations would have to be ignored. A person that has mental challenges, that is born with a disability, or that has a reason that regular work is impossible will need to continue to receive a Living Wage. A mentally challenged person may still be able to do some type of labor, but that labor may be limited, and the number of hours may not be full-time. Here is where flexibility is required on a case-by-case basis to understand individual people. Still, a majority of people in the system should be covered by Clause 6 and not Clause 7.

Today, there are a plethora of people in the system who have not provided labor for generations. In 2019, the Labor Force Participation Rate—the percentage of people who can work and who are working or seeking work—was 63% and has been trending downward since the 1990's and early 2000's, peaking in 2000 at 67%. While earlier figures were depressed because women were not in the workforce as much, from 1963 (59%) until the peak the number in 2000 it seemed to be trending much higher. The United States has an interest in getting more people actively involved in participating in labor in the private markets instead of not working or—worse—living on the wages of the government. Some people will always not be working for private companies because they are caregivers or have made enough money that they do not need to work. The rest should want to work, and hopefully with the right strategy in welfare and better wages available these people can be enticed to join the rest of the workforce. And the more people in the workforce, the more funds are available for commerce, completing the circle of continual economic growth.

BE OUR GUEST

Despite having a desire and an interest in getting more people working, the United States has not been successful even in the more recent good economic times. While every indicator coming in to 2019 showed an economy on the rise, the populous has not reflected this in the indicators as expected. One of the main measures that has surprised researchers is the birthrate within the United States.

As a general rule, the better off the macro economy is of a country or area, the less children are born and the later people wait to have children. In a country like Japan, this has led to a situation where the replacement population (children) is less than the aging population such that—for the first time in its history—Japan is opening its borders and actively trying to have immigration. Thus far, this immigration has been limited to manual labor and caregiver roles (especially with people 65+ representing 27% of the population in 2018 according to the World Bank, by far the largest in the world), but other job categories—even professional ones—will require a backfill of foreigners.

The United States is in much the same situation. Despite the so-called economic growth, the average person has not seen it in their own paychecks as the cost of living rises while paychecks are stagnant. According to Bill Chappell of NPR:

> The U.S. birthrate fell again in 2018, to 3,788,235 births — representing a 2% drop from 2017. It's the lowest number of births in 32 years, according to a new federal report. The numbers also sank the U.S. fertility rate to a record low.
>
> Not since 1986 has the U.S. seen so few babies born. And it's an ongoing slump: 2018 was the fourth consecutive year of birth declines, according to the provisional birthrate report from the Centers for Disease Control and Prevention.
>
> Birthrates fell for nearly all racial and age groups, with only slight gains for women in their late 30s and early 40s, the CDC says.

This is a direct result of not paying a Living Wage for decades. True, there are other factors like birth control, women delaying childbirth in order to advance their education and careers (hence why "women in their late 30s and early 40s" were actually growing in birthrate), lack of parental leave seen in most of the rest of the democratic world, delayed age to be married, and others. There are also societally beneficial figures, such a lower teen pregnancy rate (after seeing a bump from 2005 to 2008 as a result of President George W. Bush's abstinence only education instead of open, honest, and inclusive education of all potential options). But at the end of the day, the lower annual and trending lower birthrate has resulted in a "lifetime" birth expectancy of 1,728 for every 1,000 women. Current estimates are that in order to replace the population due to people dying for all reasons is around 2,100 children for every 1,000 women.

In other words, people are dying faster than they are being born. Further, there is no guarantee that getting a Living Wage will reverse this trend—or at least reverse it to a level that would make a difference—because the damage has been done. Several generations of people have grown up under poor and dropping wage conditions. It is in such a state that the "Millennial Generation" (debatable on the exact ages, but generally people that as the year 2019 would be in their late teens through mid-30's) is expected to have a lower standard of living and less earning potential than the generation that bore them, as well as the generations that preceded them (Generation X and Generation Baby Boom Echo). They are making the same wages as their contemporary generations, but their wages have less buying power.

It will take generations for people to feel comfortable with a Living Wage and adapt society to it. For a vast majority of working age people, the psychological damage has been done and it cannot be reversed. For some people, yes, a rise in economic conditions will reverse their thinking about child bearing, but one needs look no further than people who were young during the Great Depression who still hoard food, clothing, and money to this day to realize that you cannot change the psyche of an entire people with some policy changes and a better economic situation. No, the scar is forever there, and therefore we must face the facts of a required solution to fill the gap.

Thus, if you cannot get people to have more babies and/or participate in the labor force more, there is only one other solution:

Immigration.

The United States cannot continue to function, cannot maintain its economy, and cannot support its aging population without regular and systematic immigration. For those who fear immigrants taking jobs, the problem is how many jobs at all levels are going unfulfilled in 2020 because there are not enough people to fill them. Agriculture and health services are particularly hard hit, but so are technical and other professional jobs. The United States is far from "full", we are dying a death of a 1,000 small cuts (372 to be more correct, the difference between the amount of people dying and those being born).

Even if someone is vehemently against immigration, it is just plain necessary from a jobs and economic stability standpoint, which in turn yields protections for the American people. This could be viewed as a temporary need, though, as if birthrates rise and more people can be enticed to participate in the workforce, less immigration will be needed. For these people, consider immigration a temporary adhesive bandage strip that is being used to fill a gap until America has a self-replenishing workforce. At that time, laws may need to be updated.

For now, though, our Act requires immigrants to come here, and when they come here to be known and productive to us:

> **8:** All persons who are not citizens of the United States may register with the Census Bureau in order to become laborers within the United States.
>
> **8-A:** All non-citizens who desire to do labor within the United States and have been offered employment to do so may not be denied entry to the United States, so long as the immigration status of the laborer has not been revoked in the past.
>
> **8-B:** Should a non-citizen who has been an employed laborer within the United States be

removed from that employment, the non-citizen may remain in the United States for up to one (1) year in order to gain other employment. Should the non-citizen not find employment in that time, they may be removed from the United States at the discretion of the Census Bureau through the judicial court system as defined by Congress.

8-C: A non-citizen may petition the United Sates government for a *Living Wage* as welfare, but the United States government is not obligated to provide it.

8-D: A non-citizen may bring with him to the United States all persons within his shared asset unit—including but not limited to spouses and children—so long as those persons have not had their immigration status revoked in the past.

8-E: Within a shared asset unit, only one person is required to be acting as a laborer and the others may remain in the United States so long as one person within the shared asset unit continues to provide labor, even if it is not the original person who applied for entry.

8-F: Other persons within a shared asset unit may also provide labor, even if that person did not originally apply to do so upon entry to the United States.

8-G: Immigration status of the non-citizen may be revoked due to non-related criminal activity—whether that activity took place within the United States or abroad. Congress shall define under which criminal circumstances immigration status shall be revoked. All claims shall be pursued through the appropriate judicial venue.

8-H: Non-citizen immigrants employed as laborers or within the shared asset unit of that laborer may seek citizenship under relevant citizenship law as defined by Congress.

What we are talking about here is a "Guest Worker Program", much like the United States had for most of its history (and is not too far from what we have now). Among non-naturalized immigrants (those who have not become citizens), 49% are "Lawful Permanent Residents" and 9% are "Temporary

Lawful Residents". What we are talking about here, in part, is the 42% that are undocumented. To be clear, most of the foreign-born people are in the county legally and with documentation; and if we include those who have become citizens it is 73% lawful to 23% undocumented. As noted, too, among those undocumented people the vast majority—in a more than 2 to 1 ratio—are people who overstay their legal visas. We can suppose, then, of non-citizen immigrants around 13% are of the kind that came into the country without any kind of documentation—legal visa or otherwise.

As such, the first thing we are trying to do here is make sure those 13%—amounting to several hundred thousand a year—are documented. That is part of the reason why above we changed the role of the Census Bureau to track all people, all the time, through any method of entry or being born here. People come to the United States to take advantage of economic opportunities, safety and security, and the chance to enjoy freedom. If someone wants to come here and has been offered employment, then there is no reason to withhold that from them other than believing that immigrants drive down wages and take jobs from citizens.

If that is the case, then, this is all the more reason to ensure a Living Wage. If all jobs pay at least a Living Wage and employers cannot get citizens to take those jobs for whatever reason, they still need to fill those vacancies. Should someone who was born and lives outside the United States desire and/or have the skills for that position, the United States should want them for the economic prosperity of the masses. Since the immigrant would not be taking the job from a citizen and would not be depressing wages, then there is no conflict. The United States may still desire the hiring of citizens over non-citizens, but that can be done with incentive programs like tax breaks or the like. With everyone making fair wages, the only difference between citizens and non-citizens is who wants to and who has the ability for the job.

To be clear, this is not just about difficult physical labor jobs like agriculture, custodial work, and the like. The way immigration works for skilled labor in 2019 is a lottery system where a situation like the following can happen:

An immigrant has completed his bachelor's and master's degree in the United States, paying the full cost of his education. He has been offered and accepted a job at a high-skill technical firm and given a provisional allowance to extend his student visa for two years while the application for a working visa goes through. During that time, he gets married to another highly skilled medical professional who is also going through a similar process. Both are employed in high paying positions that require unique skills, and both of their employers are happy with them and give promotions and raises in kind to show so. They have no criminal records, not even a speeding ticket, and pay all the taxes expected of any laborer.

Yet, there is still a lottery to determine if they can stay. The first time through the lottery, neither of them gets permission to stay. It is totally up to chance. When the lottery happens a year later, they again do not receive their spot. As such, the company can no longer keep the non-citizen employed, even though they want to. They lay him off, and now he is without employment and only allowed to stay in the country for another couple of months. His spouse is about to get a different type of visa that will allow her and her spouse to stay, but then her spouse will not be able to work. This is not acceptable as he wants to work and has the skills to do so. He is trapped. What happens next?

This story is a very real situation and not uncommon. The United States literally throws out and makes life difficult for highly skilled and desirable immigrants, and for what reason? Because of capricious rules that are trying to limit the number of immigrants instead of focusing on the larger societal issues of why there is immigration and why these jobs go unfilled by citizens. Sure, the end goal can be to lower immigration and make sure there are more opportunities for citizens, but first citizens need to be willing to do the work and have the skills and knowledge to follow through with that desire. Those are multi-year if not generational solutions, and in the meantime highly skilled people who add to society and taxes are being tossed out, rejected for no other reason than random chance. What could be more the antithesis of the American ideal?

Thus, we allow the non-citizen immigrant to come here if there is a job for them. That person can bring their family as defined as a "shared asset unit". You will recall that a couple of chapters ago we said the government is not and should not be in the game of defining what a family is; it is up to a group of people to decide if they are presenting and sharing assets between them. Realistically this will mostly end up with standard monogamous (at least on paper) marriages with the chance of some children. Perhaps a family also includes an older parent that is being taken care of—all pretty standard fare and what you would see in many American and worldwide households. And if people in that family decide they want to work, too, and have something to contribute, why should we stop them? Why should only one person in a family be allowed to work and the rest are to sit on the sidelines no matter their skillset? Again, this is all being done with capricious rules and the lotteries of different systems (there are any number of distinct immigration for work methods within the United States that are in contradiction to each other).

From time-to-time, a person will lose their job for whatever reason. But they have built a life in the United States and believe they can still do more here. Should we not give them the opportunity? If someone cannot find work in a year, or no one in the household has another job or cannot find work in a year, then we should consider removing them. Still, this is just a "consideration" and not a guarantee. Perhaps economic conditions at the time would make the Census Bureau want to extend that timeline? Or perhaps this has happened before to the person and they keep getting fired so the Census Bureau has run out of patience. Whatever the case, the Census Bureau would have to make it in a court of law to have a person removed, giving them every opportunity to equal rights. Of course, this returns to the earlier chapters where we extended the Constitution to all people and no longer circumvent our own laws just because someone was not born here. Everyone is treated equally because we believe our Constitution and laws have a higher meaning for all humanity and not just for the precious few that were born with those rights and privileges.

There may still be other types of visas, like for education or asylum, that will require their existing laws to be reviewed with these changes. No matter the path for an immigrant to get here, the goal of the United States should be either that the person eventually leaves and returns to whence they came (temporary workers) or get permanently recruited to stay (citizenship). That is why this law makes specific reference to the citizenship path as defined by Congress. This is still under Congress' control and discretion and is something that Congress should discuss. Sadly, that discussion will not happen under the current oligopoly.

Despite best intentions, not all people are going to end up being law-abiding residents who contribute to society. In those situations, the Census Bureau may pursue revoking a person's immigration status—again, through the court system. It cannot be stressed enough how critical it is that the Executive Branch have no judiciary capabilities and those cases must always be pursued through the court system. A key goal of this entire journey has been to fully separate the three branches of government from each other and make sure each has co-equal power over the other two. As such, the government may say someone should no longer be here because of their crimes (whether here or abroad), but it is up to the courts to decide if that is the best solution. Should someone who gets a jaywalking ticket be kicked out of the country? They have broken the law, no doubt, but are they the same as a trafficker of illegal good or a murderer? Applying the law carte blanche with no consideration is the approach in 2020, but does it make any sense?

While there is a general focus on the illegal activities of the individual, when it comes to the employment of undocumented people the illegality is—in truth—with the employer. Yet, there are raids on facilities that see the undocumented immigrants deported while the company and the people that did the hiring getting little to no punishment (even sometimes starting a hiring spree immediately after a raid). Because of that, this Act needs to focus the blame back where it belongs:

9: An employer may not hire a non-citizen who has not registered with the Census Bureau.

9-A: Should an employer be found to be using the labor of non-citizen who is not registered with the Census Bureau, the employer shall be charged a penalty equal to ten (10) times the amount paid to the laborer for the entire lifetime of the laborer's employment. Further, if the employer was not paying the *Living Wage* and all expected taxes and benefits, the employer shall be charged the penalties as noted in prior clauses of this Act in addition to this penalty.

9-B: Other laborers of the employer shall not be protected from prosecution based on the employer being a distinct person.

9-C: The persons at an employer who are found by the courts to knowingly hire a non-citizen who was not registered with the Census Bureau—or gave direction to such persons to the same hiring type; or negligently did not investigate when claims were made of the same within the employer—shall be sentenced to no less than one (1) year and no more than five (5) years in confinement and pay a fine equal to their own gross compensation for the period the non-citizen was employed.

9-D: The non-citizen discovered to be working for an employer without proper registration with the Census Bureau shall be registered with the Census Bureau and may remain in the country for up to one (1) year in order to gain other employment. Should the non-citizen not find employment in that time, they may be removed from the United States at the discretion of the Census Bureau through the judicial court system as defined by Congress.

Let us be clear: the people who should be held responsible when undocumented immigrants work in the United States are the companies that hire them. More than that, though, the people who work for the company from the hiring managers to the CEO should not be protected just because the company is its own legal entity; instead, both should pay a significant fine. For the companies, it is a penalty of 10 times whatever they paid the undocumented immigrant plus any difference if they were not paying the Living Wage and any other taxes and benefits they were avoiding. Today, there are set levels of fees that are capped such that by an equation a company can decide the risk is worth it. If the company has multiple billions in revenue, what is even a several million-dollar fine to them? Especially if they saved millions of dollars for illegally hiring people, it could be considered just the risk of doing business and they could still end up ahead even after paying a fine. This way, a penalty will not just make a noticeable dent, it will scale and slide to the largess of the offense.

Then, the penalties can extend outward to the actual people that allowed this illegal action to happen. These people can expect at least a year and up to five years behind bars, plus pay a fine of their own equal to everything they earned at the job (at the gross level, not the net) while the undocumented immigrants were hired illegally. You cannot scare off immigrants from wanting to just work because there is no downside to them, but you can scare the people and companies that hire them with direct and very real consequences.

Meanwhile, those immigrants that just wanted to work could have simply been unaware of the law or unsure of the processes for registering. They can be given the benefit of the doubt because their only crime was trying to work and provide for themselves and their families. So long as they are willing to continue to want to work and can find someone to hire them, why can they not stay? All we care about here is that they are documented and that we know where they are, and that they pay all expected taxes and are not a cost to the system. So long as we have that information, and they are not involved with illegal activities that cause harm to others, then there should be no issue.

Hopefully, just having an easy process to register and a Living Wage for all will be enough to dissuade companies and people from avoiding the appropriate channels. But on the occasion that that does fail, then there must be severe repercussions.

OVER THERE, OVER THERE, OVER THERE

Of course, having a Living Wage is wonderful so long as there are jobs to be fulfilled. Some would argue, though, that if we extended wages like this to all people that the United States would not be competitive in the global market; that all jobs would move overseas where it is significantly cheaper. While this is largely hyperbole, there is a note of truth that plenty of jobs would move, especially in manufacturing and service support jobs. If a product or service is less expensive to make in another country and what is lost (customer service, direct oversight, a certain percentage of customers) is considered a worthwhile cost, then many companies will do exactly that.

The question becomes, as such, how do we level the playing field? The immediate idea is tariffs and the like, but those costs are just passed directly on to consumers and do almost nothing to protect American jobs (and usually cost unrelated American jobs when the impacted nations retaliate). More than that, though, they do not extend the protections American workers have to other countries. If we believe in a Living Wage, should not the people in other countries also enjoy such a benefit? We also have organizations like the Occupational Safety and Health Administration (OSHA), the Mine Safety and Health Administration (MSHA), the Office of Labor-Management Standards (OLMS), the Equal Employment Opportunity Commission (EEOC), the Women's Bureau (WB), and others that could be placed underneath the Department of Commerce and Labor (specifically under a Labor Protections rollup) that exist to ensure the safety and wellbeing of American workers. If a company can just skip town, not only can they abuse a lack of a Living Wage, but they can abuse the lack of workers' protections that Americans have literally died for. As such, the humane answer that also protects American jobs is to make sure our principles are extend to the rest of the world.

10: All products and services imported into the United States shall meet the standards heretofore within:

10-A: All products and services developed outside of the United States shall meet the requirements of the *Living Wage* as defined by this Act.

10-B: Should the Living Wage for an area be below the lowest Living Wage in the United States, the lowest *Living Wage* in the United States shall be required to be paid to the Laborer.

10-C: All employers outside of the United States must meet all safety, regulatory, certification, environmental, and any similar standard that is to be met by the domestic counterpart.

10-D: All employers outside of the United States must submit their facilities to the same level of inspection as their domestic counterpart, and these inspectors shall be the same as the ones in the United States. The employers outside of the United States shall pay the fee schedule for these inspections as defined by the relevant agencies and Congress.

10-E: Failure to submit to all inspections and meet expected standards of the domestic counterpart shall result in the product or service being banned from import and use within the United States.

10-F: Failure to pay the expected *Living Wage* shall result in a tariff equal to the difference from the wage paid to the expected *Living Wage*. The tariff collected shall be distributed back to the laborers such that they would have made the expected *Living Wage*.

10-G: Should the employer outside of the United States attempt to circumvent the rules in this Act or fail to implement corrective actions after a first violation, the employer may be banned from importing into the United States for up to ten (10) years.

What this last part of our Act is saying is that we require a factory in China or Haiti to meet the same standards that we expect in the United States proper. Employers in these foreign locations will pay the United States government for the privilege to have their sites inspected with the same rigorous expectations of their American counterparts. They will at minimum meet every single standard we set for safety, the environment, wages, working conditions, et al. If they do not want to do that, they will have their products banned from the United States.

At the end of the day, there will be absolutely no advantage to using a foreign source except if costs can be lower because they are closer to the source. For instance, many of the rare earth elements (which are not actually rare, but are "moderately abundant" according to the United States Geological Survey [USGS]) are mostly mined in China to the tune of China controlling around 90% of the collection of these elements. Now, even though these elements can be mined anywhere on Earth to the likely same distribution anywhere, China already has the mines and has the relatively beneficial situation to extract them. As such, a company involved with the extraction and use of these elements may be better off being closer to China—at least until the United States can create its own domestic market.

Meanwhile, enforcing our own regulations around the world can help workers everywhere whose own governments do not care as much for human rights. Instead of Americans exploiting people the world over for our benefit, we can use our tools to raise their standard and quality of life, perhaps making them customers of American goods in the future. The United States is the largest single consumer market in the world—larger than the European Union (EU) and China despite their vastly larger populations. The people of the United States simply buy and consume more. That is a power we can push around the world: if you want access to the largest market in the world, you need to treat your people better and play by our rules. If you do not, you will not have access to this market, and you will have nothing.

Instead of bullying the world with our military might, we can use our economic weight to better the lives of others while at the same time not just protect American jobs, but make the American lifestyle better and more secure. Economic prosperity is not a zero-sum game where there is a finite amount of it to around, resulting in some people having and some people not having in order to support those that do have. Wealth is something we have made up as humans in order to help society function—and frankly it works quite well. How many oranges is a tablet worth? That is not a question we have to answer because we have money, but money has no worth beyond itself. What use is it if we cannot extend the American dream to the rest of the world, while also propping ourselves up?

We would never need another trade negotiation again; our rules would be very clear and altruistic. Is it idealism? Of course, but that is what regular inspection and verification are for. Setting up such a system is not an end unto itself—it is just a framework in order to have the executive authority to continue to enforce it. That is the point of the Executive Branch in the first place. Here, though, we are extending that executive authority to the rest of the world as an antecedent to access the United States market. The message is clear: if you want to do business with America, you will treat your people at least as well as we treat our own. This is not do as I say, not as I do. No, it comes to the theory of "lead by example" and be the best that we purport to be.

WHEN ALL ELSE...

Sometimes, though, no matter how hard we try things do not go right. We can offer a Living Wage, we can have welfare, we can have every safety protection, we can protect families, we can enforce freedom, we can make sure every person has a say in government, we can provide every tool for a person to succeed. Despite all of that, not everyone will succeed to their hopes and dreams—or to our expectations of them. The truth is that people fail... and that is okay.

Under the direction of President Lyndon B. Johnson, starting in 1964 began the unofficial "War on Poverty". Johnson noted that the poverty rate in America remained stubbornly high, at around 19%. While the poverty rate had been dropping since 1959 and sped up under programs by Johnson's predecessor John Kennedy, Johnson wanted to see a quicker turnaround. And with laws passed by Congress, he got it such that by 1973 the poverty rate was just 11.1%. Unfortunately, that is where things stalled out.

Since 1973, the poverty rate has hung between 11% and 15% (though it is not evenly distributed among ethnic, age, and gender groups). Other measures show similar stalling points. The unemployment rate in the middle of 2019 during what is considered a strong economic epoch by almost all factors (except real wages, but we have covered that above) was around 3.7% and since the end of World War II has hardly gotten below this figure. In most good times, it hovers between 4% to 6%, but there are no resources you can throw at it besides a massive devastating war that are going to bring it down much more (as previously mentioned, the figure got as low as 1.2% during World War II).

This is what we call diminishing returns. In the simplest terms, perhaps we can invest $1 million and get 10,000 people out of poverty. If we invest another $1 million, though, only 5,000 people get pulled out of poverty. The next gets 2,500, the one after that 1,250, and so on and so forth until $1 million cannot even pull one person out of poverty. At some point, the investment is not worth it, and it is a sad truth to accept.

The most giving of us want to see everyone raised up to prosperity—or at least our definition of it. Despite these good intentions, it is not only not realistic due to diminishing returns, but also insulting to those we are trying to "help". Not everyone wants to take advantage of the programs we have, not everyone wants even the helping hand-up, and not everyone prescribes to our definitions of how they should live. This should be their right, but we are not giving it to them. Simply, we need to ensure that people have the right to do what they will and not have the preference of others forced on them, no matter if the intentions are noble. In other words, people need the right to fail.

> **By Amendment to the Constitution of the United States, Article 9, Section 1, Clause 6 shall be added:**
>
> The enumeration in the Constitution of certain responsibilities of the governments and rights retained by the people shall not guarantee that all people shall succeed at all endeavors or meet the expectations of normality and stability created by the people heretofore within. The government of the United States, the government of the States and Territories within, and all local governments within those may make all reasonable concessions for these attainments by a person, but a person through their own choice or through the will of circumstances must still be allowed to not reach these attainments. No person shall be forced into accepting the assistance of the government or others; and no government shall extend resources beyond reason to bring assistance to all people.

That does not mean it is not worth trying, but it does mean it is not worth throwing everything at every problem. We need to prioritize and live within our taxed means. In the end, not only do we have finite resources, but some statistics will not change at all no matter how much we throw at them. No amount of money in the world is going to stop some people from not being in poverty or succumbing to drug abuse or committing crimes that harm others. It is the same as no amount of money in the world will stop all terrorist attacks or create a completely safe world or ensure nothing bad will happen to anyone.

These are the risks we take to be free. The downside of freedom is that sometimes we fail, and that must be more than accepted; it has to be a right. Sure, we could keep everyone alive, safe, healthy, and employed. What would the cost of that be, though? And I am not talking just about the monetary cost (although that would be massive as well), but the cost of personal freedom to pursue your desires? In order to have that, everyone would have to be controlled to the point of there being no freedom at all. Freedom is the life-threatening dive we must accept it to be, and that does mean that sometimes we lose our life for it.

On March 23, 1775, Delegate Patrick Henry (you recall him from the introduction, he "smelt a rat") told a crowd at St. John's Church in Richmond, Virginia:

> Is life so dear, or peace so sweet, as to be purchased at the price of chains and slavery? ... I know not what course others may take; but as for me, give me liberty or give me death!

His words changed the world and inspired a mass transformation in the American consciousness. While in 1775 the colonies were trying to reconcile with the crown to end the war, in 1776 they were declaring independence. Henry is one of the most influential people in creating the American spirit and fighting for its soul during and after the creation of the Constitution. While the final draft of the Constitution was making the rounds, Henry gave a speech on June 5, 1788—just 16 days before New Hampshire became the 9th State to sign off on the Constitution to fully ratify it, followed just 4 days later by his own State of Virginia. In the speech, Henry warned of what we the people were losing by signing on to the Constitution because of what it lacked:

> Here is a revolution as radical as that which separated us from Great Britain. It is radical in this transition; our rights and privileges are endangered, and the sovereignty of the states will be relinquished: And cannot we plainly see that this is actually the case? The rights of conscience, trial by jury, liberty of the press, all your immunities and franchises, all pretensions to human rights and privileges, are rendered insecure, if not lost, by this change....
>
> You are not to inquire how your trade may be increased, nor how you are to become a great and powerful people, but how your liberties can be secured; for liberty ought to be the direct end of your Government....
>
> Is it necessary for your liberty that you should abandon those great rights by the adoption of this system? Is the relinquishment of the trial by jury and the liberty of the press necessary for your liberty? Will the abandonment of your most sacred rights tend to the security of your liberty? Liberty, the greatest of all earthly blessings—give us that precious jewel, and you may take [everything] else....

There are many on the other side, who possibly may have been persuaded of the necessity of these measures, which I conceive to be dangerous to your liberty. Guard with jealous attention the public liberty. Suspect [everyone] who approaches that jewel....

Revolutions like this have happened in almost every country in Europe: Similar examples are to be found in ancient Greece and ancient Rome: Instances of the people losing their liberty by their carelessness and the ambition of a few....

There are sufficient guards placed against sedition and licentiousness: For when power is given to this Government to suppress these, or, for any other purpose, the language it assumes is clear, express, and unequivocal; but when this Constitution speaks of privileges, there is an ambiguity, Sir, a fatal ambiguity;—an ambiguity which is very astonishing....

In some parts of the plan before you, the great rights of freemen are endangered, in other parts absolutely taken away. How does your trial by jury stand? In civil cases gone—not sufficiently secured in criminal—this best privilege is gone: But we are told that we need not fear; because those in power, being our Representatives, will not abuse the power we put in their hands: I am not well versed in history, but I will submit to your recollection, whether liberty has been destroyed most often by the licentiousness of the people, or by the tyranny of rulers? I imagine, sir, you will find the balance on the side of tyranny....

You read of a riot act in a country which is called one of the freest in the world, where a few neighbors cannot assemble without the risk of being shot by a hired soldiery, the engines of despotism. We may see such an act in America. A standing army we shall have also, to execute the execrable commands of tyranny: And how are you to punish them? Will you order them to be punished? Who shall obey these orders? ...

Nor can we ever expect to get this government amended, since I have already [shown], that a very small minority may prevent it; and that small

> minority interested in the continuance of the oppression: Will the oppressor let go the oppressed? Was there even an instance? ...
>
> Shall we imitate the example of those nations who have gone from a simple to a splendid Government? Are those nations more worthy of our imitation? What can make an adequate satisfaction to them for the loss they have suffered in attaining such a Government for the loss of their liberty? ...
>
> When the American spirit was in its youth, the language of America was different: Liberty, Sir, was then the primary object. We are descended from a people whose Government was founded on liberty....

Patrick Henry's words did have an impact and led to the Bill of Rights, but as we have shown that is not enough. Liberty must always be protected; it is the highest ideal unto itself. And part of protecting liberty is placing it above all other objectives and aspirations. When Henry said to give him liberty or give him death, the part he missed was that sometimes liberty amounts to death, or something akin it. But that is the right of the people to pursue in their own way! A tyrant need not be a despot but can be one who wishes for the betterment of the people in the way he thinks it should be done. People should not be terrorized into prosperity, but allowed to pursue it in their own way, or not at all.

This is the ultimate liberty.

BEFORE WE GO...

During this entire journey, you may have been questioning what right we may have to attack the Constitution in this way; that we can so viciously go after everything that has been written and say there are vast failures. Well, I am hardly the first person to consider the faults of the Constitution and realize that it has become terribly outdated and outmoded. In actuality, this level of skepticism goes all the way back to the writing of the Constitution, as we covered at the onset. Yet there is even more from those who were involved in its creation. Less than two years after the Constitution was presented and six months after the United States started, Thomas Jefferson wrote:

> *Letter from Thomas Jefferson to James Madison*
> *September 6, 1789*
>
> [I]t may be proved that no society can make a perpetual constitution, or even a perpetual law. The earth belongs always to the living generation. They may manage it then, and what proceeds from it, as they please, during their usufruct. They are masters too of their own persons, and consequently may govern them as they please. But persons and property make the sum of the objects of government. The constitution and the laws of their predecessors extinguished then in their natural course with those who gave them being. This could preserve that being till it ceased to be itself, and no longer. Every constitution then, and every law, naturally expires at the end of 19 years. If it be enforced longer, it is an act of force, and not of right.—It may be said that the succeeding generation exercising in fact the power of repeal, this leaves them as free as if the constitution or law has been expressly limited to 19 years only.

Here, a Founding Father has made it clear: The Constitution should have limits on time because having the dead dictate to the living what the laws are is an "act of force", not an act of freedom.

Jefferson may have been a bit extreme in this particular opinion, but there are plenty of countries that rewrite their Constitutions on a regular basis. However, this author would argue that is unnecessary as the basis of the Constitution may be reused repeatedly and provide a continuity. What matters more is not expirations but having the ability to revisit it. Previously, we created an Amendment to make sure a law is reviewed every 20 years. Just because it has been 20 years, though, does not mean the law is invalid—it just means that we need to agree to it again.

With the Constitution, though, we do not want that level of flexibility because of the chaos that can ensue. Having a contiguous government through the centuries with the same framework is an efficient means of creating stability and the peaceful transfer of power—an idea that Jefferson himself help create when he defeated incumbent President John Adams after Adams had served just one term. But it is also why we have spent so much time making the Constitution general and high level as opposed to the specifics of law. Laws are difficult and convoluted; the Constitution is simple and uncomplicated.

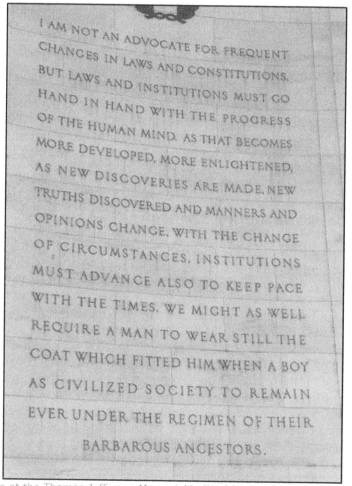

Etched in stone at the Thomas Jefferson Memorial in Washington, D.C. is this quote pictured in December 2019. Though the words are available to all, few have accepted that we should not be shackled to the Constitution and laws of the past. Instead, we continue to live under the tyranny of our forebears, even if they did not want us to.

All that matters is if we are able to recognize where there are issues and disagreements and have rational conversations about how to resolve them.

HEALTHCARE AND GUNS... OR WHERE I LOSE EVERYONE

The issues facing America are not in their own siloed boxes—everything is intertwined into a web of overlapping points. Previously, we covered how the living wage, welfare, immigration, imports, and the census are all one subject that needs to be addressed in a single line of thought. However, that is not the only such situation. Much like those particular items, though, people have become so entrenched in their singular views of "right" and "wrong" that they do not feel the need to come together on rational solutions that would serve all sides (Saying "both" would imply there are two sides to all issues, which plays into the oligopoly of the Republican and Democratic Parties. There are multiple views to all issues, not just two extremes.).

Any conflict management or negotiations book will tell you this simple idea: compromise is where everyone loses a little; collaboration is where everyone wins by creating something new together. Because each end of the political spectrum has been told they must "compromise", they know that means they would lose something, and they do not want to lose anything. With enough time and the right alignment of representatives, any niche political extremism can get what it wants. Why even talk when you can just wait to get everything you want?

One such area to explore is why the National Rifle Association (NRA) should support universal healthcare.

The NRA is well known for its far-reaching impact on politics with its vast support for its interpretation of the 2nd Amendment: the right to bear arms. The idea that the 2nd Amendment means that individuals have that right (as opposed to groups or militias, as stated in the Amendment) only became law in 2008 with the Supreme Court decision of the District of Columbia vs. Heller. The idea was further solidified in 2010's McDonald vs. City of Chicago which used the 14th Amendment to justify extending the 2nd Amendment to States and their municipalities. The results of these cases were the consequence of the NRA's decades long propaganda campaign to change the conversation and understanding of the 2nd Amendment. And as a special note, this is fine because the NRA has the right to campaign for whatever they want because the 1st Amendment guarantees that they have the "right of the people [to] peaceably to assemble, and to petition the Government for a redress of grievances." Basically, the NRA is a civil rights organization—it is just that they are for the civil rights of equal access to firearms as opposed to not being discriminated for a job based on perceived race.

Therefore, the NRA's interpretation of the 2nd Amendment is the law of the land. In order to change it, updates would need to be made to the Constitution, but that is not what we will do here. Whether the 2nd Amendment exists or does not is not a discerning factor into if the country can function on an operational level or if people can actually discuss the issues that arise from this interpretation. Contrarily, this interpretation brings up the perfect opportunity to have a dialogue and make some seemingly strange bedfellows.

One of the key arguments of the NRA is that guns do not kill people, people kill people. If that is the case, then what is the solution to the people problem? Why are people killing people?

If, as some have suggested, mental illness is to blame for gun violence, what can be done about it? After all, suicide is the 10th largest number of non-natural killer of Americans according to the Center for Dieses Control (CDC), and over half of those suicides come from firearms. As a point, those suicides-by-firearm deaths account for nearly 2/3rds of all gun-related deaths in America. It would seem there is a case to be made that mental health has a lot to do with gun-related deaths.

Given the potential correlation, the solution would be to provide better mental healthcare. But mental healthcare is very expensive in the United States and is most often not covered by health insurance—or is covered for only a few sessions. Also, mental healthcare is not tied into overall health, so a person must seek it out themselves instead of being part of their regular check-ins with medical professionals. As such, it seems that laws would be needed to make mental healthcare a part of regular healthcare, and for that healthcare to be supplemented by the government. In other words, the NRA should support universal healthcare as a right and mental care as a part of overall healthcare. This would prove their case that the issue is not gun-related but is health related. Instead of supporting candidates that do not believe in healthcare, the NRA should be working with those that do.

However, more liberal minded people who support a universal healthcare that includes mental health might not be too keen on supporting the NRA. But there are parables that can help bridge these two sides to a common understanding. While suicides are the 10th highest killer of Americans and more than half of those are from guns, "accidents" are the 3rd highest killer and around a third of those are from automobiles. One could argue that a car is an "arm" as, after all, a car is nothing but a 2-ton death machine on wheels. Among children and teenagers specifically, motor vehicles are the number one killer followed by firearms and then cancer. Over the past two decades, death by motor vehicles have been trending downward while deaths by guns have started to trend back up.

One of the reasons that motor vehicles deaths have been decreasing is because of increased safety standards and licensing. Even though a car is a death machine (and not just from accidents, but also when used in terrorist attacks and homicides), there is an understanding that a vehicle is not a right. One must be licensed, have that license renewed, be tested, and be willing to hand over the vehicle to inspection on a regular basis. Each car is individually numbered in several different ways so it can be traced back to an owner and a source. On top of all that, the government and the industry are working to continually make them safer and make sure they are not in the hands of those who have been a danger in the past.

Why does not a similar standard apply to all weapons? The Constitution just says the right to bear "arms", but it does not say what an "arm" is. A kitchen knife is an "arm" that can easily kill people; rocks have killed millions of people throughout history; mosquitos are the most dangerous animal to humans and can be weaponized; the list goes on and on. Why is "arm" equated to "gun" when it should be equated to any weapon? Is a sonic device not a weapon? Is not a biological agent? We control those, so why not guns?

Just because you have a right to bear arms, does not mean you have a right to handle and use all arms. There is no need to regulate rocks and kitchen knives, but there is a need to regulate sonic weapons and biological agents. Gun are the same, and even within the category of guns is a vast range of possibilities. Although I have a license to drive a car, I cannot get behind the wheel of a big rig without taking a specialty test to prove my ability and competence to use the vehicle. Cannot guns fall under the same categorization? Perhaps there are some guns that require a very basic level of licensing and then if you want a semi-automatic weapon you will need specialty training and licensing. Meanwhile, perhaps acid-tipped armor piercing bullets are beyond the needs of the average gamesman.

And this is where the NRA and liberal minds could theoretically find common ground. The NRA is a massive proponent of education and training, so why not take that a step further? Gun clubs associated with the NRA can, by law, become centers to train, test, license, and be the gatekeepers. Since the NRA takes safety, security, and knowledgeable firearm ownership seriously, they should be on board with a program to extend that to the next level.

The NRA and proponents of universal healthcare should be getting together as a team and coming to Congress with these proposals. With that level of clout, both would win their key agenda items (continual access to firearms | care for all people) with giving very little up (limitations on who and types of gun ownership | guns being available at all). It is better than a compromise; it is a collaboration that could shape a freer and healthier America.

Right now, these two groups refuse to talk to each other because they believe they are on different "sides", but that could not be further from the truth. They are on the same side: the side of what they feel is best for America. It is only politics that says because they lean conservative or liberal on one issue that they must align that way for all issues and all parties. That is how the oligopoly of the Republican and Democratic parties stay in power and do mostly nothing. If they ignored the political party and came together in this way, a solution would be forthcoming from the political side from both major parties because they cannot afford not to listen to a combined super-constituent.

To be clear, this entire section has not been an official recommendation or a necessary change that is needed. Instead, it is an example of how breaking down the walls of partisanship can lead to actual discussions. Having an open mind instead of a closed perspective and forcing disparate parties together has been the premise of this entire document. The question we have been answering is how we can end the walls between us and start the conversations we are not been having.

CONVERSATIONS WE ARE NOT HAVING

And what are these conversations we are not having? There are many policies and bills that have gone nowhere because of the intransigence of Congress and the President, but there are just as many issues and ideas that hardly ever come up for a deep dive. Due to how the government is set up, most of these never see the light of day or just get lost in committee.

As an overview, a significant discussion we have not had is why we support an apartheid dictatorship like Saudi Arabia. Just because Saudi Arabia is friendly to us and provides us with one resource we desire does not mean we should not only be allies, but actively protect them. Saudi Arabia has systematic discrimination against women, homosexuals, and any non-Muslim (and more specifically, even within different streams of Islam). The country is run by a royal family that has murdered members of the press and anyone they consider dissidents, even on foreign soil. Most of the terrorists involved in 9/11 came from Saudi Arabia, but they never paid any price for it like Afghanistan or Iraq—the latter of which was not involved.

The question becomes a much larger one: What are American values? If we say it is democracy, equal rights, open commerce, and a government that does not attack its people, Saudi Arabia does not check any of those boxes. Why, then, do we consider places outside our country to be areas where our values do not apply? And let us be clear: "values" are not in the Constitution; these are decision we have to make as a society.

All we have done, especially in the legislative section, has been to make sure we can not only start to ask these questions but to take action on the answers. What else have we not been able to ensue due to the continued stonewalling of the current government setup? Ahead are some examples that may be of special interest.

TIME TO MAKE THE DONUTS

While capitalism is not enshrined into the Constitution, "commerce" is, and

Congress has an obligation to protect and regulate it. Some of the furthest reaching legislation has come from anti-trust acts such as the Sherman (1890), Clayton (1914), Robinson-Patman (1936), and Celler-Kefauver (1950). All have been built on the prior acts on the theme of trying to limit monopolistic power in the marketplace. Most of this has focused on horizontal integration—that is to say, when companies take over all competitors in the same market. This is what led the United States government to break up AT&T into a long-distance company and 7 independent regional phone companies. It is also why when the NFL and AFL merged, there were multi-decade conditions on not having games on Saturday so as not to compete with college football.

Generally, though, anti-trust laws have not been used to stop or breakup companies involved in vertical integration. With vertical integration, a company may own the upstream or downstream parts of how their products are used. For instance, if a steel making company buys an iron mine, they will have lower costs of production. This has led to major conglomerates like CVS Health that own a pharmacy, a pharmacy benefits manager (a company that wholesale provides drugs), a walk-in clinic that can prescribe drugs, and are in the process of buying an insurance company. Or the aforementioned AT&T owns a cable company, a large number of cable channels, the networks to run cell phones and internet access, streaming apps, and content creation. The government sued to stop many of these integrations, but they did not have a basis because vertical integration is not anti-competitive based on current law.

But should it be? Or a much larger question: should the producers of goods and content be separated from the deliverers of goods and content. Think of companies like AT&T, Netflix, and Disney that all create their own content, have a channel to put their content on, and own the cable company and/or streaming service to distribute the channel/content (or both). Or as another example, Apple has complete control of the App Store and there is no other way to load applications on to an iPhone except through what Apple controls, of which they take a 30% cut. In the same theme, Facebook is trying to become a video service instead of using other video hosting, basically owning the content created on its platform.

All of these are examples where the company that creates the good also controls the marketplace for that good. A simpler one to think about might be Amazon that owns the marketplace to sell on, but also makes products that it sells in the marketplace and places above other similar products. If an independent seller on Amazon has a successful product, Amazon may start selling the product directly and undercut them or promote their own market page above others despite price—or they could go one step further and just make their own version of the product and drop the other product entirely. Here, Amazon makes the good, distributes the good, and sells the good all in its own marketplace.

Should this be allowed? Or should we create anti-trust law that says the creators of goods must be separate from the distributors of goods? In the case of Disney above, that would mean that they could not create a new app to distribute their shows on but would have to sell those shows to others. Yet, that does not necessarily create a competitive marketplace. If Disney signs an exclusivity agreement with Netflix (such as the one they did in the past), then those Disney programs are only available on that service and any other service from Amazon or others is not in direct competition because the product is totally different. So, should these anti-trust laws say that exclusivity contracts are anti-competitive and cannot be enforced? That would mean Disney would have its products available and Netflix, Amazon, and an independent Hulu (no longer a part of Disney) could all have the same product for the same market price. The competition between Netflix, Amazon, Hulu, and all other players, then, would be on price and service, not on exclusive content. That is real choice, not artificial when you need to go to several places to get the products desired.

This is one aspect of corporate governance that must be considered, but it is not the only one. For instance, should corporations have size limits? This could be on number of employees, percentage of the market, volume produced, or many other measures or combinations of measures. The idea here is a question of this: is there a public interest in making sure a corporation is not so large as to cause major issues in the economy or have clout beyond the size of any single "person"?

Even the fact that corporations are "persons" is an area that has never been fully addressed, so, too, is the structure of corporations. Most corporations exist as an entity that is owned by shareholders and run by a board in their stead that hires management that in turn hires and oversees employees; but what about the other way around? Why cannot more corporations be employee co-ops that hire management to run their operations and employee review boards decide whether to keep management or not. Or, at the very least, getting employee representation on the boards that run companies. In Germany, by law almost half of the representatives on a corporate board must be employee representatives. Should not all stakeholders have a say in how a company is run: owners, employees, and the communities impacted by the business?

Meanwhile, corporations—even public ones—are very secretive. Board members have had to sue their own companies to get information and check for malfeasance while the public at large may have no idea what is happening entirely. A company like Oracle can tell investors for years that their cloud business is the most important factor and then one day decide to bury the numbers in another division. Investors keep asking, but Oracle refuses to do further breakouts and sometimes says it cannot. How much should the investors in companies and the public at large be able to see into a company's finances? How much access should be allowed?

Some companies also have other questionable responsibilities. The Communications Decency Act of 1996 has a particular note in Section 230:

> No provider or user of an interactive computer service shall be treated as the publisher or speaker of any information provided by another information content provider.

What this basically means is that an internet service like Facebook or Twitter cannot be held liable for what is said on their platform. As the platform provider, they are not responsible for content except in cases where that content breaks the law. And even then, all they are required to do is remove the offending content. Therefore, if someone posts a racist and hate-filled tirade or streams a murder on YouTube, Alphabet (parent company of YouTube and Google) cannot be held complicit with the content. But should they?

By 2020, it has been well more than 20 years since the Communications Decency Act was written, so by our Amendments this law would have been up for review years ago. The technology and industry changed drastically in that time, yet because of this law we cannot force Facebook or Google or Twitter to moderate content on their platform. In order to do so, this law would have to change, and we would need new laws to describe what companies are responsible for. Within this vein, what would the punishments even be for misinformation (whether willful or via neglect)?

The question also becomes one of "if and why" we treat different types of companies in divergent ways. If a non-profit created a social media platform that became as popular as Facebook, should it be regulated in the same way? Facebook, Google, Twitter, and the rest are using their platforms to make money and thus have funds that can be attacked. But a non-profit would not have the same mission and therefore would have different capabilities. Still, this brings up a much larger question with non-profits in general and why they are treated differently at all.

At many non-profits, corporate officers make salaries that are in line with their for-profit equivalents, and sometimes then some. A football coach at a Big 10 University can make millions of dollars while a social worker might not be able to make rent. In a city like Providence, RI, non-profits own around 42% of taxable property yet do not pay taxes on any of them because of their status (some make a payment in lieu of taxes that has been negotiated by the city). Perhaps, though, exceptions for non-profits should be eliminated and all corporations should be treated the same? Then, being non-profit would just be a goal of the organization, not a designated status that requires special laws.

I'M NOT EVEN SUPPOSED TO BE HERE TODAY

Corporate structure is not the only question that needs to be answered when it comes to commerce; so are areas of workers' rights and designations.

Take for instance a "Full-Time" worker. What is it? Some people say that is a person who works 40 hours a week, but is that 40 hours of productive time, or 40 hours including breaks? Are breaks paid or not, if so for how long? The Affordable Care Act basically makes anyone who works 30 hours in a week a full-time employee, but that is only in relation to offering health insurance. There are no specific guarantees for how Paid Time Off (PTO) accrues or if it accrues at all, at least not on a Federal level (many States have such laws). This is similar to sick time and paid/unpaid family leave. Does that time come from the same bucket or are there other buckets? What happens when you have time left over in any of those buckets at the end of the year? The answers are disparate from State to State, if there are answers at all, and often from company to company within those States.

But what about other employee rights, such as the idea that an employee should not always be on call. Many salaried employees are expected to be on their phones at all hours and answer e-mails or do an assignment instantly when they come in at any time of day. This is usually not explicit in the job details but becomes expected behavior in the culture. Should laws be put into place that stops this type of behavior so as not to burn workers out and abuse their time? Someone who is salaried but working 70-90 hours a week may be making less than minimum wage (and even a Living Wage), depending upon the circumstances. And even if they are not, do they not deserve to have separation from work? Many European countries have such laws and force technology to be put in place to enforce it. For instance, in Germany a call from your manager is instantly zapped after your working hours, and all e-mails are blocked from coming in until you arrive the next day. How involved should the government be in the daily lives of workers?

Back to the subject of full-time employees, studies have shown work weeks closer to 30-32 hours are more productive and better for employees. When efficiency started increasing with technology in the early 20th century, most industrialists thought the work week and hours worked was going to continue to decline, yet it stalled out. Why is that? Should there be limits on what is expected in productivity of a single worker? If a company needs more hours filled, does that mean more employees are full time and what are the costs of that?

At the same time, what are the guidelines for even deciding if someone should be an employee at all, as opposed to an independent contractor? The IRS has a definition, but it is difficult to enforce, quite nebulous, and they often lose in court when trying to impose it. Should not there be laws to determine this? And if there are laws, what would the penalties be for trying to circumvent the law? Earlier, we discussed the penalties of a company trying to hire multiple part-time people to fill what would be singular full-time positions in order to avoid taxes and other fees, but how does that stretch out to non-employees? What if someone wants to be a contractor for those benefits but the company treats them in a way that makes them seem like an employee? How do we respond?

If companies are concerned with how they can afford these employees, should not there also be questions on executive pay? And not just the pay by itself, but also consider total compensation including non-cash related items like stock. Should there be limits on executive pay? For instance, should a law exist that the highest paid person in the company not make more than 20 times what the lowest paid full-time employee makes? Thus, if the lowest paid person makes $32,000 a year, the highest paid person would at most make $640,000 in total compensation. Therefore, if the highest paid person wants a raise, they will need to give a raise first to the lowest paid person. Bringing the lowest paid person to $35,000 a year will give the highest paid person $700,000 a year. Thus, the whole process creates an incentive to keep raising the pay at the bottom. If those people were making $50,000 a year, then the highest paid person (most likely the CEO) could then be making $1,000,000. Is this a good ratio, or should it be higher or lower? Is the answer different depending upon the type of organization (i.e., sole proprietorship vs. public corporation)? What is the right way of creating incentive to pay employees more than just a Living Wage?

But what should happen when corporations run afoul of the law? There are penalties nowadays, but most are a joke. In July 2019, the Federal Trade Commission announced a $5 billion fine for Facebook, the largest in history. But what is $5 billion to Facebook? In 2018, they had nearly $56 billion in revenue and $22 billion in net income. At the end of 2018, Facebook was sitting on $41 billion in cash that it was doing next to nothing with, so $5 billion will not impact them much at all, especially over the long term. How can penalties really make a difference so that companies change behavior? What types of laws, regulations, and fines can we pass? What if we said a violation will result in losing an entire year of top line revenue? So instead of a $5 billion fine, Facebook would have had a $56 billion fine (or more, depending upon how many years the violation took place in).

Previously, we have discussed holding government officers accountable for their actions, but what about corporate officers? Because of the laws around forming corporations and a corporation being a "person", people who work for companies are often protected from litigation. Perhaps we should look into lowering and getting rid of many of the protections that those who work for companies have? What types of laws can we pass that make people responsible, people that could be fined or imprisoned for their actions?

LIFE AFTER PEOPLE

When it comes to commerce, it goes far beyond just the companies and the people employed by them. There is also a greater question of resource management. As a thought process, in the year 2020 the United States will become a net exporter of oil and natural gas—that it, the country will export more than it imports. This begs to the question of why the United States is exporting at all if there is more need (which there seems to be because it is importing)? Should there be a law that says resources need to be used first in the U.S.A. and then—and only then—if there is an excess that it can be exported. This is the same with other commodities like corn or soybeans. Some produce is just a consequence of the time of year and what is available, but other products are not so. Should there be a policy that makes sure the United States is independent first and then involved with the rest of the world second? It must be noted this would be the least profitable method as it could create gluts at home and drive prices down. Thus, while this would be beneficial to consumers (think of gasoline at 50 cents a gallon), it might make corporate profits weak, which in turn might lower investment.

Natural resources are not the only concern when it comes to usage. There is plenty of property in American that is not being used. This takes many forms, such as a piece of land that was purchased but never developed or is being sat on for speculation; a house that was purchased but abandoned; a large downtown building that is sitting vacant because the developer is looking for handouts from the State; or an apartment in a major city that is only used for a few weeks of the year while the owner has a primary residence elsewhere. These are all examples that lead to the question of the use of Eminent Domain and for what reasons the government may want to take a property back. Can abandoned or undeveloped property just be taken back due to the lack of action on the property in order to give it use or beautify an area? How long does a city have to wait for a building to be developed? Or can they lose patience and decide to take on the project themselves or force the sale to a third party that is interested? Could New York City alleviate a housing shortage by saying someone can only own or rent a property if they are there for at least 6 months and 1 day a year?

Other resources also need to be discussed. For instance, while there is much discussion around the type of healthcare system we have, there is not as detailed discussion around how hospitals charge. The discussions keep focusing in on insurance and surprise bills, but the question also needs to be answered is why does a single anti-inflammatory pill cost $100 in a hospital and 3 cents over the counter? Should the government get involved in the hospital purchasing and billing process to control costs and keep things reasonable? How can it be regulated and what are the enforcement mechanisms going to be?

It is a similar question with education. The United States far outspends most of the rest of the world when it comes to per capita spending per student. Yet countries like South Korea that spend 2/3rd of what the United States does have far better outcomes to the point where their students are on average 2.5 years ahead of their American counterparts. Money is not the issue, effective use of money in the correct environment is. Education has been typically treated like a local issue, but should it be a national one? And if so, what does education look like? It is subject based, or competency based? How long does the school year go? How are students and teachers evaluated? How much of our resources should be dedicated to improving education, and where does education stop? What does education even mean? Is an apprenticeship in a trade education? Why are we college-focused in messaging to a group of people who do not know what they may want to do with their lives and are more likely than not to never finish? What do we even want to get out of education?

THE IRON THRONE

Considering interactions with foreign countries, it is not just comparisons in systems and how we deal with trade, but larger questions of investment. Currently in the year 2020, 30 million acres of U.S. farmland is owned by a foreign government or company (or a shell company acting on behalf of a government). Ownership extends into many other areas of real estate, including those empty buildings and pieces of land as discussed in the prior section. And more than all of that, of the $16.1 trillion in public debt the United States has, 30% to 40% of it (depending on the definition) is in foreign hands. To be even more specific, China holds $1.18 trillion and Japan holds $1.03 trillion. We have previously discussed the dangers of being in debt in general and a policy move to make sure the United States does not take on anymore, but when we need to take on debt should there be limits on what one foreign government owns? Should we allow foreign government to own the debt of the United States at all since it is a major security risk? And what about those other resource like farmland and buildings? Countries like Australia have passed laws that no longer allow foreign ownership; if you want to own the land you have to live there and use it. Should the United States have something similar?

This and many of the prior discussion have brought up the idea of government intervention and regulation. However, the United States government goes far beyond that and is an active investor. Many of those federal agencies we alluded to before act the same way any private brokerage firm would. Should the government be involved at all in investments and markets beyond being a regulatory agency? How much should the government be wrapped up in being a money-making operation?

The Constitution has not explicitly given the Federal Government the ability to create these corporations, nor has it explicitly denied them. Overall, the question is a grey one and up for debate, if only debates were happening. What is not up for debate, though, is that Congress is mandated by Article 1, Section 8, Clause 8 to:

> To promote the Progress of Science and useful Arts, by securing for limited Times to Authors and Inventors the exclusive Right to their respective Writings and Discoveries;

We know these today as copyright, patent, and trademark laws. Yet, these laws have been abused to the point where entire companies exist only to collect patents and charge others for their use—or sue them in court for seemingly using them. More often than not companies settle with these "patent trolls" because (once again) it is cheaper than going through the court process. Per the previous judicial section, we hope to alleviate this conundrum, but it does not solve the base issue of how these so-called protections work today. There is a large discussion to be had on how to fulfil the obligations of the Constitution while still allowing free creation and commerce, and a time when a discovery becomes useful for all. After all, someday even this book should be free, but with current laws it will not be public domain until 70 years after the publication date. This author will be a very, very old man then, so do I need that level of protection? Or is that protection just for my publisher and distributors (and perhaps my estate)?

This goes into further rabbit holes of how specialized some of these protections should even be. For instance, patents nowadays can be as specific as the method of alphabetically sorting content in an online feed—seemingly an idea that multiple people or groups would come to using similar if not the same methods. If everyone is using the same programming language, it is probable that the solution to many technical problems will literally be exactly the same. There are also some odd items to consider, such as the person who takes a picture is the copyright holder, not the person who is in the pictures or pays for the pictures. Thus, when you pay a photographer to take your pictures at your wedding, you still do not own the copyright on those pictures and the photographer cannot transfer that copyright to you even if she wanted to. There are countless examples of similar items and many things that we are not prepared to deal with, like custom DNA strands.

Much of how these laws become so convoluted is because of lobbying. Copyright law used to be much shorter, but Disney successfully lobbied to get extensions to the law… twice! This was mostly to protect their highly profitable mascot Mickey Mouse, but Mickey's first starring role in Steamboat Willie will enter the public domain in 2024. Is it possible that between now and then Disney will use its clout to again change the law and protect its assets? Because of Disney's actions the first time, nothing entered the Public Domain for 20 years until 2019. Now they can examine how it is working out with others while also preparing for their offensive in the years to come.

But Disney is hardly alone in its lobbying efforts. Everything from cigarettes to liquor to weapons to drugs to clothing to technology to anything else employ lobbyists of all types. These people wine and dine members of Congress and often craft the bills that Congresspeople present to the floor. Even more so, they are incredibly successful because large numbers of them are former members of Congress or worked within the government at some function that gave them close affiliation to the administration. What type of firewalls are needed to stop lobbyists from having this level of influence, or should such barriers exist at all? Are not all groups "persons" and does not every person have the right to petition the government? Or on the other end, do members of the government who get jobs with lobbyists violate their oaths of office, putting personal gain above their former job? How long does the oath of office apply for? If we limit the amount of time anyone works in government to 25 years, should we be more concerned that they will be tempted to make deals that will set them up afterwards? Are there laws we can pass that are both Constitutional and reasonable to stop the abuse of current or former placement in government?

Of course, future abuse of the system is only a symptom of many other misuses that happen while in power. For instance, the President can use Air Force One and all the taxpayer-funded resources of the United States government to travel to and take part in a campaign rally—whether for himself or for others. Should there be limits on how government protections are used in political activities? Is that a violation of 1st Amendment rights? How do we draw a line between what is a meeting on policy versus what is a political activity? How do we enforce such a difference, especially when enforcement would have to come from the Executive Branch itself?

The government does many things behind closed doors that most people are not aware of. Previously, we discussed the idea of the Federal Government sending a "receipt" to all taxpayers to explain how their funds are being used. But if we take a similar concept for transparency to the rest of the government, what type of data needs to be made available? How is it to be accessed? Could the government set up a SharePoint portal where everyone in the country has read access to every file the government produces? What about e-mails or recordings of phone calls or videos of meetings—what needs to be made available and how? What type of data needs to be protected from public view? Or are there data that in its raw form are so irrelevant that it is harmful and misleading to be released until it has been synthesized?

On the subject of data, how should it even be used? Do we need an Amendment to the Constitution that forces Congress to use empirical data to make decisions, especially in relation to funding? If we return to the CDC's list of the largest killers of Americans, number one on the list is Heart Disease, such that there is a 1 in 5 chance over a lifetime of a person dying from heart disease or a complication from it. As we move down the list, Cancer will kill 1 in 7, hospital infections 1 in 38, the flu 1 in 63, and anti-bacterial resistant diseases 1 in 197.

Terrorism accounts for around 300 deaths per year, which certainly sounds like a lot, but not in the context of other killers. Sun and Heat Exposure kills around the same number of people and has a 1 in 13,729 chance of killing you. Much more than that is Excessive Cold at 620 deaths and a 1 in 6,045 chance. Returning to the top of the list, Heart Disease is responsible for over 650,000 deaths per year. So, what does the government spend on an annual basis on these killers? Anti-Terrorism-related spending amounts to around $150 billion and Heart Disease-related spending amounts to around $2 billion. In other words, the government spends 75 times more on something that is the equivalent of the sun killing you as to something that has a 20% chance of killing you—especially when Heart Disease could be extensively limited by behavioral modifications (i.e., it is largely preventable, perhaps even with the societal taxes noted before).

To be fair, there may be more terrorist attacks if there was no funding to stop it. It is the same fallacy as those who say vaccines are unnecessary because the diseases are not prevalent. The reason the diseases are not prevalent is because of the vaccinations, in the same way terrorism is not as wide-spread due to intelligence work. However, that does not justify an imbalanced spending portfolio. Let us assume that the number of people who would have died by terrorism without the funding would be 10 times higher, so 3,000 people a year or a net of 2,700 additional deaths. That means that $150 billion is being spent to save 2,700 people which amounts to $56 million per person. Do you think it would cost $56 million to save one person from heart disease, cancer, or the flu?

If that sounds cold-hearted to the person who is killed, that is what it means to use empirical statistical analysis to make decisions. This can extend to many other areas, such as engendered species. Pandas may be cute, but they are extremely costly to try to save, especially because they are notoriously fickle with mating partners. Much uglier animals may be easier to save and a smaller investment. Is the point to save the species we like, or the species that have the greatest impact on the environment and other ones that get us the most bang for our buck? Should we let the Panda die to save the blob fish (and you know you want to save it with a name like that)?

Is this cichla (pictured at the National Zoo in Washington, D.C. in January 2020) worthy of our resources? Or is it not cute enough to garner funding? What if it was a lot cheaper to protect it instead of a koala?

The question then, is, what is the balance between our emotional responses to issues versus the basic economics and returns on our investments? Should we have such requirements, or should we continue to allow Congress to make decisions based upon how we the constituents feel at any moment? And where did we get our feelings from? What about those lobbyists and the groups behind them that set up "educational" campaigns and organizations to create a public outrage? How do we create a fair answer to governing?

FEDERALIZE AND PRIVATIZE

Along the same lines of questioning how the government should use resources and how we may want to limit them, are there ways we may want to expand the Federal Government?

For instance, every State has its own program for car licenses, registration, and emissions standards and testing. Why would something like this differ from State to State? Driving is the same across the country both in skills and in expectations of what vehicles do; so why does a person who moves between States have to get their licenses, registrations, and emissions tests redone? The cost of moving goes up significantly just because of the time and resources needed to do this. At the same time, we previously discussed having singular methods of tracking people through a continual census. If that is the case, should not a driver's license or similar ID be a federal requirement instead of a State one?

There are many costs that seem to be handled locally, but it is a question of efficiency. Why does every town have its own police department or fire department? Would it not make more sense to have a singular police or fire department that works for the Federal Government? Then, the Federal Government could place the resources where they are needed most. If a town is down a firefighter and needs additional help, the person from the next town over could be brought in on a temporary basis without having to go through a hiring process. We should have a common approach to firefighting and policing, right? Thus, should we not have a common control? The same could be said about education, as previously discussed.

But then, if the government took over certain functions, are there areas they should back out of? Back to the car example, one of the frustrating parts of the experience is the Department of Motor Vehicles (DMV) or the equivalent in each State. Some States, though, have privatized the DMV or outsourced some functions to other trusted companies, such as AAA. Why not extend this further? Instead of the government running offices that interact with the public, maybe they should outsource to private companies? And specifically, not a contract with one company, otherwise it would just be the government again. Instead, what if something like the DMV was a franchise the government could award (for a fee), and then multiple companies could compete on better, more efficient service to get customers? Now, the cost of running the government would be lower, more private jobs would be created, and the people would be served in a way they want—otherwise they will take their business elsewhere.

At the end of the day, very few people should work for the Federal Government. Cannot the goal be to limit the Federal Government to elected officials and appointed judges and other management positions as needed to function? Why cannot the government be more of an oversight committee instead of a corporation that runs things (poorly)?

Of course, a great deal of these functions that people deal with every day are more likely to be State functions today, and it becomes a question of States' Rights if they are federalized. But should not we want to eliminate economic differences between States? Should not States be on equal footing and, more so, not in competition with each other? When States compete, they give massive tax breaks to corporations to move there or build multi-billion-dollar stadiums for billionaires that should be paying for it themselves. How can we stop States from fighting each other so there is no advantage of one area over another other than the natural resources and the people who happen to live there?

DAYGLOW ORANGE VEST

Pondering how the government spends money, one of the key areas would seem to be regulation. Afterall, we have discussed how the Federal Government's role largely comes around protecting people. And we have many Agencies for just such tasks—such as the Food and Drug Administration (FDA). The FDA is charged with making sure the drugs that reach the market and the food we eat is safe; except that there are a great number of omissions. You may see on supplements and herbal remedies notes that say something to effect of "Claims have not been verified by the FDA". Should they be? Should all products that we ingest go through an FDA process? If so, how much would that cost? The FDA is stretched beyond its limits right now with its $3.9 billion budget. How much more is needed to review all the food and drugs we use, and what does that even mean? Does every batch need to go through the FDA? More so, if we say that people are responsible for everything they put in their body, should the FDA be more of a warning agency than a regulatory agency? Can the FDA just say that an item should not be ingested due to certain stated reasons, but if a person does it anyway then the consequences fall squarely on him?

The FDA is hardly the only Agency of the Federal Government that would need much deeper and further review. There are areas all over, but there are also concepts. As an example, we have a Bureau of Prisons, but what do we want out of prisons? There is often stories out in the media of "Prison Reform", but what does "Prison Reform" entail? By far, the United States locks the largest percentage of its population with rates double and triple countries like Russia, Turkey, and China that are known to incarcerate political prisoners. Why are incarcerations going up while crime rates are going down? And is prison and jail the right answer for so many crimes? If someone has a drug problem, should not rehabilitation be the sentence? Countries like Norway have limits on sentences, even for a crime like terrorism-related mass murder. Should the United States follow such models? If the goal of incarceration is to reform and pay a debt to society, what other ways can debt be paid and reform be made? Is education, community service, house arrest, and other measures a better investment? How do we get a return on enforcing the law?

Prison is not the only area where we must consider security. In 2019, the United States had 1,600 nuclear weapons deployed and at the ready of a total of 6,185 available. Are that many nuclear weapons needed to be on hand at any time? Forget the idea of matching enemies in an arms race; how many nuclear weapons are needed for deterrence? Research has shown this number to be around 100, and after that—if all were used—society would be destroyed anyway. Additionally, if they were all set off around the same time it would cause a nuclear winter and further destroy society. Using the largest nuclear bombs ever made, only 16,000 would be needed to obliterate the entire surface of the Earth (not that that would be necessary since the aforementioned nuclear winter would have already occurred). Why should we have so many at hand if it is completely unnecessary for deterrence and the damage caused when used would cost most of humanity? If others have more, does is matter if only 100 between the two is enough to end society?

This also brings a bigger question of the readiness the military is kept at. As previously discussed, the military exacts upwards of $1 trillion in spending per year, representing between a quarter and sixth of the United States budget depending upon the definition of the budget. That all said, the United States is not officially at war and has not been since World War II. If the United States is not at war, why is the military being funded so heavily? How much readiness is needed "just in case"? By all accounts, the United States Armed Forces are technologically and at staff levels far beyond any peer, and this is all in a time of peace (despite the un-Constitutional deployment of troops around the world). How much should the military be funded in times of peace, especially in relation to real threats like Heart Disease? Should military spending be capped in times of peace at a certain percentage of the budget (say 10%)?

Pictured here is the Vietnam Women's Memorial in Washington, D.C. in December 2019. The entire Vietnam War (which was not a declared war) cost around $1 trillion in 2020 dollar. However, that was over many years and the United States now spends that same amount every single year.

In order to have any of these discussions, the American people will need to be engaged in the political process. While we have talked about mandatory ballots, automatic registration, and other measures to make people vote, how do we get people more involved? How do we get people interested with what is happening in the government and want to take an active role in shaping it? And this is not talking about clicking a checkbox on a petition on Facebook, but actively participating in the everyday running and occurrences of the government at all levels.

One way the populous may have an increased involvement is if the news media presents items in a compelling way. While "if it bleeds, it leads" seems harsh, the media companies of today are well aware of what gets them views and—in turn—advertising dollars. The total story does not matter, only making sure articles are followed despite the impact. While the Flu is killing tens of thousands of people, the news will focus on items that kill 3 people a year as an epidemic. Therefore, you would assume this is about making the news more vetted.

But no, that is not the point. Whichever way the news is presented is the right of the press and those who consume it. The idea of the news needing to be objective is not in the Constitution and is not being suggested here. Actually, when the Bill of Rights was written, the idea of an objective newspaper would have been seen as peculiar; most papers existed to push a political agenda. Having a perspective is not an issue—it is a right.

That said, though, should a news source be able to call itself "fair and balanced" when it is not? Is that not the definition of false advertising? If perspective is not an issue, then what is? The problem here is that news is not labeled with its perspective. Therefore, the question is this: should the news (and other similar postings, because what is "news" anyway?) be forced to label its perspective and bias? Again, having a perspective and bias is not a negative thing, necessarily. All we are talking about here is if someone presenting data must also present the perspective from which this data is being brought?

This extends further out than just the news. Scientific studies are released all the time, but funding sources are often obfuscated. If a study that says eating 6 grams of chocolate every day is good for you, should it not be up front and center at the top of the study saying it was sponsored by a research firm that was in turn contracted by Hershey? Basically, should warning labels be put on any released material that shows potential bias and perspective? And if so, who decides what that bias is and who enforces it? What if someone has a header that says this is a liberal view, but some people read the content as a conservative view? How do you reconcile this, and what are the penalties for not doing this correctly? Is being forced to label your perspective a form of suppression of speech?

Finally, more important than all those questions, is this one:

Why are we not using the metric system?

Laugh all you want and see Presidential contenders go down in flames for suggesting it, but the United States is out of step with the entire human race on this one. Aside from the U.S.A., only Liberia (the same people still using the Grand Jury system) and Myanmar do not use the metric system as the official measuring tool for everything. And frankly, having a system that is base 10 makes far more sense than one based on differing amounts depending upon what is being calculated (16 ounces to the pound, 12 inches to the foot, 180 degrees from freezing water at sea level on Earth to boiling it). Mistakes have been made, money lost, and people hurt or killed due a lack of consistency on measurements and the conversions between them.

Even worse is that United States has spent money on making the conversion and then reversed course to spend the money again to undo the work done... more than once. The important part here is that even seemingly insignificant and low controversy items are not being discussed. If we cannot even talk about whether we should move to the metric system without a major political fallout, then how can we talk about anything?

As stated at the start of our journey, this document is not about getting the answers to all our problems—it is about having the ability to have those conversations.

THE FUTURE REFUSED TO CHANGE

Making all these Amendments to the Constitution and imagining a hopeful future full of deep discussions has been a great joy and a wonderful ride. But the sad truth is that all of it has almost no chance of coming to pass.

There are only two ways to make an Amendment to the Constitution. The first is to have Congress pass an Amendment through 2/3rd of each House and then send it to the State Legislatures and have it pass with 3/4th agreeing. As has been seen, this has happened a total of 27 times. In this day and age there is hardly anything that the majority of Congress can agree on, nonetheless a super majority, nonetheless a super-duper majority! Also, let us be very real: everything in this document has been about reining in the Government, forcing them to focus on their job, eliminating all of the benefits they get from being in the government, and holding them accountable with real consequences. Who in Congress is going to want to pass all of that? This is asking them to sacrifice everything they have campaigned for: themselves.

So, what about the other route? Well, that would have 2/3rd of the States calling for a Constitutional Convention, like the one that wrote the Constitution in the first place (completely ignoring that they were only there to amend the

Articles of Confederation and did not even have a right to create a whole new government). The main difference is that this time 3/4th of the Delegates would have to agree to the changes. In the entire 230 years of these United States, there have been approximately zero of these Conventions, and with good reason. The issue is the same one we started out with at the very beginning of this adventure when talking about the Constitutional Convention: who determines who the delegates are? Who even determines how many delegates there are? How are they selected? What can they do with or without the approval of State legislatures and the people? What happens if the States do not like what their or other delegates have agreed to?

Since this is the Constitution we are talking about, anything could be written in there and it could make the document overburdensome and way too explicit instead of the more general policies we have put in place. The special interest groups could make "compromises" to get a specific item in there for agreement elsewhere and create permanent and dangerous changes that might not be able to be undone. Or this could create a precedent for calling a Constitutional Convention on a regular basis, reshaping the Constitution with the ebbs and flows of each successive administration, making it more like law instead of the guiding principles of governmental structure.

No, that is why the very first Amendment we should pass, and perhaps one even Congress can agree to, is an Amendment (or two) to change the Amendment process.

By Amendment to the Constitution of the United States, Article 5, Section 1, Clause 1 shall read:

The Congress, whenever two thirds of both Houses shall deem it necessary, shall propose Amendments to this Constitution, or, on the Application of the Legislatures ~~of two thirds~~ of the several States, shall ~~call a Convention for proposing Amendments~~ **pass a proposed Amendment directly and send to the other States**, which, in either Case, shall be valid to all Intents and Purposes, as Part of this Constitution, when ratified by the Legislatures of three fourths of the several States~~, or by Conventions in three fourths thereof, as the one or the other Mode of Ratification may be proposed by the Congress~~; **Or when the people of the United States receive the signature of five percent of the entire population for a proposed Amendment, that Amendment must be put on the next Federal ballot for President or Congress, and if ratified by three fourths of the people shall be valid for all Intents and Purposes, as Part of this Constitution;** Provided that no Amendment which may be made prior to the Year One thousand eight hundred and eight shall in any Manner affect the first and fourth Clauses in the Ninth Section of the first Article; and that no State, without its Consent, shall be deprived of its equal Suffrage in the Senate.

By Amendment to the Constitution of the United States, Article 5, Section 1, Clause 2 shall be added:

All Amendments to the Constitution shall replace existing Clauses or be placed within a specified Article, Section, and Clause—whether adding a Clause to an existing Article and Section or creating a new one.

First, we have stripped out the Constitutional Convention idea in its entirety. Instead, we have replaced it with a mechanism whereby an Amendment does not need to start in Congress. Instead, it could be started by a State passing a proposed Amendment of its own and then passing that Amendment off directly to the other States, thus completely bypassing Congress and giving States back a power over the Federal Government that they are sorely lacking. Additionally, it would still follow the same path where once 3/4th of the States must agree to the Amendment, then it would become part of the Constitution. This is a highly likely path and would probably lead to something like a "Constitutional Convention". A State is unlikely to pass something that would be added to the Constitution without first consulting with other States and working on what would also be passed by other Legislatures. Thus, it is probable that State Legislatures would work together for these purposes before getting underway with creating the proposed Amendment for one State alone to pass.

In January of 2019, 30 State legislatures had both chambers controlled by Republicans, 18 by Democrats, 1 was split, and Nebraska only has one chamber that is considered non-partisan (although in truth it is majority Republican, so we will include it there). Even with 31 of 50 States, Republican led State legislatures could not force an Amendment through having only 62% of the necessary 75%. While the Republican Party has done an astounding job of focusing on taking control of State governments by hook or by crook (in 2010, these number were almost completely reversed with 15 Republican, 27 Democrat, and 8 split), it still has not been enough to give them this level of control. Meanwhile, the Democrats have become wise to these tactics and have put resources behind reversing the trends, though they will also not be able to create a 3/4th majority in the current climate. Most likely, if something is going to have to change, the Parties are going to have to work together.

Yet, they would still most likely not want to implement the changes that will break their Parties' oligopoly on the political discourse. Even the 3/4th rule for States creates indiscriminate power to the least populous States to block any Amendment. Representing just 14.4 million people (4% of the population), the bottom 13 States could potentially determine if an Amendment passes (however unlikely that Rhode Island and Vermont would team up with the Dakotas). That is where the final element comes into play: you! The individuals of the United States do not currently have much of a say in the Government and their responsibility stops once they cast a vote. A change in the Amendment process would irrevocably give the public a direct vote over the heads of the Federal and State governments. One would only need to gather the signatures of 5% of the entire population of the United States.

There were approximately 329 million people in the United States at the beginning of 2019. Having 5% of them would equate to 16.5 million. This is a sizeable number, for sure, and it lies somewhere between the entire populations of Pennsylvania and New York or would be almost the entire populations of the 19 least populous States and Territories combined. Despite that, it is a reasonable goal and one that can change as the population shifts over time. A coordinated grassroots campaign can get these numbers as, after all, third party and independent candidates received 5.7% of the vote in the 2016 Presidential election alone. Petitions on whitehouse.gov reach their

100,000 minimum threshold often in hours, so imagine how many signatures they could receive if they needed more than that (the White House only responds to petitions that receive 100,000 signatures in 30 days or less, and even then they often ignore or push aside the requests).

Once 5% of the people have said they want an Amendment, then the question can go to the rest of the population in the next Federal election. If 75% of the people vote for it, an Amendment is added! It is a very high threshold, but that is intentionally so as the Constitution should not be so easily changed. Of course, this author would prefer that each and every Amendment in here be passed as-is, but there is bound to be disagreement if not on content at least on language. There is more work to do be done, but you and I deserve that opportunity to decide how our government should function.

With all of that, we can finally say:

We the People of the United

States, in Order to continue to reform and build a more perfect Union, expand Justice, protect domestic Tranquility for all, share a common defense equally, ensure the general Welfare no matter one's origins and beliefs, and maintain the Boons of Liberty for ourselves and our Posterity, do ordain further Amendments to this Constitution of the United States of America.

APPENDIX: NEW AND IMPROVED CONSTITUTION

For reference, below lays out in its entirety the New and Improved Constitution of the United States, with the old and convoluted Constitution as a side-by-side comparison. While almost all the changes have been covered previously, there are a couple of small updates—mostly combining Amendments into the base document—that were not covered in depth.

PREAMBLE

We the People of the United States,

in Order to form a more perfect Union, establish Justice, insure domestic Tranquility, provide for the common defence, promote the general Welfare, and secure the Blessings of Liberty to ourselves and our Posterity, do ordain and establish this Constitution for the United States of America.

ARTICLE 1 – LEGISLATIVE

SECTION 1

Original Text	Modified Text
All legislative Powers herein granted shall be vested in a Congress of the United States, which shall consist of a Senate and House of Representatives.	No change

Original Text	Modified Text
1: The House of Representatives shall be composed of Members chosen every second Year by the People of the several States, and the Electors in each State shall have the Qualifications requisite for Electors of the most numerous Branch of the State Legislature.	**1:** The House of Representatives shall be composed of Members chosen every fourth Year on the even years opposite elections for President and Vice President by the People of the several States and Territories. Political Parties shall create Lists of one hundred persons in order of preference to be considered for Membership. The Government of the United States and the Governments of the States and Territories shall provide no support to Political Parties for determining their Lists and the Political Parties are solely responsible for determining the method of developing their Lists. Nor shall the Government of the United States nor the Governments of the States and Territories provide any other type of support or resources for internal Political Party decisions. The people of the United States and its Territories shall vote for the Political Parties directly. There shall be no criteria for a Political Party to appear on the ballots save producing the List of candidates, though the List must be limited to those people who meet the criteria for the House of Representatives as written in the Constitution.

Original Text	Modified Text
2: No Person shall be a Representative who shall not have attained to the Age of twenty five Years, and been seven Years a Citizen of the United States, and who shall not, when elected, be an Inhabitant of that State in which he shall be chosen.	**2:** No Person shall be a Representative who shall not have attained to the Age of voting maturity as defined by the Constitution and Congress and been seven Years a Citizen of the United States.

Original Text	Modified Text
3: ~~Representatives and direct Taxes shall be apportioned among the several States which may be included within this Union, according to their respective Numbers, which shall be determined by adding to the whole Number of free Persons, including those bound to Service for a Term of Years, and excluding Indians not taxed, three fifths of all other Persons.~~ The actual Enumeration shall be made within three Years after the first Meeting of the Congress of the United States, and within every subsequent Term of ten Years, in such Manner as they shall by Law direct. The Number of Representatives shall not exceed one for every thirty Thousand, but each State shall have at Least one Representative; and until such enumeration shall be made, the State of New Hampshire shall be entitled to chuse three, Massachusetts eight, Rhode-Island and Providence Plantations one, Connecticut five, New-York six, New Jersey four, Pennsylvania eight, Delaware one, Maryland six, Virginia ten, North Carolina five, South Carolina five, and Georgia three.	**3:** The number of Members of the House of Representatives shall be no less than one hundred. The Members shall be determined by taking the number of votes for a Political Party and dividing among total votes to get a proportional vote. Those attaining at least one percent of the vote shall receive a Seat and shall receive an additional Seat for each percentage point above that. Partial percentages shall always be rounded up to the next highest full number. With the number of Seats by each Party set, the Members shall be filled by the Lists provided by the Political Parties.
Also, Amendment 14, Clause 2 Representatives shall be apportioned among the several States according to their respective numbers, counting the whole number of persons in each State, excluding Indians not taxed. But when the right to vote at any election for the choice of electors for President and Vice President of the United States, Representatives in Congress, the Executive and Judicial officers of a State, or the members of	

Original Text	Modified Text
the Legislature thereof, is denied to any of the ~~male~~ inhabitants of such State~~, being twenty-one years of age~~, and citizens of the United States, or in any way abridged, except for participation in rebellion, or other crime, the basis of representation therein shall be reduced in the proportion which the number of such ~~male~~ citizens shall bear to the whole number of ~~male~~ citizens ~~twenty-one years of age~~ in such State.	

Original Text	Modified Text
4: When vacancies happen in the Representation from any State, the Executive Authority thereof shall issue Writs of Election to fill such Vacancies.	**4:** When vacancies happen in the Representation the Parties elected shall fill those vacancies from the next eligible and available names on their Lists.

Original Text	Modified Text
5: The House of Representatives shall chuse their Speaker and other Officers; and shall have the sole Power of Impeachment.	**5:** No Change

Original Text	Modified Text
1: The Senate of the United States shall be composed of two Senators from each State, ~~chosen by the Legislature thereof,~~ for six Years; and each Senator shall have one Vote. **Also, Amendment 17, Clause 1** The Senate of the United States shall be composed of two Senators from each State, elected by the people thereof, for six years; and each Senator shall have one vote. The electors in each State shall have the qualifications requisite for electors of the most numerous branch of the State legislatures.	**1:** The Senate of the United States shall be composed of at least two Senators from each State and Territory with permanent population, elected by the people thereof, for four Years on the even years opposite elections for President and Vice President; and each Senator shall have one Vote. The total number of Senators received by each State and Territory shall be one Seat for each State and zero Seats for each Territory; plus a proportional distribution of one hundred Seats based upon the total population of the States and Territories; plus a proportional distribution of one hundred Seats based upon the total land area of the States and Territories; such that each State shall have no less than three Senators and each Territory shall have no less than two Senators. The legal body of each State and Territory shall determine the method by which Senators are elected.

Original Text	Modified Text
2: Immediately after they shall be assembled in Consequence of the first Election, they shall be divided as equally as may be into three Classes. The Seats of the Senators of the first Class shall be vacated at the Expiration of the second Year, of the second Class at the Expiration of the fourth Year, and of the third Class at the Expiration of the sixth Year, so that one third may be chosen every second Year; ~~and if Vacancies happen by Resignation, or otherwise, during the Recess of the Legislature of any State, the Executive thereof may make temporary Appointments until the next Meeting of the Legislature, which shall then fill such Vacancies.~~ --- **Also, Amendment 17, Clause 2** When vacancies happen in the representation of any State in the Senate, the executive authority of such State shall issue writs of election to fill such vacancies: Provided, That the legislature of any State may empower the executive thereof to make temporary appointments until the people fill the vacancies by election as the legislature may direct.	**2:** When vacancies happen in the representation of any State or Territory in the Senate, the executive authority of such State or Territory shall issue writs of election to fill such vacancies: Provided, that the legislature of any State may empower the executive thereof to make temporary appointments until the people fill the vacancies by the method chosen by the State or Territory.

Original Text	Modified Text
3: No Person shall be a Senator who shall not have attained to the Age of thirty Years, and been nine Years a Citizen of the United States, and who shall not, when elected, be an Inhabitant of that State for which he shall be chosen.	**3:** No Person shall be a Senator who shall not have attained to the Age of voting maturity as defined by the Constitution and Congress, and been nine Years a Citizen of the United States, and who shall be a citizen of the State or Territory chosen during the election and throughout service to the Senate.

Original Text	Modified Text
4: The Vice President of the United States shall be President of the Senate, but shall have no Vote, unless they be equally divided.	**4:** The Vice President of the United States shall be President of the Senate, but shall have no Vote.

Original Text	Modified Text
5: The Senate shall chuse their other Officers, and also a President pro tempore, in the Absence of the Vice President, or when he shall exercise the Office of President of the United States.	**5:** No Change

Original Text	Modified Text
6: The Senate shall have the sole Power to try all Impeachments. When sitting for that Purpose, they shall be on Oath or Affirmation. When the President of the United States is tried, the Chief Justice shall preside: And no Person shall be convicted without the Concurrence of two thirds of the Members present.	**6:** No Change

Original Text	Modified Text
7: Judgment in Cases of impeachment shall not extend further than to removal from Office, and disqualification to hold and enjoy any Office of honor, Trust or Profit under the United States: but the Party convicted shall nevertheless be liable and subject to Indictment, Trial, Judgment and Punishment, according to Law.	**7:** No Change

Original Text	Modified Text
1: The Times, Places and Manner of holding Elections for Senators and Representatives, shall be prescribed in each State by the Legislature thereof; but the Congress may at any time by Law make or alter such Regulations, except as to the Places of chusing Senators.	**1:** The Times, Places and Manner of holding Elections for Senators and Representatives, shall be prescribed by Congress and the Day on which the people of the United States shall give their Votes; which Day shall be the same throughout the United States.

Original Text	Modified Text
2: The Congress shall assemble at least once in every Year, and such Meeting shall be on the first Monday in December, unless they shall by Law appoint a different Day. **Also, Amendment 20, Clause 2** The Congress shall assemble at least once in every year, and such meeting shall begin at noon on the 3d day of January, unless they shall by law appoint a different day.	**2:** The Congress shall assemble regularly once sworn into office, and such meetings shall begin on the 3d day of January, unless they shall by law appoint a different day.

Original Text	Modified Text
N/A	**3:** Each chamber of Congress shall set a regular schedule for itself with specific days and hours in which its members shall meet. Once set, these days and times shall not be moved, cancelled, or extended unless an emergency is declared by the President of the United States.

Original Text	Modified Text
N/A	**4:** Congress shall make all methods of debate and vote available to its members such that members need not be in the Seat of Government or any designated location to perform legislative duties. All technologies as are available shall be allowed and required to be used to limit the need for each chamber of Congress to meet in person. Representatives and Senators may respond to roll call, debate, cast votes, or perform any legislative duty by any legal method available.

Original Text	Modified Text
N/A	**5:** The Federal Government shall purchase and maintain a property or several properties to house all members of Congress when they visit the Seat of Government of the United States. The property or properties shall be sparse and utilitarian to only serve the temporary housing needs of just the members of Congress when visiting the Seat of Government. In addition to room, the Federal Government shall provide board, transportation, and all other basic needs while members of Congress travel to and from and stay in the Seat of Government.

SECTION 5

Original Text	Modified Text
1: Each House shall be the Judge of the Elections, Returns and Qualifications of its own Members, and a Majority of each shall constitute a Quorum to do Business; but a smaller Number may adjourn from day to day, and may be authorized to compel the Attendance of absent Members, in such Manner, and under such Penalties as each House may provide.	**1:** No Change

Original Text	Modified Text
2: Each House may determine the Rules of its Proceedings, punish its Members for disorderly Behaviour, and, with the Concurrence of two thirds, expel a Member.	**2:** No Change

Original Text	Modified Text
3: Each House shall keep a Journal of its Proceedings, and from time to time publish the same, excepting such Parts as may in their Judgment require Secrecy; and the Yeas and Nays of the Members of either House on any question shall, at the Desire of one fifth of those Present, be entered on the Journal.	**3:** No Change

Original Text	Modified Text
4: Neither House, during the Session of Congress, shall, without the Consent of the other, adjourn for more than three days, nor to any other Place than that in which the two Houses shall be sitting.	**4:** No Change

Original Text	Modified Text
1: The Senators and Representatives shall receive a Compensation for their Services, to be ascertained by Law, and paid out of the Treasury of the United States.6 They shall in all Cases, except Treason, Felony and Breach of the Peace, be privileged from Arrest during their Attendance at the Session of their respective Houses, and in going to and returning from the same; and for any Speech or Debate in either House, they shall not be questioned in any other Place.	**1:** The Senators and Representatives shall receive a Compensation for their Services, to be ascertained by Law, and paid out of the Treasury of the United States. No law varying the compensation for the services of the Senators and Representatives shall take effect until an election of Representatives and Senators shall have intervened.
Also, Amendment 27	Direct monetary compensation shall be limited to and equal to the Living Wage rate in the Seat of Government commiserated with the hours scheduled by each chamber of Congress. Additional non-monetary compensation may only be awarded as designated in other parts of the Constitution.
No law varying the compensation for the services of the Senators and Representatives shall take effect until an election of Representatives shall have intervened.	They shall in all Cases, except Treason, Felony and Breach of the Peace, be privileged from Arrest during their Attendance at the Session of their respective Houses, and in going to and returning from the same; and for any Speech or Debate in either House, they shall not be questioned in any other Place.

Original Text	Modified Text
2: No Senator or Representative shall, during the Time for which he was elected, be appointed to any civil Office under the Authority of the United States, which shall have been created, or the Emoluments whereof shall have been encreased during such time; and no Person holding any Office under the United States, shall be a Member of either House during his Continuance in Office.	**2:** No Change

Original Text	Modified Text
N/A	**3:** Both the House of Representatives and Senate shall be limited in the number of days they may meet per legislative year and the number of hours they shall meet in any single day. While either chamber of Congress is in session, each shall meet no more than three days per calendar week. All sessions must begin after seven o'clock in the morning and must end before ten o'clock in the evening at the Seat of Government. Furthermore, each session shall last no longer than six hours. Additional days and times may only be granted if an emergency is declared by the President of the United States.

Original Text	Modified Text
N/A	**4:** Congress may appropriate funds for a staff to cover the organizational and functional needs of Congress. Organizational and functional staff shall be shared by all members of Congress equally. Congress may not appropriate funds for staff assigned to individual members of Congress or groups of members of Congress. No staff member of the Government of the United States may be assigned to a single Representative or Senator or any group of Representatives or Senators.

Original Text	Modified Text
N/A	**5:** No person shall be elected to the House of Representatives more than twice nor to the Senate more than twice, and not more than four times for all of Congress. And no person who has held a position in Congress for more than two years of a term to which some other person was elected shall be elected to the House of Representatives or the Senate more than once. But this clause shall not apply to any person holding a position in Congress at the time of ratification until the end of his current term.

SECTION 7

Original Text	Modified Text
1: All Bills for raising Revenue shall originate in the House of Representatives; but the Senate may propose or concur with Amendments as on other Bills.	**1:** No Change

Original Text	Modified Text
2: Every Bill which shall have passed the House of Representatives and the Senate, shall, before it become a Law, be presented to the President of the United States; If he approve he shall sign it, but if not he shall return it, with his Objections to that House in which it shall have originated, who shall enter the Objections at large on their Journal, and proceed to reconsider it. If after such Reconsideration two thirds of that House shall agree to pass the Bill, it shall be sent, together with the Objections, to the other House, by	**2:** No Change

Original Text	Modified Text
which it shall likewise be reconsidered, and if approved by two thirds of that House, it shall become a Law. But in all such Cases the Votes of both Houses shall be determined by yeas and Nays, and the Names of the Persons voting for and against the Bill shall be entered on the Journal of each House respectively. If any Bill shall not be returned by the President within ten Days (Sundays excepted) after it shall have been presented to him, the Same shall be a Law, in like Manner as if he had signed it, unless the Congress by their Adjournment prevent its Return, in which Case it shall not be a Law.	

Original Text	Modified Text
3: Every Order, Resolution, or Vote to which the Concurrence of the Senate and House of Representatives may be necessary (except on a question of Adjournment) shall be presented to the President of the United States; and before the Same shall take Effect, shall be approved by him, or being disapproved by him, shall be repassed by two thirds of the Senate and House of Representatives, according to the Rules and Limitations prescribed in the Case of a Bill.	**3:** No Change

Original Text	Modified Text
N/A	**4:** Any bill that thus has been passed by both Chambers of Congress and approved by the President of the United States, or reconsidered by Congress after the President has returned it shall then be sent to the Supreme Court or a Federal Court designated by the Supreme Court. The designated Court will review the bill and confirm that it meets the requirements of the Constitution and other relevant laws. No Bill shall become Law nor be in effect before this review.

Original Text	Modified Text
N/A	**5:** Any law that has passed the local process within each State or Territory shall be reviewed by the Federal Court designated by the Supreme Court before the law may go into effect. The designated Federal Court shall review that the new law does not violate the Constitution, existing Federal Law, existing State or Territory Law, or prior judicial interpretation of the law. Should the law be found in violation thereof, the Courts shall return the law to the State or Territory and not allow the law to go into effect.

Original Text	Modified Text
N/A	**6:** Any law that has been put into effect shall expire twenty years past the day it was put into effect, unless another date prior to twenty years has been set for its expiration. The law must be repassed via the process as laid out for a new Bill by the Constitution and relevant law prior to expiration in order to remain in effect. Upon the passing of this Amendment, all existing laws shall expire on a schedule unless another date had already been set for its expiration within twenty years of its passing. Those laws that have passed in the prior twenty years shall come up for expiration as if this Amendment were already in effect. For those laws that passed prior to twenty years before this Amendment has gone into effect, each shall expire in the proceeding ten years such that the last digit of the year the law was originally passed in becomes the year in which the law shall expire.

SECTION 8

Original Text	Modified Text
1: The Congress shall have Power To lay and collect Taxes, Duties, Imposts and Excises, to pay the Debts and provide for the common Defence and general Welfare of the United States; but all Duties, Imposts and Excises shall be uniform throughout the United States;	**1:** No Change

Original Text	Modified Text
2: To borrow Money on the credit of the United States;	**2:** No Change

Original Text	Modified Text
3: To regulate Commerce with foreign Nations, and among the several States, and with the Indian Tribes;	**3:** No Change

Original Text	Modified Text
4: To establish an uniform Rule of Naturalization, and uniform Laws on the subject of Bankruptcies throughout the United States;	**4:** No Change

Original Text	Modified Text
5: To coin Money, regulate the Value thereof, and of foreign Coin, and fix the Standard of Weights and Measures;	**5:** No Change

Original Text	Modified Text
6: To provide for the Punishment of counterfeiting the Securities and current Coin of the United States;	**6:** No Change

Original Text	Modified Text
7: To establish Post Offices and post Roads;	**7:** To establish, maintain, and support the existence and safe usage of systems of delivering communications, goods, and people; and the methods by which those communications, goods, and people are moved between locations; and shall ensure both of these are available to all people at a reasonable expense without limitations and available equally without preferential treatment;

Original Text	Modified Text
8: To promote the Progress of Science and useful Arts, by securing for limited Times to Authors and Inventors the exclusive Right to their respective Writings and Discoveries;	**8:** No Change

Original Text	Modified Text
9: To constitute Tribunals inferior to the supreme Court;	**9:** No Change

Original Text	Modified Text
10: To define and punish Piracies and Felonies committed on the high Seas, and Offences against the Law of Nations;	**10:** No Change

Original Text	Modified Text
11: To declare War, grant Letters of Marque and Reprisal, and make Rules concerning Captures on Land and Water;	**11:** No Change

Original Text	Modified Text
12: To raise and support Armies, but no Appropriation of Money to that Use shall be for a longer Term than two Years;	**12:** No Change

Original Text	Modified Text
13: To provide and maintain a Navy;	**13:** No Change

Original Text	Modified Text
14: To make Rules for the Government and Regulation of the land and naval Forces;	**14:** No Change

Original Text	Modified Text
15: To provide for calling forth the Militia to execute the Laws of the Union, suppress Insurrections and repel Invasions;	**15:** No Change

Original Text	Modified Text
16: To provide for organizing, arming, and disciplining, the Militia, and for governing such Part of them as may be employed in the Service of the United States, reserving to the States respectively, the Appointment of the Officers, and the Authority of training the Militia according to the discipline prescribed by Congress;	**16:** No Change

Original Text	Modified Text
17: To exercise exclusive Legislation in all Cases whatsoever, over such District (not exceeding ten Miles square) as may, by Cession of particular States, and the Acceptance of Congress, become the Seat of the Government of the United States, and to exercise like Authority over all Places purchased by the Consent of the Legislature of the State in which the Same shall be, for the Erection of Forts, Magazines, Arsenals, dock-Yards, and other needful Buildings;— And	**17:** No Change

Original Text	Modified Text
18: To make all Laws which shall be necessary and proper for carrying into Execution the foregoing Powers, and all other Powers vested by this Constitution in the Government of the United States, or in any Department or Officer thereof.	**18:** No Change

SECTION 9

Original Text	Modified Text
1: ~~The Migration or Importation of such Persons as any of the States now existing shall think proper to admit, shall not be prohibited by the Congress prior to the Year one thousand eight hundred and eight, but a Tax or duty may be imposed on such Importation, not exceeding ten dollars for each Person.~~	Removed by Amendment 13

Original Text	Modified Text
2: The Privilege of the Writ of Habeas Corpus shall not be suspended, unless when in Cases of Rebellion or Invasion the public Safety may require it.	**1:** No Change except modification of Clause number

Original Text	Modified Text
3: No Bill of Attainder or ex post facto Law shall be passed.	**2:** No Change except modification of Clause number

Original Text	Modified Text
4: No Capitation, or other direct, Tax shall be laid, unless in Proportion to the Census or Enumeration herein before directed to be taken. **Also, Amendment 16** The Congress shall have power to lay and collect taxes on incomes, from whatever source derived, without apportionment among the several States, and without regard to any census or enumeration.	**3:** Maintains the text of Amendment 16 only.

Original Text	Modified Text
5: No Tax or Duty shall be laid on Articles exported from any State.	**4:** No Change except modification of Clause number

Original Text	Modified Text
6: No Preference shall be given by any Regulation of Commerce or Revenue to the Ports of one State over those of another: nor shall Vessels bound to, or from, one State, be obliged to enter, clear, or pay Duties in another.	**5:** No Change except modification of Clause number

Original Text	Modified Text
7: No Money shall be drawn from the Treasury, but in Consequence of Appropriations made by Law; and a regular Statement and Account of the Receipts and Expenditures of all public Money shall be published from time to time.	**6:** No Change except modification of Clause number

Original Text	Modified Text
8: No Title of Nobility shall be granted by the United States: And no Person holding any Office of Profit or Trust under them, shall, without the Consent of the Congress, accept of any present, Emolument, Office, or Title, of any kind whatever, from any King, Prince, or foreign State.	**7:** No Change except modification of Clause number

SECTION 10

Original Text	Modified Text
1: No State shall enter into any Treaty, Alliance, or Confederation; grant Letters of Marque and Reprisal; coin Money; emit Bills of Credit; make any Thing but gold and silver Coin a Tender in Payment of Debts; pass any Bill of Attainder, ex post facto Law, or Law impairing the Obligation of Contracts, or grant any Title of Nobility.	**1:** No Change

Original Text	Modified Text
2: No State shall, without the Consent of the Congress, lay any Imposts or Duties on Imports or Exports, except what may be absolutely necessary for executing it's inspection Laws: and the net Produce of all Duties and Imposts, laid by any State on Imports or Exports, shall be for the Use of the Treasury of the United States; and all such Laws shall be subject to the Revision and Controul of the Congress.	**1:** No Change

Original Text	Modified Text
3: No State shall, without the Consent of Congress, lay any Duty of Tonnage, keep Troops, or Ships of War in time of Peace, enter into any Agreement or Compact with another State, or with a foreign Power, or engage in War, unless actually invaded, or in such imminent Danger as will not admit of delay.	**1:** No Change

SECTION 11

Original Text	Modified Text
N/A	**1:** The Speaker of the House of Representative and the President or President pro Tempore of the Senate shall be responsible for scheduling all debate and voting of their respective chambers.

Original Text	Modified Text
N/A	**2:** Any legislation proposed by individual members of each chamber should be considered for schedule and voting by the leaders of the respective chambers. The leader of the chamber may refuse to add the legislation to the schedule, however if the legislation is sponsored by ten percent or more of the chamber it must be added to the schedule within thirty days of presenting the required sponsorship to the leader of the chamber.

Original Text	Modified Text
N/A	**3:** The Vice President of the United States—as President of the Senate—may propose legislation that must be added to the schedule and voted on within thirty days.

Original Text	Modified Text
N/A	**4:** Any order by the Supreme Court or delegated Federal Court to create new law or modify existing bills and law must be done within the timeframe designated by the Court.

Original Text	Modified Text
N/A	**5:** Any legislation that shall pass through either chamber of Congress must be scheduled and voted on by the other chamber within ten days.

Original Text	Modified Text
N/A	**6:** All legislation must consist of single clauses directly related to the same subject at hand. Each clause and amendment must be passed separately in its own approval process.

Original Text	Modified Text
N/A	**7:** All Representatives and Senators, save for vacancies or physical inability, are required to cast a vote on all legislation presented before that chamber of Congress.

Original Text	Modified Text
N/A	**8:** All legislation must have at minimum sixty-one percent of the vote of all legislators in the chamber in order to pass to the next phase of the bill's process.

Original Text	Modified Text
N/A	**9:** Congress shall make no rules or exceptions to circumvent the process of scheduling and conducting a vote.

Original Text	Modified Text
N/A	**10:** Failure to follow the guidelines of Article One, Section Eleven of the Constitution and any future amendments shall be considered Treason of the United States of America. The Vice President of the United States is responsible for enforcement of this clause and bringing forth charges of Treason against individual members of Congress.

ARTICLE 2 – EXECUTIVE

SECTION 1

Original Text	Modified Text
1: The executive Power shall be vested in a President of the United States of America. He shall hold his Office during the Term of four Years, and, together with the Vice President, chosen for the same Term, be elected, as follows	**1:** No Change

Original Text	Modified Text
2: Each State shall appoint, in such Manner as the Legislature thereof may direct, a Number of Electors, equal to the whole Number of Senators and Representatives to which the State may be entitled in the Congress: but no Senator or Representative, or Person holding an Office of Trust or Profit under the United States, shall be appointed an Elector. **Also, Amendment 23** **1:** The District constituting the seat of government of the United States shall appoint in such manner as the Congress may direct: A number of electors of President and Vice President equal to the whole number of Senators and Representatives in Congress to which the District would be entitled if it were a state, but in no event more than the least populous state; they shall be in addition to those appointed by the states, but they shall be considered, for the purposes of the election of President	**2:** The President and Vice President of the United States shall be directly elected by the people of all States and Territories here within.

Original Text	Modified Text
and Vice President, to be electors appointed by a state; and they shall meet in the District and perform such duties as provided by the twelfth article of amendment. **2:** The Congress shall have power to enforce this article by appropriate legislation.	

Original Text	Modified Text
3: ~~The Electors shall meet in their respective States, and vote by Ballot for two Persons, of whom one at least shall not be an Inhabitant of the same State with themselves. And they shall make a List of all the Persons voted for, and of the Number of Votes for each; which List they shall sign and certify, and transmit sealed to the Seat of the Government of the United States, directed to the President of the Senate. The President of the Senate shall, in the Presence of the Senate and House of Representatives, open all the Certificates, and the Votes shall then be counted. The Person having the greatest Number of Votes shall be the President, if such Number be a Majority of the whole Number of Electors appointed; and if there be more than one who have such Majority, and have an equal Number of Votes, then the House of Representatives shall immediately chuse by Ballot one of them for President; and if no Person have a Majority, then from the five highest on the List the said House shall in like Manner chuse the President. But in chusing the President, the Votes shall be taken by States, the Representation from each State having one Vote; A quorum for this Purpose shall consist of a Member or~~	**3:** The President and Vice President shall run together on a single ticket and there shall be no criteria for a President or Vice President to appear on the ballots save for meeting the criteria for each position as stated in the Constitution. Eligible voters of the States and Territories shall rank their top three choices for President and Vice President and shall also be granted a single vote against a choice for President and Vice President. A value shall be added to each vote such that the first choice gets three points, the second choice gets two points, and the third choice gets one point. Furthermore, the vote against shall subtract two points. The candidates that receive the net most amount of points shall be the President and Vice President of the United States.

Original Text	Modified Text
~~Members from two thirds of the States, and a Majority of all the States shall be necessary to a Choice. In every Case, after the Choice of the President, the Person having the greatest Number of Votes of the Electors shall be the Vice President. But if there should remain two or more who have equal Votes, the Senate shall chuse from them by Ballot the Vice President.~~	

Also, Amendment 12

The Electors shall meet in their respective states, and vote by ballot for President and Vice-President, one of whom, at least, shall not be an inhabitant of the same state with themselves; they shall name in their ballots the person voted for as President, and in distinct ballots the person voted for as Vice-President, and they shall make distinct lists of all persons voted for as President, and of all persons voted for as Vice-President, and of the number of votes for each, which lists they shall sign and certify, and transmit sealed to the seat of the government of the United States, directed to the President of the Senate;—The President of the Senate shall, in the presence of the Senate and House of Representatives, open all the certificates and the votes shall then be counted;—The person having the greatest number of votes for President, shall be the President, if such number be a majority of the whole number of Electors appointed; and if no person have such majority, then from the persons having the highest numbers not exceeding three on the list of those voted for as President, the House of Representatives shall choose

Original Text	Modified Text
immediately, by ballot, the President. But in choosing the President, the votes shall be taken by states, the representation from each state having one vote; a quorum for this purpose shall consist of a member or members from two-thirds of the states, and a majority of all the states shall be necessary to a choice. And if the House of Representatives shall not choose a President whenever the right of choice shall devolve upon them, before the fourth day of March next following, then the Vice-President shall act as President, as in the case of the death or other constitutional disability of the President.14 —The person having the greatest number of votes as Vice-President, shall be the Vice-President, if such number be a majority of the whole number of Electors appointed, and if no person have a majority, then from the two highest numbers on the list, the Senate shall choose the Vice-President; a quorum for the purpose shall consist of two-thirds of the whole number of Senators, and a majority of the whole number shall be necessary to a choice. But no person constitutionally ineligible to the office of President shall be eligible to that of Vice-President of the United States.	

Original Text	Modified Text
4: The Congress may determine the Time of chusing the Electors, and the Day on which they shall give their Votes; which Day shall be the same throughout the United States.	4: The Congress may determine the Time of holding elections for the President and Vice President, and the Day on which the people of the United States shall give their Votes; which Day shall be the same throughout the United States.

Original Text	Modified Text
5: No Person except a natural born Citizen, or a Citizen of the United States, at the time of the Adoption of this Constitution, shall be eligible to the Office of President; neither shall any Person be eligible to that Office who shall not have attained to the Age of thirty five Years, and been fourteen Years a Resident within the United States.	**5:** No Person except a natural born Citizen, or a Citizen of the United States, at the time of the Adoption of this Constitution, shall be eligible to the Office of President or Vice President; neither shall any Person be eligible to that Office who shall not have attained to the Age of voting maturity as defined by the Constitution and Congress, and been fourteen Years a Resident within the United States.

Original Text	Modified Text
6: ~~In Case of the Removal of the President from Office, or of his Death, Resignation, or Inability to discharge the Powers and Duties of the said Office, the Same shall devolve on the Vice President, and the Congress may by Law provide for the Case of Removal, Death, Resignation or Inability, both of the President and Vice President, declaring what Officer shall then act as President, and such Officer shall act accordingly, until the Disability be removed, or a President shall be elected.~~ **Also, Amendment 25, Clause 1** In case of the removal of the President from office or of his death or resignation, the Vice President shall become President. **Also, Amendment 20, Clause 3** If, at the time fixed for the beginning of the term of the President, the President elect shall have died, the Vice President elect shall become President. If a President shall not	**6:** Shall be the text of Amendment 25, Clause 1 **7:** Shall be the text of Amendment 20, Clause 3 **8:** Shall be the text of Amendment 20, Clause 4

Original Text	Modified Text
have been chosen before the time fixed for the beginning of his term, or if the President elect shall have failed to qualify, then the Vice President elect shall act as President until a President shall have qualified; and the Congress may by law provide for the case wherein neither a President elect nor a Vice President elect shall have qualified, declaring who shall then act as President, or the manner in which one who is to act shall be selected, and such person shall act accordingly until a President or Vice President shall have qualified. **Also, Amendment 20, Clause 4** The Congress may by law provide for the case of the death of any of the persons from whom the House of Representatives may choose a President whenever the right of choice shall have devolved upon them, and for the case of the death of any of the persons from whom the Senate may choose a Vice President whenever the right of choice shall have devolved upon them.	

Original Text	Modified Text
7: The President shall, at stated Times, receive for his Services, a Compensation, which shall neither be encreased nor diminished during the Period for which he shall have been elected, and he shall not receive within that Period any other Emolument from the United States, or any of them.	**9:** No Change except modification of the Clause number

Original Text	Modified Text
8: Before he enter on the Execution of his Office, he shall take the following Oath or Affirmation:—"I do solemnly swear (or affirm) that I will faithfully execute the Office of President of the United States, and will to the best of my Ability, preserve, protect and defend the Constitution of the United States."	**10:** No Change except modification of the Clause number

Original Text	Modified Text
Amendment 20, Clause 1: The terms of the President and Vice President shall end at noon on the 20th day of January, and the terms of Senators and Representatives at noon on the 3d day of January, of the years in which such terms would have ended if this article had not been ratified; and the terms of their successors shall then begin.	**11:** No Change

Original Text	Modified Text
Amendment 22: No person shall be elected to the office of the President more than twice, and no person who has held the office of President, or acted as President, for more than two years of a term to which some other person was elected President shall be elected to the office of the President more than once. But this article shall not apply to any person holding the office of President when this article was proposed by the Congress, and shall not prevent any person who may be holding the office of President, or acting as President, during the term within which this article becomes operative from holding the office of President or acting as President during the remainder of such term.	**12:** No Change

Original Text	Modified Text
Amendment 25, Clause 2: Whenever there is a vacancy in the office of the Vice President, the President shall nominate a Vice President who shall take office upon confirmation by a majority vote of both Houses of Congress.	**13:** No Change

Original Text	Modified Text
Amendment 25, Clause 3: Whenever the President transmits to the President pro tempore of the Senate and the Speaker of the House of Representatives his written declaration that he is unable to discharge the powers and duties of his office, and until he transmits to them a written declaration to the contrary, such powers and duties shall be discharged by the Vice President as Acting President.	**14:** No Change

Original Text	Modified Text
Amendment 25, Clause 4: Whenever the Vice President and a majority of either the principal officers of the executive departments or of such other body as Congress may by law provide, transmit to the President pro tempore of the Senate and the Speaker of the House of Representatives their written declaration that the President is unable to discharge the powers and duties of his office, the Vice President shall immediately assume the powers and duties of the office as Acting President. Thereafter, when the President transmits to the President pro tempore of the Senate and the	**15:** No Change

Original Text	Modified Text
Speaker of the House of Representatives his written declaration that no inability exists, he shall resume the powers and duties of his office unless the Vice President and a majority of either the principal officers of the executive department or of such other body as Congress may by law provide, transmit within four days to the President pro tempore of the Senate and the Speaker of the House of Representatives their written declaration that the President is unable to discharge the powers and duties of his office. Thereupon Congress shall decide the issue, assembling within forty-eight hours for that purpose if not in session. If the Congress, within twenty-one days after receipt of the latter written declaration, or, if Congress is not in session, within twenty-one days after Congress is required to assemble, determines by two-thirds vote of both Houses that the President is unable to discharge the powers and duties of his office, the Vice President shall continue to discharge the same as Acting President; otherwise, the President shall resume the powers and duties of his office.	

Original Text	Modified Text
1: The President shall be Commander in Chief of the Army and Navy of the United States, and of the Militia of the several States, when called into the actual Service of the United States; he may require the Opinion, in writing, of the principal Officer in each of the executive Departments, upon any Subject relating to the Duties of their respective Offices, and he shall have Power to grant Reprieves and Pardons for Offences against the United States, except in Cases of Impeachment.	**1:** No Change

Original Text	Modified Text
2: He shall have Power, by and with the Advice and Consent of the Senate, to make Treaties, provided two thirds of the Senators present concur; and he shall nominate, and by and with the Advice and Consent of the Senate, shall appoint Ambassadors, other public Ministers and Consuls, Judges of the supreme Court, and all other Officers of the United States, whose Appointments are not herein otherwise provided for, and which shall be established by Law: but the Congress may by Law vest the Appointment of such inferior Officers, as they think proper, in the President alone, in the Courts of Law, or in the Heads of Departments.	**2:** No Change

Original Text	Modified Text
3: The President shall have Power to fill up all Vacancies that may happen during the Recess of the Senate, by granting Commissions which shall expire at the End of their next Session.	**3:** No Change

SECTION 3

Original Text	Modified Text
He shall from time to time give to the Congress Information of the State of the Union, and recommend to their Consideration such Measures as he shall judge necessary and expedient; he may, on extraordinary Occasions, convene both Houses, or either of them, and in Case of Disagreement between them, with Respect to the Time of Adjournment, he may adjourn them to such Time as he shall think proper; he shall receive Ambassadors and other public Ministers; he shall take Care that the Laws be faithfully executed, and shall Commission all the Officers of the United States.	No Change

SECTION 4

Original Text	Modified Text
The President, Vice President and all civil Officers of the United States, shall be removed from Office on Impeachment for, and Conviction of, Treason, Bribery, or other high Crimes and Misdemeanors.	No Change

Original Text	Modified Text
N/A	**1:** The President, Vice President, and heads of the Executive Departments shall form a body known as the Cabinet that shall meet at the discretion of the President.

Original Text	Modified Text
N/A	**2:** The President may ask or appoint other officers or persons to take part in the discussions of the Cabinet, but these persons shall not be members of the Cabinet.

Original Text	Modified Text
N/A	**3:** All other agencies of the Federal Government shall be organized underneath the Executive Departments, or the President or Vice President directly. All other agencies shall be subordinate to the heads of the Executive Departments, or the President or Vice President directly.

Original Text	Modified Text
N/A	**4:** The President shall be responsible for organizing all Agencies within each Federal Department, or Agencies within Federal Departments, or to the President or Vice President directly.

Original Text	Modified Text
N/A	**5:** The President may temporarily delegate specific Executive Duties to a Governor from a State or Territory such that the Governor may act as the President in that regard.

ARTICLE 3 – JUDICIAL

SECTION 1

Original Text	Modified Text
The judicial Power of the United States, shall be vested in one supreme Court, and in such inferior Courts as the Congress may from time to time ordain and establish. The Judges, both of the supreme and inferior Courts, shall hold their Offices during good Behaviour, and shall, at stated Times, receive for their Services, a Compensation, which shall not be diminished during their Continuance in Office.	No Change

SECTION 2

Original Text	Modified Text
1: The judicial Power shall extend to all Cases, in Law and Equity, arising under this Constitution, the Laws of the United States, and Treaties made, or which shall be made, under their Authority;—to all Cases affecting Ambassadors, other public Ministers and Consuls;—to all Cases of admiralty and maritime	**1:** No Change except where already removed

Original Text	Modified Text
Jurisdiction;—to Controversies to which the United States shall be a Party;—to Controversies between two or more States; ~~between a State and Citizens of another State;~~ between Citizens of different States, —between Citizens of the same State claiming Lands under Grants of different States, and between a State, or the Citizens thereof, and foreign States, Citizens or Subjects.	

Original Text	Modified Text
2: In all Cases affecting Ambassadors, other public Ministers and Consuls, and those in which a State shall be Party, the supreme Court shall have original Jurisdiction. In all the other Cases before mentioned, the supreme Court shall have appellate Jurisdiction, both as to Law and Fact, with such Exceptions, and under such Regulations as the Congress shall make.	**2:** No Change

Original Text	Modified Text
3: The Trial of all Crimes, except in Cases of Impeachment, shall be by Jury; and such Trial shall be held in the State where the said Crimes shall have been committed; but when not committed within any State, the Trial shall be at such Place or Places as the Congress may by Law have directed.	**3:** The Trial of all Crimes, except in Cases of Impeachment, shall be by a panel of Judges acting as a Jury; and such Trial shall be held in the State or Territory where the said Crimes shall have been committed; but when not committed within any State or Territory or committed in multiples States and/or Territories, the Trial shall be at such Place or Places as the Congress may by Law have directed.

Original Text	Modified Text
N/A	**4:** The Panel of Judges acting as a Jury shall consist of an odd number of Judges. The lowest inferior courts shall consist of three Judges, the appeal courts shall consist of five Judges, and the Supreme Court shall consist of seven Judges.

Original Text	Modified Text
N/A	**5:** All Judges shall be in a common Pool by area of the court or by type of court as determined by Congress. Each Panel of Judges shall be filled from these Pools; shall share cases except when a substitute is needed due to a conflict of interest, movement to a different Pool, personal leave, death, retirement, or any other reason determined by Congress; and shall serve for a term of five years. Assignment from the Pool to a Panel shall be at random in a method determined by the President. The Pool must consist of more Judges than necessary to fill Panels in order to have Judges in reserve in case a substitution is necessary. At the end of a five-year term, Judges are to return to the Pool for re-assignment or moved to another Pool and may not again serve in the same physical or specialized area.

Original Text	Modified Text
N/A	**6:** A Judge may only act as a permanent member of four Panels over the course of the Judge's service.

Original Text	Modified Text
N/A	**7:** The States, Territories, and Local Governments shall have Court Systems set up in the same model as the Federal Court System as laid out in the Constitution and its Amendments. Any Amendment to the Judicial Branch at the Federal Level should be reflected at the State, Territory, and Local Level.

SECTION 3

Original Text	Modified Text
1: Treason against the United States, shall consist only in levying War against them, or in adhering to their Enemies, giving them Aid and Comfort. No Person shall be convicted of Treason unless on the Testimony of two Witnesses to the same overt Act, or on Confession in open Court.	**1:** Treason against the United States, shall consist only in levying War against them, or in adhering to their Enemies, giving them Aid and Comfort, or any specific way defined elsewhere in the Constitution. No Person shall be convicted of Treason unless on the Testimony of two Witnesses to the same overt Act, or on Confession in open Court.

Original Text	Modified Text
2: The Congress shall have Power to declare the Punishment of Treason, but no Attainder of Treason shall work Corruption of Blood, or Forfeiture except during the Life of the Person attainted.	**2:** No Change

Original Text	Modified Text
Amendment 4: The right of the people to be secure in their persons, houses, papers, and effects, against unreasonable searches and seizures, shall not be violated, and no Warrants shall issue, but upon probable cause, supported by Oath or affirmation, and particularly describing the place to be searched, and the persons or things to be seized.	**1:** No Change

Original Text	Modified Text
Amendment 5: No person shall be held to answer for a capital, or otherwise infamous crime, unless on a presentment or indictment of a Grand Jury, except in cases arising in the land or naval forces, or in the Militia, when in actual service in time of War or public danger; nor shall any person be subject for the same offence to be twice put in jeopardy of life or limb; nor shall be compelled in any criminal case to be a witness against himself, nor be deprived of life, liberty, or property, without due process of law; nor shall private property be taken for public use, without just compensation.	**2:** No person shall be held to answer for a capital, or otherwise infamous crime, unless on a presentment or indictment of the appropriate and relevant Executive Department or Agency, except in cases arising in the land or naval forces, or in the Militia, when in actual service in time of War or public danger; nor shall any person be subject for the same offence to be twice put in jeopardy of life or limb no matter if the offence was tried at the Federal, State, Territory, Local, or any other jurisdiction within the United States and foreign courts recognized and designated by Congress; nor shall be tried in a civil court when found not guilty in a criminal court; nor shall be compelled in any criminal case to be a witness against himself, nor be deprived of life, liberty, or property, without due process of law; nor shall private property be taken for public use, without just compensation.

Original Text	Modified Text
Amendment 6: In all criminal prosecutions, the accused shall enjoy the right to a speedy and public trial, by an impartial jury of the State and district wherein the crime shall have been committed, which district shall have been previously ascertained by law, and to be informed of the nature and cause of the accusation; to be confronted with the witnesses against him; to have compulsory process for obtaining witnesses in his favor, and to have the Assistance of Counsel for his defence.	**3:** In all criminal, civil, or other judicial prosecutions, the accused and the accuser shall enjoy the right to a speedy and public trial, by an impartial jury of judges of the State or Territory and district wherein the crime shall have been committed, which district shall have been previously ascertained by law. Further, the accused is to be informed of the nature and cause of the accusation; to be confronted with the witnesses against him; to have compulsory process for obtaining witnesses in his favor, and to have the Assistance of Counsel for his defence.

Original Text	Modified Text
Amendment 7: In Suits at common law, where the value in controversy shall exceed twenty dollars, the right of trial by jury shall be preserved, and no fact tried by a jury, shall be otherwise re-examined in any Court of the United States, than according to the rules of the common law.	**4:** No Change

Original Text	Modified Text
Amendment 8: Excessive bail shall not be required, nor excessive fines imposed, nor cruel and unusual punishments inflicted.	**5:** No Change

Original Text	Modified Text
Amendment 11: The Judicial power of the United States shall not be construed to extend to any suit in law or equity, commenced or prosecuted against one of the United States by Citizens of another State, or by Citizens or Subjects of any Foreign State.	**6:** No Change

Original Text	Modified Text
Amendment 14, Clause 1: All persons born or naturalized in the United States, and subject to the jurisdiction thereof, are citizens of the United States and of the State wherein they reside. No State shall make or enforce any law which shall abridge the privileges or immunities of citizens of the United States; nor shall any State deprive any person of life, liberty, or property, without due process of law; nor deny to any person within its jurisdiction the equal protection of the laws.	**7:** All persons born or naturalized in the United States, and subject to the jurisdiction thereof, are citizens of the United States and of the State or Territory wherein they reside. No State, Territory, Local government, or Federal authority shall make or enforce any law which shall abridge the privileges or immunities of citizens of the United States or any other person within or in the care of the United States; nor shall any government or government body deprive any person of life, liberty, or property, without due process of law; nor deny to any person within its jurisdiction the equal protection of the laws.

Original Text	Modified Text
N/A	**1:** When standing in judgement of a law or lack thereof, neither the Supreme Court nor any inferior court may create law, modify the meaning of existing law, or remove existing law. The Supreme Court or the designated inferior court must send the law or need for a law back to the appropriate legislature—whether that be Congress or the legislatures of a State or Territory—to create, modify, or remove the law entirely.

Original Text	Modified Text
N/A	**2:** Should the Supreme Court or a designated inferior court send to Congress or the legislature of a State or Territory a demand for the creation, modifications, or removal of law within a specific timeframe and criteria, and the legislature does not act in accordance with the orders of the Supreme Court or designated inferior court, the Supreme Court or designated inferior court may hold any or all members of the legislature in contempt and implement any procedures and penalties as defined by law.

Original Text	Modified Text
N/A	**3:** Should Congress or the legislature of a State or Territory knowingly and willfully pass a law that is in violation of the Constitution, existing Federal Law, existing State or Territory Law, or prior judicial interpretation of the law—with the express intent of using the judicial system to challenge existing law and judicial interpretation—the Supreme Court or designated inferior court may hold any or all members of the legislature in contempt and implement any procedures and penalties as defined by law.

Original Text	Modified Text
N/A	**4:** Should the President of the United States or the Governor of a State or Territory knowingly and willfully sign a law passed by their legislature or give an Executive Order that is in violation of the Constitution, existing Federal Law, existing State or Territory Law, or prior judicial interpretation of the law—with the express intent of using the judicial system to challenge existing law and judicial interpretation—the Supreme Court or designated inferior court may hold the President or Governor in contempt and implement any procedures and penalties as defined by law.

Original Text	Modified Text
N/A	**5:** The Supreme Court or its designated inferior court may directly bring a criminal Case against the President, Vice President, Department Heads, Agency Heads, or any other person in the employ of the Executive Branch should—in the course of performing duties—that individual violate the Constitutional rights and rights granted by law to any person.

Original Text	Modified Text
N/A	**6:** Congress shall have the ability to create law that governs the proceedings of the Supreme Court and all inferior federal courts. This includes, but is not limited to, designating where trials may take place, how long a person may be detained before trial, how much time may be spent on arguments, and how long trials may proceed.

Original Text	Modified Text
N/A	**7:** The President of the United States may order the Supreme Court or the appropriate designated inferior federal court to start a trial within the timeframe decreed by Congress when the court is in session, so long as the Supreme Court has not already ruled on the issue at hand.

Original Text	Modified Text
N/A	**8:** Judges on the Supreme Court and inferior federal courts shall be removed from Office on Impeachment for, and Conviction of, Treason, Bribery, abusing the powers granted by the Constitution and law, failure to follow the procedural law as set by Congress, failure to start a trial when ordered by the President, or other high Crimes and Misdemeanors.

SECTION 6

Original Text	Modified Text
N/A	**1:** All parties presenting or intending to present a case—whether criminal or civil—to the Supreme Court, inferior courts, or any court belonging to a State, Territory, or Local government shall have a Counsel assigned to them by the appropriate government body.

Original Text	Modified Text
N/A	**2:** All Counsel who are to present a case to the Supreme Court, inferior courts, or any court belonging to a State, Territory, or Local government must be in the employ of the Federal Government or the Government of a State, Territory, or Local municipality. The Counsel may not receive funding, services, or support of any kind from any party directly or indirectly involved with a case before any court system. Congress shall have power to enforce, by appropriate legislation, the provisions of this clause.

Original Text	Modified Text
N/A	**3:** Any party who prosecutes a case—whether criminal or civil—to the Supreme Court, inferior courts, or any court belonging to a State, Territory, or Local government shall be held liable if they do not prove their case and will pay reparations to the defending party, Counsel, and Court for the harms suffered as determined by the hearing Court. This only applies to the originating party and does include assigned prosecuting Counsel.

ARTICLE 4 – STATES' RELATIONS

SECTION 1

Original Text	Modified Text
Full Faith and Credit shall be given in each State to the public Acts, Records, and judicial Proceedings of every other State. And the Congress may by general Laws prescribe the Manner in which such Acts, Records and Proceedings shall be proved, and the Effect thereof.	**1:** No Change except making a Clause

Original Text	Modified Text
Amendment 10: The powers not delegated to the United States by the Constitution, nor prohibited by it to the States, are reserved to the States respectively, or to the people.	**2:** No Change

Original Text	Modified Text
1: The Citizens of each State shall be entitled to all Privileges and Immunities of Citizens in the several States.	**1:** No Change

Original Text	Modified Text
2: A Person charged in any State with Treason, Felony, or other Crime, who shall flee from Justice, and be found in another State, shall on Demand of the executive Authority of the State from which he fled, be delivered up, to be removed to the State having Jurisdiction of the Crime.	**2:** No Change

Original Text	Modified Text
3: ~~No Person held to Service or Labour in one State, under the Laws thereof, escaping into another, shall, in Consequence of any Law or Regulation therein, be discharged from such Service or Labour, but shall be delivered up on Claim of the Party to whom such Service or Labour may be due.~~ **Also, Amendment 13** Neither slavery nor involuntary servitude, except as a punishment for crime whereof the party shall have been duly convicted, shall exist within the United States, or any place subject to their jurisdiction. Congress shall have power to enforce this article by appropriate legislation.	**3:** Shall reflect the text of Amendment 13

Original Text	Modified Text
1: New States may be admitted by the Congress into this Union; but no new State shall be formed or erected within the Jurisdiction of any other State; nor any State be formed by the Junction of two or more States, or Parts of States, without the Consent of the Legislatures of the States concerned as well as of the Congress.	**1:** No Change

Original Text	Modified Text
2: The Congress shall have Power to dispose of and make all needful Rules and Regulations respecting the Territory or other Property belonging to the United States; and nothing in this Constitution shall be so construed as to Prejudice any Claims of the United States, or of any particular State.	**2:** No Change

Original Text	Modified Text
N/A	**3:** Populated Territory may be added to the United States only via a treaty—whether the treaty is made ensuing peace, surrender, intent to join the Union, purchase, or trade—and only if the majority of the population has voted to join the United States. Unpopulated and claimed Territory may be added to the United States through the same method and only requires the agreement of the governing body. Unpopulated and unclaimed Territory may be added to the United States through an act passed by Congress.

Original Text	Modified Text
N/A	**4:** Should a Territory be added to the United States that has a population, the people of that Territory shall be granted automatic citizenship of the United States. This citizenship shall be retroactive to that person's birth such that each new citizen shall be regarded as if that person were born in the United States and has resided there for as long as the person has resided within the Territory or any other part of the United States.

Original Text	Modified Text
N/A	**5:** The entirety of the Constitution and the Laws of the United States shall apply immediately when any Territory is added to the United States. Any reference to a State within the Constitution or the Laws of the United States shall apply equally to all Territories.

Original Text	Modified Text
N/A	**6:** Once a Territory has been added to the United States, it may remain a Territory in perpetuity within its existing boundaries. By agreement of a majority of the people in the Territory, the Territory may become its own State, be added to an existing State, combined with another Territory to make a single Territory, or any combination thereof. Should a Territory have no population, Congress may make the same decisions for the Territory.

Original Text	Modified Text
N/A	**7:** Over time, all Territory of the United States should be incorporated into the Union as a State or part of another State. Should it not be possible or desirable to maintain a Territory, a Territory may be divested by an act of Congress and—if populated—by a vote of a majority of the people in the Territory. Congress may grant the Territory to another nation or full sovereignty. Should the divested Territory be populated, the people shall remain citizens of the United States unless they individually relinquish that citizenship and all the rights that citizenship ensues.

Original Text	Modified Text
N/A	**8:** Once a State is in the Union of the United States, neither the State nor any land within the State may secede or be divested to another nation.

SECTION 4

Original Text	Modified Text
The United States shall guarantee to every State in this Union a Republican Form of Government, and shall protect each of them against Invasion; and on Application of the Legislature, or of the Executive (when the Legislature cannot be convened) against domestic Violence.	No Change

ARTICLE 5 – MODE OF AMENDMENT

Original Text	Modified Text
The Congress, whenever two thirds of both Houses shall deem it necessary, shall propose Amendments to this Constitution, or, on the Application of the Legislatures of two thirds of the several States, shall call a Convention for proposing Amendments, which, in either Case, shall be valid to all Intents and Purposes, as Part of this Constitution, when ratified by the Legislatures of three fourths of the several States, or by Conventions in three fourths thereof, as the one or the other Mode of Ratification may be proposed by the Congress; Provided that no Amendment which may be made prior to the Year One thousand eight hundred and eight shall in any Manner affect the first and fourth Clauses in the Ninth Section of the first Article; and that no State, without its Consent, shall be deprived of its equal Suffrage in the Senate.	**1:** The Congress, whenever two thirds of both Houses shall deem it necessary, shall propose Amendments to this Constitution, or, on the Application of the Legislatures of the several States, shall pass a proposed Amendment directly and send to the other States, which, in either Case, shall be valid to all Intents and Purposes, as Part of this Constitution, when ratified by the Legislatures of three fourths of the several States; Or when the people of the United States receive the signature of five percent of the entire population for a proposed Amendment, that Amendment must be put on the next Federal ballot for President or Congress, and if ratified by three fourths of the people shall be valid for all Intents and Purposes, as Part of this Constitution; Provided that no Amendment which may be made prior to the Year One thousand eight hundred and eight shall in any Manner affect the first and fourth Clauses in the Ninth Section of the first Article; and that no State, without its Consent, shall be deprived of its equal Suffrage in the Senate.

Original Text	Modified Text
N/A	**2:** All Amendments to the Constitution shall replace existing Clauses or be placed within a specified Article, Section, and Clause—whether adding a Clause to an existing Article and Section or creating a new one.

ARTICLE 6 - PRIOR DEBTS, NATIONAL SUPREMACY, OATHS OF OFFICE

Original Text	Modified Text
1: All Debts contracted and Engagements entered into, before the Adoption of this Constitution, shall be as valid against the United States under this Constitution, as under the Confederation.	**1:** No Change

Original Text	Modified Text
Amendment 14, Clause 4: The validity of the public debt of the United States, authorized by law, including debts incurred for payment of pensions and bounties for services in suppressing insurrection or rebellion, shall not be questioned. But neither the United States nor any State shall assume or pay any debt or obligation incurred in aid of insurrection or rebellion against the United States, or any claim for the loss or emancipation of any slave; but all such debts, obligations and claims shall be held illegal and void.	**2:** No Change

Original Text	Modified Text
2: This Constitution, and the Laws of the United States which shall be made in Pursuance thereof; and all Treaties made, or which shall be made, under the Authority of the United States, shall be the supreme Law of the Land; and the Judges in every State shall be bound thereby, any Thing in the Constitution or Laws of any State to the Contrary notwithstanding.	**3:** No Change except modifying the Clause number

Original Text	Modified Text
3: The Senators and Representatives before mentioned, and the Members of the several State Legislatures, and all executive and judicial Officers, both of the United States and of the several States, shall be bound by Oath or Affirmation, to support this Constitution; but no religious Test shall ever be required as a Qualification to any Office or public Trust under the United States.	**4:** No Change except modifying the Clause number

ARTICLE 7 – RATIFICATION

Ratification is only valid to the original document.

ARTICLE 8 – LIMITATIONS OF GOVERNMENT

SECTION 1

Original Text	Modified Text
N/A	**1:** No person shall serve more than a combined twenty-five years in total in any elected or appointed position or combination thereof within any part of government, with no differentiation between local, State or Territory, Federal, or Foreign government. But this clause shall not apply to any person holding an elected or appointed position at the time of ratification until the end of his current term. Additionally, this Clause does not apply to staff and civil servants that support the functions of Government, nor those serving in the military or militia.

Original Text	Modified Text
Amendment 14, Clause 3: No person shall be a Senator or Representative in Congress, or elector of President and Vice President, or hold any office, civil or military, under the United States, or under any State, who, having previously taken an oath, as a member of Congress, or as an officer of the United States, or as a member of any State legislature, or as an executive or judicial officer of any State, to support the Constitution of the United States, shall have engaged in insurrection or rebellion against the same, or given aid or comfort to the enemies thereof. But Congress may by a vote of two-thirds of each House, remove such disability.	**2:** No Change

SECTION 2

Original Text	Modified Text
N/A	**1:** The Day chosen by Congress for holding Elections for Senators and Representatives shall be the same Day for holding Elections for the President and Vice President; only separated by the Years as prescribed in the Constitution and relevant Amendments.

Original Text	Modified Text
N/A	**2:** Elections for Senators, Representatives, and the President and Vice President shall start at least three weeks before the Day chosen by Congress for holding Elections. The Election timeframe may be extended by law but shall not be shortened for any reason. Election polling must be made available as most convenient for the People of the United States and include hours and days in which the majority do not make labor.

Original Text	Modified Text
N/A	**3:** The governing body of each election—Federal or otherwise—shall maintain the secrecy of ballot results until at least seven full days have passed from the Day of Election. This timeframe may be extended by law or in order to have the appropriate time to verify the results, but shall not be shortened for any reason. No member of the governing body of each election may share results or estimates of the elections during this timeframe under penalty of treason.

Original Text	Modified Text
N/A	**4:** All eligible voters of the United States shall be automatically registered to Vote and be provided all necessary materials and information in order to give their vote.

Original Text	Modified Text
N/A	**5:** All eligible voters of the United States shall be provided a ballot at the commencement of the Election timeframe. This ballot shall be able to be submitted by all methods as have been made available by law during the Election timeframe.

Original Text	Modified Text
N/A	**6:** All eligible voters within the United States are required to vote in Federal elections unless unable to physically or mentally do so or have been granted an exception by law. Congress shall lay a levy on those who fail to submit ballots without meeting an exception.

SECTION 3

Original Text	Modified Text
N/A	**1:** No Branch of the Federal Government may delegate any duties, responsibilities, or powers as laid out by the Constitution to any other Branch.

Original Text	Modified Text
N/A	**2:** The Executive Branch and Judicial Branch may not create any new law or rules on top of existing law. Each may suggest and present wording for such laws to Congress, but only Congress shall have the ability to make changes to existing law and create new law.

Original Text	Modified Text
N/A	**3:** The Executive Branch and Legislative Branch may not create or run any judiciary function except where designated by the Constitution. Any judicial function must be vested within the Judicial Branch in the Supreme Court or an inferior Court as ordained and established by Congress.

Original Text	Modified Text
N/A	**4:** The Judicial Branch and Legislative Branch may not create or run any agency, department, or any other division of the Federal Government underneath each Branch save those granted by the Constitution.

Original Text	Modified Text
N/A	**5:** While acting as Commander in Chief of the Armed Forces of the United States, the President may not deploy any part of the military without the expressed consent of Congress. Should the President declare an emergency session, Congress must respond to a President's request for military services within forty-eight hours. Congress must renew any use of military services every ninety days or within the limits set by Congress at no more than ninety days. The President may only deploy military services without the expressed consent of Congress in Cases of Rebellion or Invasion as a defensive measure only, and then only until Congress is able to convene and officially declare intent.

Original Text	Modified Text
N/A	**1:** Congress shall pass an appropriations budget for the entire Federal Government before the start of the fiscal year.

Original Text	Modified Text
N/A	**2:** The appropriations budget passed by Congress shall not exceed in total cost the amount of Taxes, Duties, Imposts, Excises, and revenue amassed by self-funded agencies collected in the prior fiscal year— though appropriated budget costs may be less than what was collected in the prior fiscal year. Taking on debt to cover the planned cost of the government is prohibited and the intaking of debt cannot be included in the planned budget.

Original Text	Modified Text
N/A	**3:** The United States may take on debt only in the event that war is declared by Congress or if the President has declared an emergency and Congress has passed legislation to support said emergency.

Original Text	Modified Text
N/A	**4:** Once debt has been accumulated, Congress is directed to pay off the debt as fast as possible without limiting the operational functions of the Federal Government. This includes paying off principle debt ahead of schedule so as not to incur future interest fees.

Original Text	Modified Text
N/A	**5:** Expected and real penalties and fines collected by a government agency—whether a federal agency, State or Territory agency, or local agency—cannot be included in the appropriated budget of said agency or any other part of the same government. Penalties and fines are to be consider extraordinary income and shall not be included as planned income.

Original Text	Modified Text
N/A	**6:** Expected and real penalties and fines collected by a government agency—whether a federal agency, State or Territory agency, or local agency—may not be used at the agency that collects the penalties or fines, nor at any agency that receives direct or indirect benefits from the agency; nor may penalties and fines collected be transferred to the general treasury. Penalties and fines may be transferred to an unrelated agency for use as a one-time revenue for a specific purpose that will not directly or indirectly benefit the agency that originally collected the penalty or fine.

Original Text	Modified Text
N/A	**7:** Excess penalties and fines that have not been distributed, as well as excess tax collected but not needed to run federal agencies or held for a specific planned future use, shall be returned to the people of the United States or the local area from which the penalties, fines, or taxes have been collected and shall not be kept in the Treasury for general use.

Original Text	Modified Text
N/A	**8:** The heads of federal agencies shall be held personally financially responsible should the agency of which they have charge spends more than appropriated by Congress unless granted additional funding by Congress through legislation or a declared emergency. Congress may pursue the recovery of the excess spending directly from the agency head through the courts. Similarly, Congress may make an allotment such that if an agency spends below what is appropriated that a portion of the unspent funds may be distributed to the agency head and other members of the agency, with the remainder returned to the treasury.

Original Text	Modified Text
N/A	**9:** All departments, agencies, companies, organizations, and any other entity that is run by or owned by the Federal Government must be included in the appropriations budget—even if the entity is self-funding. All sources of revenue must be shown in the appropriations budget, including expected revenue from self-funded entities.

Original Text	Modified Text
N/A	**10:** With the erection of Forts, Magazines, Arsenals, dock-Yards, and other needful Buildings—or any other asset built by any government—the legal body responsible for the creation of the asset must also pass an act such that the costs of maintaining the asset for the asset's expected lifetime will automatically be a part of the appropriations budget of the future and cannot be diminished.

Original Text	Modified Text
N/A	**11:** All government authorities that collect Taxes, Duties, Imposts, Excises, Penalties, Fines, or Fees shall send to the people from which these were collected a receipt that fully lays out how the funding was collected and used. These receipts shall be made available at least once per fiscal year and be as specific to the individual as possible and be understandable to the layperson.

Original Text	Modified Text
N/A	**12:** Failure to follow the guidelines of Article Eight, Section Four of the Constitution and any future amendments shall be considered Treason of the United States of America. The Vice President of the United States is responsible for enforcement of this clause and bringing forth charges of Treason against individual members of Congress or the responsible legal body forthwith.

ARTICLE 9 – PEOPLE RELATIONS

SECTION 1

Original Text	Modified Text
Amendment 9: The enumeration in the Constitution, of certain rights, shall not be construed to deny or disparage others retained by the people.	**1:** No Change

Original Text	Modified Text
N/A	**2:** No edict by any government nor rule—whether official or understood—by any private persons or businesses shall be created, maintained, or enforced that denies or abridges the equality in law and treatment of the many people of the United States and the people in care of the United States on the basis of age, ethnicity, race, color, physical attributes, religion or lack thereof, gender or gender identity, sexuality, language, origin, family origin, national origin, citizenship status, immigration status, political affiliation, group affiliation, personal affiliation, employment status, economic situation, or any other known or unknown way of categorizing people, except in cases where a person is unable to be treated equally due to physical or mental limitations, or where necessary knowledge and skills are required.

Original Text	Modified Text
N/A	**3:** No law of any government, nor any Amendment to this Constitution, shall allow the will of the majority to hold tyranny over the minority.

Original Text	Modified Text
Amendment 1: Congress shall make no law respecting an establishment of religion, or prohibiting the free exercise thereof; or abridging the freedom of speech, or of the press; or the right of the people peaceably to assemble, and to petition the Government for a redress of grievances.	**4:** No Change

Original Text	Modified Text
N/A	**5:** The rights of the people shall not be abridged or denied until the actions of the person brings harm to another. Each person has the inalienable rights to take any action with himself and his property, so long as that will does not violate the rights of another. No law shall be created, maintained, or enforced by any government that may abridge or deny the rights of a person unless this principal is taken into consideration.

Original Text	Modified Text
N/A	**6:** The enumeration in the Constitution of certain responsibilities of the governments and rights retained by the people shall not guarantee that all people shall succeed at all endeavors or meet the expectations of normality and stability created by the people heretofore within. The government of the United States, the government of the States and Territories within, and all local governments within those may make all reasonable concessions for these attainments by a person, but a person through their own choice or through the will of circumstances must still be allowed to not reach these attainments. No person shall be forced into accepting the assistance of the government or others; and no government shall extend resources beyond reason to bring assistance to all people.

Original Text	Modified Text
Amendment 26: The right of citizens of the United States, who are 18 years of age or older, to vote, shall not be denied or abridged by the United States or any state on account of age. The Congress shall have the power to enforce this article by appropriate legislation.	**1:** No Change

Original Text	Modified Text
Amendment 15: The right of citizens of the United States to vote shall not be denied or abridged by the United States or by any State on account of race, color, or previous condition of servitude. The Congress shall have power to enforce this article by appropriate legislation.	**2:** No Change

Original Text	Modified Text
Amendment 19: The right of citizens of the United States to vote shall not be denied or abridged by the United States or by any State on account of sex. Congress shall have power to enforce this article by appropriate legislation.	**4:** No Change

Original Text	Modified Text
Amendment 24: The right of citizens of the United States to vote in any primary or other election for President or Vice President, for electors for President or Vice President, or for Senator or Representative in Congress, shall not be denied or abridged by the United States or any state by reason of failure to pay any poll tax or other tax. The Congress shall have power to enforce this article by appropriate legislation.	**4:** No Change

SECTION 3

Original Text	Modified Text
Amendment 2: A well regulated Militia, being necessary to the security of a free State, the right of the people to keep and bear Arms, shall not be infringed.	**1:** No Change

Original Text	Modified Text
Amendment 3: No Soldier shall, in time of peace be quartered in any house, without the consent of the Owner, nor in time of war, but in a manner to be prescribed by law.	**2:** No Change

Original Text	Modified Text
N/A	**3:** Congress shall create laws or direct the States and Territories to create laws that shall allow persons to combine into a single unit and present as a single person for the purposes of commerce and all other rights attained by such a union. No law shall limit the merger of persons save for those protected by other clauses of the Constitution. Further, Congress shall create laws or direct the States and Territories to create laws that shall allowed the dissolution of such unions.

SECTION 4

Original Text	Modified Text
N/A	**1:** An actual Enumeration or Census of all the peoples within the United States shall be made on a continual basis, in such manner as Congress shall by law direct through an agency created and assigned by Congress to do so.

Original Text	Modified Text
N/A	**2:** The Enumeration or Census of all the peoples shall include not just citizens, but shall also include all peoples who have made residence within the United States—whether on a permanent or temporary basis—as well as those calling upon the United States for an impermanent period of time.

Original Text	Modified Text
N/A	**3:** The agency assigned by Congress for the Enumeration or Census shall also be responsible for tracking all residents—whether permanent or temporary—that are not citizens and those calling upon the United States for an impermanent period of time to ensure compliance with the uniform Rule of Naturalization as defined by law by Congress.

Original Text	Modified Text
N/A	**4:** Upon leaving the United States, a person shall not be struck from the Enumeration or Census but shall be maintained in a separate list such that the person is known not to be within the borders of the United States but may return in the future and continue as the same record—whether the person is a citizen of the United States or otherwise.

Original Text	Modified Text
N/A	**5:** For the Enumeration or Census, the main domicile and pertinent contact information—as defined by Congress—for each person within the United States shall be maintained by the agency assigned by Congress and updated immediately upon a change to that domicile or any pertinent contact information.

Original Text	Modified Text
N/A	**6:** Upon the main domicile or any pertinent contact information being updated by the agency assigned by Congress, the agency shall in turn alert all government, public, and private institutions that use that domicile or pertinent contact information to update their records to align to the Enumeration or Census.

Original Text	Modified Text
N/A	**7:** The domicile and pertinent contact information maintained by the agency assigned by Congress shall be considered protected information and shall only be released to organizations agreed to by the person related directly. Congress shall make law such that individually identifying information within the Enumeration or Census shall only be accessible by those within the agency assigned and punishments for unauthorized access or release of this information up to and including treason.

APPENDIX: NEW AND IMPROVED LAW

For reference, below lays out the new laws that were previously added to support the updated Constitution and to enforce the clauses that already exist.

EXECUTIVE BRANCH COMMUNICATIONS ACT

1: The United States Executive Branch shall provide singular messaging for the entire executive government through the President or the President's designated representative(s).

2: All communications to the public, other branches of government, foreign bodies, or any other like institutions shall go through the Office of the President or the representative(s) designated by the President. No Agency, Department, or any other sub-division of the Executive Branch shall provide its own communications outside of this method unless designated as a representative of the President.

3: Should the President or the President's designated representative(s) refuse to publish a communication authored by a person in the employee of the federal government, by an Agency, by a Department, or by any other sub-division of the Executive Branch, the communication may be presented to Congress and Congress may vote to release the communication under normal voting procedures. When voted upon, the President or the President's designated representative(s) must release the communication as originally presented.

4: Once the President or a designated executive representative has released a communication, that communication may be responded to by any employee, civil servant, contractor, appointee, or anyone else in service to the Federal Government whose work is directly impacted or referenced by the communication. If the communication was released against the President's wishes, the President may also respond to the original communication.

5: There shall be no restrictions on those persons responding to an executive communication save for reasons of national security. Elsewise, no person shall be restricted by any form for non-disclosure agreement.

6: The President, the President's representatives, supervisors, department heads, agency heads, or any other persons in the employ of Executive Branch shall be forbidden from making any reprisal for a person responding to an executive communication. Congress shall create law for the penalties of enforcement and the Judicial Branch shall adjudicate in claims of reprisal.

7: The President or the President's designated representative(s) shall create methods by which these responses can be attached to executive communications without restriction, censorship, editing, or any other constraint.

PERPETUAL CONSUMPTION TAX AND PRICE REQUIREMENTS ACT

1: The Federal Government shall lay no taxes directly on the income of workers, but instead shall tax consumption.

2: The tax rate on consumption shall be set by Congress each year.

3: All transactions—whether a good, a service, a fee, or any other method of selling—shall be taxed at minimum the rate set by Congress. No good, service, or any other type of transaction shall be exempt from having a tax on it. Only other taxes are exempt.

4: Taxes shall always be collected by the seller and be the responsibility of the seller to withhold and transfer to the Treasury of the United States in the times, manners, and methods as defined by law.

5: If a third party entity is acting as a seller or a marketplace for another seller and is collecting money for the initial seller, the third party entity shall be the party that is held responsible for collecting, withholding, and transferring the tax to the Treasury of the United States.

6: Prices shown to consumers must always include taxes, fees, and any other additional costs—no matter the source or reasonings for those additional costs. When a price is shown, that is what the purchaser shall pay in total and no additional costs can be collected at any point before, during, or after the transaction.

7: All types of legal tender shall be charged the same amount and no additional fees may be charged for using any specific form of payment.

8: Failure to collect and return taxes to the Treasury of the United States shall result in a penalty equal to double the original sale price including all taxes and fees.

9: Congress may create levels for higher taxes on certain products, categories of products, services, or categories of services—or charge another Federal Department or Agency with creating higher taxes on the same—so long as the taxes are in addition to the standard tax that must be paid on all products and services.

10: Additional taxes put on certain products, categories of products, services, or categories of services may only be added if it is deemed that the same has a cost to society or the varied peoples of the United States.

11: Additional taxes put on certain products, categories of products, services, or categories of services shall be directed into regulation, education, and rehabilitation programs with the intent of lowering consumption of the same or paying for the costs of society because of the same.

UNIFORM LABOR, WELFARE, IMMIGRATION, AND IMPORTS ACT

1: The laborers within the United States shall at a minimum make a *Living Wage*.

1-A: A *Living Wage* is defined such that a household that contains two adults and the average number of children within the county or equivalent area, and one adult is working *Full-time* for wages, the wage received shall cover the *Cost of Living* for all individuals within said household.

1-B: The *Cost of Living* is defined as the median cost of housing, food, clothing, utilities, healthcare, and any other such measure as deemed necessary by Congress.

1-C: *Full-time* is defined by Congress as the amount of time necessary for a laborer at a single job to be considered so.

2: The *Living Wage* for a laborer shall be calculated in the method as determined by Congress.

2-A: The *Living Wage* for a laborer shall be calculated at the county or equivalent level, such that all those who live or labor within a county shall have at minimum that Living Wage.

2-B: Should a laborer live in a county with a different *Living Wage* than the county that the laborer is employed in, the higher *Living Wage* of the two shall be required to be paid.

2-C: Should a laborer live within 20 kilometers of another or several counties, the highest *Living Wage* of all of the counties within 20 kilometers shall apply to that laborer.

2-D: Congress shall recalculate the Living Wage once per year such that the new *Living Wage* shall take effect on the date the last one has expired, as defined by Congress. The *Living Wage* shall automatically take effect without further legislation from Congress.

2-E: Should the *Living Wage* decrease from the prior calculation laborers may not have their wages reduced to match this lower amount. Should an employer attempt to do so or induce a laborer to accept a reduction, the employer shall be penalized twice the expected annual wages of the laborer.

3: The States and Territories—and the municipalities within those States and Territories should they be allowed to by the law of that State or Territory—may set a wage rate above the definition within this Act, but may not set a wage rate below the definition within this Act.

4: An employer may not hire multiple *Part-time* laborers when a single *Full-time* laborer could perform the required tasks and a *Full-time* laborer is available for hire.

4-A: *Part-time* is defined as any time threshold that eliminates any benefits provided by the employer or eliminates any taxes or benefits required by law for *Full-time* laborers as defined by either Congress, the State/Territory legislature, or the local municipal law-making body.

4-B: Should an employer attempt to circumvent hiring *Full-time* laborers and instead hire multiple *Part-time* laborers, the employer shall be penalized twice the expected annual wages of each *Part-time* laborer as if each were a *Full-time* laborer, as well as pay any tax or benefit not paid because of not meeting the necessary threshold. Additionally, the employer shall pay each *Part-time* laborer the difference in wages from being *Part-time* to *Full-time* for the lifetime of that laborer's employment.

5: The laborers and employers of the United States may bring a case to the courts of the United States if they surmise that Congress has incorrectly defined or calculated *Living Wage*, *Cost of Living*, *Full-time*, *Part-time*, average number of children, distance from county borders, or any other measure used in determining the Living Wage. Should the party bringing the case succeed, the Treasury of the United States shall be responsible for paying out the difference in either lost wages or cost of wages to the originating party.

6: In the event a laborer is unable to find employment and decides to do so, the laborer may petition for the welfare of the government to provide a *Living Wage*.

6-A: The government is obligated to provide a *Living Wage* for any person that petitions and meets the criteria heretofore:

6-B: In return for a *Living Wage*, the government must require an act of labor or an advancement of education deemed necessary that is within the physical and mental capabilities of the laborer.

6-C: A laborer may only collect the *Living Wage* provided as welfare for a maximum of one (1) contiguous year. In the event of declared emergency or Act of Congress, this may be extended up to three (3) contiguous years.

6-D: A laborer may only collect the *Living Wage* provided as welfare once within a contiguous term.

6-E: At the end of collecting the *Living Wage* provided as welfare, the laborer must wait at least six (6) months before being allowed to collect the *Living Wage* provided as welfare again.

6-F: A laborer may only collect the *Living Wage* provided as welfare for a maximum of five (5) years within a lifetime.

6-G: The government may refuse to allow the *Living Wage* provided as welfare for a laborer if the laborer has refused to do assigned tasks or has fraudulently claimed completion of tasks when not done so.

7: A continuous *Living Wage* as welfare may be provided with no expiration only for a person without the physical or mental capabilities of doing any labor or will never be able to be hired by any employer for other reasons as defined by law.

7-A: In the event that a person will never be to be hired by any employer for any reason defined by law, but the person has the physical and/or mental ability to do labor, the government may assign labor to that person, though may not end welfare should that person not complete labor.

8: All persons who are not citizens of the United States may register with the Census Bureau in order to become laborers within the United States.

8-A: All non-citizens who desire to do labor within the United States and have been offered employment to do so may not be denied entry to the United States, so long as the immigration status of the laborer has not been revoked in the past.

8-B: Should a non-citizen who has been an employed laborer within the United States be removed from that employment, the non-citizen may remain in the United States for up to one (1) year in order to gain other employment. Should the non-citizen not find employment in that time, they may be removed from the United States at the discretion of the Census Bureau through the judicial court system as defined by Congress.

8-C: A non-citizen may petition the United Sates government for a *Living Wage* as welfare, but the United States government is not obligated to provide it.

8-D: A non-citizen may bring with him to the United States all persons within his shared asset unit—including but not limited to spouses and children—so long as those persons have not had their immigration status revoked in the past.

8-E: Within a shared asset unit, only one person is required to be acting as a laborer and the others may remain in the United States so long as one person within the shared asset unit continues to provide labor, even if it is not the original person who applied for entry.

8-F: Other persons within a shared asset unit may also provide labor, even if that person did not originally apply to do so upon entry to the United States.

8-G: Immigration status of the non-citizen may be revoked due to non-related criminal activity—whether that activity took place within the United States or abroad. Congress shall define under which criminal circumstances immigration status shall be revoked. All claims shall be pursued through the appropriate judicial venue.

8-H: Non-citizen immigrants employed as laborers or within the shared asset unit of that laborer may seek citizenship under relevant citizenship law as defined by Congress.

9: An employer may not hire a non-citizen who has not registered with the Census Bureau.

9-A: Should an employer be found to be using the labor of non-citizen who is not registered with the Census Bureau, the employer shall be charged a penalty equal to ten (10) times the amount paid to the laborer for the entire lifetime of the laborer's employment. Further, if the employer was not paying the *Living Wage* and all expected taxes and benefits, the employer shall be charged the penalties as noted in prior clauses of this Act in addition to this penalty.

9-B: Other laborers of the employer shall not be protected from prosecution based on the employer being a distinct person.

9-C: The persons at an employer who are found by the courts to knowingly hire a non-citizen who was not registered with the Census Bureau—or gave direction to such persons to the same hiring type; or negligently did not investigate when claims were made of the same within the employer—shall be sentenced to no less than one (1) year and no more than five (5) years in confinement and pay a fine equal to their own gross compensation for the period the non-citizen was employed.

9-D: The non-citizen discovered to be working for an employer without proper registration with the Census Bureau shall be registered with the Census Bureau and may remain in the country for up to one (1) year in order to gain other employment. Should the non-citizen not find employment in that time, they may be removed from the United States at the discretion of the Census Bureau through the judicial court system as defined by Congress.

10: All products and services imported into the United States shall meet the standards heretofore within:

10-A: All products and services developed outside of the United States shall meet the requirements of the *Living Wage* as defined by this Act.

10-B: Should the Living Wage for an area be below the lowest Living Wage in the United States, the lowest *Living Wage* in the United States shall be required to be paid to the Laborer.

10-C: All employers outside of the United States must meet all safety, regulatory, certification, environmental, and any similar standard that is to be met by the domestic counterpart.

10-D: All employers outside of the United States must submit their facilities to the same level of inspection as their domestic counterpart, and these inspectors shall be the same as the ones in the United States. The employers outside of the United States shall pay the fee schedule for these inspections as defined by the relevant agencies and Congress.

10-E: Failure to submit to all inspections and meet expected standards of the domestic counterpart shall result in the product or service being banned from import and use within the United States.

10-F: Failure to pay the expected *Living Wage* shall result in a tariff equal to the difference from the wage paid to the expected *Living Wage*. The tariff collected shall be distributed back to the laborers such that they would have made the expected *Living Wage*.

10-G: Should the employer outside of the United States attempt to circumvent the rules in this Act or fail to implement corrective actions after a first violation, the employer may be banned from importing into the United States for up to ten (10) years.

ABOUT THE AUTHOR

J.P. Prag is a Pisces, even though that does not mean anything. However, ten of the stars in Pisces are known to host planets, though these stars are nowhere near each other. One of the planets (GU Pisces b) takes around 80,000 Earth years to circle its sun. Of note, some of the stars are not stars at all, but are entire galaxies! Further scientific examination has discovered many other faint galaxies, nebulae, stars, and other stellar objects within the Pisces general area. A couple of those galaxies are on a collision course, so look out for that over the next several hundred million years or so.

When not observing the stars at the Ladd Observatory, J.P. Prag can be found several blocks away at his home and office in Providence, RI, U.S.A. with his partner Caroline and their many tall ferns and philodendrons, lazy lying down cacti, outside pet squirrels (including Squirrel the Raccoon), and a stuffed pet sloth named Peeve.

For more irreverent details (and perhaps some pertinent ones, too?) and contact information, please visit www.jpprag.com.

Please visit www.jpprag.com to see all upcoming works, prior works, general articles, and current status.

Upcoming works include:

- **New & Improved: The President of the United States of America:** How can you change the world in 254 days or less? That is all the time between when the President of the United States takes the Oath of Office and when the budget is due. As a tangential sequel to "NEW & IMPROVED: THE UNITED STATES OF AMERICA", we follow the aftermath of an election of a truly independent President. What happens when an idealist sits in the most powerful chair in the world while an entire bureaucracy fights to stay relevant? This mixed-media story and political thesis follows just that, beginning with what should be just a mundane inauguration ceremony that instead abruptly changes everything. From there, we follow the actions of the White House just as we would in the real world: through a variety of media sources and perspectives. When we reach that 254-day mark and a standoff ensues, the question simply becomes: can a new way of doing politics truly supplant the entrenched system?

- **Compendium of Humanity's End:** Humanity's scientific and societal achievements have reached unprecedented heights and now people are populated on distant planets throughout the galaxy. Despite the vast distances and technology required, no life has been found at all—not even a microbe or a fossil of one. Colonists have never discovered an Earth-like planet, no matter how exactly close it is to the real thing, but work tirelessly to keep a fragile balance in the ones they have created through terraforming. If thousands of years have been spent looking for life to no avail, what would that do the psyche of those who have been tasked to find it? If we are truly alone in the cold emptiness of the universe, then is life a mistake?

- **Herrenvolk:** During World War II, Hitler managed to set up an underground lair that the Nazis populated with "perfect" people. As the war turned, the secret society was forgotten about and everyone who knew about them was killed. Nearly a century later, they are discovered by accident. As archaeologist, psychologists, historians, and others are exposed to the lost nation, they are impressed with how peaceful the Nazi descendants are and how well their society runs. The Nazis do not know much about the war and do not carry a hatred of other people. They just know they are the chosen ones destined to be the best.

- **Lost Rumors:** What would happen to you if you woke up to find several days of your life are completely missing? As you go out in the world and speak with others, you slowly realize this, but something more:

everyone has distinct memories of you; and they do not align to who you think you are. Told entirely from your perspective, you have many questions: What is real? What is just a rumor or perception? How do you separate facts from fiction, and how do you even know which one is which? What does is mean about you personally? And, most of all, what are you going to do now?

Prior works include:

- **In Defense Of...:** Certain people, events, organizations, and storylines in history have gotten a bum rap. Some have presented overtly critical comments and outright lies as fact, and others have followed suit. "In Defense of..." had one reason to exist: to bring the truth to the people!

- **Hidden Highlights:** Hidden Highlights was about the small, hardly noticeable acts in entertainment that made large, positive differences. This could be camera people catching things perfectly, announcers making deep references, or even just interesting people in the audience. There were just so many unsung heroes that deserved to be highlighted for making what we watch that much better!

- **The Hamilton Ave Journal:** The Hamilton Ave Journal was the _only_ professional wrestling news report focused solely on the business side of the industry. Looking not only at the stories that were important to investors and business-minded people, the Journal also delved into reports that most fans of wrestling would overlook. That was because the Journal was about getting the heart of the matters that affected the companies and outlooks of the wrestling world.

DEDICATIONS AND NOTES

First and foremost, all my gratitude goes to my bestedest partner Caroline for her patience, understanding, support, and health insurance as I have embarked on this crazy journey. I love you^3!

Next up, my deep appreciation goes to my editor Mary Rockwell. Mary came out of semi-retirement as a favor for me; what can be a greater compliment than that? You should "actually" believe that (I apparently have a predilection for the word that Mary tirelessly edited out)!

To my alpha readers, you have my biggest thanks. To my beta readers, you have slightly less thanks. I'm kidding beta readers, you are wonderful! Among the list of alpha and/or beta readers includes Adi Srinivas, Alan Prag, Andrew Smith, Doug Prag, Ed Tang, Jen Gerofsky, Kelly Prag, Kendi Johnson, Marianne Smith, Marci Prag, May Sennewald, Mirka Schroeder, Patrick Lehner, Rachel Rausch, Rob Hasek, Ron Correia, Sarah Morse, Steve Gilman, and Sue Huling.

And finally, I am grateful to you for being a patriot and not only reading this work but using it as a call of action to help preserve our country as a free and just nation. Whether you use this to form a new political coalition, write your representative for change, vote for a third party candidate, sign a petition, or just leave a review on Amazon, anything will help to spread the message that the Constitution and the United States can be so much better, not just good enough. Of course, leaving a review will help me eat, so I do have a greater personal interest in that one.

VERSION HISTORY

Version Number	Version Date	Version Notes
0.00	2019-04-30	Draft Started
0.10	2019-05-03	Shell Outline Transfer Complete
1.00	2019-10-01	Alpha Draft
1.50	2020-01-31	Alpha Draft – Edited
2.00	2020-02-11	Beta Draft
2.50	2020-05-18	Beta Draft – Edited
3.00	2020-06-29	Final Release Form

COPYRIGHTS AND DISCLAIMERS

Printed in the United States of America

First Edition October 2020

Edited by Mary Rockwell

Cover design by Saul Fineman
SelfPubBookCovers.com/finecomm
finemancommunications.com

ISBN 978-1-7353287-0-6 // ebook
ISBN 978-1-7353287-1-3 // hardcover
ISBN 978-1-7353287-2-0 // paperback

Basil Junction Publishing
11 S. Angell St. #366
Providence, RI 02906

www.jpprag.com

Made in the USA
Monee, IL
23 June 2022